ALASTAIR SAWDAY'S
SPECIAL PLACES TO STAY

BRITISH
BED AND
BREAKFAST

Design:	Caroline King
Maps & Mapping:	Bartholomew Mapping, a division of HarperCollins, Glasgow
Printing:	Canale, Italy
UK Distribution:	Portfolio, Greenford, Middlesex
US Distribution:	The Globe Pequot Press, Guilford, Connecticut

Published in 2003

Alastair Sawday Publishing Co. Ltd
The Home Farm Stables, Barrow Gurney, Bristol BS48 3RW
Tel: +44 (0)1275 464891 Fax: +44 (0)1275 464887
E-mail: info@specialplacestostay.com Web: www.specialplacestostay.com

The Globe Pequot Press
P. O. Box 480, Guilford, Connecticut 06437, USA
Tel: +1 203 458 4500 Fax: +1 203 458 4601
E-mail: info@globe-pequot.com Web: www.GlobePequot.com

Eighth edition

ISBN 1-901970-36-1 in the UK
ISBN 0-7627-2854-X in the US

Printed in Italy

A WORD FROM ALASTAIR SAWDAY

1984 is long gone, but do you ever feel that humans are being shuffled out of the picture? We are all achingly familiar with the call-centre syndrome, where the poor soul at the end of the line dares not stray off the script, and with the computer voices that ask us strange and personal questions. Those of us who enjoy a bit of a whinge take delight in the survival of the old London buses; if the conductor sees you dropping your purse as you leap on, she might let you off the fare. A computer wouldn't.

In a computer-mad world it is fun to come across people ditching the script. Humans will try to be human, of course, and I can see it in our office, where a gale of laughter can overwhelm the demands of any system. We are dependent, of course, on computers and systems, but if we ever do computer-talk, or fail to repsond as warm, human beings, then ditch us.

One aspect of Special Places of which I am proud is the way our owners insist on being themselves. We welcome all sorts of mild eccentricity – no trace of a script here. And whatever their specialists skills – and they are often prodigious – they bend in every direction to make you happy and comfortable. Many are the stories of medicine collected, favourite food cooked, children cosseted and whims indulged. Many, too, are the tales of friendships forged – and even lives changed.

There's little that's ordinary about these houses, and much is extraordinary. If you're weary of sameness and the culture of box-ticking, go and see for yourselves. We are firmly convinced that our own selection process, firmly run by human beings, is the magic that makes this book work. There is no script at this end, either.

Alastair Sawday

ACKNOWLEDGEMENTS

In spite of my wariness of systems – see my Introduction – this book comes together so successfully, with all its fiendish complexity, because the admin systems work. For this we owe much to Jackie King, who has patiently steered the project through the minefields – for the sixth time. She has worn all available hats: writer, inspector, manager and general factotum. She has been patient, full of ideas and hugely professional – and she never loses her sense of humour.

Laura Kinch as Assistant Editor has co-ordinated inspections (and done some herself), efficiently juggled mountains of paperwork and has also put her pen to paper for some of these vivid and colourful descriptions. She has risen magnificently to every challenge. And talking of challenges, this year has seen the re-launch of our web site – with every one of our properties listed – a magnus opus conducted with skill and composure by Russell Wilkinson.

Behind the scenes are too many other devoted souls for me to mention here, but their names are below. Thank you, all of you.

Alastair Sawday

Series Editor:	Alastair Sawday
Editor:	Jackie King
Assistant Editor:	Laura Kinch
Editorial Director:	Annie Shillito
Production Manager:	Julia Richardson
Web & IT:	Russell Wilkinson, Matt Kenefick
Editorial:	Sarah Bolton, Roanne Finch, Jessica Hughes, Danielle Williams
Production:	Rachel Coe, Paul Groom, Beth Thomas
Copy Editor:	Jo Boissevain
Accounts:	Bridget Bishop, Sheila Clifton, Jenny Purdy, Sandra Hassell
Sales & Marketing:	Siobhan Flynn, Julia Forster
Writing:	Jackie King, Tom Bell, Jo Boissevain, Viv Cripps, Laura Kinch
Inspections:	Jan Adams, David Ashby, Tom Bell, Bridget Bishop, Sarah Bolton, Lucinda Carling, Gillian Charlton-Meyrick, Nicola Crosse, Trish Dugmore, Jonathan Goodall, Sandra Hassell, Deborah Jacobs, Laura Kinch, Jackie King, Auriol Marson, Hazel Martin

A special thank you, too, to the other inspectors who saw just one or two houses for us – often at short notice.

WHAT'S IN THE BOOK?

CONTENTS

england

CONTENTS

CONTENTS

scotland

CONTENTS

wales

INTRODUCTION

Each year we sift through hundreds of applications, weigh up reader recommendations and owners' reports and decide which houses we should visit.

So what excites us? Good taste does, as do sympathetic renovations of ancient buildings, natural materials, a respect for the environment, comfort at bath-time and bedtime, good local food, thoughtful anticipation of your needs. Every place in this guide has a combination of these elements. Some have it all, others are so strong in some areas that they compensate for others in which they are weaker. Dustiness or crumbling walls can be acceptable if architecture or view is exceptional. Untidiness, even a touch of chaos can be acceptable – griminess is never – if the owner serves food fits for kings or treats your children like princes.

These subjective preferences are hard to measure. Many other guide books concentrate on the measurable, the variety of things on the tea tray, the TV, the hangers, the availability of tourist info, the co-ordination of the furnishings. Taste and style don't get a look in. We like comfort and things that work, but we are keener still on surroundings that will please the senses, whether they are luxurious or rustic. We like owners who know what they're doing but perhaps more importantly we like owners who enjoy what they are doing and who are generous: a drink before dinner, the offer of a lift, the loan of maps and guides. We like flexibility and a willingness to consider your needs. We know that an encounter with genuine kindness and an easy welcome live longer in the memory than any number of 'facilities' that have earned gold or silver awards.

Many of our owners go to great lengths to make your stay that little bit more special. They don't skimp or cut corners. You often won't know to which lengths they've gone, for many just do, without trumpeting the fact. They may get up early to collect your breakfast eggs, or cycle to the village shop for your morning paper, they may source the very best coffee, test all varieties of local bacon and sausages to ensure the best, pay that bit more for organic milk or for the bread which makes exceptional toast.

INTRODUCTION

How we go about it

We have visited every place here — most of them several times. Without a visit there can be no proper evaluation of friendliness, taste, authenticity or style. The sort of detail that cannot be gleaned during a phone call is important to us. We like to know what the owners were like, how they were with guests, what the house felt like, what was memorable.

Writing each entry is the most challenging part of putting the book together. Why do we do the writing ourselves? We want a lively, vibrant book that avoids the estate agents' language and cliché of other guide books. In order that you trust what you read we try to draw attention to drawbacks or quirks of taste or personality.

We avoid those owners who want you to feel privileged to be staying in their historic, beautiful home, or those who have succumbed to 'C.G.H.S.' (see below).

Creeping Guest House Syndrome

The term is our in-house summing up of what separates our B&Bs from guest-houses. 'Private' signs on doors leading to 'their' part of the house, piles of tourist pamphlets in the hallway and laminated information, large exterior B&B signs, strict timetables for meals or arrivals or departures, separate dining tables. These things confirm the C.G.H.S. diagnosis.

We call it 'Creeping' because the change from the house being a home first and B&B second, to being first and foremost a business can be slow but steady. Some of the above may be sensible measures, but C.G.H.S. is a subtle shift away from 'looking after' to 'processing' guests.

What to expect

We hope that you will be enriched by the whole experience of staying in someone's home. Unlike hotel staff who separate their personal lives from their work, these folk do both at the same time. You are IN their life, among their friends and family, children and pets, phone calls and unexpected visitors. Many guests love this feeling of involvement.

Most houses run on well-oiled wheels but occasionally there will be a spanner in the works. Most of you are tolerant but if your needs aren't being met please do say so — your hosts want you to be happy.

INTRODUCTION

Our favourite owners are unselfconsciously easy about having guests around. Some need to set rules about arrivals and departures and, if such things bother you, discuss them beforehand. You are embarking on a B&B 'contract' and anything extra is a bonus; time in the garden or pool, or early or late breakfasts, need to be negotiated.

We have masses of feedback from owners expressing delight at their Sawday guests who clearly understand B&B. You don't expect your bags to be carried, rooms to be 'serviced', or snacks brought to your room. By the same token, you are right to expect to feel more like a 'human being' than a 'bed night'.

Do read between the lines and be canny about interpreting our descriptions. Let us know if a house isn't what we led you to expect.

Finding the right place for you

Quick reference indices

At the back of the book we list those owners:

* with single rooms or those who charge no single supplement

* willing to collect you from local train or bus stations

* with houses suitable for wheelchair users or for those of limited mobility.

* who have pools or tennis courts

* who can stable your horse

* who charge £50 or less for a room for two

Map

If you know where you want to stay, look at the map at the front of the book first for the nearest houses. Focusing on counties alone can be misleading. You may not realise that the christening in Cheshire is very close to an excellent B&B in neighbouring Flintshire. In cities, check individual entries for their position. www.multimap.com is a useful web site.

Rooms

We tell you if rooms are double, twin, family or single. Most owners are flexible and can juggle things to suit you – just ask.

Bathrooms

If a bedroom is 'en suite' we say 'WITH' bath or shower. If it is not en suite, we follow the description of the room with details of private or shared bathrooms.

INTRODUCTION

Prices

Please note that we give prices PER ROOM. Afterwards we usually tell you the price singles will pay, i.e. the single room rate or the amount one person has to pay to stay in a double room.

Some owners vary their prices during the year. Double check if any supplements or discounts apply.

Breakfasts

Unless we say otherwise, a full, cooked breakfast is included. Some owners – particularly in London – will give you a prodigious continental breakfast instead.

Symbols

On the inside back cover we explain our symbols. Use them as a guide, not as a statement of fact. Owners may occasionally bend their own rules.

Types of houses

If you are heading for a large, ancient country house, be prepared for the odd draught. Our city places and working farms may be noisy at times, so light sleepers should pack ear plugs. Some houses have rooms in annexes or stables or barns or garden 'wings', some of which feel part of the house, some of which don't. If you have strong preferences for being in the thrub of things or quietly private, check where your bedroom is.

We hope you'll find good value for money in all of our houses – including the most expensive ones.

Practical Matters

Meals

Apart from breakfast, no meals should be expected unless you have arranged them – all our owners need advance notice for packed lunch, lunch or dinner.

When booking, discuss your diet and mealtimes. Prices are quoted per person, and dinner is most often a shared event with your hosts and other guests.

You'll find some talented cooks in this book and we urge you to eat in if you can – at the end of a long day it is good to amble downstairs for a meal rather than set out again.

Very few of our houses are licensed, so do ask the owner if you may bring wine to drink with your meal. Some entries state B.Y.O. (Bring Your Own).

INTRODUCTION

Seasons and public holidays

We have given a price range for each B&B that covers high and low season but many owners offer discounts for longer stays or for winter weekends. Others may charge supplements at certain times (houses in Edinburgh at Festival time, for example); others ask for a two-night minimum stay at weekends. Do ask about any special deals/expensive times. Book early for bank and school holidays.

Bookings

There are various ways of booking, but phoning enables you to 'get the feel' of people and place. Do, if you can, get written confirmation of the room booked and the price for B&B and for meals. Say roughly what time you will arrive, as most hosts want to welcome you personally.

Be on time if you have booked dinner; if despite best efforts you are delayed, phone to give warning.

Requests for deposits vary, too; some are non-refundable, especially in our London homes, and some homes may charge you for the whole of the booked stay in advance (see below).

Cancellations

If you have to cancel your booking, please phone the owner as soon as possible. You may lose your deposit or have to pay part of the cost of your booking. Some owners will charge you the total cost if you cancel at short notice.

If an owner holds your credit card details he/she may deduct a (widely varying) cancellation fee from it and not contact you to discuss this. This is rare, but be aware of the legalities of this in the eyes of your credit or debit card company.

Payment

All our owners take cash and cheques with a cheque card. If they also take credit cards, we have given them the appropriate symbol. Check that your credit card is acceptable.

Children

The 🐫 symbol is given to houses which accept children of any age. They may or may not have all the equipment you need.

INTRODUCTION

If an owner welcomes children, but only those of a certain age, we have put the lowest age limit on their entry. These houses do not have the teddy symbol.

It can be difficult for owners to balance the needs of mixed age groups. Nevertheless, many owners love having children to stay and will bend their own rules, particularly if parents encourage 'best' behaviour.

Dogs

The ✎ symbol is given to places where your pet can sleep in the bedroom (but not on the bed) with you. Please be honest about your pet – if it is nervous or excitable or unsociable, then say so.

Smoking

A ✎ symbol means no smoking anywhere – even hanging out of the window! The ✎ symbol means you can smoke in certain rooms, but probably not in bedrooms.

Tipping

Owners do not expect tips. If you have been treated with extraordinary kindness, write to them, or leave a present. (We love to hear about it, too.)

Environment

We try to reduce our impact on the environment by:

* planting trees. We are officially Carbon Neutral®. The emissions directly related to our office, paper production and printing of this book have been 'neutralised' through the planting of indigenous woodlands with Future Forests.

* re-using paper, recycling stationery, tins, bottles, etc.

* encouraging staff use of bicycles (they're loaned free) and car sharing.

* celebrating the use of organic, home-grown and locally-produced food.

* publishing books that support, in however small a way, the rural economy and small-scale businesses.

* running an Environmental Benefit Trust to stimulate business interest in the environment.

* working to establish an organic standard for B&B's (preliminary meetings have taken place).

INTRODUCTION

- publishing *The Little Earth Book*, a collection of essays on environmental issues and *The Little Food Book*, a hard-hitting analysis of the food industry. *The Little Money Book* is under way, too. See our web site www.fragile-earth.com for more information on any of these titles.

Subscriptions Owners pay to appear in this guide. Their fee goes towards the high costs of a sophisticated inspection system and producing an all-colour book. We only include places and owners that we find positively special. It is not possible for anyone to buy his/her way into our guides.

Internet Our web site www.specialplacestostay.com has online pages for all the places featured here and from all our other books – around 3,500 Special Places in total. There's a searchable database, a taster of the write-ups and colour photos.

For more details see the back of the book.

Disclaimer We make no claims to pure objectivity in choosing our Special Places to Stay. They are here because we like them. Our opinions and tastes are ours alone and this book is a statement of them; we hope that you will share them.

We have done our utmost to get our facts right but apologise unreservedly for any mistakes that may have crept in. Feedback from you is invaluable and we always act upon comments. With your help and our own inspections we can maintain our reputation for dependability.

You should know that we do not check such things as fire alarms, swimming pool security or any other regulation with which owners of properties receiving paying guests should comply. This is the responsibility of the owners.

And finally... Our book celebrates Britain and its people. You'll find hosts who share your passions, interests and quirks. One Sawday convert said she had had such fun in the places that she had visited, she regarded all the others as "friends she hadn't yet met".

If you have a yen to do something while away, to pick up a long-lost skill, to go riding, to throw a pot, to climb, pot-hole, sail, paint, ask your hosts if they have any leads. Most will know what is available locally and, thus, can add a whole other dimension to your break.

Jackie King

INTRODUCTION

The important bits, in summary...

Bathrooms
We do not use the words 'en suite'.

WITH bath or WITH shower = en suite.
If a room is not en suite, we follow the room description
with details of PRIVATE or SHARED bathrooms.

Prices
We give prices PER ROOM usually followed by the amount
one person has to pay to stay in a double room. Some owners
vary their prices during the year. Double check if any
supplements or discounts apply.

Symbols
On the inside back cover we explain our symbols. Use them
as a guide, not as a statement of fact. Owners may occasionally
bend their own rules.

Meals
Apart from breakfast, no meals should be expected unless
you have arranged them – all our owners need advance
notice for packed lunch, lunch or dinner.

When booking, discuss your diet and mealtimes. Prices are
quoted per person, and dinner is most often a shared event
with your hosts and/or other guests.

Very few of our houses are licensed, so ask the owner if you
may bring wine to drink with your meal; some entries state
B.Y.O. (Bring Your Own).

Payment
All our owners take cash and cheques with a cheque card. If
they also take credit cards, we have given them the appropriate
symbol. If you have an obscure card, check that it is acceptable.

Children
The 🏫 symbol is given to houses which accept children of any
age. They may or may not have all the equipment you need.

Pets
The 🐾 symbol is given to places where your pet can sleep
in the bedroom (but not on the bed) with you.

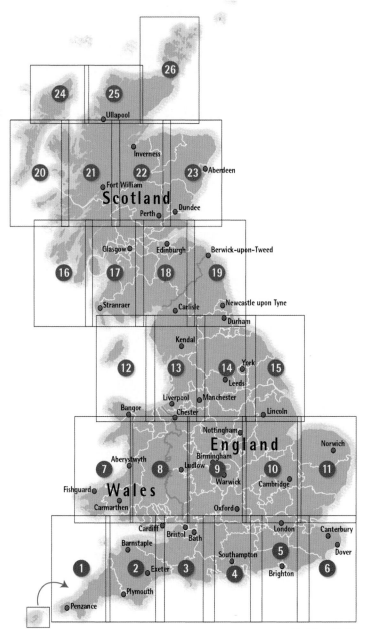

A guide to our map page numbers

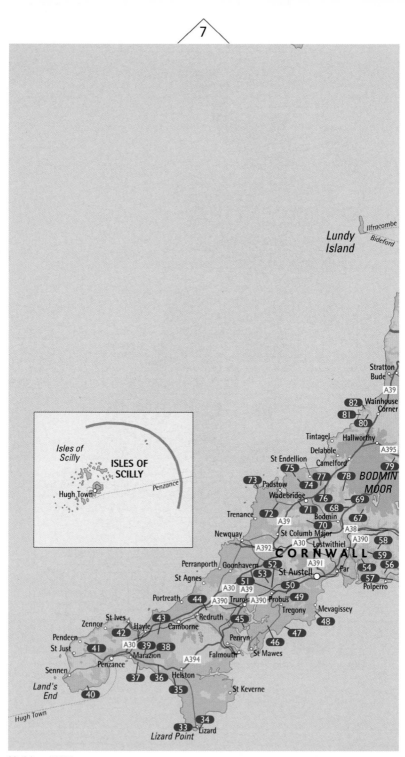

Lundy
Island

Ilfracombe
Bideford

Isles of
Scilly

**ISLES OF
SCILLY**

Hugh Town

Penzance

Stratton
Bude

A39

82 Wainhouse
        Corner
81 80

Tintagel   Hallworthy
                        A395
         Delabole
St Endellion   Camelford   79
    75   77   78 BODMIN
73   MOOR
   Padstow   74
   Wadebridge
            76   69
Trenance 72   71   68   67
         A39   Bodmin   A38
Newquay   St Columb Major   70   A390 58
         A392   A30   Lostwithiel
                CORNWALL   59
Perranporth Goonhavern   Par   54   56
          52   St Austell   57
St Agnes   51 53   Polperro
         A30 A39   50
Portreath 44 A390 Truro A390 Probus   49
         43   Redruth   Tregony   Mevagissey
Zennor   42   Hayle Camborne   45   48
Pendeen   Penryn   47
St Just 41 A30 39 38   46
         Marazion   St Mawes
Sennen Penzance   A394 Falmouth
        37   36 Helston
Land's
End   40   St Keverne
Hugh Town   35

           34
    33 Lizard
Lizard Point

Map 1

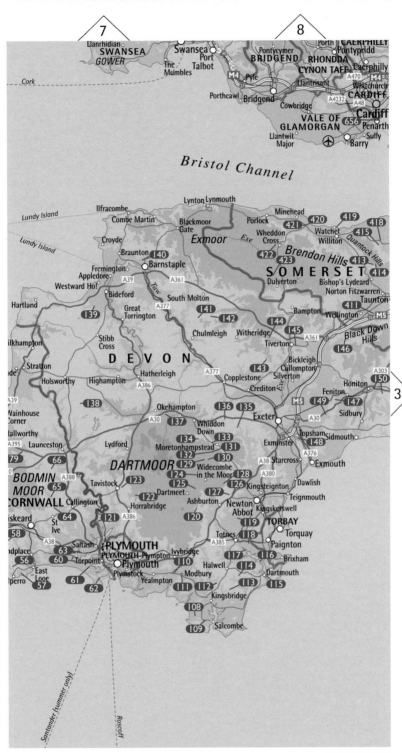

Map 2

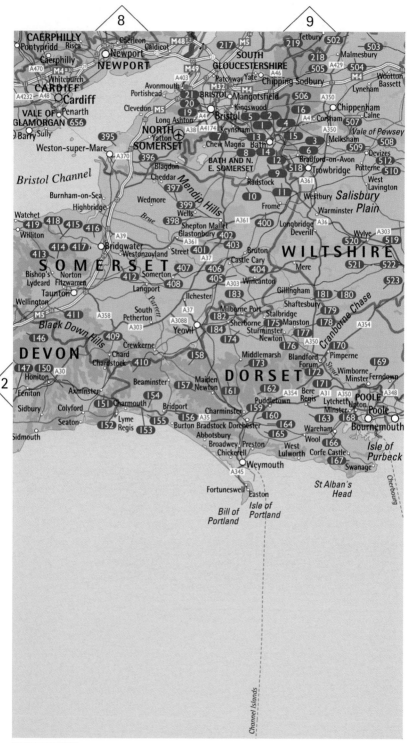

Map 3

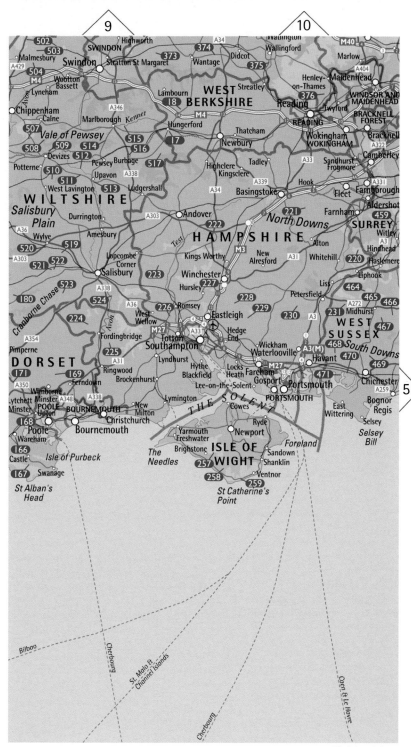

Map 4

High Wycombe
Marlow
Beaconsfield
M40
A355
BUCKINGHAMSHIRE
Maidenhead
Henley-on-Thames
A404
A40
Uxbridge
Hendon
M1
A41
A1
303
302
304
310
Romford
Brentwood
Ilford
A127
Basildon
A130
Wickford
Canvey Island
A13
THURROCK
A1089
Thames
MEDWAY

Twyford
WINDSOR AND MAIDENHEAD
Slough
M4
A4
299
301
295
313
300
297
298
305
306
LONDON
308
Grays
Tilbury
Gravesend
A2
Rochester
Chatham

Windsor
A30
A316
A308
294
296
291
292
A205
309
312
307
Dartford
A20
A226

Bracknell
Staines
293
314
GREATER LONDON
311
Orpington
A21
M25
North Downs
M20
West Malling
A228
Maidstone
A26
262
263

Wokingham
A322
Weybridge
Walton-on-Thames
A243
Epsom
A23
New Addington
Caterham
A25
M26
Sevenoaks
A26

M3
457
Camberley
Woking
Leatherhead
M25
A217
7
Oxted
260
261
Tonbridge
Southborough
Staplehurst
264

Sandhurst
Frogmore
A331
Farnborough
Dorking
Reigate
Redhill
Royal Tunbridge Wells
265
266
Pembury
A229

Fleet
HAMPSHIRE
Aldershot
458
Guildford
461
463
Horley
M23
A22
East Grinstead
Crowborough
266

A31
Farnham
North Downs
459
Godalming
SURREY
462
Crawley
M23
Worth
A264
A26
The Weald
Hawkhurst
Hurst Green
267

220
A3
Hindhead
Witley
Cranleigh
460
Horsham
A264
485
486
483
Ashdown Forest
E A S T

Whitehill
Haslemere
Liss
Liphook
464
Billingshurst
A24
A23
Cuckfield
484
Maresfield
Uckfield
Heathfield
479
480
A21

231
A272
465
WEST
Petworth
Pulborough
Cowfold
A272
Haywards Heath
476
475
S U S S E X
477
A22
Herstmonceux
478
Battle
Hollington

Midhurst
467
466
473
Storrington
Henfield
Burgess Hill
Lewes
Beddingham
Hailsham
Polegate
Bexhill
Pevensey

468
SUSSEX
South Downs
474
Steyning
Findon
BRIGHTON & HOVE
A26
Willingdon
A27
Eastbourne

470
469
472
Arundel
A280
A283
Hove
A27
Shoreham-by-Sea
Peacehaven
Seaford
Beachy Head

Chichester
471
Littlehampton
A259
Worthing
Brighton

East Wittering
Bognor Regis
Middleton-on-Sea

Selsey
Selsey Bill

Dieppe (summer only)

ENGLISH CHANNEL

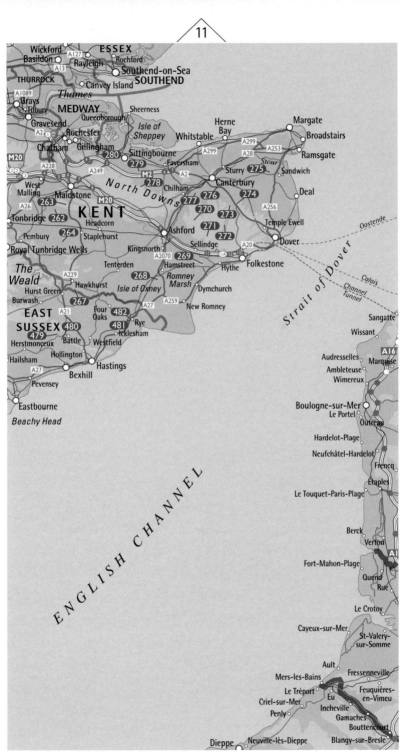

Map 6

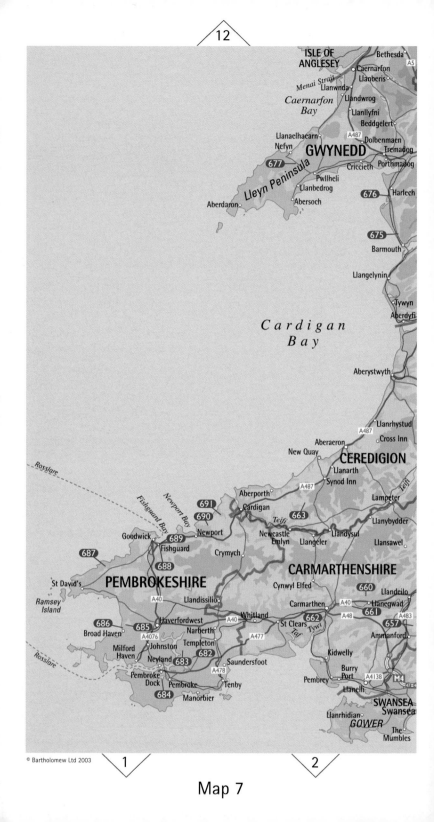

ISLE OF ANGLESEY
Bethesda
Caernarfon
A5
Menai Strait
Llanberis
Llanwnda
Caernarfon Bay
Llandwrog
Llanllyfni
Beddgelert
Llanaelhaearn
A487
Dolbenmaen
Nefyn
GWYNEDD
Tremadog
677
Criccieth
Porthmadog
Lleyn Peninsula
Pwllheli
676
Harlech
Llanbedrog
Abersoch
Aberdaron
675
Barmouth
Llangelynin
Tywyn
Aberdyfi

Cardigan Bay

Aberystwyth

Llanrhystud
A487
Cross Inn
Aberaeron
New Quay
CEREDIGION
Llanarth
Rosslare
Synod Inn
A487
Lampeter
Teifi
Aberporth
691
Llanybydder
Newport Bay
690
Cardigan
663
Fishguard Bay
Teifi
Llandysul
Llansawel
Goodwick
689
Newport
Newcastle Emlyn
Llangeler
Fishguard
Crymych
687
688
CARMARTHENSHIRE
St David's
PEMBROKESHIRE
Cynwyl Elfed
660
Llandeilo
Ramsey Island
A40
Llandissilio
Carmarthen
A40
Llanegwad
A483
661
686
685
Haverfordwest
A40
Whitland
662
A48
657
Broad Haven
Narberth
St Clears
Tywi
Ammanford
A4076
Templeton
A477
Milford Haven
Johnston
682
Kidwelly
Rosslare
Neyland
683
Saundersfoot
A478
Burry Port
Pembroke Dock
Pembrey
A4138
M4
684
Pembroke
Tenby
Llanelli
Manorbier
SWANSEA
Swansea
Llanrhidian
GOWER
The Mumbles

© Bartholomew Ltd 2003

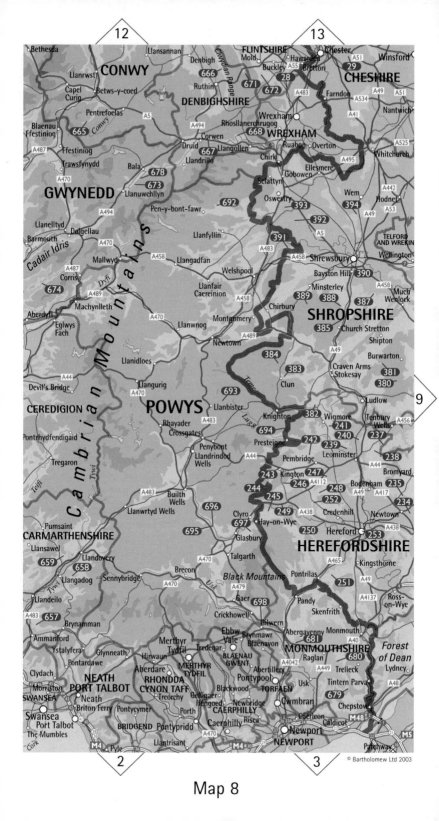

Map 8

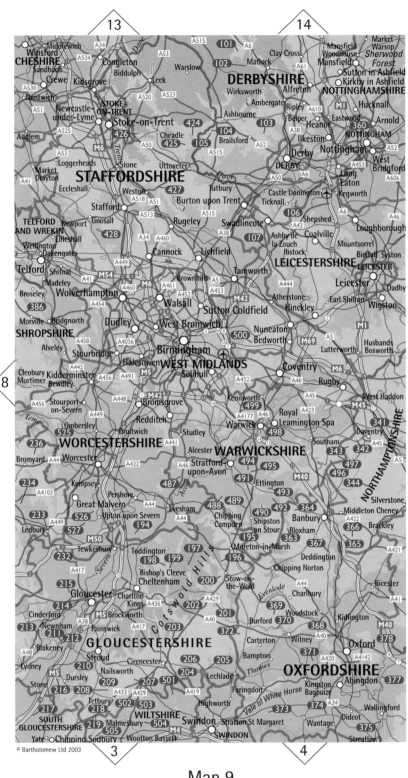

Map 9

Map 10

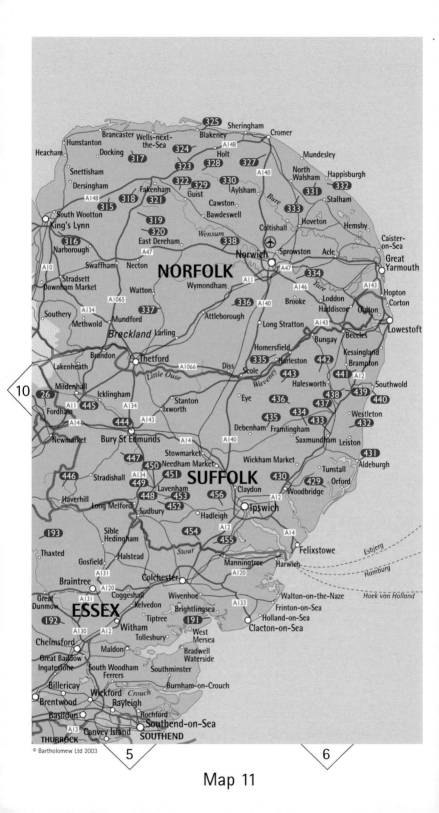

Map 11

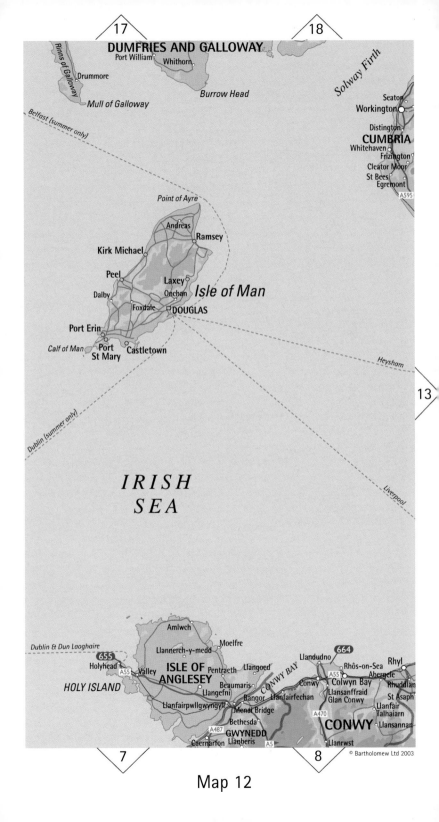

Map 12

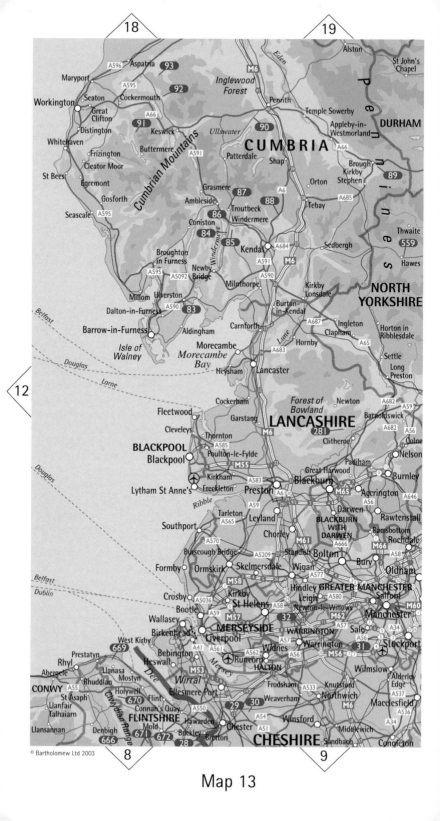

Map 13

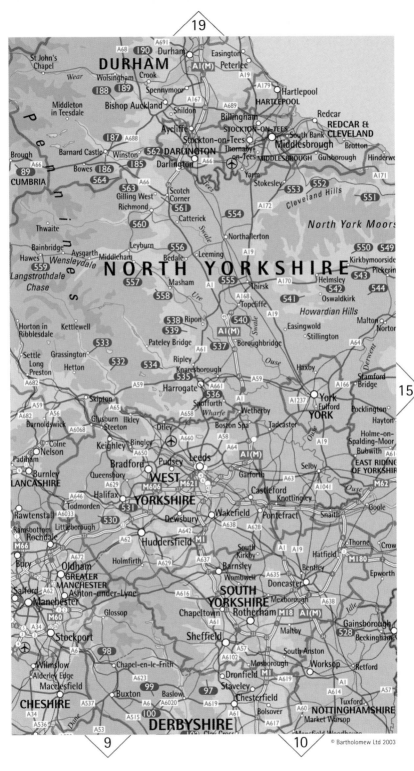

Map 14

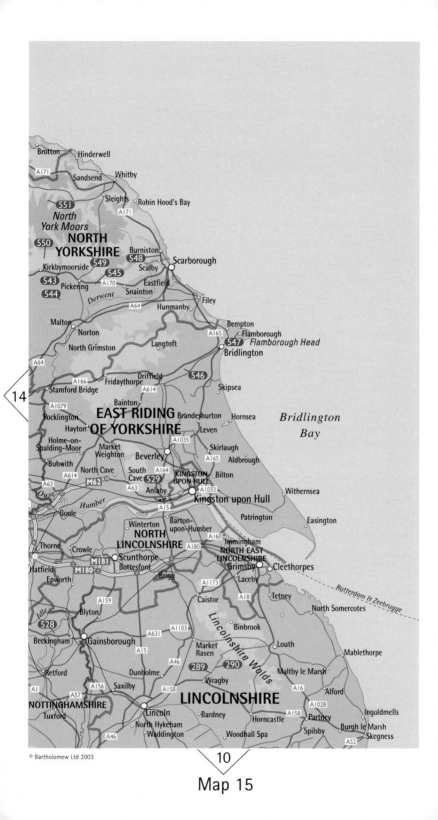

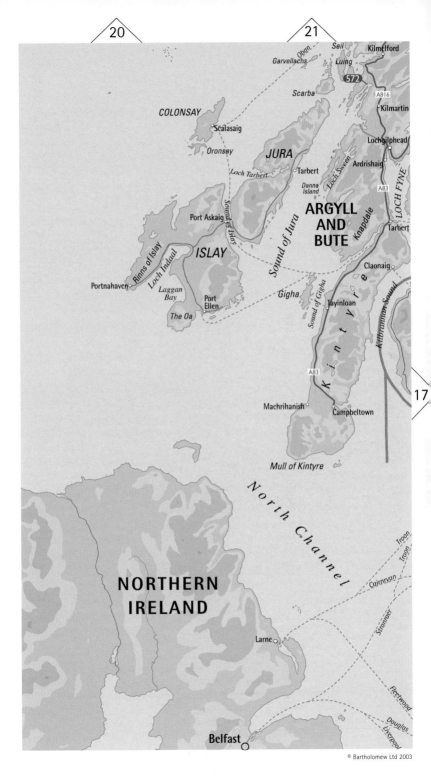

Map 16

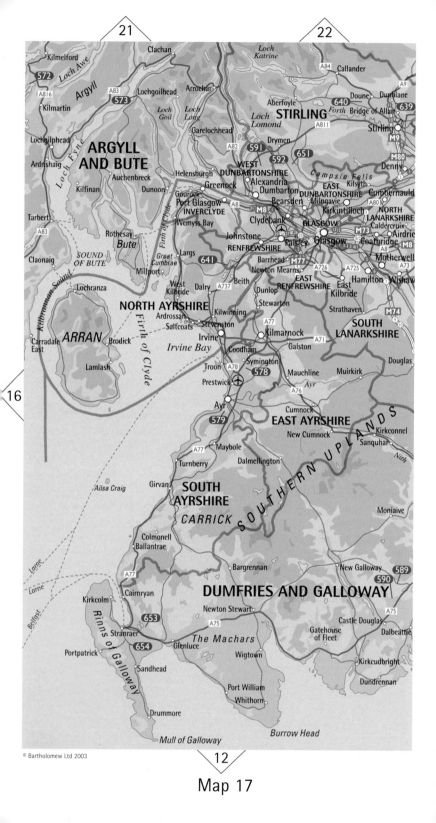

Map 17

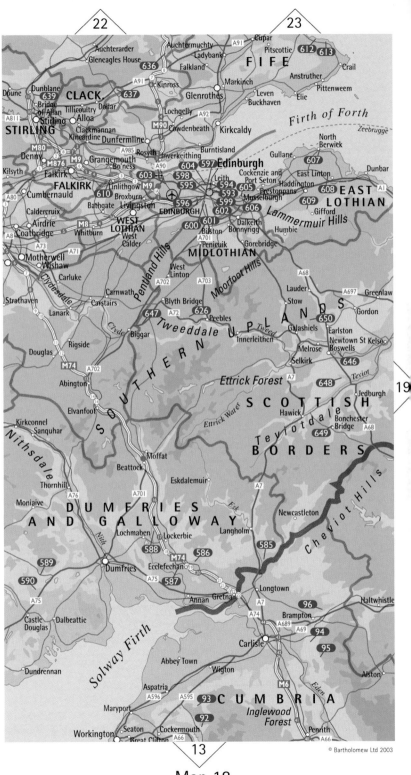

19

© Bartholomew Ltd 2003

Map 18

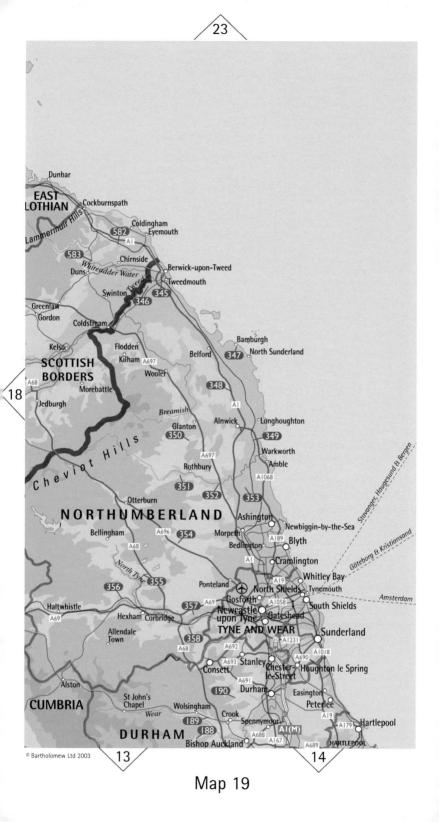

Dunbar
EAST LOTHIAN
Cockburnspath
Lammermuir Hills
Coldingham
582 Eyemouth
A1
583
Whiteadder Water
Chirnside
Duns
Berwick-upon-Tweed
Swinton *Tweed*
346 345
Tweedmouth
Greenlaw
Gordon
Coldstream
Kelso
Flodden
SCOTTISH BORDERS
Kilham A697
Bamburgh
Belford
North Sunderland
347
Wooler
348
A68
18
Morebattle
Jedburgh
Breamish
A1
Glanton
Alnwick
Longhoughton
350
349
Cheviot Hills
Rothbury
Warkworth
351
Amble
352
A697
A1068
Otterburn
353
NORTHUMBERLAND
Bellingham
A696
354
Ashington
Newbiggin-by-the-Sea
A68
Morpeth
A189
Bedlington
Blyth
A1
Cramlington
North Tyne
356 355
Ponteland
A19
Whitley Bay
Stavanger, Haugesund & Bergen
Göteborg & Kristiansand
Haltwhistle
357
A69
Gosforth
North Shields
Tynemouth
A69
A1058
Amsterdam
Hexham Corbridge
Newcastle upon Tyne
Gateshead
South Shields
Allendale Town
TYNE AND WEAR
Sunderland
A68
358
A1231
A692
A693
Stanley
A690
A1018
Consett
Chester-le-Street
Houghton le Spring
A691
Alston
190
Durham
Easington
Peterlee
CUMBRIA
St John's Chapel
Wolsingham
Wear
Crook
A19
A179
Hartlepool
189
Spennymoor
A1(M)
188
A688
A167
A689
HARTLEPOOL
DURHAM
Bishop Auckland

© Bartholomew Ltd 2003

Map 19

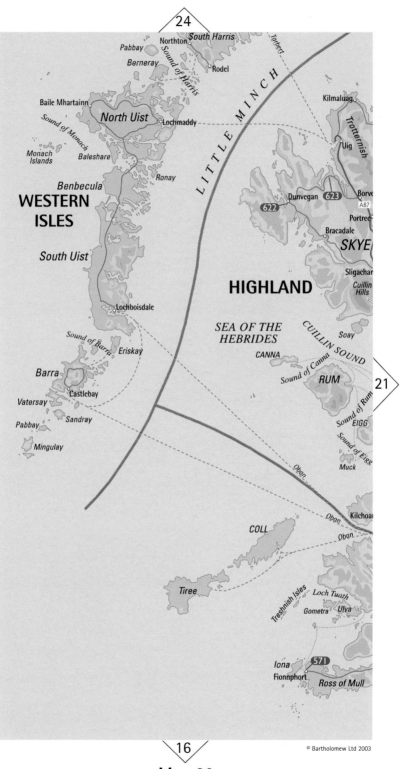

South Harris
Pabbay
Northton
Berneray
Sound of Harris
Rodel
Tarbert
LITTLE MINCH
Kilmaluag
Baile Mhartainn
North Uist
Trotternish
Sound of Monach
Lochmaddy
Uig
Monach Islands
Baleshare
Dunvegan
623
Borve
Benbecula
622
A87
WESTERN
ISLES
Ronay
Bracadale
Portree
SKYE
South Uist
Sligachan
Cuillin Hills
HIGHLAND
Lochboisdale
SEA OF THE
HEBRIDES
CUILLIN SOUND
Sound of Barra
Soay
Eriskay
CANNA
Sound of Canna
Barra
RUM
Vatersay
Castlebay
Sound of Rum
Sandray
EIGG
Pabbay
Sound of Eigg
Mingulay
Oban
Muck
Oban
Kilchoan
Oban
COLL
Tiree
Treshnish Isles
Loch Tuath
Gometra
Ulva
Iona
571
Fionnphort
Ross of Mull

Map 20

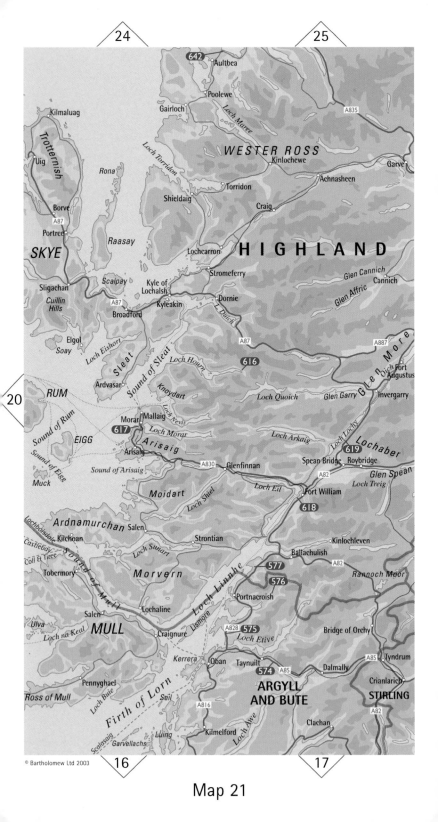

Map 21

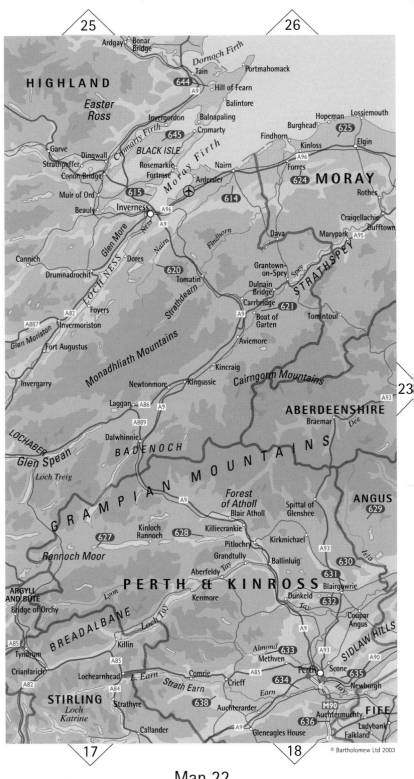

Map 22

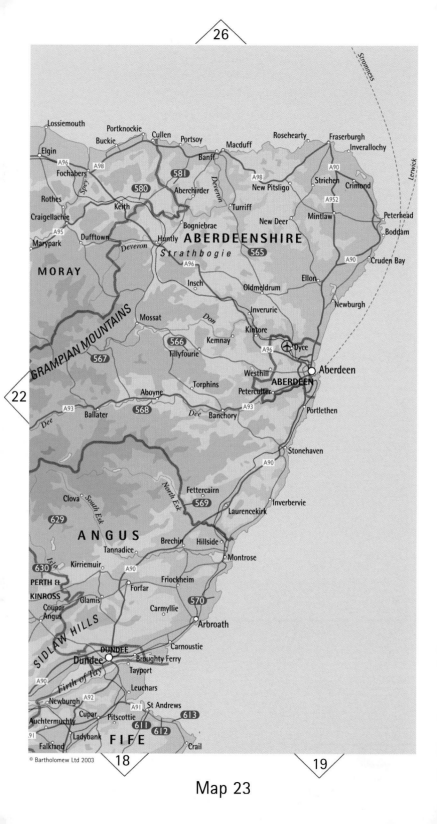

Lossiemouth
Portknockie
Buckie
Cullen
Portsoy
Macduff
Rosehearty
Fraserburgh
Inverallochy
Elgin
A96
A98
Banff
Fochabers
581
Strichen
Crimond
Spey
Deveron
A98
New Pitsligo
A90
Rothes
580
Aberchirder
Keith
Turriff
A952
Mintlaw
Peterhead
Craigellachie
A95
Bogniebrae
New Deer
Boddam
Maryculter
Dufftown
Deveron
Huntly
ABERDEENSHIRE
Cruden Bay
Strathbogie
565
Ellon
A90
Insch
Oldmeldrum
Newburgh
Mossat
Inverurie
Don
Kintore
GRAMPIAN MOUNTAINS
566
Kemnay
Dyce
Aberdeen
567
Tillyfourie
A96
Torphins
Westhill
ABERDEEN
Aboyne
Peterculter
22
A93
Ballater
568
Dee
Banchory
A93
Portlethen
Dee
Stonehaven
A90
Clova
Fettercairn
Inverbervie
South Esk
569
629
North Esk
Laurencekirk
ANGUS
Brechin
Hillside
Tannadice
Montrose
630
Kirriemuir
A90
Isla
Friockheim
PERTH &
Forfar
KINROSS
570
Glamis
Carmyllie
Coupar
Angus
Arbroath
SIDLAW HILLS
Carnoustie
DUNDEE
Dundee
Broughty Ferry
Tayport
A90
Firth of Tay
Leuchars
Newburgh
A92
St Andrews
Auchtermuchty
A91
Cupar
613
91
Pitscottie
Falkland
Ladybank
611
612
Crail
FIFE

Stromness
Lerwick

© Bartholomew Ltd 2003

Map 23

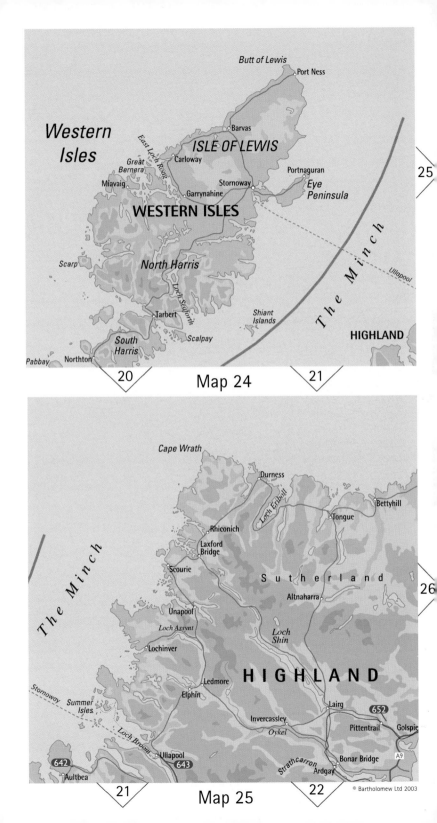

Map 24

Western Isles

Butt of Lewis
Port Ness
Barvas
ISLE OF LEWIS
East Loch Roag
Carloway
Great Bernera
Stornoway
Portnaguran
Miavaig
Eye Peninsula
Garrynahine
WESTERN ISLES
Ullapool
The Minch
Scarp
North Harris
Loch Seaforth
Shiant Islands
Tarbert
Scalpay
HIGHLAND
Pabbay
Northton
South Harris

20   21   25

Map 25

Cape Wrath
Durness
Bettyhill
Loch Eriboll
Tongue
Rhiconich
Laxford Bridge
Scourie
Sutherland
The Minch
Altnaharra
Unapool
Loch Assynt
Loch Shin
Lochinver
HIGHLAND
Stornoway
Summer Isles
Ledmore
Elphin
Lairg
652
Pittentrail
Golspie
Loch Broom
Invercassley
Oykel
A9
642
Ullapool
643
Strathcarron
Bonar Bridge
Aultbea
Ardgay

21   22   26

© Bartholomew Ltd 2003

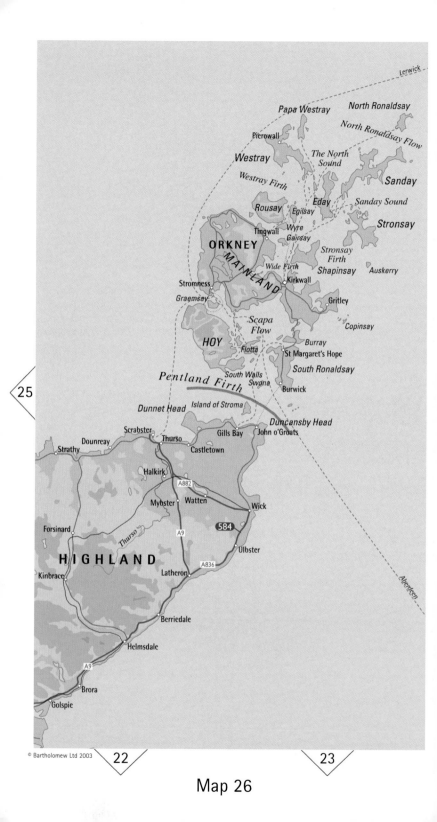

Map 26

HOW TO USE THIS BOOK

sample entry

CONWY

A haven for musicians, walkers and those who love the simple life. Fresh air, birdsong, good conversation and hot scones for breakfast – could you want more? Alan is a pianist who might play after your (excellent) supper; Irish Ger plays the fiddle and the organ. The small bedrooms in this long, low, wonky-floored granite cottage are whitewashed and simple, personalised with cheerful rugs and friends' paintings. The bathroom is overlooked only by sheep – and there's a guests' sitting room with a woodburner. An atmospheric, riverside retreat. *Children over 10 welcome.*

rooms	3: 1 double with bath/shower; 1 twin with private shower. Single room also available.
room price	£45. Singles £22.50.
meals	Dinner £12.50-£15. Supper £7.50. B.Y.O.
closed	November-March.
directions	From A5, B4406 through Penmachno. Left at The Eagles pub. On for 2 miles until 'S' bend sign; cottage on left just before bridge.

	Ger Tunstall
	Rhyd-y-Grô,
	Cwm Penmachno, Betws-y-Coed,
	Conwy LL24 0RB
tel	01690 760144
fax	01690 760144
e-mail	afonig@btinternet.com
web	www.afonig.com

❻ 🚲 📝 🥾

❼ map: 8 entry: 665

explanations

❶ rooms
We do not use the words 'en suite'.
WITH bath or **WITH shower** = **en suite**

If a room is not 'en suite' we say with private bathroom or with shared bathroom: the former you will have to yourself, the latter may be shared with other guests or family members; both will have a wc, basin and either a bath or a shower.

❷ room price
The price shown is for B&B for two people sharing a room. A price range incorporates room/seasonal differences. We also give single occupancy rates – the amount payable by one person staying in a room for two.

❸ meals
Prices are per person. All meals must be booked in advance. Ask the owner if you may bring your own wine. Some entries say B.Y.O.

❹ closed
When given in months, this means for the whole of the named months and the time in between.

❺ directions
Use as a guide; the owner can give more details.

❻ symbols
see the last page of the book for fuller explanation:

🐄 working farm
🚲 all children welcome
🐾 pets can sleep in your bedroom
🥗 vegetarians catered for with advance warning
♿ step-free access to bathroom/bedroom
♿ wheelchair facilities for one bedroom/bathroom
🚭 no smoking anywhere
🐾 this house has pets
💳 credit cards accepted
🍷 licensed premises
🚬 smoking permitted in certain rooms only
🚲 borrow or hire bikes here
🥾 good hiking from house or village

❼ Map & entry numbers
Map number; entry number.

www.thirdangle.com

ENGLAND

Step inside and forget the city bustle – serenity pervades the Smiths' Grade I-listed Bath apartment. A Chinese lantern with hand-painted silk, a fascinating mix of furniture and pottery, and framed embroideries and art from all over the world hint at a life of travel; he was with the British Council, both are charming and multi-lingual. The calm bedroom – pale walls, Delft chandelier, cream counterpanes – has a collection of books on art/tea/opera; choose one to browse, then wander into the courtyard garden where the colourful pots are arranged as artfully as the treasures in the house.

rooms	1 twin/double with bath.
room price	£60. Singles £45–£50.
meals	Breakfast until 8.45am. Good restaurants within walking distance.
closed	Christmas & New Year.
directions	A46 to Bath, then A4 for city centre. Left onto A36 over Cleveland Bridge; follow signs to Holburne Museum. Gt Pulteney St opp. museum. Down steps to basement. Parking £1 per day.

Chan Loo Smith
Apartment One,
60 Great Pulteney Street, Bath,
Bath & N.E. Somerset BA2 4DN

tel	01225 464134
fax	01225 483663
e-mail	chanloosmith@aptone.fsnet.co.uk

A very English house (1820 and listed) on the edge of this most English of cities. Mrs Bowman is charming, and fun, and gives you the freedom to come and go as you please. Rooms are quietly old-fashioned with some elegant touches and furniture that has evolved over the years. Views from the largest bedroom are unforgettable: the glorious Abbey lit up at night; more panoramas from the guests' drawing room, where French windows open to a lovely walled garden. Fresh fruit and croissants for breakfast, flowers from the garden, and the Roman city a 15-minute stride downhill.

rooms	2 twins, both with private bath.
room price	£56. Singles £32.
meals	Dinner 15-minute walk or short bus ride.
closed	Christmas & New Year.
directions	From Bath centre, 15-minute walk. Quarter way up Bathwick Hill. Pass Cleveland Walk on left, house one of big ones on right.

Mrs Elspeth Bowman
9 Bathwick Hill,
Bath,
Bath & N.E. Somerset BA2 6EW

| tel | 01225 460812 |

Simone has a natural sense of hospitality. Hers is a French-Caribbean welcome and she spoils you with cross-cultural colour: breakfasts of fruit, yogurt and cereals, as well as traditional English; the décor and even the pretty crockery have an exotic flavour. Bedrooms feel luxurious with embroidered cotton, fluffy towels and thick curtains in beautiful fabrics. The garden looks French and formal, with box parterre, lavender and roses. You are less than 10 minutes' walk from the city centre and there are views to the floodlit Abbey and National Trust land. *Babies and children over 10 welcome.*

Come for fine hilltop views of Bath or walk up through the large gardens to Solsbury Hill where the views get even better. Naomi and Austin are chatty and fun: he used to be a dairy farmer and she is a reiki healer and can treat you at the house. Behind the modern exterior are family antiques and pretty furnishings – a distinctly elegant feel. The bedrooms have deep, dark-blue carpets, Farrow & Ball papers and paints, pine furniture, rattan lamp shades and watercolours; bathrooms are newly done. You are no distance from Bath city centre: 12 minutes by car, 35 by foot.

rooms	3: 1 double with bath/shower; 1 twin, 1 single, both with private bath.
room price	£65. Singles £45.
meals	Breakfast 7.30-9am. Pubs & restaurants close by.
closed	Christmas Day.
directions	From Bath centre follow signs to American Museum. Pass Mercedes garage (300 yds up Bathwick Hill on right). 1st road on right after garage. On right, 300 yds down.

rooms	3: 1 twin, 1 double, 1 single, all with private bath.
room price	£40-£75.
meals	Packed lunch £6. Pub 500 yds.
closed	Christmas.
directions	M4 exit 18, A46 south to Batheaston r'bout & Bath exit. Left towards Batheaston; after 0.5 miles left into Bailbrook Lane; house last on right.

Mrs S Johnson
47 Sydney Buildings,
Bathwick Hill, Bath,
Bath & N.E. Somerset BA2 6DB

tel	01225 463033
fax	01225 461054
e-mail	sydneybuildings@bigfoot.com
web	www.sydneybuildings.co.uk

Naomi Chamberlain
Highfields,
207 Bailbrook Lane, Batheaston,
Bath,
Bath & N.E. Somerset BA1 7AB

tel	01225 859782
e-mail	acham@supanet.com
web	www.highfieldsbath.co.uk

Such a gorgeous, mullion-windowed, rambler-rose-strewn home. It sits in 450 acres with views to Bristol on a clear day. Graham runs the farm, now converted to organic status, and he makes Bath soft cheese – "delicious", said our inspector – and helps the sweet, sunny Gabrielle run the B&B. Quiet guest bedrooms are in their own wing; they overlook the village gardens and are carpeted, cottagey and decorated in soft colours. You can breakfast beside the inglenook fireplace, or in the garden on a warm summer's day. The guest book overflows with praise for Gabrielle's cooking – and her welcome.

There's city convenience (Bath's only five miles), but this feels a world away from… most places! In fact, there's a total other worldliness about the Lock Cottage and its pretty, rose-filled garden: colourful narrow boats drift lazily up the old Somerset Coal Canal that runs through the garden, and idling feels compulsory. There's a peaceful towpath walk to the local pub and a café/restaurant, or you can hire an electric launch for a day's pootling, or a bike. It's an easy place for families to be happy together. Bedrooms are simple and cottagey with watery views and Wendy gives an easy welcome.

rooms	2: 1 double with bath/shower; 1 twin with shower.
room price	£60. Singles £45.
meals	Good pubs in village.
closed	Rarely.
directions	From Bath A431 (Upper Bristol Rd), signed Bitton. Kelston 2.5 miles. 1st left into 1st turning in village by cul-de-sac sign. House 1st on right.

rooms	2: 1 double, 1 twin/double, both with private bath/shower.
room price	£52–£57. Singles by arrangement.
meals	Breakfast until 9am. Pub 1 mile.
closed	Christmas & New Year.
directions	5 miles south of Bath just off A36, 50 yds north of Suzuki garage. Entrance at an oblique angle. Turn in road opposite or approach from south.

Gabrielle Padfield
Park Farm,
Kelston, Bath,
Bath & N.E. Somerset BA1 9AG

tel 01225 424139
fax 01225 331906
e-mail parkfarm.b.b@amserve.net
web www.parkfarm.co.uk

Tim & Wendy Wheeldon
Dundas Lock Cottage,
Monkton Combe, Bath,
Bath & N.E. Somerset BA2 7BN

tel 01225 723890
fax 01225 723890
e-mail dundaslockcottage@freenet.co.uk

map: 3 entry: 5

map: 3 entry: 6

The Addicotts have given over a generous swathe of their farm to the creation of a natural habitat for indigenous wildlife; they have a Gold Award under the Duke of Cornwall's Habitat Award 2002 scheme to boot. Utterly committed to the environment, they use flax from the vibrant blue linseed crops to heat their sturdy listed house. There are stone mullion windows, dressers with old china, Chinese rugs on wooden floors, open fires, a smattering of Africana and big bedrooms with all mod cons. Your affable hosts manage the mix of B&B-ing and farming with easy-going humour and a passion for Bath rugby.

Duchy of Cornwall farmland stretches as far as the eye can see – the views from this neatly-converted, open-plan barn are magnificent by any standards, but remarkable considering you are so close to Bath. There's much wildlife, too: sparrowhawks nest in the gable end and buzzards circle above the valley. Spruce guest rooms with houseplants and excellent beds are painted in pale colours. Giles and Sue serve delicious breakfasts on the terrace when the weather is fine… and the glories of Bath are a short ride away – by bus or by car.

rooms	4: 1 double with bath; 2 doubles, 1 twin, all sharing bath/shower.
room price	From £54. Singles £32.
meals	Pub 300 yds.
closed	Christmas & New Year.
directions	From A4 west of Bath, A39 through Corston. 1 mile on, just before Wheatsheaf Pub (on right), right. Signed 200 yds along lane on right.

rooms	2: 1 twin/double with bath; 1 double with private shower.
room price	£55-£60. Singles £37.50-£40.
meals	Excellent restaurants nearby.
closed	Christmas & New Year.
directions	From Bath, A367 (Wells Rd). At Odd Down r'bout right (Bristol A4). Straight on, past Culverhay School on left. After 100 yds left to Englishcombe. There, right after postbox to church, fork right, follow road; last on right.

Gerald & Rosaline Addicott
Corston Fields Farm,
Corston, Bath,
Bath & N.E. Somerset BA2 9EZ
tel   01225 873305
fax   01225 874421
e-mail corston.fields@btinternet.com
web   www.corstonfields.com

Sue & Giles Barber
Manor Farm Barn,
Englishcombe, Bath,
Bath & N.E. Somerset BA2 9DU
tel   01225 424195
fax   01225 427434
e-mail info@manorfarmbarn.com
web   www.manorfarmbarn.com

A delicious place, managing to combine elegance with cosiness and comfort. Logs smoulder in the fire, the colours are warm, the dresser is Welsh, the stones are flagged. And such a lovely kitchen, with Aga, terracotta tiles and inviting cherrywood table. There are winding stairs, an old bread oven, quirky touches everywhere – and the double bedroom is pure magic, with gorgeous furniture and a quilt made by Angharad. She is an aromatherapist (treatments can be booked) and has the same warmth and offbeat elegance as the house. Only a couple of doors away is an excellent village pub. *Children over five welcome.*

rooms	2: 1 double with shower, 1 single with bath.
room price	From £55. Singles £35.
meals	Light supper from £10. Excellent pub close by.
closed	Rarely.
directions	From Bath A367 Exeter road. After 3 miles, left opp. Strydes Inn, signed 'Wellow 3 miles'. Park in square by Fox & Badger pub. House 2 doors down in Railway Lane.

Angharad Rhys–Roberts
Honey Batch Cottage,
Railway Lane, Wellow, Bath,
Bath & N.E. Somerset BA2 8QG
tel 01225 833107
e–mail angharad@waitrose.com

map: 3 entry: 9

Interesting, child-friendly hosts who are entirely natural and un-businesslike make this place special; it's excellent value, too. The large old Mendip-style 'long cottage' with mullioned windows and beams made of ships' timbers is fronted by a vineyard and is temptingly close to Babington House, the treasures of Bath and Wells, the gardens and concerts at Stourhead and Gregorian chant in Downside Abbey. Fresh, simple bedrooms have sloping ceilings and fresh flowers; jams and marmalades are home-made. No sitting room, but tea in the beautiful walled garden is rich compensation. *Children over five welcome.*

rooms	3: 1 twin with shower; 1 double, 1 single, both with shared bath.
room price	£35-£45. Singles £22.50.
meals	Pub 2 miles.
closed	Rarely.
directions	From Bath A367, Wells road, through Radstock. After 3 miles, at large r'bout, B3139 for Trowbridge. 1.1 miles on, right up drive. House at top, visible from road.

Virginia & Hugh Pountney
Melon Cottage Vineyard,
Charlton, Radstock, Nr. Bath,
Bath & N.E. Somerset BA3 5TN
tel 01761 435090
e–mail v.pountney@virgin.net

map: 3 entry: 10

Meandering lanes lead to this 17th-century cottage, with roses round the door, a grandfather clock in the hall and an air of genteel tranquillity. The cottage charm has been updated with Regency mahogany and sumptuous sofas. There's even a four-poster bed for a single guest and the bedrooms have long views over farmland and undulating countryside. Behind the cottage is a newly enlarged conservatory – a lovely place for breakfast – and a sloping, south-facing garden with a pond and some rare trees and shrubs. Escorted children will enjoy visiting the farm opposite. Bath is 20 minutes away; Julia knows the city well.

You are in a conservation area, yet only five minutes from the centre of Bath – the views are breathtaking from wherever you stand. The steep valley rolls out ahead of you from most of the rooms, and from the garden comes a confusion and a profusion of scents and colours – a glory in its own right. The friendly and likeable Sticklands are conservationists as well as gardeners and have a Green Certificate to prove it. Breakfasts are a feast: bacon and eggs, cereals, home-grown jam, kedgeree. Jane will tell you all about wonderful local gardens to visit.

rooms	4: 1 twin, 1 single four-poster, 1 double, all with bath/shower; 1 double with shared bath & shower.
room price	From £60. Family suite (2 rooms) £85. Singles £30.
meals	Dinner from £15.
closed	Rarely.
directions	From Bath, A36 to Woolverton. Just past Red Lion, turn for Laverton. 1 mile to x-roads, & towards Faukland. Downhill for 80 yds. House on left, just above farm entrance on right.

rooms	3: 2 twins/doubles, 1 family, all with shower.
room price	£65-£75. Singles £35-£45.
meals	Breakfast 7-9.30am. Pub/restaurant 2 miles.
closed	Rarely.
directions	From A36 about 3 miles out of Bath on Warminster road, take uphill road by lights & Viaduct Inn. 1st left, approx. 100 yds, signed Monkton Combe. After village, house 1st on left, 0.5 miles on.

Mrs Julia Naismith
Hollytree Cottage,
Laverton, Bath,
Bath & N.E. Somerset BA2 7QZ
tel   01373 830786
fax   01373 830786
e-mail   julia@naismith.fsbusiness.co.uk

Jane & Anthony Stickland
Grey Lodge,
Summer Lane, Combe Down, Bath,
Bath & N.E. Somerset BA2 7EU
tel   01225 832069
fax   01225 830161
e-mail   greylodge@freenet.co.uk
web   www.greylodge.co.uk

map: 3 entry: 11

map: 3 entry: 12

O n warm summer mornings you can come to, peacefully, on the terrace – it's bliss, with amazing views over the Mendips' rolling hills. Views from the bedroom are of the walled garden and will encourage you to explore… immaculate lawns, deep herbaceous borders, croquet lawn, masses of roses and clematis and a burgeoning fruit and vegetable garden. The Stevens have poured a huge amount of love into it all. There are home-made biscuits on the bedroom tea tray and you have exclusive use of the drawing room. You are minutes from Bath and Bristol and Julia has much local knowledge. *Children over 12 welcome.*

rooms	1 twin/double with extra single bed, bath & shower.
room price	£60. Singles £35.
meals	Dinner £15-£20. Excellent pubs/restaurants nearby.
closed	Mid-December-mid-January.
directions	From Bath, A4 west. At r'bout by Globe Inn, left onto A39 for Wells. Through Corston, after 0.5 miles B3116, sharp right. After 1 mile left for Burnett & next right. House 100 yds on left.

Patrick & Julia Stevens
Brooklands,
Burnett, Keynsham, Bath,
Bath & N.E. Somerset BS31 2TF
tel   0117 986 8794
fax   0117 986 8794
e-mail   patrick@micamail.com

T he Bath stone of this Georgian replica will soon be swathed in rambling roses and who wouldn't have chosen this spot to build? It is close to the centre of Bath, yet wonderfully secluded in its elevated grounds and the views are tremendous. The house, named after one of Andrew's illustrious forbears, is pristine with handsome furniture and family portraits in gilt frames. Your lovely hosts enjoy entertaining and will spoil you with an excellent dinner from the Aga – Philippa is an experienced Cordon Bleu cook.

rooms	2: 1 twin/double with bath/shower; 1 twin/double with basin & private shower.
room price	£75. Singles £50.
meals	Breakfast until 9am. Dinner £25.
closed	Rarely.
directions	A4/A46 Bath, then ring-road clockwise, signed A4, for Bristol. Left for Claverton Down just before White Hart. 0.5 miles up Widcombe Hill on left.

Philippa & Andrew Gordon-Duff
Blantyre House,
Widcombe Hill, Bath,
Bath & N.E. Somerset BA2 6AE
tel   01225 480682
fax   01225 789543
e-mail   blantyrebath@aol.com
web   www.blantyre-house.co.uk

Stroll easily into Bath... or stay above the fray, with fine mature trees all around you, a croquet lawn and a summer house. Your affable, well-travelled hosts' Victorian family home is smartly decorated – pale fitted carpets, ruched curtains, Regency stripes. Peaceful, big-windowed bedrooms are comfortable, with space to sit, original fireplaces and cosy touches. Albert has views of Bath Abbey, magnificently illuminated at night; Palmerston has its own baby grand paino that you're welcome to play. Breakfasts include fresh fruit and home-baked bread served on family china.

Owl House has the best of both worlds: a rural setting yet it's only three miles from Bath. Breakfast on the terrace and gaze over the honey-coloured collage of the city below – a stunning spectacle from this lofty vantage point. Old Cotswold stone outside, modernity within; there are good beds in comfortable rooms, a striking selection of art and a décor spiced with a touch of the orient. Anne has spent many years in the East and rooms are bedecked with batiks and other Malaysian memorabilia. She enjoys sharing her home with guests.

rooms	4: 1 twin/double, 1 double, both with shower; 1 double, 1 single, both with private bath/shower.
room price	£65-£75. Singles £40-£60.
meals	Breakfast 7.30-9am. Excellent choice of restaurants in Bath.
closed	Christmas.
directions	A36 (Warminster road) from Bath. At boundary Bath/Bathampton, right on to North Rd, pass Golf Club entrance on left, house 200 yds further on right.

rooms	3: 1 twin/family with shower; 1 double with bath & shower; 1 double/single with private shower.
room price	£52-£65. Singles £38.
meals	Breakfast 8.30-9.30am. Excellent pub within walking distance.
closed	Rarely.
directions	M4 exit 18, A46. A46 joins A4, left for Chippenham. At r'bout, A363. Under bridge, bear left at Crown pub into Bathford. 1.5 miles uphill, left after Swan pub (Lower Kingsdown Rd). Bear right at bottom, house 300 yds on left.

Patrick & Hilary Bryan
Ravenscroft,
North Road, Bathwick, Bath,
Bath & N.E. Somerset BA2 6HZ
tel   01225 461919
fax   01225 461919
e-mail   patrick@ravenscroftbandb.co.uk
web   www.ravenscroftbandb.co.uk

Anne Venus
Owl House,
Kingsdown, Nr. Box, Bath,
Bath & N.E. Somerset SN13 8BB
tel   01225 743883
fax   01225 744450
e-mail   venus@zetnet.co.uk
web   www.owlhouse.co.uk

map: 3 entry: 15

map: 3 entry: 16

The welcome is the same, the house is new – and what a place! The Welfares moved here from another Special Place and Pevsner described this as "the most ambitious house in Hungerford". It is a classic townhouse with a Queen Anne façade and, inside, wood panelling and beams, wonky floors, period furniture and family portraits. Bedrooms are fresh, traditional, perfect; so is breakfast in the 18th-century dining room. The Welfares give a terrific welcome. Antique shops to the front and a walled garden with cordon-trained fruit trees behind. *Children over eight welcome.*

If you want to swim, there's an indoor heated pool; if you want to walk, there are 650 acres of farmland and a dog to keep you company. Both hosts are multilingual and enjoy their guests: Henry works less on the farm now and has turned his hand to breakfasts, served in the beamed kitchen. Some of the guest rooms date back to the 16th century and are large, bright, airy, simply and attractively decorated and have views of well-tended garden and fields. The sitting room has a large open fire and there is a huge selection of books and classical CDs.

rooms	2: 1 double, 1 twin/double, both with bath.
room price	£58. Singles £39.
meals	Breakfast until 9am Mon-Fri; flexible Sat-Sun. Packed lunch £5. Dinner within walking distance.
closed	Christmas.
directions	Junc. 14 from M4. Follow A338 to A4; right for Marlborough. Turn off A4 at Bear Hotel onto Salisbury road (A338). Over canal bridge into High St. House 200 yds past Town Hall on right.

rooms	3: 2 twins/doubles, both with bath/shower; 1 twin/double with private bath/shower.
room price	£52-£60. Singles £35-£50.
meals	Breakfast 7.30-9am; continental until 10am. Good pub 0.5 miles.
closed	Rarely.
directions	From M4 junc. 14, A338 north for Wantage. After 0.5 miles, 1st left (B4000). 1st farm road on right after Pheasant Inn to house.

	Deborah & Jonathan Welfare
	Wilton House,
	33 High Street, Hungerford,
	Berkshire RG17 0NF
tel	01488 684228
fax	01488 685037
e-mail	welfares@hotmail.com
web	www.wiltonhouse.freeserve.co.uk

	Mary & Henry Wilson
	Fishers Farm,
	Shefford Woodlands, Hungerford,
	Berkshire RG17 7AB
tel	01488 648466
fax	01488 648706
e-mail	mail@fishersfarm.co.uk
web	www.fishersfarm.co.uk

BRISTOL

BRISTOL

An easy-going family house and hostess; you'll feel at home in the city and have enough privacy to ensure a peaceful stay. Anne has furnished the freshly-painted bedrooms with modern paintings, stunning wall hangings, antiques, pretty china and comfy sofas; light and airy, the sky-blue room with white muslin curtains and white linen is a delight. Luxurious bathrooms have large mirrors, fluffy towels and seriously strong showers. Breakfast (as organic as possible) is served on a raspberry silk tablecloth on white china. It's a short walk to Clifton village, the Suspension Bridge and the thriving harbourside.

The first house to be built in Clifton Park in 1797, now surrounded by busy streets, it is imposing, delightful and ivy-clad. Fight your way past a beautiful muddle of things – books, pictures, shells, fossils and pre-war wooden sports gear – to your pretty, old-fashioned bedroom. The upstairs one has views over one of the walled gardens around which two white breeding Call ducks plod and the downstairs twin is next to a library stuffed with books. A light sitting-room has a large table for breakfast and a view of the other garden. Delia is wise, friendly and kind and you are within walking distance of everything.

rooms	3: 2 doubles, 1 twin, all with shower.		rooms	2: 1 double, 1 twin, both with shower.
room price	From £70. Singles from £50.		room price	£65. Singles £50.
meals	Breakfast from 7.30am. Many places to eat within 10-minute walk.		meals	Excellent restaurants within walking distance.
closed	Rarely.		closed	24 December-2 January; 1 week over Easter.
directions	M5 junc. 18; A4 signs to Bristol West & airport; under Suspension Bridge & follow city sign. Follow lane signed Clifton; left into Clifton Vale before church; 1st right into Camden Terrace; on right.		directions	Directions given when booking. From Temple Meads Station, take 8 or 9 bus to Student Union, Queens Road, Clifton.

Anne Malindine
14 Camden Terrace,
Clifton Vale, Bristol BS8 4PU
tel   0117 914 9508
fax   0117 914 9508
e-mail anne@amalindine.freeserve.co.uk
web   www.roseberyhouse.net

Mrs Delia Macdonald
Park House,
19 Richmond Hill, Clifton, Bristol,
Bristol BS8 1BA
tel   0117 973 6331

BRISTOL

Unabashedly 1920s mock-Tudor with an oak-panelled hall and a great engraved fireplace. This is a generous house on the edge of the Bristol Downs, perfectly placed for country quiet in the evening after daytime city bustle. Light from the garden floods in and Philippa, with long experience of five-star hotels, does an efficient, professional job. The breakfast menu is mouthwatering and the morning papers come with it. Rooms are 'fully-equipped' and comfortable, but if you prefer a family house feel, ask for a room in the house; other rooms are in the annexe. *Children over seven welcome.*

rooms	6: 4 doubles, all with shower & private wc; 1 twin with bath; 1 single with private bath.
room price	£65-£69. Singles £45-£49.
meals	Dinner 10-minute walk.
closed	Christmas & New Year.
directions	From M5, exit 17 onto A4018. At 4th r'bout 3rd exit into Parry's Lane. Left into Saville Rd. 3rd right into Hollybush Lane. 1st left immed. after 2nd road hump into Downs Edge. Drive to end.

Alan & Philippa Tasker
Downs Edge,
Saville Road, Stoke Bishop,
Bristol BS9 1JA

tel	0117 968 3264
fax	0117 968 7063
e-mail	welcome@downsedge.com

BUCKINGHAMSHIRE

This is a one-off. Sarah's conversion, architectural rather than religious, has turned a fascinating church into a fascinating home, complete with tower and spiral staircase, original stained glass and stone mullion windows. It has a charm all of its own – the Winnie the Pooh mural in one bedroom and the fish swimming around the bathroom walls are amusing touches. The bedrooms are compact but each has its own church window. The old schoolroom is now a kitchen/dining room – impressively big and a great place for breakfast. Sarah is ease personified and this is really good value.

rooms	3: 1 double, 1 twin, 1 single, sharing bath & shower.
room price	£45. Singles £30.
meals	Excellent restaurants & pubs nearby.
closed	Rarely.
directions	From Aylesbury, A413 for Buckingham. In Winslow centre, left into Horn St between Bell Hotel & The George. On left.

Sarah Hood
The Congregational Church,
15 Horn Street, Winslow,
Buckinghamshire MK18 3AP

tel	01296 715717
fax	01296 715717
e-mail	sarahhood@waitrose.com

CAMBRIDGESHIRE

CAMBRIDGESHIRE

One cosy and very private bedroom is up its own spiral stair – a lovely conversion and sure winner of first prize in any Loo With A View competition. In the main house is a fresh blue and white bedroom; a lovely big new room on the ground floor has its own entrance. All are spotless. You will unwind quickly here, as the Barlows' relaxed 'take-us-as-you-find-us' approach pervades the whole house. There are fruit trees and bees and home-made jam and honey for breakfast and, although this is an arable farm, sheep still graze the land. Beautifully quiet, and close to Cambridge.

Roman remains, Saxon hamlet, 13th-century church, Georgian house... The estate has been in the family for nearly 600 years but the present house was built in 1820. Very much a family home, it's big, comfortably furnished, informal and friendly, with three dogs and an African grey parrot. You eat in the impressive dining room, under the gaze of oil-painted ancestors; you may use the cosy family sitting room, too. Pleasant bedrooms look out over big gardens to peaceful Cambridgeshire countryside; the only sound is the cawing of rooks in the ancient trees nearby.

rooms	3 doubles all with shower.
room price	£50. Singles up to £30.
meals	Breakfast 7.30-9.30am. Pub/restaurant 3 miles.
closed	Christmas.
directions	From A1198 at Longstowe onto B1046. House on right after 3 miles, before Little Gransden.

rooms	3: 1 twin with bath; 1 twin with shower; 1 double with private bath.
room price	£60. Singles £45.
meals	Dinner £15; 3 courses, £18. Good pub 300 yds.
closed	Christmas & New Year.
directions	From Royston A505 towards Baldock. Right to Litlington; at church, fork right to Abington Pigotts. After Pig & Abbott Pub, left up Church Lane; house on left of church.

Sue Barlow
Model Farm,
Little Gransden,
Cambridgeshire SG19 3EA

tel	01767 677361
fax	01767 677883
e-mail	bandb@modelfarm.org.uk
web	www.modelfarm.org.uk

Guy & Eleanor Sclater
Abington Pigotts Hall,
Nr Royston,
Cambridgeshire SG8 0SH

tel	01763 852310
e-mail	guysclater@aol.com

map: 10 entry: 23

map: 10 entry: 24

A happy combination of elegance and a bustling family atmosphere in a large 1840 Regency-style home. The former school house hugs the bend of a river on the edge of the quiet, ancient village of Linton and the rooms overlook the large gardens and the river. The conservatory, draped with a mimosa tree, is exceptional and a wonderful spot for summer breakfasts, while in winter one 'repairs' to the dark green dining room. Bedrooms are large, so are the beds, and are stocked with books. This is exceptional value, and Cambridge is nearby.

Breakfasts here are something of a legend: soft cheeses, hams, black puddings, kippers and haddock – the freshest, locally sourced produce is served at 7am if you like. The Ropers bend over backwards to meet guests' needs and many that come to stay are here for the horsey connection: Malcolm's an equine buff and organises racing packages and, of course, the racecourse is close by. Jan, formerly an illustrator, cooks and attends to the décor – old pine, huge cushions, handsome wallpapers and fresh flowers. The Georgian home has a croquet lawn and a conservatory, too. *Minimum stay 2 nights in high season.*

rooms	2: 1 double with bath; 1 double with bath/shower.
room price	£50–£60. Singles £27–£35.
meals	Breakfast 7.30-9.30am. Pub 150 yds.
closed	Rarely.
directions	A1307 from Cambridge, left into High St. 1st right after The Crown (on left) into Horn Lane. House on right next to chapel, before ford.

rooms	2: 1 twin with bath; 1 double with shower.
room price	From £60. Singles from £40. Occasionally, min. stay 2 nights.
meals	Breakfast 7-9.15am. Restaurants within walking distance.
closed	Rarely.
directions	A142 Newmarket to Ely road, through Fordham & right at Murfitts Lane; at end, right into Carter St; Queensberry 200 yds on left next to Fordham Moor Road.

Judith Rossiter
Springfield House,
14-16 Horn Lane, Linton,
Cambridgeshire CB1 6HT
tel 01223 891383
fax 01223 890335

Jan & Malcolm Roper
Queensberry,
196 Carter Street, Fordham, Ely,
Cambridgeshire CB7 5JU
tel 01638 720916
fax 01638 720233
e-mail queensberry@queensberry196.demon.co.uk

CAMBRIDGESHIRE

You are in the middle of an ancient market town with narrow streets and medieval buildings, yet have a beautiful one-acre garden in which to wander, with lawns, shrubbery, orchard and vegetable garden. The Friend-Smiths have retained the original Edwardian garden design. The feel in the bedrooms is traditional English with good quality linen and country antiques and you have lovely views of the garden and cathedral. Sheila serves locally baked bread and home-made marmalade at the long mahogany dining table. The cathedral is only five minutes' walk and Cambridge 15 miles.

rooms	2: 1 double with private bath; 1 twin with bath.
room price	£52. Singles £35–£42.
meals	Breakfast until 9.30am. Dinner 4-minute walk.
closed	Christmas, New Year, & for annual holiday.
directions	From Cambridge, A10. Entering Ely, left at lights by Lamb Hotel. Left at next lights, after 200 yds into Egremont Street. House last on left. Off-street parking just beyond.

Sheila & Jeremy Friend-Smith
Old Egremont House,
31 Egremont Street, Ely,
Cambridgeshire CB6 1AE
tel 01353 663118
fax 01353 614516

CHESHIRE

Rachel is delightful, warm and friendly. This is Britain at its best with rare trees planted in 1860, flowers everywhere, a pond and a fruitful vegetable garden. The Victorian house is furnished in elegant and traditional style, with garden views from every angle. The proportions of the light-filled drawing room and the big, high-ceilinged dining room feel just right. The bedrooms are inviting, bright and large with attractive fabrics, art and lovely furniture. This is a haven for garden buffs, walkers and birdwatchers and there's tennis, too. Easy access to Chester and North Wales.

rooms	3: 2 twins/doubles, both with bath; 1 double with shower.
room price	From £52. Singles by arrangement.
meals	Good pub/restaurant 0.5 miles.
closed	Christmas & New Year.
directions	From Chester, A55 west, then A5104 to Broughton. Through Broughton & over A55. 1st left to Kinnerton down Lesters Lane. On right, 0.75 miles down, opp. Mount Farm.

Jonathan & Rachel Major
The Mount,
Higher Kinnerton, Chester,
Cheshire CH4 9BQ
tel 01244 660275
fax 01244 660275
e-mail major@mountkinnerton.freeserve.co.uk

Explore the intriguing city of Chester with its Roman history and 900-year-old cathedral... before returning the short distance (four miles) to the farm. You have 250 acres to explore and geese, sheep, and, maybe, otters to watch. Parts of the farm are cared for under the Countyside Stewardship Scheme. Bedrooms are 'stylish farmhouse' with lovely fabrics and touches of luxury, such as huge bath towels, but best of all is the relaxed, family atmosphere created by the Hills. Breakfasts are excellent, cooked by Clare who was trained by Prue Leith.

Light-filled rooms are furnished with style and restraint, and have views over five counties. A wide, graceful hall runs from one end of the house to the other, past old prints, alcoves of china and a spinet. Polished stairs lead to delightful bedrooms overlooking the Welsh hills; bathrooms are new and superb. Ardmore is in a leafy, rural setting (there are two good pubs in walking distance) and was built in the 1930s in the Arts & Crafts style. The lovely gardens, in the same idiom and are being restored by Flossy, yield fresh fruit for breakfast; there's home-baked bread, too. *Children over 10 welcome.*

rooms	3: 2 doubles, 1 twin, all with bath/shower.
room price	From £52. Singles £32.
meals	Pub 1.5 miles.
closed	Rarely.
directions	From Chester, A51 east, signed Nantwich. 1.5 miles from city outskirts, right, down Cotton lane, signed Cotton Edmunds. 1.5 miles, on sharp right-hand bend, left. Farm 2nd drive on right.

rooms	2: 1 double with bath/shower; 1 twin with shower.
room price	£70. Singles from £35.
meals	Pub & fish restaurant within walking distance.
closed	Christmas & occasionally.
directions	A51 from Chester; at Stamford Bridge traffic lights, left to Barrow (B5132); house 1.5 miles, on left with pointed oak gateposts.

Clare & Nigel Hill
Cotton Farmhouse,
Cotton Edmunds, Chester,
Cheshire CH3 7PG
tel   01244 336616
fax   01244 336699
e-mail info@cottonfarm.co.uk
web   www.cottonfarm.co.uk

Neil & Flossy Dixon
Ardmore,
Station Lane, Great Barrow, Chester,
Cheshire CH3 7JN
tel   01829 740257
e-mail fdixon@ardmore2000.freeserve.co.uk

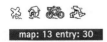

David designed some of the furniture, including the vast bed that needs nine pillows. The rooms are sumptuous (TV and video hidden in wooden cabinets) and have great country views; bathrooms have towelling robes and other spoiling extras. You are on a quiet country lane with the village pub at the end of the drive and Dunham Massey Deer Park five minutes' walk away. David was a professional snooker player. Good value so close to the city (Manchester and its airport are six minutes), yet the feel is rural. Breakfasts are superb and your hosts are great fun.

Stylish and uncluttered, with well-proportioned rooms and lots of light and space... not what you'd expect from a neo-Georgian townhouse on a new development – but then, it's not your average estate. Separated from the village by a swathe of parkland, it is rather grand. The house is three-storeyed and elegant, with attractive bedrooms, excellent bathrooms and a big, cream-and-white guest sitting room decorated with Fiona's fine photos. Your hosts are young and friendly, there's a mouthwatering breakfast menu and only the occasional rumble from the M6/M62.

rooms	3: 1 double with shower; 1 double with private bath; 1 four-poster with bath/shower.
room price	£60–£71. Singles £46–£53.
meals	Breakfast until 9.30am. Pub/restaurant 5 minutes away.
closed	Christmas & New Year.
directions	A556 NE to Manchester, then left on A56 for Lymm. At 1st pub, right down Park Lane. Next to The Swan With Two Nicks.

rooms	2: 1 double with bath; 1 twin/double with shower.
room price	£48. Singles £30.
meals	Dinner, 3 courses, £25.
closed	Rarely.
directions	M6 exit 22. Follow signs for Newton-le-Willows. At r'bout, 2nd exit into Winwick Park. On over two r'bouts & formal square to last house on right before T-junction.

David & Janice Taylor
Ash Farm Country Guest House,
Park Lane, Little Bollington,
Nr. Altrincham, Cheshire WA14 4TJ
tel   0161 929 9290
fax   0161 928 5002
e-mail   jan@ashfarm97.fsnet.co.uk
web   www.ashfarm.co.uk

Fiona & Steve Heaton
34 Winwick Park Avenue,
Winwick, Warrington,
Cheshire WA2 8XA
tel   01925 654496
e-mail   winwick@tiscali.co.uk

CORNWALL

CORNWALL

The setting deserves the word 'dramatic'. The little bungalow is perched on the last strip of land before the Atlantic which swirls around the Lizard at England's most southerly point. Breakfasts – continental and delicious as they are – have to fight for your attention, for your table is set at the big picture window to take in the beauty of it all. The bedroom has picture windows and overlooks your private patio – waking is a delight. John works in broadcasting and is about to launch a radio station; Jane works locally and both are gentle, easy and so hospitable. It's a five-minute walk to the shoreline.

All is immaculate – the vegetable garden, the decoration, the flower arrangements – and runs like clockwork thanks to Marion, who loves this special place. The views to the sea are heart-stopping and the ever-changing light casts a spell over the landscape. The dining room is illuminated by fire and candle; the yellow drawing room, with wooden floors and deep sofas, is perfect. Good linen, a regal four-poster and a luxurious half-tester... bedrooms are exquisite. Swim in the sheltered pool, laze in the pavilion and gaze across the superb garden to the sea – just a three-minute walk.

rooms	1 double with private bath/shower.
room price	£50. Singles by arrangement.
meals	Pub & restaurant 0.25 miles.
closed	Rarely.
directions	From Helston to the Lizard. 1st right at Lizard Green (head for Smugglers Fish & Chips). 1st right & pass wc on left. Road unmade; on for 400 yds. Double bend. 2nd bungalow on right.

rooms	2: 1 double, 1 twins/double, both with bath/shower.
room price	£84-£98. Singles £59-£64.
meals	Breakfast until 9.30am. Dinner, 3 courses, £26.
closed	Christmas.
directions	From Helston, A3083 south. Just before Lizard, left to Church Cove. Follow signs for about 0.75 miles. House on left behind blue gates.

Jane and John Grierson
Carmelin,
Pentreath Lane, The Lizard,
Nr. Helston, Cornwall TR12 7NY

tel	01326 290677
e-mail	pjcarmelin@aol.com
web	www.carmelin.ukf.net

Peter & Marion Stanley
Landewednack House,
Church Cove, The Lizard,
Cornwall TR12 7PQ

tel	01326 290909
fax	01326 290192
e-mail	landewednackhouse@amserve.com

map: 1 entry: 33

map: 1 entry: 34

The 1903 house in its sylvan setting is half a mile from the sea; on stormy nights, you can hear the sound of the rollers pounding. You are surrounded by 1,200 acres of National Trust land, minutes from breathtaking coastal paths and magical Loe Pool. Christine spoils you at breakfast at the pine table polished with wax and time; country bedrooms have bags of old-fashioned comfort – sofas, dressing-tables, big beds, colourful Cornish art. The new garden, Mike's domain, will be wonderful. All feels settled with no one to rush you… the house is filled with good cheer and you'll leave with a spring in your step.

Two – perhaps three – 200-year-old miners' cottages have combined to create a sturdy granite home in a quiet hamlet. Narrow staircases, low ceilings, pine doors, inglenooks and unpretentious flowery decoration give a typically Cornish feel. There's crisp, ironed cotton in the bedrooms and fresh garden flowers. Moira, a retired midwife, has a passion for gardening; Goff, a potter, joins in, too, and has created a warm, sheltered potager. They are both immensely kind and will bring an early-morning tea tray; Aga cooked breakfasts and home-made preserves await at the breakfast table.

rooms	2 doubles/twins, both with private bath.
room price	£70. Singles by arrangement.
meals	Excellent restaurants nearby in Porthleven. Dinner occasionally available.
closed	Christmas.
directions	B3304 Porthleven road from Helston. Past Duck Pond for a mile; on sharp right-hand bend, left for Loe Bar. Left after 150 yds; follow track past NT car park; left through gate.

rooms	3: 2 doubles, both with bath & shower; 1 twin/double with private bath.
room price	£44–£50. Singles £22–£25.
meals	Early breakfast for people going to Scillies. Packed lunch from £5.50. Dinner from £13. Seafood restaurant, 10-minute drive.
closed	Christmas & New Year.
directions	A394 Helston to Penzance, 2nd right after Ashton Post Office for Tresowes Green. After 0.25 miles, sign for house on right.

Christine Harvey
Parc Mean,
Helston, Penrose Estate,
Cornwall TR13 0RB
tel   01326 574290
e-mail   parcmean@btopenworld.com

Moira & Goff Cattell
The Gardens,
Tresowes, Ashton, Helston,
Cornwall TR13 9SY
tel   01736 763299
e-mail   thegardens@amserve.com

CORNWALL

CORNWALL

There's a terrace for each pristine bedroom with views to the wild blue yonder and St Michael's Mount Bay – an enchanting prospect that changes with the passage of the day. Come for peace, space and privacy. There are honey-coloured timbers, pretty tea sets, good fabrics and colours, delicious toiletries and fluffy towels. Choose either full English breakfast in the woody kitchen-diner or a continental tray brought to your room. Your hosts are busy people yet will help you discover local walks; a footpath through the field below leads to the village, and Prussia Cove and Cudden Point are walkable, too.

An outstanding Grade II* listed 17th-century granite manor. The approach, down a tree-lined avenue, is majestic; beyond, 102 acres of grass and woodland. The river runs by and there are wonderful walks. Bedrooms are stunning – one is panelled, all have exceptional beds – and the bathrooms amaze: oak floors and big fireplaces, a slipper bath in the centre of one, an enormous shower in another. Downstairs are flagstones, mullioned windows, a sumptuous, sunny dining room with gold curtains at floor-to-ceiling windows, and a breakfast room with a big old French oak table. Expect excellent dinners.

rooms	3: 1 double with bath; 2 doubles with bath/shower.
room price	£65-£77. Singles £45-£60.
meals	Breakfast until 9am. Dinner available within walking distance.
closed	Christmas.
directions	From A30 after Crowlas r'bout, A394 to Helston. 0.25 miles after next r'bout, 1st right for Perranuthnoe. Farm drive on left, signed.

rooms	3: 1 double with private bath & shower; 1 double with bath & shower; 1 double with bath/shower.
room price	£90-£98. Singles £64.
meals	Dinner, 3 courses, £25.
closed	Rarely.
directions	From A394 Helston/Penzance road, B3280 through Goldsithney & St Hilary to hamlet of Relubbus. House last on right.

Christine & Charles Taylor
Ednovean Farm,
Perranuthnoe, Nr. Penzance,
Cornwall TR20 9LZ

tel	01736 711883
fax	01736 710480
e-mail	info@ednoveanfarm.co.uk
web	www.ednoveanfarm.co.uk

David & Lesley Berkeley
Tregembo,
St Hilary, Penzance,
Cornwall TR20 9EW

tel	01736 761881
fax	01736 761882
e-mail	tregembo@tiscali.co.uk
web	www.tregembo.co.uk

Prepare to be spoiled. A fire smoulders in the sumptuous sitting room, afternoon tea is laid out in the farmhouse kitchen gratis, bedrooms are luxurious – the four-poster has pretty *toile de Jouy* wallpaper, a powerful shower and fat pillows. Everywhere there are fascinating artefacts and curios from Gill's travels, designer fabrics and antique pieces. The road ends at Ennys, so the rural bliss is entirely yours. Walk down to the river and along the old towpath, or simply stay here; play tennis, swim in the heated pool sunk deep into the tropical gardens. *Children over three welcome.*

Kenneth is a rich mixture of talent and enthusiasm, a baritone and a BBC singer. He also cooks divinely and imaginatively (e.g. gunpowder sauce!). He and his delightful mother live on the wildest cliffs, a stroll from some of Cornwall's loveliest places. It is windswept, traditional and fun – a wash basin from an Edwardian train carriage, bedroom views to the Lizard, views to the sea and two lighthouses from your sitting room, smart old Victorian beds. Old-fashioned charm, books and Kenneth, chatty, expansive and larger than life. *Children over 12 welcome. Self-catering available. See back of book.*

rooms	5: 1 twin with bath; 2 four-posters, both with shower; 2 family suites in barn.
room price	£65-£90. Singles from £50.
meals	Breakfast until 9.15am. Good pub 3 miles.
closed	November-February.
directions	2 miles east of Marazion on B3280, look for sign leading down Trewhella Lane between St Hilary & Relubbus. Continue to Ennys.

rooms	2: 1 double with shower; 1 twin with private shower.
room price	£60-£70. Singles by arrangement. Christmas breaks available.
meals	Occasional dinners, for four or more. Pubs/restaurants 2-6 miles.
closed	Rarely.
directions	A30 to Land's End. 3 miles from Penzance left at Catchall, onto B3283. Through St Buryan (towards Porthcurno). After 0.5 miles, left for Lamorna by phone box on green. 2nd right 0.75 miles on, on left-hand bend by woods. Right into drive.

Gill Charlton
Ennys,
St Hilary, Penzance,
Cornwall TR20 9BZ

tel	01736 740262
fax	01736 740055
e-mail	ennys@ennys.co.uk
web	www.ennys.co.uk

Kenneth Fraser Annand
Burnewhall House,
Nr. St Buryan, Penzance,
Cornwall TR19 6DN

tel	01736 810650
fax	01736 810650
e-mail	burnewhall@btconnect.com

map: 1 entry: 39

map: 1 entry: 40

Ahead, the Atlantic stretches to infinity; behind is the wild moorland of West Penwith, dotted with ancient sites. Keigwin is a 200-year-old stone farmhouse, simple, unpretentious and delightful. Whitewashed rooms contain natural fabrics, much-loved, much-used Welsh country furniture, and books; the refreshingly plain bedrooms have iron bedsteads and white linen. There's much to catch the eye in the house, the courtyard art gallery (contemporary fine and applied art) and in the two acres outside. Gilly's cooking is vegetarian and uses food from her organic farm and potager.

Sea-loving style-seekers look no further. This is a perfect seaside B&B run by the charming John who, until recently, ran the perfect country house hotel. Meticulous attention to detail has made this St Ives house what it is. There are just two bedrooms for guests — the best rooms in the house — and in each, a bay window and a table set with fresh flowers where breakfast is brought to you. The feel is luxurious and contemporary, colours are muted and pebble-pale and the captivating harbour views will launch dreams of living by the sea. Designer bathrooms, organic soaps and shampoos, and the Tate a short stroll away.

rooms	2: 1 double, 1 single, sharing bath/shower.
room price	£40. Singles £20.
meals	Breakfast until 9.30am. Packed lunches £5. Excellent pub/restaurant 3 miles.
closed	Rarely.
directions	A30 Penzance. At r'bout near Tesco, up hill towards Land's End; 2nd r'bout, right for Madron, Morvah. At junc. with B3306, left through Morvah; house on left 1 mile on, with gatepost.

rooms	2 doubles/twins, both with bath/shower.
room price	£90.
meals	Pubs/restaurants nearby.
closed	Rarely.
directions	Fom Carbis Bay, on to St Ives. At Porthminster Hotel, continue. left until Dunmar Hotel; sharp left, then 1st right to Sea View Terrace. Private parking.

Gilly Wyatt-Smith
Keigwin Farmhouse,
Keigwin, Morvah, Penzance,
Cornwall TR19 7TS
tel   01736 786425
fax   01736 786425
e-mail g.wyatt-smith@virgin.net
web   www.yewtreegallery.com

John Charlick
1 Sea View Terrace,
St Ives, Cornwall TR26 2DH
tel   01736 798001
fax   01736 791802
e-mail oneseaviewterrace@hotmail.com
web   www.seaview-stives.co.uk

An island of calm – it sits, as it has for 500 years, in its own five acres in a wild and lovely part of Cornwall. The mood is now artistic for the Halls are devoted to the encouragement of the arts in the area. Once a vicarage (the church stands next door), the house has polished wooden floors, oriental rugs, faded blue carpet, bird-print curtains, Italian prints. The pretty bedroom and sitting room are in a separate part of the house and overlook an Italianate courtyard. The gardens are part of the mood, traditional and beautiful. Your hosts are generous and fun.

The grounds are full of delights: an oval walled garden, camellia walks, a Cornish garden, magnolias... And beyond, parkland, woods and farmland, the peace broken only by the occasional whinny from one of Richard's racehorses. The house is similarly grand – weddings with up to 100 guests can be catered for – and very lovely. A double stone staircase leads to big, elegant bedrooms (night storage heaters, so you might want to bring a hottie), and there's a sitting room for guests. The Williams family have lived here since George III's reign; you will be greeted with old-style kindness.

rooms	1 twin/double with bath & private sitting room.
room price	£60.
meals	Dinner sometimes available. Pub 1.5 miles.
closed	Rarely.
directions	From A30 exit Hayle (Pickfords r'bout); 100 yds left at mini-r'bout; 400 yds left for Gwinear; 1.5 miles, top of hill, driveway on right, just before 30mph Gwinear sign.

rooms	2: 1 double with bath/shower; 1 twin with private bath/shower.
room price	£60–£70. Singles £35–£45.
meals	Pubs nearby.
closed	Rarely.
directions	A30; then A3047 to Scorrier. On for 0.5 miles to mini-r'bout; left. Large drive on right (about 200 yds); signs.

Charles & Diana Hall
House at Gwinear,
Gwinear, St Ives, Cornwall TR27 5JZ
tel   01736 850444
fax   01736 850031

Richard & Caroline Williams
Scorrier House,
Scorrier, Redruth,
Cornwall TR16 5AU
tel   01209 820264
fax   01209 820677
e-mail rwill10442@aol.com

CORNWALL

The sea and the peninsula wrap themselves around you – Trevilla House is a great family home in an enviable position, with expansive views over the Fal Estuary. The King Harry ferry gives you easy access to the delights of the Roseland peninsula, too. Your bedroom is comfortable and unfrilly; recline on your high, antique basketwork twin beds with their French polished frames and gaze out on those wonderful views. There is also a small sitting room just for you. Breakfast is usually served in the south-facing conservatory overlooking the sea. Trelissick Gardens are just next door.

rooms	1 twin with bath. Extra single for members of the same party.
room price	From £60. Singles by arrangement.
meals	Breakfast until 9.30am. Restaurants/pubs 1-2 miles.
closed	Christmas & New Year.
directions	A390 to Truro, left onto A39 to Falmouth. At double r'bout with garage, left off 2nd r'bout (B3289). Pass pub on left. At x-roads, left (B3289). 200 yds on, fork right to Feock. On to T-junc., then left. 1st on right.

Jinty & Peter Copeland
Trevilla House,
Feock, Truro, Cornwall TR3 6QG

tel	01872 862369
fax	01872 870088
e-mail	jinty@trevilla.com
web	www.trevilla.clara.net

map: 1 entry: 45

CORNWALL

A footpath leads from the garden to a big sandy beach – this is a great spot for seaside hols. There's no shortage of spare welly boots for the children either; a sense of fun echoes around Polsue. Rooms are huge, bedrooms have eiderdowns, good beds and countryside views, the traditional lounge has floral sofas and a bar. Annabelle has cooked professionally and her breakfasts are special. Outside: big trees, camellias, a pond, field views. You are not far from the Eden Project, and there are lots of fine National Trust gardens nearby.

rooms	3 twins/doubles, all with bath.
room price	£80. Singles £50.
meals	Breakfast until 9.30am. Pub 1 mile.
closed	Rarely.
directions	A3078 south from Tregony. In Ruan High Lanes, 2nd right (for Philleigh & King Harry Ferry). House 1 mile up on left.

Graham & Annabelle Sylvester
Polsue Manor,
Ruan High Lanes, Truro,
Cornwall TR2 5LU

tel	01872 501270
fax	01872 501177
web	www.polsuemanor.co.uk

map: 1 entry: 46

CORNWALL

Catch a tantalising glimpse of the sea from your room and wake to the sound of a bubbling stream. Clare's sunny nature is reflected in her home, with its shelves of books, rose-strewn wallpapers and delicious smells of beeswax and baking. She used to run a restaurant and is a superb cook who loves to treat guests to locally-caught bass, brill, mullet, sole. Bedrooms are filled with light: an elegant double/twin and a sweet double with that glimpse of the sea. All this, a garden full of birdsong, a (real) fishing village 500 yards below and the Eden project close by. *Children by arrangement.*

rooms	3: 1 twin/double with bath/shower; 1 double with private bath/shower; 1 single occasionally available.
room price	£70–£76. Singles by arrangement.
meals	Packed lunch £7.50. Dinner, 2-3 courses, £20–£25.
closed	Rarely.
directions	From Tregony, A3078 to St Mawes. After 2 miles, at Esso garage on left, left to Portloe. Through village to Ship Inn. Right fork after pub car park. Cottage immed. on left between white gate posts up drive under trees.

Clare Holdsworth
Pine Cottage,
Portloe, Truro, Portloe,
Cornwall TR2 5RB
tel 01872 501385
web www.pinecottage.net

map: 1 entry: 47

CORNWALL

Everything's just right – the setting, the gentle activity of the farm, the windy lanes, and delightful hosts who look after you with huge enthusiasm. What's more, there are freshly decorated rooms, good bathrooms, family antiques and the promise of good food. The dining room is huge: even with sofas and a woodburner, you could turn a cartwheel. An ancient lane leads to Colona Bay: small, secluded and full of rock pools. There's an indoor pool and sauna, too, and Heligan and the Eden Project nearby. Blissful. *Guided walks by arrangement. Children over 12 welcome.*

rooms	3: 1 double, 1 twin, both with private bath/shower; 1 double with shower.
room price	£70. Singles £35.
meals	Breakfast 8-9am. Packed lunch from £5. Supper £15. Dinner £25.
closed	Christmas & New Year.
directions	St Austell B3273 for Mevagissey. At x-roads on hill, right to Heligan, avoiding Mevagissey. Through Gorran, bend left to Portmellon. After 1.5 miles, right at grass triangle into farm, before hill.

Sally & Tim Kendall
Bodrugan Barton,
Mevagissey, Cornwall PL26 6PT
tel 01726 842094
fax 01726 844378
e-mail bodruganbarton@ukonline.co.uk

map: 1 entry: 48

CORNWALL

CORNWALL

Lally and William have transformed a jungle into one of Cornwall's loveliest gardens, where secret paths tempt you into the woodland's dappled delights. Inside the lovely 1730s house shimmering wooden floors are covered with Persian rugs and light pours into every elegant corner; large guest rooms are gloriously furnished with antiques. Breakfast in the large dining room often turns into an early morning house-party, such is Lally's sense of fun and spontaneity. You are in deep and tranquil countryside, and the Eden Project and Heligan are nearby.

Stunning rooms lead onto a pretty private garden with banked lawns – take your breakfast tray and revive gently in the morning sun. The house has been in the family since the 1600s and the young Croggons have renovated this private barn extension thoughtfully and with flair: Floris soaps, pretty china, Colefax & Fowler fabrics, seagrass matting, a sofa in the bedroom, beautiful greys and greens. Annabel stocks your fridge with chopped exotic fruits, walnut bread, jams and yogurts, local butter and milk (cooked breakfasts are sometimes available). You are minutes from the Heligan Gardens and the Eden Project – perfect.

rooms	3: 1 twin/double with bath/shower; 2 twins/doubles, both with private bath.
room price	£70-£80. Singles by arrangement.
meals	Breakfast until 9.30am. Pub/restaurant 1 mile.
closed	Christmas & New Year.
directions	From St Austell, A390 to Grampound. Just beyond clock tower, left into Creed Lane. After 1 mile left at grass triangle opp. church. House behind 2nd white gate on left.

rooms	1 suite with twin/double, breakfast room & bath.
room price	£70. Singles £45.
meals	Breakfast anytime. Village restaurant 10-minute walk.
closed	Christmas, New Year & Easter.
directions	From Truro, A390 for St Austell. 6 miles on, through Grampound; on leaving village, at top of hill, right at speed limit sign into Bosillion Lane. House 150 yds on left.

Lally & William Croggon
Creed House,
Creed, Grampound, Truro,
Cornwall TR2 4SL
tel   01872 530372

Jonathon & Annabel Croggon
Bosillion,
Bosillion Lane, Grampound, Truro,
Cornwall TR2 4QY
tel   01726 883327

map: 1 entry: 49

map: 1 entry: 50

CORNWALL

Surrounded by a lovely garden open to the public, both by appointment and under the National Gardens Scheme, a classical late-Regency English country house that contains the occasional hint of eastern promise. In the drawing room, where tea is served, a beautiful Chinese cabinet occupies one wall; in the dining room is a Malaysian inscribed silk-screen – a thank-you present from Empire days. Upstairs, comfortable bedrooms have antique furniture, views onto the glorious garden and generous baths. The Eden Project and Heligan are nearby.

rooms	3: 1 four-poster, 1 twin, both with bath; 1 double with private bath.
room price	£74–£94. Singles £47–£57.
meals	Dinner, 4 courses, £27. B.Y.O.
closed	Christmas & Easter.
directions	A30 for Truro, then left for Grampound Rd. After 3 miles, right onto A390 for Truro. After 200 yds, right where double white lines end. Pass between reflector posts towards house, 200 yds down private lane.

Alison O'Connor
Tregoose,
Grampound, Truro,
Cornwall TR2 4DB
tel   01726 882460
fax   01872 222427

map: 1 entry: 51

CORNWALL

Sir John Betjeman mentions Treworyan in his Guide to Cornwall. It's a pretty, slate-hung farmhouse, built in 1745 in a peaceful, rural setting – a great spot from which to explore. The Sharps have converted an outbuilding adjoining the house to provide attractive accommodation: a private entrance, a light, chintzy bedroom and a bathroom with a double shower – all very new and fresh, and with easy access for the disabled or partially mobile. Cornish watercolours, old polished floorboards, comfortable yellow sofas and a woodburning stove make the private sitting room a cosy retreat. You may use the tennis court, too.

rooms	1 twin with shower.
room price	£70. Singles £45.
meals	Good pubs/restaurants nearby.
closed	Rarely.
directions	From A30 at Fraddon, B3275 to Ladock. Left after pub, signed Ladock church/Grampound Rd; 1st right to Probus; cont. 0.5 miles; 1st on right, set back from lane.

Mrs Carey Sharp
Treworyan,
Ladock, Truro, Cornwall TR2 4QD
tel   01726 882491
fax   01872 222487

map: 1 entry: 52

CORNWALL

Barbara is a B&B professional, and kind, too – she is the fourth generation of her family to have welcomed guests. The house was purpose-built for the Holts; circled by young trees it sits in a delightful position above Ladock. It is big, light and well-thought-out, its furniture and fittings brand new; beds have immaculate floral valances and masses of cupboard space, the sitting room – comfortable, plush even – has French windows leading to a terrace with views. A blissful corner of peace and quiet from which to explore. Breakfasts are as generous as you would expect.

rooms	2: 1 double with private bath/shower; 1 twin/double with bath/shower.
room price	£48–£58. Singles by arrangement.
meals	Breakfast 8-9am. Good village pub 200 yds.
closed	December.
directions	From A30, B3275 south to Ladock. There, turn opposite Falmouth Arms & follow road uphill for 200 yds. Right 70 yds after 'End 30mph' sign. House on right.

Ian & Barbara Holt
Oxturn House,
Ladock, Truro, Cornwall TR2 4NQ
tel 01726 884348
fax 01726 884248

CORNWALL

An intriguing 18th-century farmhouse of great character and with outstanding views over unspoiled countryside and the pretty creek side village of Lerryn. A farm with ewes, lambs, chickens and even otters. It is an artistic household: Anne sells huge dried hydrangeas and the house is full of their sons' art. The cheerful bedrooms are on the second floor and there is an elegant drawing room for guests. Iain and Anne give a big welcome and serve generous breakfasts on the large Cornish slate table. Good walks all around and the Eden Project is only 20 minutes away. *Children and pets by arrangement.*

rooms	2: 1 twin, 1 twin/double, 1 with shower, 1 with private bath.
room price	£64–£66. Singles £33, by arrangement.
meals	Pub 2-minute walk.
closed	Christmas & Easter.
directions	From Plymouth, A38 then A390 west. 1 mile before Lostwithiel, 2nd left after Downend garage to Lerryn. Before bridge, left for Couch's Mill, then 1st left into cul-de-sac, up hill for 0.25 miles.

Anne & Iain Mackie
Collon Barton,
Lerryn, Lostwithiel,
Cornwall PL22 0NX
tel 01208 872908
fax 01208 873812
e-mail iainmackie@btconnect.com

CORNWALL

The super-rich may think they have everything: king-size beds raise you from your slumbers to tip you into the heated pool; beds vibrate and play your favourite music at the touch of a button; luxury hotels perch over lagoons, spoiled only by the super-celebs in the next 'hut'. We have outsmarted the lot. How about a Cornish hut that is genuinely celeb-free and has a brilliant and unique device? The mere pull on a lever tips your bed towards the sea and propels you down a specially built ramp into the thundering surf. Forget Hawaii – this is fabulous enough for the most world-weary travel cynic. You are close to the Eden Project and Heligan.

rooms	3 king-size vibrating beds, all with shower.
room price	By arrangement. Credit cards accepted.
meals	Fresh fish and freshly-picked mussels a speciality.
closed	High tide.
directions	Head towards Eden Project; right at sign to disused launching point, down bumpy track; on left.

	Professor RNL Idling
	Surf's Up
	Oldquay,
	Cornwall
tel	01892 SOS SOS
e-mail	surfsup@luxuryincornwall.com
web	www.itsaripper.com

map: 505 entry: 55

CORNWALL

You are at the head of the old smuggling route and an ancient right of way leads you to Polperro's little harbour. The Macartneys have breathed new life into the 14th-century Grade II*-listed hall house, where ancient charm blends with creature comforts. There are three dressing-gowns in descending order of size and you have a cosy timbered A-frame sitting room with woodburner, candles, wild flowers; it's stylish, good value and, thanks to your hosts' kindness, memorably special. Food is delicious, and organic and free-range where possible. A favourite among guests.

rooms	2: 1 double, 1 single, with shared shower room & sitting room.
room price	£50–£64. Singles £25–£32.
meals	Dinner, 4 courses, £21.50. B.Y.O.
closed	Rarely.
directions	A387 through Looe & approx. 3 miles beyond, then B3359 for Pelynt. Less than a mile on, 2nd of 2 turnings on left. After 0.5 miles, left at T-junc., then fork left, signed.

	Michael & Ann Macartney
	Penellick,
	Pelynt, Nr. Looe, Cornwall PL13 2LX
tel	01503 272372
fax	01503 272372
e-mail	penellick@hotmail.com

map: 2 entry: 56

CORNWALL

A 1939 dower house built by the watercolourist Sir Francis Cook who reputedly had a pink Rolls Royce and several wives. He chose the plot well: the views to the headland of Talland Bay have you rooted to the spot. Hotel standards and a smart retreat, free of family bustle – pretty fabrics and soft creams in the bedrooms, mineral water, robes and wildflowers, too. The Rosiers are (between them) three-quarters French, and home-made brioches and croissants add a continental touch to breakfast. As the sun goes down, head for the ancient coastal inns and imagine the days when jubilant smugglers crowded the bars.

rooms	3: 2 doubles with private bath; 1 twin/double with private shower.
room price	£60-£90. Singles from £40.
meals	Good restaurants within 5 miles.
closed	December.
directions	From Looe towards Polperro; 2nd turning to Talland, on left after 2 miles; cont. down lane for 1 mile.

Mr & Mrs B Rosier
Allhays,
Porthallow, Talland Bay, Looe,
Cornwall PL13 2JB

tel	01503 273188
e-mail	info@allhays.co.uk
web	www.allhays.co.uk

map: 2 entry: 57

CORNWALL

D own a wild-flowered drive in a hidden fold, inland from the Fowey river, this is a farmhouse in the true sense of the word, a synthesis of style, stone, wood and colour. A Shaker simplicity is sprinkled with pretty touches such as flowers, candles and printed fabrics. Relax on the settle by the Rayburn; sip an espresso in the garden where chickens and ducks potter. Helen is an aromatherapist and reflexologist (book a treatment); she and Richard are young, enthusiastic and gentle. Wooden-floored bedrooms, reached up a steep stair, are pleasingly simple. Organic breakfasts, home-made biscuits and fresh fish dinners.

rooms	2: 1 double, 1 twin, both with basins, sharing bath.
room price	£60-£80. Singles £40.
meals	Dinner with wine, £30-£40. Packed lunch, cream teas & drinks available.
closed	Rarely.
directions	From Liskeard on A38. At Dobwalls take left fork, A390 for St Austell. After East Taphouse, left onto B3359 for Looe. After 2 miles, right signed Botelet.

The Tamblyn Family
Botelet,
Herodsfoot, Liskeard,
Cornwall PL14 4RD

tel	01503 220225
fax	01503 220225
e-mail	stay@botelet.co.uk
web	www.botelet.co.uk

map: 1 entry: 58

CORNWALL

CORNWALL

A country house dream of a place. The Varcoes have piled energy into a superb renovation – unpretentiously stylish and full of light – with plenty of white and off-white in fabrics and paints. The open-plan kitchen/sitting room has an open wood fire, big comfy sofas and a fascinating collection of paintings; bedrooms are charming, bathrooms have fresh flowers. Emma is an art agent and used to be in catering; Justin, a designer, rents out Indian tents for special events. Unspoilt countryside stretches out in all directions… go boating up the River Fowey with a picnic, or have dinner in one of the Indian tents.

This is Cornwall's 'Forgotten Corner' and the countryside is gorgeous. The house sits opposite the church, rooted in time and space; its massive walls echo their 400 years of history. All is welcoming and comfortable within, from the farmhouse kitchen, with its blue Aga and Welsh dresser, to the beautifully elegant and flagstoned sitting room. There, Farrow & Ball Library Red walls contrast with heavy calico curtains, off-white sofas and church candles. Bedrooms have crisp cotton and great comfort. Your hosts are easy and fun and there is a games room too, with bar billiards and table tennis. Excellent value.

rooms	3: 2 doubles with private bath; 1 twin/double with private shower.
room price	£60-£70. Singles from £45.
meals	Dinner £20.
closed	Christmas.
directions	A38 from Plymouth-Dobwalls. There, A390 to E. Taphouse. There, B3359 left. Past Calamazag Nursery (3.4 miles). Right signed Couch's Mill. Immed. left for C. Mills. On 1.6 miles to T-junc. right for C. Mills. Immed. left for same. 0.5 miles on house, signed.

rooms	4: 2 doubles with shower (1 with extra bed); 1 double with bath & shower; 1 twin with private bath & shower.
room price	£50. Singles £30.
meals	Pub/restaurant 0.5 miles.
closed	Christmas & Boxing Day.
directions	To Sheviock on A374. House opposite church.

Emma Varcoe
Hill Farmhouse,
Boconnoc, Lerryn, Lostwithiel,
Cornwall PL22 0RU

tel 01503 220517
e-mail emmavarcoe@aol.com
web www.hill-farmhouse.co.uk

Carol & Tony Johnson
Sheviock Barton,
Sheviock, Torpoint,
Cornwall PL11 3EH

tel 01503 230793
fax 01503 230793
e-mail thebarton@sheviock.freeserve.co.uk
web www.sheviockbarton.co.uk

CORNWALL

CORNWALL

The idyllic valley setting and your hosts' warm professionalism make this the perfect retreat. Two hundred years ago the Navy used to test cannons in the creek at the end of the garden — now you hear only wildlife. There's an understated elegance here and the 1744 house is lovingly tended by Button and Clive. Bedrooms have fine views from both high brass bed and antique four-poster, and are hugely comfortable. You are brought scones in a sitting room full of colour and light; morning kippers and free-range eggs are served in a room that looks over the sub-tropical garden. *Minimum stay two nights.*

Ann is huge fun and a natural entertainer — you'll settle in quickly. This is a comfortable house, artistically yet classically decorated, with great views over Plymouth Sound. It is at the top of a steep hill overlooking a charming seaside village of some 600 souls. Ann cooks superb meals with wholefood ingredients and local produce and makes her own muesli, bread, yogurt and ice-cream (and can cater for vegans). Bring your own music... there's a 'boudoir grand' to be played and a music centre, too. And a superb first-floor drawing room with those sea views.

rooms	3: 1 double with private bath; 1 four-poster, 1 twin/double, both with shower.
room price	£75-£100. Singles from £52.50.
meals	Breakfast 9-10.30am. Choice of pubs/restaurants 300 yds-4 miles.
closed	Occasionally.
directions	Please contact hosts for directions.

rooms	3: 1 double with bath; 1 twin/double, 1 twin, both with shower.
room price	From £45. Singles by arrangement.
meals	Dinner £16-£25; light supper £10.
closed	Rarely.
directions	B3247 for Mount Edgcumbe. Right, before school, for Kingsand. Down hill to right, left fork on bend into Kingsand, 2nd left, then left again. House on left with yellow door. Avoid single track road.

	Clive & Button Poole
	The Old Rectory,
	St John-in-Cornwall, Nr. Torpoint,
	Cornwall PL11 3AW
tel	01752 822275
fax	01752 823322
e-mail	clive@oldrectory-stjohn.co.uk
web	www.oldrectory-stjohn.co.uk

	Ann Heasman
	Cliff House,
	Devonport Hill, Kingsand,
	Cornwall PL10 1NJ
tel	01752 823110
fax	01752 822595
e-mail	chkingsand@aol.com
web	www.cliffhse.abel.co.uk

CORNWALL

CORNWALL

All of our inspectors have been bowled over by this house. The approach, surrounded on three sides by tidal estuaries, makes your heart leap. The Grade II-listed manor has its own chapel in which a 14th-century fresco still clings to the walls. Its many rooms are filled with thousands of books, pictures and some slightly worn, but massively stylish, fine furniture. Guy is eccentric, funny and passionate about horses; if you can't bring your own, some may be available to competent riders. Rooms, reached via four staircases, are simple and bright with old rugs and scattered books. *Children over 12 welcome.*

An old corn mill with the original water wheel now in the farmhouse kitchen. Bedroom views sweep down the garden to the salmon/sea trout river; Richard is a keen fly-fisherman and can fix up rods for visitors. Mariebel is a professional portrait painter who taught for many years and is still happy to teach individuals or groups. Bicton is an informal, comfortable and relaxing place to stay. Meals are eaten in that huge, cosy kitchen or in the impressive slate-floored dining/sitting room. The Lynher Valley is unspoilt and enchanting. *Children by arrangement.*

rooms	3: 2 doubles, both with bath; 1 twin with private bath.
room price	£70. Singles £40.
meals	Breakfast until 9.30am. Dinner £20. B.Y.O.
closed	Rarely.
directions	From Plymouth A38, cross Tamar Bridge. Through bypass tunnel over r'bout. On top of next hill left to Trematon; through village. Road forks, take right. After 2 miles at white cottage with post box, right at sign to Erth Barton.

rooms	2: 1 double with shower; 1 double with private bath.
room price	£50-£60. Singles by arrangement.
meals	Pubs/restaurants within 5 miles.
closed	Rarely.
directions	On A388 Callington-Launceston, left at Kelly Bray (opp. garage) to Maders. 400 yds after Maders, left to Golberdon & left at x-roads. After 400 yds, right down unmarked lane. 0.75 miles to Mill by bridge.

Guy Bentinck
Erth Barton,
Saltash, Cornwall PL12 4QY
tel 01752 842127
fax 01752 842127

Richard & Mariebel Allerton
Bicton Mill,
Bicton, Nr. Liskeard,
Cornwall PL14 5RF
tel 01579 383577
fax 01579 383577

map: 2 entry: 63

map: 2 entry: 64

CORNWALL

CORNWALL

Spectacular views of Bodmin Moor from the listed 17th-century farmhouse – the Hallidays farm organically and derive quiet pleasure from sharing this peaceful place. No frills or fuss: a pine table, Windsor chairs, white walls, flagged floors, books, plants, no TV and an owl at night. Bedrooms are gently old-fashioned: plain curtains at mullioned windows, William Morris wallpaper, a mahogany bed. The plank-floored bathroom with claw-foot bath is shared. There's a walled garden for summer breakfasts of home eggs and bread; glorious walks start from the door.

The garden has seats positioned to catch the evening sun: perfect after a day exploring the gardens and beaches of Cornwall. The peaceful house is named after the hill and you have a private entrance to your fresh, roomy suite: a twin-bedded room and a large, square, high sitting room with double doors look onto the wooded valley. There's a CD player, music, chocolates and magazines and you are utterly private; Jos, a kitchen designer, and Mary-Anne really want you to enjoy your stay. Local produce and free-range eggs are yours for breakfast.

rooms	4: 2 doubles, 1 single, 1 room with bunk-beds, all sharing bath/shower & extra wc.
room price	£54–£58. Singles £27–£29.
meals	Light supper £7.
closed	Rarely.
directions	A388 Callington-Launceston for 3 miles; fork left onto B3257. At Bray shop, 2nd left. 1st left, 1st right, then next left. Next right (just before village). 1.5 miles to bottom of valley; on left.

rooms	2: 1 twin with bath/shower, sitting room & child single next door, if required.
room price	£70. Singles £45.
meals	Dinner, 3 courses, £18. B.Y.O.
closed	Christmas.
directions	From Launceston, B3254 towards Liskeard. Through Daw's House & South Petherwin, down steep hill & last left before little bridge. House 1st on left.

	Mrs Lavinia Halliday
	Browda,
	Linkinhorne, Callington,
	Cornwall PL17 7NB
tel	01579 362235

	Jos & Mary-Anne Otway-Ruthven
	Hornacott,
	South Petherwin, Launceston,
	Cornwall PL15 7LH
tel	01566 782461
fax	01566 782461
e-mail	otwayruthven@btinternet.com

map: 2 entry: 65

map: 2 entry: 66

CORNWALL

There's a treasure round every corner of this fine old manor on the edge of Bodmin Moor. Rich, exotic rugs, cushions and artefacts from around the world, and Louella's sumptuous hand-stencilled fabrics and furniture. Huge beds, coir on the floors and garden flowers in your rooms, and a guest sitting room, crammed floor to ceiling with books, many of them Robin's (he's a writer and explorer). A conservatory for breakfast/dinner overlooks elegant lawns, garden, tennis court... and heavenly views. There's even an opera house in a converted barn. Everyone waxes lyrical – you will, too.

rooms	4: 1 double with bath; 2 doubles, 1 twin, sharing 2 baths.
room price	£70. Singles £35.
meals	Packed lunch from £5. Dinner, 3 courses, £18.
closed	Christmas & New Year.
directions	6 miles after Jamaica Inn on A30, left for Cardinham. Through Millpool & straight on, ignoring further signs to Cardinham. After 2.5 miles, left to Cabilla Manor 0.75 miles; house right down drive.

	Robin & Louella Hanbury-Tenison
	Cabilla Manor,
	Nr. Mount, Bodmin,
	Cornwall PL30 4DW
tel	01208 821224
fax	01208 821267
e-mail	louella@cabilla.co.uk
web	www.cabilla.co.uk

map: 1 entry: 67

CORNWALL

Charles's family has lived here for hundreds of years – a period gem packed with detail and delight. The Grade II*-listed mansion is a family home whose owners, now that their children have flown the nest, are keen to share its faded, much-loved patina. Meet the relatives over breakfast – they hang from every wall; relax over a game of backgammon by a log-fuelled stove. Views onto sloping lawns and sheep-dotted hills sail into bedroom windows. The nine acres are planted with unusual trees, and the village has a real ale pub and a beautiful church – one of John Betjeman's favourites.

rooms	2: 1 twin with bath/shower; 1 twin with private bath.
room price	£60-£70. Singles £35.
meals	Pub 1 mile & good restaurants nearby.
closed	Rarely.
directions	A30 towards Bodmin, turn towards Blisland. At T-junction left (ignoring signpost to Blisland); down to bottom of hill, right up drive.

	Victoria & Charles Edward-Collins
	Trewardale,
	Blisland, Nr Bodmin,
	Cornwall PL30 4HS
tel	01208 821226
fax	01208 821766
e-mail	vicky@cornish-trad-cottages.com

map: 1 entry: 68

An exquisite house in a magical setting: 33 acres of ancient woods, Celtic crosses, a holy well and a water garden. Catherine has decorated the house (part-15th-century) with enormous care and flair, matching fabrics and antique pieces. One bedroom was part of the old chapel and has interesting stone lintels; all are sunny, with proper bathrooms and lovely old baths. Catherine is a warm hostess and her guest sitting room full of books and fresh flowers; there's a piano, too. In the walled garden, amid lavender, rosemary and yew, is a heated pool. *Children over 10 welcome.*

rooms	3: 2 doubles, both with private bath; 1 twin/double with bath.
room price	£70–£85. Singles £35–£45.
meals	Dinner £25. Pub 0.25 miles.
closed	Rarely.
directions	From A30, turn for Blisland. There, past church on left & pub on right. Take lane at bottom left of village green. 0.25 miles on, drive on left (granite pillars & cattle grid).

Christopher & Catherine Hartley
Lavethan,
Blisland, Bodmin,
Cornwall PL30 4QG
tel   01208 850487
fax   01208 851387
e-mail   chrishartley@btconnect.com
web   www.lavethan.com

map: 1 entry: 69

Micky and Gelda farm 450 acres at the head of the beautiful Ruthern Valley. There are stunning views, grassy fields, grazing cattle and horses; recline in the garden hammock, drink in the peace. Gelda has decorated the house with flair and there's a generous feel to everything: designer fabrics hang in thick folds at the windows, bathroom towels are large and soft, sofas are satisfyingly squishy. Gelda also makes special efforts to source local produce and her meals have been much praised; enjoy breakfast in the garden in summer. *Children by arrangement.*

rooms	2 doubles, both with private bath.
room price	£70–£80. Singles £35–£40.
meals	Dinner £20–£25.
closed	Rarely.
directions	From M5, A30 to r'bout south of Bodmin. On A30 for Redruth. 2.2 miles on, right to Withiel. Through Withiel, down hill, over bridge, left at T-junc., for Wadebridge. Drive on right, 0.5 miles on.

Gelda Madden
Higher Tregawne,
Withiel, Bodmin,
Cornwall PL30 5NS
tel   01208 831257
fax   01208 831257
e-mail   highertregawne@btinternet.com

map: 1 entry: 70

Rosina modestly refers to her home as offering "simple comfort"; it has so much more. Views of, and walks to, the tidal Camel Estuary, a spot in the garden for sunny summer breakfasts, space to unload sporting gear and gumboots, a sitting room snug with winter fire: uncomplicated cottage charm. It's mid-eighteenth-century, uncluttered and unfussy, with 30 acres of woodland and 40 of grassland. Rosina is a dear and will make sure guests of all ages enjoy their stay. The Camel cycle trail is nearby and you can hire bikes in Padstow or Wadebridge – perfect for a car-free family outing.

Stone slabs, planked floors and deep sash windows in this dear little house five minutes from Padstow. Generous, artistic Amanda serves breakfasts and dinner in a duck-egg-blue room elegant with fresh flowers and small chandelier. The double bed wears modern checks in a slopey-ceilinged room that's light and fresh; the bathroom charms with its roll-top bath, spoiling smellies and dressing gown from Indonesia. Views are to village and countryside. The garden is a series of hedged 'rooms' and the kitchen garden gives blackcurrants and gooseberries for perfect fruit fools.

rooms	2: 1 double with private bath; 1 double sharing bath, only let to members of same party.
room price	From £50. Singles £25.
meals	Excellent pubs/restaurants 0.5-6 miles.
closed	Rarely.
directions	Bypass Wadebridge on A39 for Redruth. Over bridge, pass Esso garage on left; then immed. right to Edmonton. Pass modern houses; then immed. right to Roskear over cattle grid.

rooms	3: 1 double with bath; 1 double, 1 twin, sharing bath.
room price	£60. Singles £40.
meals	Light supper £12.50. Excellent pubs/restaurants nearby.
closed	Rarely.
directions	A39 after Wadebridge, signed A389 Padstow. Reach Little Petherick; over hump bridge to whitewashed cottage at corner of unmarked lane; turn up lane bearing right; on right, opp. pink house.

Rosina Messer-Bennetts
Roskear,
St Brock, Wadebridge,
Cornwall PL27 7HU
tel   01208 812805
e-mail   rosinamesserbennetts@ukonline.co.uk

Amanda Fearon
Ballaminers House,
Little Petherick, Padstow,
Cornwall PL27 7QT
tel   01841 540933
fax   01841 540933
e-mail   pandafearon@aol.com
web   www.ballaminershouse.co.uk

CORNWALL

A homely refuge with family furniture and oil paintings and so close to the sea that you might spot dolphins or a lazy basking shark. You are almost at sea – crashing surf and Atlantic winds in a stunning Daphne du Maurier setting; this is rugged North Cornwall with surfing beaches all around. The cottage, which has been in the family for four generations, was once a 'fish cellar' for processing catches. There's a woodburner in the drawing room and the bedrooms are simple and unfrilly; it will be their views that rivet you. A good choice for families.

rooms	3: 2 twins, both with bath. A single bed can be added to make 1 triple.
room price	From £50. Singles by arrangement.
meals	Packed lunch from £5. Dinner from £15.
closed	Rarely.
directions	From St Merryn, right for Trevose Head. Over sleeping policemen. After toll gate ticket machine, right through farm gate. On towards sea; cottage gate at end, on right.

Phyllida & Antony Woosnam-Mills
Mother Ivey Cottage,
Trevose Head, Padstow,
Cornwall PL28 8SL

tel	01841 520329
fax	01841 520329
e-mail	woosnammills@compuserve.com

CORNWALL

Tea in the garden or the drawing room when you arrive; Sarah and her family are easy and you will immediately feel at home. The grandeur is soft: Empire sofa, good oils, faded rugs on wooden floors, lovely lamps, an old oak chest – just what you might hope for from a 1780s, creeper-clad vicarage... not forgetting, in the dining room, Sydney the polar bear skin rug. Bedrooms have good period furniture, fresh flowers, a quilted bedspread; the children's room, off the twin, with its miniature beds, is charming. Breakfast on local produce, taken at your leisure.

rooms	2: 1 double suite, 1 twin with children's room, both with bath.
room price	£56–£66. Singles £25–£35.
meals	Breakfast until 10.30am. Good pub 200 yds.
closed	Christmas Day.
directions	From Wadebridge, B3314 for Rock & Polzeath. After 3.5 miles, left for St Minver. In village, left into cul-de-sac just before Four Ways Inn. House at bottom on left.

Graham & Sarah Tyson
The Old Vicarage,
St Minver, Nr. Rock,
Cornwall PL27 6QH

tel	01208 862951
fax	01208 863578
e-mail	g.tyson2@tiscali.co.uk

The Bloors manage to be kind and helpful without being intrusive. "They are doing a perfect job," says our inspector. The converted barn hunkers down in its own secluded valley and a path leads you through woods to delightful Epphaven Cove. Inside it is elegantly uncluttered and cool; new seagrass contrasts with old oak and the downstairs bedrooms have fresh flowers, quilted bedspreads and doors opening to the garden. The shower room – a mix of rusty red and Italian marble – is magnificent.

Easy to see why Sir John Betjeman and historian A L Rowse loved this 15th-century manor. It is so relaxed and unselfconsciously beautiful. Delightful hosts, an Elizabethan tithe barn, a wonderful garden with croquet, tennis and special trees add to the magic. The interior is an exhilarating mix of the traditional and the exotic, with more than a touch of luxury. Late afternoon sun streams into the lovely drawing room, illuminating yellow stencilled walls, fine pictures and a vast fireplace. Betjeman's beloved St Enodoc Church is a quarter of an hour's drive away and so are surfing beaches.

rooms	3: 1 double, 2 twins, sharing 1 bath & 1 shower.
room price	£60. Singles by arrangement.
meals	Breakfast 8-9.30am. Pub 1.5 miles.
closed	Rarely.
directions	A39 to Wadebridge. At roundabout follow signs to Polzeath, then to Porteath Bee Centre. Through Bee Centre shop car park, down farm track; signed on right after 150 yds.

rooms	3: 1 double with bath; 1 double, 1 twin, both with private bath.
room price	From £70. Singles by arrangement.
meals	Pub 1 mile.
closed	Rarely.
directions	On A39, 7 miles south of Camelford at St Kew Highway, through village on Trelill Road. (Avoid St Kew.) 1 mile on, pass white cottage on right, left over cattle grid past white bungalow, house 0.25 miles down drive.

Jo Bloor
Porteath Barn,
St Minver, Wadebridge,
Cornwall PL27 6RA

tel	01208 863605
fax	01208 863954
e-mail	mbloor@ukonline.co.uk

Maggie & Lawrence Gordon Clark
Bokelly,
St Kew, Bodmin,
Cornwall PL30 3DY

tel	01208 850325
e-mail	bokelly@gordonclark.freeserve.co.uk

CORNWALL

Cornish slate and stone, a real candelabra over the big breakfast table, pretty rugs, a leather Chesterfield, original art, open fires and a lovely family dog ready to help you settle. The lines of the farmhouse are elegant Georgian, the atmosphere relaxed. There's a huge billiard room with polished slate floor, and a garden for those who like to pass their leisure time less competitively. White cotton on an antique brass bed with handmade patchwork quilt, wild flowers on the breakfast table and views of horses in the paddock. The watery delights of Rock and Polzeath are nearby.

rooms	1 double with private bath.
room price	From £60. Singles £35.
meals	Wonderful pub 0.25 miles.
closed	Christmas & New Year.
directions	From Camelford, A39 to Wadebridge. After 10-15 mins, at brow of hill, right, past Esso garage, then immed. left at pub for 0.75 miles. Post, rails & fir trees on left; bear left to house.

Daphne Gough
Tregoid Manor Farm,
Trequite, St Kew, Bodmin,
Cornwall PL30 3EU

tel   01208 841580
e-mail   philip-gough@uknetworks.co.uk

CORNWALL

From January to October you may only come if you have a child under five! This is a marvellous, unpretentious haven for families. Children adore playing in the roofed sandpit and miniature farmyard, and there are piglets and chicks, a pony to groom and eggs to collect. Nursery teas begin at 5pm (don't miss cream tea in the garden) and Lucy will babysit while you slink off later to the local pub – the highest in Cornwall. One bedroom is modern with new pine; the other two are more traditional. Celtic crosses in the garden and original panelling hint at the house's 500-year history.

rooms	3 family, all with bath/shower.
room price	From £60. Singles by arrangement.
meals	Packed lunch £5. Nursery tea £3.50. Supper £13. Dinner £16 (Sat only).
closed	Christmas.
directions	From Launceston, A395, then A39 through Camelford. Left onto B3266 to Bodmin. 4 miles on, left signed Wenfordbridge Pottery; over bridge, past pottery & on brow of hill, left into lane; house at top.

Lucy Finnemore
Higher Lank Farm,
St Breward, Bodmin,
Cornwall PL30 4NB

tel   01208 850716
e-mail   a_finnemore@lineone.net

CORNWALL

A Grade II-listed, slate-hung Georgian farmhouse in 30 acres of pastoral loveliness with its own (ancient) Holy Well. Your immensely likeable hostess Gillian is full of enthusiasm for her home where guest rooms have beautiful antique bedspreads and glorious views. (Bask in the morning sun with your head on your pillow.) The vegetable garden is her passion; the freshest produce ends up on the supper table in the Moroccan-look dining room. Guests share a private sitting room. The perfect spot on the way to surf, sand and the Eden Project. *Children over five welcome.*

rooms	3: 1 double with shower; 1 double with basin & wc, 1 twin, sharing separate bath with members of same party.
room price	£46–£50. Singles £30.
meals	Dinner £15. B.Y.O. Pub 1.5 miles.
closed	Christmas.
directions	Heading west, right off A30 onto A395 for Wadebridge. Through Pipers Pool & 3rd left for Laneast. Left again, before church, wooden gates on left.

Gillian & Anthony ffrench Blake
Laneast Barton,
Laneast, Launceston,
Cornwall PL15 8PN
tel   01566 880104
e-mail   affb@totalise.co.uk

CORNWALL

The Domesday-listed property of Duke William's half-brother sits alongside fine outbuildings in the most glorious garden with manicured lawns: the setting is stunning. Inside there is sober luxury. Muriel runs the house with irreproachable efficiency and plans her menus with elaborate care; if you stay in to eat, you meet fellow guests for drinks before dining in dinner party style. There are fine paintings, stone-silled windows onto garden views, carefully decorated rooms. Your hosts pride themselves on running an immaculate, peaceful, totally English home.

rooms	3 twins/doubles all with bath/shower.
room price	£60–£70. Singles £40.
meals	Breakfast 8.30am. Dinner £23.
closed	Christmas Day.
directions	From Wainhouse Corner on A39, follow sign to Crackington Haven. At beach, turn inland for 1 mile, left into Church Park Road & 1st right into lane.

Muriel Knight
Manor Farm,
Crackington Haven, Bude,
Cornwall EX23 0JW
tel   01840 230304

CORNWALL

CORNWALL

Built around a cobbled courtyard and tucked into a sheltered hollow, ancient Trevigue hunkers down against the gustiness of the North Cornish coast. Inside there's little evidence of the original farming activity: all is spick, span and spotless, yet the stone mullions, flagstones and slate are authentic. Breakfasts, using local produce, are generous and at weekends you can eat at the restaurant across the courtyard. Head for Strangles Cove for absolute seclusion; Crackington beach – big at low tide – is wonderful for families. *Children over 12 welcome. Self-catering available. See back of book.*

The road twists and turns, the driveway falls through the spring-fed wooded valley... then, suddenly, the secret is yours. The former vicarage – part-16th-century with Georgian and Edwardian additions – is beautiful; at the end of its intriguing garden lie, wonderfully, coastal path and sea. Sandy beaches are nearby. Lots of light, sea views, seagrass matting, paintings, books, comfy sofas, pretty fabrics and the feel of a family home; bedrooms are fresh and peaceful, bathrooms are charming. Jane and Anthony are lovely and share their house without fuss. *Children over five welcome.*

rooms	3: 2 doubles, both with shower; 1 twin with bath.
room price	£70. Singles £40.
meals	Breakfast until 9.30am. Dinner available in farmhouse restaurant.
closed	Rarely.
directions	From Crackington Haven follow coastal road keeping sea on right. Up hill & right for Trevigue. Farm 1.5 miles on left on top of cliffs.

rooms	4: 1 double, 1 twin, both with private bath; 1 further twin only let to same party; 1 small single for child.
room price	£48–£64. Singles £34–£42.
meals	Simple supper or dinner, 3 courses, £12–£20. B.Y.O.
closed	Christmas.
directions	Leave A39 at Wainhouse Corner, south of Bude, for St Gennys Church. 2 miles on, fork right by white cottage towards St Gennys Church. Before church, right into lane/drive.

Janet Crocker
Trevigue,
Crackington Haven, Bude,
Cornwall EX23 0LQ

tel	01840 230418
fax	01840 230418
e-mail	trevigue@talk21.com
web	www.trevigue.co.uk.

Anthony & Jane Farquhar
St Gennys House,
St Gennys, Bude,
Cornwall EX23 0NW

tel	01840 230384
fax	01840 230537
e-mail	ac.farquhar@btopenworld.com

The dark red door admits you to a glorious, eclectic mix of styles. Antiques, modern sculptures, paintings, books and Denise's own pots proliferate in colourful confusion, with Persian or rag rugs covering stripped or painted floorboards. In the striking bedrooms, beds have antique quilts; one dates back to 1780, when the house was built. Guests have their own sitting/dining room, too. It's a warm, friendly, elegant house – the ideal setting for Denise's entertaining. She cooks with organic ingredients where possible and once a month does a special, themed evening meal (Turkish, Thai, Lebanese...).

Louise and Stephen are bubbly and fun and give a big, generous welcome with not a hint of stuffiness. Bedrooms are sunny and bright with huge comfy beds, fat pillows and super quilted throws, and overlook a wonderful variety of trees – open the windows and let the birdsong in. The suite up in the loft is a real hideaway. You'll find it easy to relax by the fire in the winter with a glass of wine, or in the secluded garden in summer. After a splendid breakfast – lots of choice and home-made bread and Aga pancakes too – stroll to lake, fells or village, only five minutes away. *Children by arrangement.*

rooms	3: 1 double, 1 family (1 double & 2 singles) with bath & shower; 1 twin with private bath.
room price	£55-£75. Singles from £30.
meals	Dinner, 4 courses, £22. B.Y.O.
closed	Christmas & New Year.
directions	From A590, over 1st r'bout by Booths; on through 2nd r'bout with Ulverston sign. Through 1st set of lights; at 2nd set, left into Prince's St. House on left after 100 yds.

rooms	3: 1 twin/double with shower; 1 family suite (1 double, 1 twin) with bath.
room price	£56-£80. Singles from £38. Half price for children.
meals	Breakfast 8.30-9.30am. Pubs/restaurants 5-minute walk.
closed	Christmas.
directions	From Kendal, A591 to Windermere & follow signs to Bowness. There, bear left at bottom of hill & 1st left opp. church. Follow road past garage on left. House 50 yds on, on right.

Denise Barnes
Lightburne Georgian Town House,
13 Prince's Street, Ulverston,
Cumbria LA12 7NB
tel   01229 581930
e-mail   enquiries@lightburne.co.uk
web   www.lightburne.co.uk

Louise & Stephen Broughton
Low Fell,
Ferney Green, Bowness-on-
Windermere, Windermere,
Cumbria LA23 3ES
tel   015394 45612
fax   015394 48411
e-mail   lowfell@talk21.com
web   www.low-fell.co.uk

map: 13 entry: 83

map: 13 entry: 84

The magnificent Edwardian Arts & Crafts-style house has been built with huge attention to detail: vast airy rooms have leaded windows, panelled walls, oak floors, beautiful oak doors with wooden latches and motifs moulded into plaster. Bedrooms, reached via a spiral staircase, are simple; like the guest sitting room, they allow the architecture to breathe. Blueberries and damsons from the garden in season, distant views of mountains and lakes. Your hosts really are delightful and are passionate about conservation and the wildlife that populates their 14 acres of woodland and grounds. *Babies and children over six welcome.*

A pretty stone terrace built in 1849 by August Pugin, the architect famous for his ornamentations on the House of Parliament – and more evidence of his work in the fine woodwork and in a stunning copy of the fireplace at Westminster Palace. A Victorian feel has been created with period furniture, china and watercolours – even stuffed animals. Immaculately decorated bedrooms have comfortable, hand-painted four-posters or half-testers and modern shower rooms. Pauline and John, a wildlife painter who trained at the Glasgow School of Art, enjoy their guests and the door to the Aga-kitchen is ever open.

rooms	3: 1 double with shower; 1 twin with bath; 1 further double for members of same party.
room price	£55. Singles from £37.50.
meals	Excellent pubs/restaurants nearby.
closed	Christmas & New Year.
directions	From M6, junc. 36, A590 & A591 to r'bout, then B5284 for Hawkshead (via ferry) for 6 miles. After Windermere golf club, right for Heathwaite. Bear right up hill past nursery. Next drive on right; central part of manor.

rooms	4: 2 four-posters, 1 double, 1 triple, all with shower.
room price	£70-£78. Singles from £70.
meals	Breakfast 8.30-9am. Packed lunch £4.75. Dinner, 3 courses, £15, by prior arrangement. Pubs/restaurants short walk.
closed	Christmas & New Year.
directions	From M6, junc. 36; A591 to Windermere; past Boston House sign, left into 1st private lane The Terrace; red front door.

Rhoda M & Tony Graham
Gillthwaite Rigg,
Heathwaite Manor,
Lickbarrow Road, Windermere,
Cumbria LA23 2NQ

tel	01539 446212
fax	01539 446212
e-mail	tony_rhodagraham@hotmail.com

John & Pauline MacDonald
Boston House,
The Terrace, Windermere,
Cumbria LA23 1AJ

tel	01539 443654
e-mail	stay@bostonhouse.co.uk
web	www.bostonhouse.co.uk

CUMBRIA

An ancient cottage so pretty that artists have painted it. It is just about perfect with tumbling roses, dry stone walls, slate roof and views that lift the soul; the conservation village of Troutbeck lies below and the bumpy bridleway approach is part of the charm. The interior of the 1626 shepherd's cottage is simple and cosy with electric heaters and, in the sitting room, an inglenook fire; its windows look up and down the hill. Revel in your privacy – you'll not be disturbed. If you don't fancy tumbling out of bed too early, Anne will slip in quietly and leave a continental breakfast tray for you downstairs.

rooms	2: 1 double with shower; 1 twin with private shower.
room price	£60. Singles £30.
meals	Good pub 0.5 miles.
closed	Christmas & New Year.
directions	Facing Post Office in Troutbeck up Robin Lane, turn left. 1st cottage on right, 100 yds from Post Office.

Stephen & Anne Kelly
Dorothy's Cottage,
Robin Lane, Troutbeck,
Cumbria LA23 1PF
tel   01539 432780
e-mail   skelly99@hotmail.com
web   www.robinlane.co.uk

map: 13 entry: 87

CUMBRIA

You feel wrapped in the warmth of Philip and Alison's welcome, just as Low Jock Scar is folded into the leafy valley. (The scar in question is the escarpment on the far side of the stream.) This is a comfortable, homely, country guest house, built of stone, with a conservatory, cosy sitting area and bright, attractive bedrooms. The six acres of woodland and gardens are the Midwinters' pride and joy. Enjoy a five-course feast at dinner – the food is wonderful and uses locally available produce – then wander down the garden to the burbling beck and relax on the pretty bank.

rooms	5: 1 twin, with bath; 2 doubles, 1 with bath, 1 with shower; 1 twin, 1 double, sharing bath.
room price	£50-£62. Singles from £35.
meals	Packed lunch £3.75. Dinner £19.
closed	November-mid-March.
directions	From Kendal, A6 to Penrith. After 5 miles, Plough Inn on left. After 1 mile turn into lane on left.

Alison & Philip Midwinter
Low Jock Scar,
Selside, Kendal, Cumbria LA8 9LE
tel   01539 823259
fax   01539 823259
e-mail   ljs@avmail.co.uk

map: 13 entry: 88

We can tell you that it is grand, lavish, breathtaking, yet you will arrive unprepared for the luxury and the scale. There is no stinting on *anything*, be it fabric, colour, food or welcome. It is an 1841 Victorian folly with panelled hall, vast drawing room, grand piano, tumbling curtains, rugs on polished floors. There are turreted rooms, soaring fairy-tale castle windows and vaulted ceilings. Wendy and Simon spoil you with a happy, family atmosphere, magnificent feasts, huge pillows, handmade chocolates, sherry and massive tubs. Fancy getting married here? You can. *Self-catering available. See back of book.*

Wordsworth's brother-in-law lived here and the great man visited frequently. The views that he enjoyed, over to Barton Fell, are as glorious as ever. The mood is genuine – uncomplicated country hospitality at its best, with communal dining and no ceremony. Much of the atmosphere comes from Mary herself; she is great fun, down-to-earth and friendly, a real farmer's wife. The home-made biscuits in the rooms are a typical gesture. The bedrooms are simple and unfussy, with bathrobes for you, and those wonderful views. There are 300 acres, 850 sheep and a lovely walled garden... all in the National Park.

rooms	8: 2 twins/doubles, 3 doubles, 3 four-posters, all with bath/shower.
room price	£140. Singles £100.
meals	Breakfast from 9am. Dinner £30, Fri/Sat only; can cater for groups.
closed	Christmas.
directions	M6 junc. 38, then A685 through Kirkby Stephen. Just before Brough, right signed South Stainmore; house signed on left after 1 mile.

rooms	3: 1 double with shower; 1 twin/double with shower; 1 double sharing bath.
room price	£48. Singles £25.
meals	Breakfast until 9am. Pub 1 mile, restaurant 3 miles.
closed	December-February.
directions	From M6 junc. 40, A66 west. At r'bout left on A592. Follow signs to Dalemain house, through car park into courtyard ignoring 'No car' signs. Right for 0.5 miles & right again, at farm building.

Simon & Wendy Bennett
Augill Castle,
Brough, Kirkby Stephen,
Cumbria CA17 4DE

tel 017683 41937
e-mail augill@aol.com
web www.augillcastle.co.uk

Mrs Mary Milburn
Park House Farm,
Dalemain, Penrith,
Cumbria CA11 0HB

tel 01768 486212
fax 01768 486212
e-mail mail@parkhousedalemain.freeserve.co.uk
web www.parkhousedalemain.co.uk

Everything's well above average... the large and comfortable beds, the linen, the fabrics, the pillows. Feel cossetted. You'll appreciate the sensitivity of the renovations, too – the plasterwork stops here and there to reveal old beam, slate or stone. Peaceful bedrooms are free from clutter and each is named after the mountain that it faces; Swinside brings the 1650s house its own spring water. The breakfast room has separate tables, woodburner, hunting prints and a grandfather clock. Walkers will fall gratefully into the hot spring spa. *Children over six welcome.*

Gaze across rooftops towards the towering mass of Skiddaw, the Lake District's third highest mountain. Here is a cottage garden with sweet peas, herbs, vegetables and flowers... all suitably rambling. Roy and Chris have kept most of the buildings' original features; there are wooden floorboards and lofty bedroom ceilings. Dried flowers, cast-iron tubs, antique linen and patchwork quilts, a collection of christening gowns... television is delightfully absent and classical music plays. The Beatys are very hospitable. *Self-catering available. See back of book.*

rooms	5: 2 doubles, 3 twins/doubles, all with bath/shower.
room price	£92–£100. Singles by arrangement.
meals	Breakfast 8.30-9.30am. Packed lunch £7. Dinner £22. Tea rooms next door April-October.
closed	Rarely.
directions	From M6 junc. 40 west on A66. Past Keswick & on A66 for Cockermouth. Left at Braithwaite onto B5292, Whinlatter Pass. Through forest to Lorton. Left onto B5289 to farm, 1.5 miles on.

rooms	2: 1 double, 1 twin, both with bath.
room price	£47–£55. Singles £33.50–£35.
meals	Breakfast 8-9am. Inn 300 yds.
closed	December-January.
directions	From Keswick A591 to Carlisle (approx. 6.5 miles). Right at Bassenthwaite Chapel into village (0.5 miles). Straight on at village green for 170 yds.

Hazel Thompson
New House Farm,
Lorton, Cockermouth,
Cumbria CA13 9UU
tel 01900 85404
fax 01900 85421
e-mail hazel@newhouse-farm.co.uk
web www.newhouse-farm.co.uk

Roy & Chris Beaty
Willow Cottage,
Bassenthwaite, Keswick,
Cumbria CA12 4QP
tel 01768 776440
web www.willowbarncottage.co.uk

map: 13 entry: 91   map: 13 entry: 92

A rustic, 1669 yeoman's residence with an array of chunky wooden beams, wooden floors, bare stone and rough-plastered walls, inglenook fireplaces, flagged floors. Bedrooms are simple yet with pleasing touches; one has a four-poster, another a cerise velvet eiderdown and cream, gold and brown colourings, and there's a cockloft for children to play in. Jill is intent on your having a good time and spoils you with home-cured bacon, local sausages, free-range eggs and home-grown organic veg. There's a shoot on the farm, and venison, pheasant, duck, partridge or trout may be on the dinner menu. Special indeed.

W hite, 18th-century and pretty, Sirelands was once a gardener's cottage. It stands among spreading trees on a sunny, peaceful slope, lifting its eyes to the fells. A beck runs through the gardens, regularly visited by roe deer, red squirrels and an array of birds. The Carrs have lived here for nearly 35 years and their home has an attractive, lived-in feel. The pale green dining room is delightfully full of books and old, well-polished country furniture; the bedrooms are pleasant and comfortable. Angela enjoys cooking; much of the fruit and veg is home grown, and game and venison are sometimes available.

rooms	3: 1 four-poster with bath/shower; 1 twin/double, 1 twin/double with mezzanine for children, sharing bath/shower.
room price	£60. Singles £30.
meals	Packed lunch £5. Lunch £10-£15. Supper £15. Dinner, 3-4 courses, £25.
closed	Rarely.
directions	On A591, right for Whitrigg, Ireby, Torpenhow. After 2 miles, steep hill & squirrel signs; right over cattle grid for Snittlegarth, bear right after 2nd grid; half mile up lane.

rooms	2: 1 double with private bath/shower; 1 twin with bath.
room price	£50-£60. Singles £40.
meals	Dinner, 2-3 courses, £15-£20.
closed	Christmas & New Year.
directions	M6 north to junc. 43; A69 Newcastle; 3 miles to traffic lights. Turn right, on to Head's Nook; house 2 miles after village.

Miss Jill Green
High Houses,
Snittlegarth, Ireby, Carlisle,
Cumbria CA7 1HE

tel   01697 371549
e-mail   enquiries@highhouses.co.uk
web   www.highhouses.co.uk

Angela Carr
Sirelands,
Head's Nook, Brampton, Carlisle,
Cumbria CA8 9BT

tel   01228 670389
fax   01228 670389
e-mail   carr_sirelands@btinternet.com

The house echoes the enthusiasm poured into it by this young couple. Built in 1753, it has a classic Georgian façade and original features remain, including ornate ceilings, flagstones and shutters. Seek out the secret door to the billiard room, play tennis, or settle on the terrace for a sundowner. A soft sandstone arch leads to a lawned courtyard and two guest rooms; all bedrooms and bathrooms are large and fresh. Long views over this AONB, and shooting, fishing, sailing or riding can be arranged. Breakfast on local produce - maybe asparagus and poached egg?
House parties a speciality.

Rustic chic at its best — exposed stone or rough-plastered walls, open fireplaces, stylish, simple furnishings, rooms at different levels... The water mill was built around 1600, fell into ruin in the early 1900s and was converted into this unusual house in 1991. A wrought-iron spiral stair winds up through a beautiful dining room to the guest sitting room, comfortable with sofas, candles and an uncluttered air. Bedrooms lead off here (more unexpected steps!) and are as pleasing. Beyond the patio is a garden that takes you straight into the woods or to the River Irthing. A haven for those walking Hadrian's Way.

rooms	3: 1 double with shower; 1 double, 1 twin/double, both with bath.
room price	£70. Singles £40.
meals	Supper tray, £20. Dinner, 3 courses, £25. Pub/restaurant 0.3 miles.
closed	Christmas & New Year.
directions	From M6 junc. 41, follow A6 to High Hesket, right to Armathwaite & follow signs to Newbiggin. There, left at T-junc. 0.5 miles on, right into Cumrew. House straight ahead.

rooms	2: 1 double, 1 twin/double, both with bath/shower.
room price	£78. Singles £49.
meals	Dinner, 2 courses, £14.50.
closed	Christmas, New Year & occasionally.
directions	Exit M6 junc. 43, east on A69 Newcastle. At Brampton, follow Heritage signs for Lannercost Priory; a mile out of town, Abbey Mill on right, opp. Abbey Bridge Hotel.

Roddy & Isabel Duff
Cumrew House,
Cumrew, Head's Nook, Carlisle,
Cumbria CA8 9DD
tel	01768 896115
fax	01768 896117
e-mail	rabduff@aol.com
web	www.countrysport-lodge.com

Anthony Peacock
Abbey Mill,
Lannercost, Brampton,
Cumbria CA8 2HG
tel	01697 742746

DERBYSHIRE

DERBYSHIRE

Explore the two acres of herbaceous beds, jungle garden, kitchen garden, lovely terraces of stone walls, hidden patios, sculptures and streams. This is garden heaven. Hens, ponies and doves animate the charming old stable yard and, inside the 1783 house, Margaret has created more magic. Her fine eye for detail has brought together perfect colours, fabrics and pieces of furniture to create a house that is inviting throughout. Breakfast is served in the old schoolroom — organic eggs, honey, home-made jams and, of course, garden fruit. Glorious setting... and place.
Children over five welcome.

Farmhouse life at its luxurious best in the heady surroundings of the Peak District. Water from the spring, breakfasts with eggs and fruit from the farm, local sausages, oat cakes and home-made preserves, views in every direction. The farmhouse was built by the family in 1880 and has been deftly and smartly decorated — all rooms are closely carpeted and well lit and have elaborate window treatments. Bedrooms are pristine yet homely and one takes in views of the Peaks. Pam, South African, capable and welcoming, serves home-made cake and tea on arrival.
Self-catering available. See back of book.

rooms	3: 1 double with bath/shower; 1 family, 1 twin sharing bath & separate wc.
room price	£48-£55. Singles from £35.
meals	Breakfast 8-9am. Pub 1 mile.
closed	23 December-4 January.
directions	M1, junc. 29, A617 to Chesterfield, then B6051 to Millthorpe. Horsleygate Lane 1 mile on, on right.

rooms	3: 1 double with shower; 1 double, 1 twin/double with bath/shower.
room price	£50-£70. Singles £35.
meals	Many pubs & restaurants within 3 miles.
closed	December-February.
directions	From A6 follow Chinley signs. At Chinley Lodge Hotel leave B6062, over bridge, left into Stubbins Lane. After 0.25 miles, left fork onto farm road, over cattle grid & almost 0.5 miles into farmyard.

Margaret Ford
Horsleygate Hall,
Horsleygate Lane, Holmesfield,
Derbyshire S18 7WD
tel 0114 289 0333
fax 0114 289 0333

Pamela & Nick Broadhurst
Cote Bank Farm,
Buxworth, High Peak,
Derbyshire SK23 7NP
tel 01663 750566
fax 01663 750566
e-mail cotebank@btinternet.com.
web www.cotebank.co.uk

DERBYSHIRE

You are on the precipice of a spectacular limestone gorge – on some days, cloud is at window level. This is a former mill owner's house, a magnificent William IV property with truly panoramic views over the River Wye and to the green hills beyond. Don't be surprised if you see Len in the sky – he is famed for his hang-glider landings in the 30 acres of parkland. Inside, bedrooms are simple, but sympathetic renovation is ongoing; the orangery has just been completed. The Hall buzzes with family life – four generations live here and dynamic Bobby is central to it all. *Self-catering available. See back of book.*

rooms	3: 2 doubles, 1 twin, all with bath or shower.
room price	£65-£95. Singles from £55.
meals	Packed lunch & dinner by arrangement.
closed	Christmas & New Year.
directions	From Ashford-in-the-Water, B6465 to Monsal Head. Left at Monsal Head Hotel, follow valley to Cressbrook Mill, fork left. Left, at lodge building with white fence & 'Private Drive' sign.

Bobby & Len Hull-Bailey
Cressbrook Hall,
Cressbrook, Nr. Buxton,
Derbyshire SK17 8SY
tel 01298 871289
fax 01298 871845
e-mail stay@cressbrookhall.co.uk
web www.cressbrookhall.co.uk

map: 14 entry: 99

DERBYSHIRE

Elisabeth is an avid gardener and bird lover and has designed her garden to encourage wildlife. She also bakes bread, buys 'best-local' and has generally made this big country house a pleasure to stay in. The bedrooms are large and south-facing, with wonderful views. The double is chintzy, with walnut furniture and silk flowers, and you bathe in a cast-iron bath; the twin has Victorian/Edwardian furniture to match this wing of the house (the rest is much older). Elisabeth's garden is a joy and she is immensely kind. This is great walking country and Chatsworth is a 10-minute drive.

rooms	2: 1 double with private bath; 1 twin with private shower.
room price	£55. Singles £40.
meals	Breakfast 8-9am. Pubs & restaurants within walking distance.
closed	Christmas & New Year.
directions	On A6, 1.5 miles from Bakewell, right to Ashford-in-the-Water. Immediately left, then right to Monsal Head & right at Monsal Head Hotel into Little Longstone. Pass Pack Horse pub on left. House almost opposite.

Elisabeth Chadwick
The Hollow,
Little Longstone, Bakewell,
Derbyshire DE45 1NN
tel 01629 640746

map: 14 entry: 100

DERBYSHIRE

The whole village is listed, and most of it is estate-owned – but Sarah and Ray own the house. Hence the passionate commitment to restoring the best bits to their original splendour, such as flagstoned hall, fireplaces and big old iron bath. There are some beautiful pieces of furniture – an 18-foot dining table and handsome beds – and some striking decorations that are mostly Georgian with some earlier Tudor bits. Originally Tudor, this was the Master's House where tenants came to pay their rent. Wonderful countryside, fine walking and a bubbly hostess who buys local produce for your breakfast.

rooms	2 doubles/twins, both with private bath/shower.
room price	£60. Singles £35.
meals	Good pubs 10-minute walk.
closed	Rarely.
directions	A6 East of Bakewell; right onto B5006 to Ashbourne. Follow signs to Youlgreave & Alport 1.75 miles. House 1st on right in hamlet.

Sarah Copley & Ray Shannon
Rock House,
Alport, Bakewell,
Derbyshire DE45 1LG
tel   01629 636736

map: 9 entry: 101

DERBYSHIRE

How could the rooms of this 16th-century house match the beauty of its façade? Yet the interior surpasses all expectations: Marsha has flair, and the white-painted beams, vibrant colours and interesting pictures give the house a stylish, contemporary feel. There's an elegant dining room that looks onto a walled garden, a pretty guest sitting room with low stone fireplace and part-flagged floor, and large, warmly comfortable bedrooms with conservation-village views. Winster (near Bakewell and Chatsworth) is a gem. Big, fluffy towels, farm-cured bacon for breakfast, delightful hosts – perfection.

rooms	3: 1 double with bath/shower; 1 double, 1 twin, both with private bath.
room price	£85. Singles £60.
meals	Breakfast 7.30-9.30am. Packed lunch £3.75. Pub/restaurant 300 yds.
closed	Christmas & New Year.
directions	3 miles from Matlock on A6 for Bakewell. Left on B5057 signed Winster for 3 miles. House at end of Main Street.

John & Marsha Biggin
The Dower House,
Main Street, Winster,
Derbyshire DE4 2DH
tel   01629 650931
fax   01629 650932
e-mail   fosterbig@aol.com

map: 9 entry: 102

Y ou'll be hit by the wow factor. One of the four-poster rooms is *huge*, decadent, lavish – revel in the generosity of it all. Soft white robes, masses of pillows, a chandelier and a vast white-and-pink bathroom in which an enticing tub takes pride of place... new-laid eggs for breakfast, fresh fruits and home-made breads are the finale to a grand performance. The solid Victorian farmhouse sits in 370 peaceful acres and Kedleston Hall Park with its Robert Adam masterpiece provides a stunning backdrop. The generosity extends to the price: this is good value. *Children over eight welcome.*

A beautiful house, generously furnished with fine pieces to admire. There are two sitting rooms with books and antiques, some oriental; a twin with mahogany beds and Regency chair; a double with rose-patterned fabrics and deep cast-iron bath. Sue's competence does not overshadow her sense of humour: she's frank and friendly and guests love staying here. The garden is an added treat – rose walkways, a brook and lawns that open onto fields: a tranquil setting for tea. Breakfast fruit platters, scrambled eggs and smoked salmon will tempt you from your bed. *Self-catering available. See back of book.*

rooms	3: 1 double with bath/shower; 1 double with shower; 1 double with private bath.
room price	£65-£80. Singles £40-£45.
meals	Good eating places within 20-minute drive; closest 1 mile.
closed	Christmas.
directions	From A52/A38 r'bout west of Derby, A38 north. 1st left for Kedleston Hall. House 1.5 miles past Park on crossroads in Weston Underwood.

rooms	2: 1 twin, 1 double, both with private bath.
room price	£72. Singles £46.
meals	Dinner £22.
closed	Christmas & New Year.
directions	From Ashbourne A515 for Lichfield. 3 miles on, right to Snelston. Follow road for 1.25 miles to centre of village. House opp. War Memorial. Drive to rear.

Linda & Michael Adams
Park View Farm,
Weston Underwood, Ashbourne,
Derbyshire DE6 4PA
tel	01335 360352
fax	01335 360352
e-mail	enquiries@parkviewfarm.co.uk
web	www.parkviewfarm.co.uk

Edmund & Sue Jarvis
Oldfield House,
Snelston, Ashbourne,
Derbyshire DE6 2EP
| tel | 01335 324510 |
| e-mail | s-jarvis@tiscali.co.uk |

Lush greenness surrounds the house up a tiny country lane with glorious views over the Dove Valley. An ancestor of Peter was Lord Mayor of London in 1681, hence the memorabilia; Cynthia is Australian – they are a delightful couple for whom nothing is too much trouble. Although elegant, the house is nevertheless a home and guests are treated as friends – no off-limits, and there is even a small, book-lined sitting room just for guests. The hall sets the tone: white tiles, Indian rugs, woodburning stove and ancestral paintings. The bedrooms are impeccable, and there's a fine garden.

They are the kindest, most gracious hosts. Robert, who has a connection with Beatrix Potter, races vintage cars and Patricia, who tends the beautiful garden, anticipates your needs. Their splendid Georgian mansion, listed by Pevsner, was 'improved' in 1840 with pillars and again, later, with a high Victorian conservatory; breakfast here, overlooking the beautiful garden, is not to be missed. Shutters, antique furniture and fine country or garden views sit well with the elegant Georgian proportions. The bedrooms are in keeping, with plenty of space, traditional quilts and excellent bathrooms.

rooms	2: 1 double with bath; 1 double with private bath.
room price	£52-£56. Singles £35.
meals	Good pub 2 miles.
closed	Christmas.
directions	From Ashbourne, A515 Lichfield road. After 4 miles, right onto B5033. After 1 mile, 2nd lane on right. Cottage 0.5 miles on, on right.

rooms	3: 2 doubles, both with bath/shower; 1 twin with shower.
room price	£64-£70. Singles from £45.
meals	Dinner, 3 courses, £20.
closed	Christmas.
directions	Leave M1 at junc. 23a on to A453. At Isley Walton, right to Melbourne. Left in centre of village, then on Ashby road. Right at Melbourne Arms on to Robinsons Hill.

Peter & Cynthia Moore
Rose Cottage,
Snelston, Ashbourne,
Derbyshire DE6 2DL
tel   01335 324230
fax   01335 324651
e-mail   pjmoore@beeb.net

Robert & Patricia Heelis
Shaw House,
Robinsons Hill, Melbourne,
Derbyshire DE73 1DJ
tel   01332 863827
fax   01332 865201
e-mail   rheelis@onetel.net.uk

DERBYSHIRE

The former monastery dates from 1644 but the linen-fold panelling in the dining room could be older. It's a smart Grade-II* listed house with large, warm, generously furnished bedrooms and Victorian claw-footed baths. Bold chintzy designs complement classic English furniture and Clemmie has imbued every corner with a genuine warmth. Hot water bottles, flowers, early morning tea, relaxed suppers — she's a great cook — are typical of her natural inclination to spoil guests. Stroll in 18 acres of peaceful, rolling lakeside gardens, with woodland and countryside beyond, play croquet or just flop in a quiet corner with a book.

rooms	3: 2 doubles with bath; 1 twin with private bath.
room price	£62-£68. Singles £35-£45.
meals	Packed lunch £3-£5. Dinner from £18.
closed	Christmas & New Year.
directions	M42, junc. 11; A444 Burton-on-Trent for 2 miles; left immediately before Cricketts Inn for Netherseal. Gate 0.5 miles on right at end of long brick wall.

Clemency Wilkins
The Old Hall,
Netherseal, Swadlincote,
Ashby de la Zouch,
Derbyshire DE12 8DF
tel   01283 760258
fax   01283 762991
e-mail   clemencywilkins@hotmail.com

map: 9 entry: 107

DEVON

A beautifully renovated cottage/former bakery for which local materials have been sourced — beams from wood from Plymouth docks and panelling in the bedrooms from Dartmouth church. Farmhouse breakfasts of local produce are taken in a small book-filled, geranium-scented conservatory. Bedrooms are cosy and low ceilinged, the bathroom is tongue-and-groove panelled, and you have your own entrance and key. You are on a narrow lane and less than a mile from the coastal path at Hope Cove (once a smugglers' den) and four from the magnificent Salcombe estuary. Paddy and Griselda are delightful.

rooms	3: 2 doubles with bath; 1 double with shower.
room price	£50-£55. Singles from £35.
meals	Pub/restaurant in Hope Cove, 1 mile.
closed	Christmas.
directions	From Kingsbridge on A381, right to Hope Cove. In Galmpton, cottage is 200 yds on left, past village sign.

Paddy & Griselda Daly
Rose Cottage,
Galmpton, Salcombe,
Devon TQ7 3EU
tel   01548 561953
fax   01548 561953
web   www.rosecottagesalcombe.co.uk

map: 2 entry: 108

A Listed 16th Century thatched longhouse sitting at the head of its own secluded valley with wonderful walking and beaches nearby. There's hotel luxury here and you will be pampered. Lots of attention to detail – a fridge for BYO drinks, Molton Brown toiletries in the bathroom, lavender-scented linens and clotted cream teas on arrival. Elegant traditional furnishings and fresh flowers everywhere and a lovely beamed sitting room for guests with roaring log fires in Winter. Enormous breakfasts will be free-range, organic and seasonal; bread is baked daily and preserves and muesli are home-made. The nearest sandy cove is under a mile-a delightful 20-minute walk.

The woodpecker comes at 8.10 every morning; this is a haven for wildlife. Even the cat enters the mood, keen to join you in your room, and there is a goat to take for a walk. The 1860s house was part of the Flete estate – 5,000 acres which run from the South Hams to the sea – and has big, bright bedrooms with velux windows and cheerful colours. Carol and Peter couldn't be nicer and are clearly happy in their chosen spot. Dinner is good; and there's cream tea if you arrive before 5pm, gin and tonic after. *Children over 10 welcome.*

rooms	3: 1 twin/double, 1 double, both with shower; 1 four-poster with bath.
room price	£80-£130. Singles £55-£75.
meals	Breakfast 9-10am. Dinner, from £35, minimum 6 people. B.Y.O.
closed	Christmas.
directions	In Marlborough, turn opp. Texaco garage into Collaton Rd. Approx. 0.3 miles on, left for Collaton. Keep left at grass island, for Higher Collaton. House at end of private lane.

rooms	3: 1 double, 1 twin/double, both with bath & shower; 1 double with private shower.
room price	£50-£55. Singles £27.50.
meals	Packed lunch £5. Dinner £15.
closed	Rarely.
directions	From Modbury, A379 for Plymouth. After 1.5 miles, left to Orcheton. Right after 50 yds. 3rd on right.

Mark Andrews
The Yeoman's Country House,
Collaton, Salcombe, Devon TQ7 3DJ
tel   01548 560085
fax   01548 562070
e-mail   yeomanshouse@aol.com
web   www.yeomanshouse.co.uk

Peter Foster & Carol Farrand
Goutsford,
Ermington, Nr. Ivybridge,
Devon PL21 9NY
tel   01548 831299
fax   01752 601728
e-mail   carolfarrand@tiscali.co.uk

map: 2 entry: 109

map: 2 entry: 110

W alk through the pretty garden – past seats placed to soak up the sun – to your own entrance and private terrace, outside your bedroom door. The room is large, with wooden floors, an extremely comfortable brass bed, pretty pieces of Spanish pottery, biscuits on the tea tray. It's immaculate yet homely. The Ewens are friendly and easy company, their two spaniels equally so, and you are brilliantly sited – just above the rural town of Modbury and three miles from the sea. Generous breakfasts are served in the oak-beamed dining room. *Children over 10 welcome.*

B reakfast, served at a table by the sitting room's French windows, is a hearty affair with own free-range eggs and home-made marmalade and jam. The bright, spotless bedrooms have sofas and super bathrooms, one with a double-sized shower and the other a luxuriously large corner bath. Scented roses and climbers flourish on the local stone walls of this pleasing barn conversion and you cross a primrose-banked stream to an old orchard. Petrina and Kevin, easy-going and friendly, harvest apples for cider which they sell at the local farmer's market. *Self-catering available. See back of book.*

rooms	1 double with shower.
room price	£45. Singles £30.
meals	Good inn 300 yds.
closed	Christmas.
directions	A379 from Plymouth for Modbury. On reaching Church St. at top of hill, before Modbury, fork left at Palm Cross, then 1st right by school into Back St. Cottage 3rd on left, past village hall.

rooms	2: 1 double with shower; 1 twin/double with bath.
room price	£56–£70. Singles £38–£45.
meals	Excellent pub 2 miles.
closed	Christmas & New Year.
directions	From M5, A38 for Plymouth, A384 for Totnes, A381 for Kingsbridge; through Harbertonford, Halwell & The Mounts. 0.25 miles on, right for Grimpstonleigh. On left at end of lane.

Maureen Ewen
Orchard Cottage,
Palm Cross Green, Modbury,
Devon PL21 0QZ

tel 01548 830633
fax 01548 831127

Petrina & Kevin Frost
Lower Grimpstonleigh,
East Allington, Kingsbridge,
Devon TQ9 7QH

tel 01548 521258
fax 01548 521258
e-mail grimpstonleigh@ukgateway.net
web www.grimpstonleigh.com

map: 2 entry: 111

map: 2 entry: 112

DEVON

DEVON

Travel by train and Peter will chauffeur you home in his vintage Bentley (tours available). If sailing's your thing, he can take you out on the yacht. You can ride one of their horses, bring your own… or just mooch around the house and garden all day. Whichever appeals, Peter and Glynis want you to enjoy your stay. The house is Georgian, though in parts much older, and stands at the head of a lovely green valley with great views. The entire place has been beautifully renovated and the Farrow & Ball colours are easy on the eye. Sleep in an antique French or Italian bed, take breakfast on the terrace in summer.

From a narrow decorative window you see a charming vignette of Devon: a winding country lane edged by fat hedgerows, a hillside dotted with cows. The 18th-century former gamekeeper's cottage is folded into Devon's gentle green softness. Bedrooms are fresh and charming, the drawing and dining rooms formal and immaculate with fine furniture. Tim and Sally serve tea and home-made cake on arrival; they used to run a clematis nursery and the terraced garden is lovely. An excellent pub and the sea are nearby; at night you can see the beam from Start Point lighthouse.

rooms	3: 1 double, 1 twin, both with shower; 1 double with bath/shower.
room price	£55. Singles from £35.
meals	Dinner, 3 courses, £21. Lunch £7.50. Packed lunches £6.
closed	Rarely.
directions	From A381 at Halwell, 3rd left signed Slapton; 4th right after 2.3 miles signed Valley Springs Fishery at Wallaton Cross. House down 3rd drive on left.

rooms	3: 1 double, 1 twin/double, both with shower; 1 double with bath.
room price	From £50. Singles by arrangement.
meals	Breakfast 8.30-9.30am. Packed lunch £5. Pubs 600-800 yds.
closed	Christmas.
directions	A381 from Totnes to Halwell, then A3122 for Dartmouth. After Dartmouth Golf Club, right at sign to house & Blackawton. 0.3 miles before Blackawton, on right.

Peter & Glynis Bidwell
Lower Norton Farmhouse,
East Allington, Totnes,
Devon TQ9 7RL
tel 01548 521246
fax 01548 521246
e-mail lowernorton@tiscali.co.uk

Tim & Sally Adams
Woodside Cottage,
Blackawton, Nr. Dartmouth,
Devon TQ9 7BL
tel 01803 712375
fax 01803 712761
e-mail stay@woodsidedartmouth.co.uk
web www.woodsidedartmouth.co.uk

map: 2 entry: 113

map: 2 entry: 114

DEVON

The views from Nonsuch are glorious – from the conservatory or the lovely terraced garden watch the ever-fascinating spectacle of boats sailing up and down the estuary. The delights of Dartmouth lie across the water – a five-minute walk brings you to the ferry that transports you (and your car) to the other side. But Nonsuch does not rest on its natural laurels: everything here is captivating. The guests' sitting room has its own balcony, breakfasts are wonderful, bedrooms – all with views – are big, fresh and comfortable, bathrooms are perfect. *Children over 10 welcome.*

rooms	3: 2 twins/doubles with shower; 1 twin/double with bath.
room price	From £80. Singles by arrangement.
meals	Dinner, 3 courses, £24; cheese course £3.50. Not Tues, Wed or Sat.
closed	Rarely.
directions	2 miles before Brixham on A3022, take A379. After r'bout, fork left (B3205) downhill, through woods, left up Higher Contour Rd, down Ridley Hill. At hairpin-bend.

Christopher Noble
Nonsuch House,
Church Hill, Kingswear, Dartmouth,
Devon TQ6 0BX

tel	01803 752829
fax	01803 752357
e-mail	enquiries@nonsuch-house.co.uk
web	www.nonsuch-house.co.uk

DEVON

Gaze down to the sparkling Dart estuary from the snug warmth of your double bed. A maritime theme plays throughout this 18th-century home with its pebble collections and flotilla of model ships. Fresh, flower-filled bedrooms have tea, coffee and chocolates and your guest sitting/breakfast room is cosy with open fire, comfortable chairs, masses of books, and French windows that open onto the terrace. Gulls wheel overhead; a ferry transports you to Dartmouth and Totnes. Hugh and Jill are lovely and couldn't do more for their guests. *Children by arrangement.*

rooms	2: 1 double with bath & shower; 1 double with private bath.
room price	£65-£70. Singles £40-£50.
meals	Good pubs a short walk away.
closed	Christmas.
directions	Coming downhill into Dittisham, sharp right immed. before Red Lion Inn. Along The Level, up narrow hill & house entrance opp. at junc. of Manor Street & Rectory Lane.

Hugh & Jill Treseder
The White House,
Manor Street, Dittisham,
Devon TQ6 0EX

tel	01803 722355
fax	01803 722355

Your generous host has given you the best room in the house. The twin bedded room opens onto a large terrace high above the spectacular garden: 11 wondrous acres of rhododendron, magnolia, fuchsia, a lily-strewn pond, lawns and paths that dip and rise through areas of wild flowers. Richard is a gifted gardener and the archetypal gardener's modesty and calm have penetrated the house itself. It is uncluttered, comfortable and serene. There's a sheltered corner for breakfasts and you are welcome to find a spot to read or simply sit and absorb the tranquillity.

William of Orange is said to have held his first parliament here. The ancient, rambling house has blossomed thanks to the attention to detail that you'd expect from two designers. Wallpapers, napkins, *toile de Jouy* — they're all to Carole's own design; fresh white walls and plain painted wood form the perfect backdrop for many pretty touches. Breakfast feasts — bacon and eggs, home-made marmalade, yogurts, fruit — are served on pretty china. Bedrooms are supremely comfortable, one with a cast-iron fireplace and hand-stencilled paper. The garden, with many enchanting corners, is a joy.

rooms	2: 1 double sharing shower; 1 twin with bath.
room price	£50–£66. Singles £30–£38.
meals	Excellent pub in village.
closed	Rarely.
directions	From Totnes A381 to Kingsbridge for 1 mile. Left, for Ashprington. Into village then left by pub ('Dead End' sign). House 0.25 miles on right.

rooms	3: 1 twin/double, 1 double, both with private bath; 1 single sometimes available.
room price	From £55. Singles £35.
meals	Pubs/restaurants within 2 miles.
closed	Rarely.
directions	From Totnes, A385 Paignton rd. 2 miles on, look for South Hams Motors on right. Right. House 1st on right. Just past house to parking area on right.

Richard Pitts
Avenue Cottage,
Ashprington, Totnes,
Devon TQ9 7UT
tel   01803 732769
e–mail   richard.pitts@dial.pipex.com

Carole & Harry Grimley
Parliament House,
Longcombe, Totnes, Devon TQ9 6PR
tel   01803 840288
fax   01803 840288
e–mail   parliamenthouse@btopenworld.com

map: 2 entry: 117

map: 2 entry: 118

Sarah's a fanatical gardener – and a successful one, producing vegetables that will find their way onto your dinner plate, and fresh raspberries for your cereal. She keeps bees so there's honey – and eggs – for breakfast, too, taken in the smart red dining room. The farmhouse is part- 14th-century, and twists and turns around unexpected nooks and crannies. Sarah is capable, breezy and well-used to looking after people. The two bedrooms are large and painted sunny yellow; each has a tray with pretty china, two types of tea, coffee and local spring water. Excellent food in the pub up the road.

You come for the glory of the setting and the unpretentiousness of it all, not for huge luxury or sterile scrupulousness. The 17th-century longhouse has a gorgeous cobbled yard (laid by Judy), a bridge across to the island (shades of Monet) and goats. The family produces its own moorland water and all its fruit and vegetables; eggs come free-range from happy hens. The rooms are in simple, country style, the atmosphere laid-back, the attitude 'green' – hedge-laying, stone wall-mending – and the conversation fascinating. You can wander through two acres of young woodland, too. *Self-catering available. See back of book.*

rooms	2: 1 double with bath/shower; 1 twin with private bath.
room price	£50–£60. Singles £28–£32.
meals	Packed lunch £3–£4. Dinner £12–£15.
closed	Rarely.
directions	From Newton Abbot, A381 for Totnes. After approx. 2.5 miles, right for Broadhempston. Past village sign, down hill & 2nd left. Pass pub on right & left 170 yds on into courtyard.

rooms	4: 2 twins, 2 singles, all with basins, sharing bath.
room price	£25–£50. Under 2s free; under 5s half price in parents' room.
meals	Dinner occasionally available, £12.50. Good pub nearby.
closed	Christmas.
directions	Leave A38 at 2nd Ashburton turning for Princetown. After 2 miles, fork left to Holne. Pass inn & church. After 240 yds, right; after another 150 yds, left to Michelcombe. Over bridge & left. 200 yds on right.

Sarah Clapp
Manor Farm,
Broadhempston, Nr Totnes,
Devon TQ9 6BD

tel	01803 813260
fax	01803 813260
e-mail	clappfamily@members.shines.net

Judy Henderson
Dodbrooke Farm,
Michelcombe, Holne,
Devon TQ13 7SP

tel	01364 631461
e-mail	judy@dodbrooke.freeserve.co.uk
web	www.dodbrookefarm.com

Fascinating! The Tamar is magnetic and there's an ivy-clad ruin of an engine house and mine count house. The lovely Trish makes bread and will procure beef and lamb, or salmon fresh from the river below. Martha the donkey helps Trish win the battle with nature but prefers to have her front feet in the kitchen. Sail in, through the SSSI and AONB – there are moorings and a jetty – or book in for a writing or poetry course. It's characterful, fun, charming. Local branch line connects with Plymouth. *Babes in arms and children over eight welcome. Self-catering available. See back of book.*

History oozes from every cranny of this Devonshire manor farmhouse which predates the Domesday Book: granite mullioned windows, slate floors and beamed ceilings are all impressive. Rosalind gives a big welcome; she loves her ancient smallholding with chickens and carthorse. Guest bedrooms have their own entrance and a lovely feel – pretty fabrics and a sofa in the double, apricot walls and crocheted bedspreads in the twin. This is beautiful walking and riding country, and there's stabling and grazing for your horse. If you're looking for privacy and peace you'll be smitten.

rooms	2: 1 double with bath; 1 twin/double with bath & extra single/dressing room.
room price	£50–£60. Singles £25–£30.
meals	Dinner £18, occasionally available. Pub 3 miles.
closed	Rarely.
directions	Into Bere Alston on B3257, left for Weir Quay. Over x-roads. Follow Hole's Hole sign, then right for Hooe. Fork left for South Hooe Farm. 300 yds on, turn sharply back to your left & down track.

rooms	2: 1 double with private bath; 1 twin with private shower.
room price	From £50. Singles from £25.
meals	Packed lunch £5. Dinner £15.
closed	Rarely.
directions	From Tavistock B3357 for Princetown. At 1st x-roads, right for Whitchurch Down. Next x-roads 'Warren's Cross', left for Sampford Spiney. 2nd right at national speed limit sign, past 1 cottage on left. Next house on left.

Trish Dugmore
South Hooe Mine,
Hole's Hole, Bere Alston, Yelverton,
Devon PL20 7BW
tel   01822 840329
e-mail southhooe@aol.com

Rosalind Spedding
Sampford Manor,
Sampford Spiney, Yelverton,
Tavistock, Devon PL20 6LH
tel   01822 853442
fax   01822 855691
e-mail manor@sampford-spiney.fsnet.co.uk
web   www.sampford-spiney.fsnet.co.uk

An enchanted guest wrote: "If your life is full of stress, there's no better place to recover." Everything here is geared to your comfort – pretty rooms, four-poster and half-tester beds, deep, free-standing baths. Joanna and Graham, a lovely Devon couple, have worked hard to restore this former gardener's bothy, Graham making much of the furniture himself. Two new bedrooms have been created in the potting shed across the courtyard, where you can bed and breakfast in glorious seclusion. Outside are ponds, a stream and a walled Victorian garden… and Nelson, newly retired from the rigours of the Pony Club.

You will be captivated by the 17th-century Devon longhouse, whose windows peep onto a fascinating corner of Dartmoor. Generous, artistic Isabelle has added sophistication to lowly origins: a gilt-framed painting on a bare stone wall, luscious curtains thickly lined, big old fireplaces left intact, colour from patchwork quilt and garden flower, wood in beam and floor. It is like a warm, soft nest, and you are greeted as a friend. Breakfast on homegrown sausages, walnut muffins, coffee from a silver pot. Only the bleat of the sheep breaks the peace in these 23 bucolic acres, and the walks are glorious.

rooms	3: 1 four-poster, 2 twins/doubles, all with private bath.
room price	From £50. Singles from £25.
meals	Dinner, 3 courses, £15.
closed	Rarely.
directions	From Tavistock B3357 towards Princetown. 0.25 miles on, after Mount House School, left. Drive past lake to house.

rooms	2: 1 double with private bath/shower; 1 twin/double with bath/shower.
room price	£50. Singles £35.
meals	Packed lunch £7.
closed	Rarely.
directions	A38 south. Take Drumbridges r'bout, A382 Newton Abbott. At 2nd r'bout, 2nd exit A382 Bovey Tracey; 3rd r'bout left, B3387 to Widecombe. There, 1st right after post office; right at x-roads; farm 0.75 miles on right.

Mr & Mrs G H Moule
Mount Tavy Cottage,
Tavistock, Devon PL19 9JL
tel 01822 614253
e-mail graham@mounttavy.fsnet.co.uk
web www.mounttavy.freeserve.co.uk

Isabelle & David Meek
Old Langworthy Farm,
Widecombe in the Moor,
Devon TQ13 7UB
tel 01364 621319
e-mail isabelle@ic24.net

map: 2 entry: 123   map: 2 entry: 124

The bleat of sheep, the stamp of hooves — come to be engrossed in the routines of a wild, engagingly chaotic haven. Ann and William are friendly, kind and extrovert; guests adore them and keep coming back. There is comfort, too: warm curtains, a four-poster with lacy drapes, early morning tea... and a steep circular stair to rooms. Gentle giant shire horses live at the shippon end where the cows once stood; Bronze Age foundations lend medieval magic. A place for those who love the rhythm of real country life — and the Two Moors Way footpath is on the doorstep. *Children over 10 by arrangement.*

rooms	2: 1 four-poster, 1 twin, sharing bath.
room price	£40–£50. Singles £20–£25.
meals	Pubs 2 miles.
closed	Rarely.
directions	From A38 2nd Ashburton turn for Dartmeet & Princetown. In Poundsgate pass pub on left; 3rd signed turning right for Corndon. Straight over x-roads, 0.5 miles further, farm on left.

Ann & William Williams
Corndonford Farm,
Poundsgate, Newton Abbot,
Devon TQ13 7PP
tel 01364 631595
e-mail corndonford@btinternet.com

map: 2 entry: 125

The charm of this well-hidden miner's cottage will soothe stressed souls. Brave the long, bumpy track to a green oasis carved out of the woodland: 12 acres to explore, spectacular when the bluebells are out, with an enchanting garden. The house is filled with the mellifluous song of bird and river. Gently-spoken Mary loves to see guests unwind; both she and Dick have a finely-judged sense of humour. Bedrooms are simply furnished, the double with a brass bed and American patchwork quilt. Sip your Pimms by the pool in summer, tuck into local sausages and bacon at breakfast. Dinner, too, has been praised.

rooms	2: 1 double, 1 twin, both with bath/shower and separate wc.
room price	From £46. Singles £25.
meals	Supper £12.50. B.Y.O.
closed	Rarely.
directions	From A38, A382 at Drumbridges for Newton Abbot. 3rd left at r'bout for Bickington. There, down hill & past garage on left. Right for Haytor. Under bridge, 1st left & down long, bumpy track, past thatched cottage to house.

Mrs Mary Lloyd-Williams
Hooks Cottage,
Bickington, Nr. Ashburton,
Devon TQ12 6JS
tel 01626 821312
e-mail hookscottage@yahoo.com

map: 2 entry: 126

Architect Clough Williams-Ellis (of Portmeirion fame) did more than design an elegant house, he made sure it communed with nature. Light pours in from every window, and the most lovely views of the enchanting woodland garden and Devon farmland lift the spirits. The proportions and spaces work and the deep comfort gilds the lily. At every turn, antiques and heirlooms, elegant furniture, inviting sofas. The Gregsons take huge pride in having created an idyllic retreat and love guests to enjoy the house and the garden; they are charming, excellent hosts. You are welcome to play tennis on the all-weather court.

Bagtor House appears in the Domesday Book, though today's house dates from the 15th century; dramatist John Ford was born here in 1586. The dining room, with its wonderful oak panelling and granite inglenook, makes a fine setting for breakfasts. (Sue's home-made bread and marmalade are pretty good, too.) The double, red-painted and elegant, overlooks the garden and on the top floor is a huge and comfortable family room. The house is a leafy and lush retreat with chickens and ducks and you can walk to the moor from behind. You'd never know you were just 10 minutes from the A38.

rooms	3: 1 twin/double with private bath; 1 double, 1 double/family with private shower.
room price	£54–£60. Singles from £37.
meals	Dinner occasionally available. Good pub 1 mile, excellent pub 5 miles.
closed	Rarely.
directions	A38 west to Plymouth, A382 turn off, & 3rd turning off r'bout, signed Bickington. There, right at junc. (to Plymouth), right again (to Sigford & Widecombe). Over top of A38. 1st entrance on right.

rooms	2: 1 double, 1 family, both with private bath.
room price	From £54. Singles by arrangement.
meals	Excellent restaurant 1 mile & real-ale pub 0.75 miles.
closed	Christmas.
directions	From Bovey Tracy, B3387 for Widecombe-in-the-Moor. After 2.5 miles, left for Ilsington. After 0.75 miles, fork right to Bickington. Next right to Bagtor. On right 0.75 miles on.

Madeleine & Michael Gregson
Penpark,
Bickington, Newton Abbot,
Devon TQ12 6LH
tel   01626 821314
fax   01626 821101
e-mail   maddy@penpark.co.uk
web   www.penpark.co.uk

Nigel & Sue Sawrey-Cookson
Bagtor House,
Ilsington, Dartmoor,
Devon TQ13 9RT
tel   01364 661538
fax   01364 661538
e-mail   sue@bagtor.freeserve.co.uk

The house in the woods is small, cosy, unpretentious – it fits around you like a well-worn glove. Christina is welcoming and plies you with tea and well-travelled companionship. The walking and riding are outstanding in this fascinating corner of Devon – take your binoculars and catch the birds. Bedrooms are modest, and have quilted bedspreads and fabulous views: the garden and stream from one, the wild open moor from the other. Come not for luxury but for the setting, the hospitality (home-made soups, lovely people) and the peace. There's real warmth here.

There is a peacefulness about Easdon Cottage that strikes you the moment you enter. Replenish your soul in this light and beautifully proportioned cottage; if the room is taken, you may stay in the warm, peaceful barn; both have moor views. An enchanting interior with a mix of good pictures, oriental rugs, books, plants and some handsome Victorian finds. Liza and Hugh are vegetarian and dedicated users of organic produce. You are in a classic Devon valley yet the wilderness of Dartmoor lies just beyond the door. *Children and pets by arrangement. Self-catering available. See back of book.*

rooms	2: 1 twin/double with bath; 1 twin/double with shower.
room price	£40. Singles £20.
meals	Packed lunch £5. Light supper £12. Dinner, 3 courses, £20.
closed	Mid-March–mid-November.
directions	From Bovey Tracey signs to Manaton/Becky Falls; from Kestor Inn in Manaton, signs to Moretonhampstead for 3.3 miles. Lane to house 2nd on left after Heatree Cross.

rooms	1 twin/double with bath.
room price	£50. Singles £25.
meals	Packed lunch £3-£5. Supper from £12. Pubs/restaurants 10-minute drive.
closed	Rarely.
directions	A38 from Exeter; A382 for Bovey Tracey. There, left at 2nd r'bout for Manaton. 2 miles beyond Manaton, right at x-roads signed M'hampstead. 0.5 miles on, right, signed Easdon. Cottage on left up track.

John & Christina Everett
Vogwell Cottage,
Manaton, Newton Abbott,
Devon TQ13 9XD
tel 01647 221302

Liza & Hugh Dagnall
Easdon Cottage,
Long Lane, Manaton,
Devon TQ13 9XB
tel 01647 221389
fax 01647 221389
e-mail easdondown@btopenworld.com

DEVON

DEVON

Walks from the house are reason enough to come here – the atmosphere and the house (a 17th-century ex-wool-mill) are a bonus. On the edge of one of Dartmoor's prettiest villages, the mill's lawned gardens run down to the Bovey river. There are sparkling wooden floors, walking sticks for hikers, whitewashed walls, wood carvings, stone fireplaces and candlelight at dinner. The bedrooms have superb views over woodland and river, and your delightful, and delightfully modest, hosts provide superb organic and local produce. Peter makes honey and spins wool from their own Jacob sheep.

Such care is taken with everything that you can't fail to feel spoiled; John and Sheila are keen hosts and clearly love sharing their 15th-century hall house with guests. Dinners here are a real treat – maybe free-range chicken breasts cooked in sherry and served on a bed of celeriac with home-grown veg; you dine by candlelight off the crispest white linen. There's a sitting room for guests with a vast, granite fireplace; bedrooms are traditional with floral fabrics. A pool in the large, secluded gardens overlooks woodland and moors, and the historic village is delightful.

rooms	3: 2 doubles with bath; 1 twin/double with shower.
room price	£80-£84. Singles £48.
meals	Breakfast 8.30-9am. Light suppers by arrangement. Dinner £26, not Sun/Mon. Good pub in village.
closed	January-February.
directions	From M5, A30 to Okehampton. Look for Marsh Barton sign onto B3212 to Moretonhampstead. There, take Princetown road, left at newsagent for North Bovey.

rooms	3: 1 twin/double with bath/shower; 1 twin/double with shower; 1 double with private bath/shower.
room price	£62. Singles £38.
meals	Breakfast 7.30-8.45am. Packed lunch available. Dinner, 4-5 courses, £18. B.Y.O.
closed	Rarely.
directions	From Moretonhampstead via Pound Street to North Bovey (1.5 miles). House 25 yds off village green, down Lower Hill past inn on left.

Peter Hunt & Hazel Phillips
Black Aller,
North Bovey, Moretonhampstead,
Devon TQ13 8QY
tel 01647 440322
fax 01647 441131
e-mail peter@blackaller.fsbusiness.co.uk
web www.blackaller.co.uk

John & Sheila Williams
The Gate House,
North Bovey, Devon TQ13 8RB
tel 01647 440479
fax 01647 440479
e-mail gatehouseondartmoor@talk21.com
web www.gatehouseondartmoor.co.uk

map: 2 entry: 131

map: 2 entry: 132

Winding, high-hedged Devon lanes lead to Great Sloncombe – a working Dartmoor farm with milking cows and a pedigree Aberdeen Angus herd. There are few traces of its 13th-century origins – the house is listed – but there are pieces of old oak and granite everywhere, to which the Merchants have added their own antiques and old photographs. Doorways are tiny, bedrooms are country-style cosy – one has a pine four-poster – and all have views to meadows teeming with wildlife. Trudie, who is very involved with carriage driving, cooks dinners of home-grown meat and vegetables.

A charming terraced cottage full of 16th-century nooks and crannies and beams worth ducking. The setting is exquisite: the garden leads into fields of sheep, the Dartmoor Way goes through the town and the Two Moors Way skirts it. Shelagh, a lovely lady, gives guests their own sitting room with a fire, lit on cool nights; breakfasts, served in the cosy dining room, are fresh and free-range. Up the narrow stairs and into flowery bedrooms – a small double and a tiny twin. A perfect house and hostess, and a perfect little town, with its pubs, fine restaurant and delicatessen for picnickers.

rooms	3: 1 double, 1 twin, 1 four-poster, all with shower.
room price	£50-£54. Singles by arrangement.
meals	Dinner £15.
closed	Rarely.
directions	From Bovey Tracey A382. After Moretonhampstead, look for signs to farm.

rooms	2: 1 double with private bath; 1 twin with shower.
room price	£45-£50. Singles £25-£27.
meals	Good pub & restaurant 400 yds.
closed	Christmas.
directions	In Chagford leave church on left; 1st right beyond Globe Inn. House 150 yds on right.

Trudie Merchant
Great Sloncombe Farm,
Moretonhampstead,
Devon TQ13 8QF

tel	01647 440595
fax	01647 440595
e-mail	hmerchant@sloncombe.freeserve.co.uk
web	www.greatsloncombefarm.co.uk

Shelagh Weeden
Cyprian's Cot,
47 New Street, Chagford,
Devon TQ13 8BB

| tel | 01647 432256 |
| e-mail | shelagh-weeden@lineone.net |

Watch hares cavort from your bedroom window in picture-perfect Devon. The thatched cottage has a calming, uncluttered mood of whitewashed walls, old pine and traditional chintz. There's a lovely big conservatory, a flowered garden, and tennis to play; in winter, logs crackle in a huge hearth. Bedrooms have charming windows, white candlewick bedspreads, and framed samplers on the walls. Judi looks after you with unflappable friendliness and her cooking is superb — breakfast is an ever-changing treat. You will feel folded into the countryside and utterly content.

Over 900 years old and still humming with life; goats, ponies, cats, guinea-fowl, rabbits and foxes share the rambling gardens. Sally-Anne and family are artistic, fun, slightly zany and dizzy. It's an adventure to stay here, so keep an open mind: the house is an historic gem and so robustly rustic that the BBC twice filmed *Down to Earth* here. Huge flagstone fireplaces, interesting art, books, pianos, wellies, muddle and charm; Sally Anne will take children to collect eggs and may babysit. Expect to be wrapped in perfect peace and immersed in a panorama of forest, hills and fields of waving wheat.

rooms	3: 1 double with bath/shower; 2 doubles with private bath/shower.
room price	£60-£80. Singles £35.
meals	Supper £15. Dinner, 3 courses, £27.50.
closed	Rarely.
directions	B3212 to Dunsford; turn for Dunsford, follow road for 1.5 miles; on edge of village, turn for Cheriton Bishop. Right towards C. Bishop at Wild Banks; driveway 0.5 miles up lane on right.

rooms	2: 1 twin, 1 double, sharing bath.
room price	£50. Singles £30.
meals	Restaurants 0.5 miles.
closed	Christmas & New Year.
directions	A30 to Okehampton. After 10 miles left exit into Cheriton Bishop, 2nd left between 2 cottages. Down & up hill. Road turns sharp left. Down lane; signed.

Judi Smith
Symonds,
Dunsford, Exeter, Devon EX6 7DR
tel   01647 24510
fax   01647 24084
e-mail   judithsmith@symondsdunsford.co.uk
web   www.symondsdunsford.co.uk

Carter-Johnson Family
Higher Eggbeer Farm,
Cheriton Bishop, Nr Exeter,
Devon EX6 6JQ
tel   01647 24427

Your warm and expansive hosts, he a garden designer, she a painter, have created an enchanting and atmospheric home from a thatched longhouse that once belonged to the author Doris Lessing. You'll love this 14th-century, Grade II-listed house in the heart of Dartmoor National Park; each of the beamy, low-ceilinged bedrooms overlooks a cottage garden resplendent with wild flowers. Woodburning stoves, oriental rugs, warm-coloured walls, four-poster beds and, outside, a boules pitch, duck pond and the moor with all its wild treasures.

Sonia and Geoffrey are natural hosts; they have lived all over the world and are now extremely happy in their converted mill in this corner of Devon. You can walk, ride or sail on or around the Roadford Reservoir which is close by – or put your artistic inhibitions to one side and set off with Sonia, a keen landscape painter, to capture the natural beauty of your surroundings. You'll be folded in human warmth, offered a glass of wine in the large, homely kitchen and be given masses of ideas for exploring the area. *Children by arrangement.*

rooms	2: 1 four-poster with shower, 1 four-poster with bath.
room price	£80. Singles £50.
meals	Breakfast 8.30-9.30am. Excellent pubs/restaurants 0.75 miles.
closed	Christmas & New Year.
directions	Exit A30 for Okehampton & Belstone. Follow signs to Belstone. In centre of village right after phone box. After 0.75 miles cross cattle grid. House on left.

rooms	1 twin with bath/shower & sitting room. Bed in studio also available, with shower.
room price	£50. Studio, only available if twin is full, £30.
meals	Light supper £10, not Sundays. Excellent pubs/restaurants within 2 miles.
closed	Christmas & New Year.
directions	North from Launceston on A388, right for Ashwater. After 1.75 miles, left by post-office. 1 mile north, at Thorney Cross, 1st drive on left, then right down driveway.

John & Maureen Pakenham
Tor Down House,
Belstone, Okehampton,
Devon EX20 1QY
tel   01837 840731
fax   01837 840731
e-mail   info@tordownhouse.co.uk
web   www.tordownhouse.co.uk

Geoffrey & Sonia Archer
Renson Mill,
Ashwater, Devon EX21 5ER
tel   01409 211665
fax   01409 211665
e-mail   soniaarcher@globalnet.co.uk

You reach the traditional Devon farmhouse across open farmland; within minutes of entering you feel the love that Ann and Richard have for the old place. They are vastly talented and artistic and have worked in harmony to restore it all. Richard made the dresser and uncovered everything of ancient beauty; he's also created a pond that's now home to a family of mallards and two pairs of geese. Ann has laid brick paths, stencilled, stitched and painted, all with a wonderful eye for colour. Charming rooms, place and people, and free-range home eggs for breakfast, taken in the lovely garden room.

The Bradiford Valley is pretty and lush and runs down towards the glorious beaches of North Devon and the biosphere of Braunton Burrows. The 17th-century home – creaky, comfortable, deceptively big – is wrapped in the most lovely garden that stretches up the hill. Old rugs give a warm passage over slate floors, and chintz and pretty wallpapers add to the snug feel. The main bedroom has wiggly walls and wicker furniture; the bathroom, with its long sloping ceiling, a huge bath in which to soak. The house has been in the family for 200 years and your hosts are easy, unstuffy people who love and know the area well.

rooms	2: 1 double with shower; 1 twin with bath & shower.
room price	£50. Singles £30.
meals	Breakfast 8-9am. Dinner, 2 courses, £15.
closed	20 December-5 January.
directions	From A39, left into Bideford, round quay, pass old bridge on left. Follow signs to Torrington. 1.5 miles on, right for Buckland Brewer. 2.5 miles on, left. 0.5 miles on, right over cattle grid & down track.

rooms	3: 2 doubles, 1 twin, all with basins, sharing bath & separate shower.
room price	£40-£50. Singles £20-£25.
meals	Breakfast until 9.30am. Good pubs nearby.
closed	Christmas & New Year.
directions	From Barnstaple, A361 for Braunton. At 2nd set of lights, right for Bradiford. Next T-junc., sharp left, over bridge, up hill for 50 yds, 2nd lane to right. House 1st on left.

Ann & Richard Dorsett
Beara Farmhouse,
Buckland Brewer, Bideford,
Devon EX39 5EH

tel   01237 451666

Jane & Tony Hare
Bradiford Cottage,
Bradiford, Barnstaple,
Devon EX31 4DP

tel   01271 345039
fax   01271 345039
e-mail   holidays@humesfarm.co.uk
web   www.humesfarm.co.uk

map: 2 entry: 139

map: 2 entry: 140

Bright, clear colours, antique furniture and charming decorative touches. Fresh fruit and flowers in the bedrooms (one with an inviting king-size bed) and two guest sitting rooms. Delicious, organically-reared meat, veg and eggs, fresh fish, home-made cakes… As if that were not enough, this Georgian farmhouse has a stunning formal garden which Liz, a weaver, and Tony, a painter, have created from a green field: spring-fed pools, lime walk, pergola, arches, herbaceous beds and ongoing parterre. A bold, grassy avenue leads to the three ponds, which attract lots of wildlife. Look – and listen – for the tawny owl.

Folded into the Devon hills, the 30-year-old house is full of light and surprises. David is a designer, Rosie a florist and their home a hymn to contemporary texture and colour. One bedroom is lilac, the other yellow – a French sleigh bed here, a chic 60s armchair there, new art, crisp linen, ethnic treasures. Bathrooms are pure delight. Surrounded by bluebell woods and badgers, the garden yields flowers for your room, vegetables for your table; there's even a solar-heated pool for summer swims. Surf the north Devon coast, ramble the two moors, walk the Tarka Trail… return for deep sleeps.

rooms	2 doubles, both with bath.
room price	£58. Singles £29.
meals	Dinner £20.
closed	Rarely.
directions	From Tiverton, B3137 west; 3 miles on, B3042 to Eggesford; there, right onto A377. 5 miles on, B3226 on right; 1 mile on, right for Kings Nympton; through village, over x-roads; house 0.75 miles on left.

rooms	2: 1 twin/double with bath/shower; 1 double with shower.
room price	£90. Singles £45.
meals	Packed lunch from £7.50. Dinner from £17.50.
closed	Rarely.
directions	From South Molton, B3137 for 4.5 miles; right at Odam Cross to Romansleigh; next left at Buckam Cross signed 'No through road'; steep hill, ford, 2nd right, house on left at top of hill.

Tony & Liz Williams
Lower Hummacott,
Kings Nympton, Umberleigh,
Devon EX37 9TU
tel 01769 581177
fax 01769 581177

Rosemary Ames
Catsheys,
Romansleigh, South Molton,
Devon EX36 4JW
tel 01769 550580
fax 01769 550395
e-mail rose.ames@mailbox.co.uk
web www.catsheys.co.uk

map: 2 entry: 141

map: 2 entry: 142

Fun, hugely surprising, simple, refreshingly different – and the food is brilliant. Michael has a deserved reputation as an inspired cook and his meals in the kitchen-cum-dining room are great value. The adventure begins as you meander down a lane towards this former 18th-century wheelwright's shop… it's three miles from a numbered road in any direction, but what rewards. Bedrooms have polished wooden floors and whitewashed walls, bathrooms are rag-rolled and fluorescent and the stairs are painted green. Jellicoe's is fresh, vibrant, Mediterranean. Come for restorative peace and great views.

Total immersion in beauty – fields on either side of the long drive, Dartmoor views, bluebells in spring, sparkling stream, pretty garden. Privacy, too, in the 18th-century upside-down barn on the side of the 17th-century Devon longhouse. A handmade oak staircase, oak floors, rugs, woodburner, a big bed and a good sofabed. How tempting to have Phillida bring breakfast to your pretty kitchen with French doors; you can also eat in the farmhouse dining room. There will be home-made something on arrival – flapjacks, cake, biscuits, brownies – and a gentle, genuine welcome. Excellent riding, and stabling for your own horse.

rooms	3: 2 doubles, both with shower; 1 twin/family with bath.
room price	£44. Singles £22.
meals	Breakfast 7.30-9.30am. Packed lunch £2.50. Dinner, 3 courses, £12.
closed	Rarely.
directions	Leave A396 at Bickleigh, right for Crediton, then immed. right again for Cadeleigh. Through Cadeleigh. Left at 'Post Box Cross', & right for Upham. House 2nd on left.

rooms	1 twin/double with bath/shower.
room price	£70. Singles £35.
meals	Good pubs nearby.
closed	Rarely.
directions	B3137 Witheridge road out of Tiverton; cont. towards Rackenford/Calverleigh. After pink thatched cottage (2 miles), fork left to Templeton; West Bradley 2 miles; on left before village hall.

Michael Jellicoe
Jellicoe's,
Higher Holn, Upham,
Cheriton Fitzpaine, Crediton,
Devon EX17 4HN
tel   01363 866165
fax   01363 866165
e-mail   enquiries@jellicoes.co.uk
web   www.jellicoes.co.uk

Martin & Phillida Strong
West Bradley,
Templeton, Nr Tiverton,
Devon EX16 8BJ
tel   01884 253220
fax   01884 259504
e-mail   martin.strong@btinternet.com

map: 2 entry: 143

map: 2 entry: 144

Lofty ceilings and large windows bring light and space to this traditional family house. The former coaching inn stands at the top of a steep hill (how the horses must have toiled) with exhilarating views of farmland and Exe Valley. Dining and drawing rooms are on a grand scale with antique furniture. One bedroom has a Victorian four-poster; the ground floor double opens onto the gardens. A good place for breaking a journey or for those on business in Tiverton. Barbara is an efficient, kind, no-fuss hostess.

rooms	3: 1 double with shower; 1 four-poster with private bath/shower; 1 twin with private bath.
room price	From £48. Singles £27.
meals	Breakfast 7-9am. Dinner, 4 courses, £15. Pub 2 miles.
closed	Rarely.
directions	At junc. 27 (M5), A361 for approx. 4.5 miles. Turn off at Gornhay Cross, for Grand Western Canal. At Canal Hill, 1st right into Exeter Hill. House at top on left.

Barbara Pugsley
Hornhill,
Exeter Hill, Tiverton,
Devon EX16 4PL
tel 01884 253352
fax 01884 253352
e-mail hornhill@tinyworld.co.uk
web www.hornhill-farmhouse.co.uk

map: 2 entry: 145

An Irish attitude to life dominates the house, says Charlotte – that means friends, family and guests mingle with ease. There's plenty of company and activity to enjoy: polo ponies (tuition available), fishing, the garden to explore. Or sit and catch the morning sun in the dining room, then enjoy the privacy of your suite. You have handsome, traditional furniture, fat pillows, new mattresses, cotton bed linen and a tray with whisky decanter and mineral water. For breakfast, home-reared, additive-free sausages and bacon, and home-made breads. Your horse can come, too. *Children over 10 welcome.*

rooms	1 twin with bath, sitting room & kitchenette.
room price	£70. Singles from £45.
meals	Breakfast until 9.30am. Picnic lunch £15. Dinner £25.
closed	Christmas & New Year.
directions	From M5, junc. 26 or 27, A38 for Exeter for 6 miles, then left to Culmstock. There, over bridge, first right into Silver Street. Last drive on right.

Roger & Charlotte Horne
Woodhayne Barton,
Culmstock, Devon EX15 3JG
tel 01884 840708
fax 01884 841479
e-mail rogercharlotte@homewoodhayne.demon.co.uk
web www.hornewoodhayne.demon.co.uk

map: 2 entry: 146

You couldn't better the position: deep in the country, yet near airport, cathedral and coast. The Victorian farmhouse breathes an air of well-being – sparkling sash windows fill big rooms with light, stripped floors shine, the grandfather clock ticks away the hours. Guests are spoiled with the best: goosedown duvets on king-size beds, exceptional bathroom goodies and home-baked bread, contemporary luxury in fabric and fitting and bathroom mirrors mist-free! Charlie, Savoy-trained, is charming and easy – you are in perfect hands. Stylish, fun and without pretension. *Children sleep in parents' room free of charge.*

Lapping, almost, at the riverside garden is the Exe estuary, wide and serene. Birds and boats, the soft hills beyond, a gorgeous Georgian house on the river and kind hosts – silly to wish for more. Yet the garden, too, is beautiful, full of topiary, old apple trees and box hedging; you may breakfast there or in the conservatory. Every corner of the house has been considered. The bedrooms are luxurious, peachy, soft, chintzy and have antique white bedspreads. Topsham is an unspoilt conservation area. A remarkable marriage of nature and human intervention.

rooms	3: 2 doubles both with bath/shower; 1 twin/double with bath/shower.
room price	£70–£85. Singles from £55.
meals	Dinner, 3 courses, from £21.50.
closed	Rarely.
directions	From A30 Exmouth & Ottery St Mary junction. At mini-r'bouts follow Whimple signs. After 0.25 miles, right; 0.5 miles, then left signed Larkbeare. 1 mile on left.

rooms	2: 1 twin, 1 double, both with bath.
room price	£60. Singles £35.
meals	Good pubs & restaurants a short walk away.
closed	Christmas & New Year; January–March.
directions	M5, junc. 30, follow signs to Exmouth. Right at George & Dragon. After about 1 mile immed. left after level crossing. At mini roundabout, left down The Strand. House last on left by beach.

Charlie & Julia Hutchings
Larkbeare Farmhouse,
Larkbeare, Talaton, Exeter,
Devon EX5 2RY
tel   01404 822069
fax   01404 823746
e-mail   stay@larkbeare.net
web   www.larkbeare.net

Trevor & Jane Coleman
Beach House,
The Strand, Topsham, Exeter,
Devon EX3 0BB
tel   01392 876456
fax   01392 873159
e-mail   janecoleman45@hotmail.com

The round-headed oak door frame in the back bedroom hints at this Grade II-listed farmhouse's 16th-century origins — James will tell you about its history. Orchards, paddocks and ponds outside; homeliness and comfort within. You'll want for nothing with Sîan (once a nurse) your attentive yet unobtrusive hostess. Pale-walled bedrooms, with charming old windows and deep sills, are attractively furnished with some antiques. The odd beam to be ducked, a soppy black labrador to be fussed over, eight miles from Exeter and a dream for walkers, too. Wholly delightful. *Children and pets by arrangement.*

Privacy, peace and stylish comfort in stunning surroundings. After much travelling, these ex-TV producers had a clear vision of the perfect place to stay. They've achieved it here, using local craftsmen and local material in the renovations. Each bedroom is self-contained, two with private terraces, one tucked under the roof beams. The beds are firm, the linen luxurious and the chrome shower-heads the size of dinner plates. Woodland, valley and bluebell walks start outside the door and the views are unimaginably glorious. If Frank's teatime nut torte is anything to go by, his breakfasts will be pretty good too.

rooms	3: 1 double with bath; 1 double with private bath; 1 twin with shower.
room price	£50-£58. Singles £33-£36.
meals	Breakfast until 9.30am. Packed lunch £4. Excellent pub 2 miles.
closed	Rarely.
directions	From A30, B3180 for Exmouth. 0.75 miles on, right at crossroads for Marsh Green. House 1st on left on entering village.

rooms	3 doubles, all with shower.
room price	£70. Singles £35.
meals	Packed lunch from £7.50. Restaurants in Honiton.
closed	Christmas.
directions	3 miles from Honiton & signed off A35 Honiton-Axminster road. In centre of village, at church, down hill. Farm 0.5 miles on.

	Mr & Mrs J B Wroe
	Lower Marsh Farm,
	Marsh Green, Exeter,
	Devon EX5 2EX
tel	01404 822432
fax	01404 822062
e-mail	lowermarshfarm@eclipse.co.uk
web	www.lowermarshdevon.co.uk

	Frank & Carol Hayes
	West Colwell Farm,
	Offwell, Honiton, Devon EX14 9SL
tel	01404 831130
fax	01404 831769
e-mail	stay@westcolwell.co.uk
web	www.westcolwell.co.uk

DEVON

Breakfast in the conservatory – or a drink there before dinner – will seduce you: it's awash with colour, plants and *objets de curiosité*. The garden is outrageously lovely: specimen trees, a fountain and two ponds, mature trees of all kinds, spring carpets of aconites, crocuses, snowdrops and bluebells, huge rhododendrons and camellias. Simon was a pilot, Gill a nurse – the house has lovely paintings, done by Gill when they lived in Japan. It is a splendid place with large rooms, high corniced ceilings, antiques and fine things, and your generous hosts encourage you to feel thoroughly at home.

rooms	1 double with private bath.
room price	£80–£90. Singles £45.
meals	Packed lunch £5. Dinner £15–£25. Good pubs/restaurants nearby.
closed	Occasionally.
directions	From Tesco/Station r'bout in Axminster, A358 Seaton road up hill. 0.5 miles on, left into Woodbury Lane, after bus stop. House on right 0.5 miles up lane.

Gill Boston
Chattan Hall,
Woodbury Lane, Axminster,
Devon EX13 5TL

tel	01297 32365
fax	01297 32365
e-mail	boston@chattanhall.co.uk
web	www.chattanhall.co.uk

DORSET

On a clear day ask for breakfast on the balcony: you'll be wowed by stupendous views across Lyme Bay and beyond. Years of travel and naval lifestyle lie behind the Normans' meticulous and old-fashioned hospitality; they have settled happily in this large 1920s house. Bedrooms under the eaves are thoroughly comfortable; all have chairs, a writing desk and flowers from the garden. Two of the rooms are large and have wonderful coastal views and the third is cottagey; one of the bathrooms is small. *Children over eight welcome.*

rooms	3: 1 double, 2 twins, all with bath.
room price	£44–£58. Singles £33–£40.
meals	Breakfast 8.15–9am. Supper tray £9.50 (1st night only). Pub/restaurant 400 yds.
closed	Mid-November–mid March.
directions	From Lyme Regis, up Pound St & Sidmouth Rd, past 'Morgans Grave' & Somers Road; house up 1st driveway on right, abreast of junction sign & 'SLOW' sign on road.

Tony & Vicky Norman
The Red House,
Sidmouth Road, Lyme Regis,
Dorset DT7 3ES

tel	01297 442055
fax	01297 442055
e-mail	red.house@virgin.net

In the parlour, deep sofas, a woodburner and piles of magazines and cookery books – a real foodie haven. A thatched working farmhouse in 80 acres of bio-dynamic, organic farmland on which the Bells, specialist food suppliers, graze Aberdeen Angus cattle, Portland sheep and Tamworth pigs (they supply Nigella Lawson and other top chefs). Large bedrooms have a simple country feel with pure Irish bed linen and views of the Jurassic coastline and Golden Cap. The farm's field overlook Lyme Bay and walks and wild flowers abound. A very relaxing home and gardens: not a place to rush through. *Children and pets by arrangement.*

rooms	2 doubles, sharing bath & separate wc.
room price	£150. Reduced 3-night rates.
meals	Hampers & packed lunch from £15. Dinner, 3 courses, £30. Excellent local restaurants.
closed	Occasionally.
directions	Directions given at time of booking.

Denise & Ian Bell
Shedbush Farm,
Muddy Ford Lane,
Stanton St Gabriel, Lyme Regis,
Dorset DT6 6DR
tel   01297 489304
fax   01297 489531
e-mail   heritageprime@aol.com
web   www.heritageprime.co.uk

map: 3 entry: 153

An impeccably furnished 17th-century house so steeped in history that the Royal Commission included it in its inventory of Historical Monuments. A cherished home, too, with stacks of atmosphere. Attractive fabrics and paints compliment the more architectural charms of flagstones, window seats and original beams, and there is a fascinating collection of prints and china. Books, comfortable beds, and your own delightful sitting room with inglenook fire spoil further. Absolute quiet – an orchard leads to a stream and the sea is one mile away. Mrs Tennant is a gentle, thoughtful hostess. *Children over 10 welcome.*

rooms	2: 1 double with private bath; 1 twin sharing bath, let to members of same party.
room price	£60-£70. Singles by arrangement.
meals	Many pubs & restaurants 0.75 miles.
closed	Christmas & New Year.
directions	From Bridport, A35 into Chideock. Right at church. 0.75 miles up 'No Through Road' to T-junc. Right, house 7th on right (thatched with 2 porches). Drive to end of house, through gate to yard.

Mrs Miranda Tennant
Champ's Land,
Brighthay Lane, North Chideock,
Bridport, Dorset DT6 6JZ
tel   01297 489314

map: 3 entry: 154

DORSET

What views! Catch them from the bedrooms and the sweeping gardens. This handsome house stands in a glorious position up and away from the summer crowds and joins National Trust land; the Jurassic Coast – a World Heritage Site – lies below. Jane and Adrian, good company and well-travelled, have created a hugely comfortable home and B&B: antique furniture and books in the main rooms, bedrooms with colour-washed walls and pretty fabrics. You are a five-minute walk from Seatown beach and the Anchor Inn, in an Area of Outstanding Natural Beauty.

rooms	3: 2 doubles sharing bath; 1 twin/double (+ single bed) with shower.
room price	From £55. Singles by arrangement.
meals	Breakfast 8-9.30am. Good pub 5-minute walk.
closed	Christmas & New Year.
directions	Into Chideock on A35, take Bridport & Honiton road. Left at sign to Seatown, then right fork. At top of hill take access road on right-hand side. Signed on right.

Jane & Adrian Tamone
Seahill House,
Seahill Lane, Seatown, Chideock,
Dorset DT6 6JT
tel   01297 489801
e-mail   jane@seahill.co.uk
web   www.seahill.co.uk

DORSET

Sydney and Jayne share a gift for unwinding stressed souls – and producing memorable food and wine. Ten acres of orchard, valley and wooded hills, wrapped in peace and quiet; inside, 17th-century stone walls, low-beamed ceilings and a warm French flair. Bedrooms have antique French beds, bold colours and crisp linen; in the sitting room are books, a log fire and soft, deep chairs. Jayne makes compotes from the orchard fruit; try them at breakfast with cured ham, pains au chocolat and American pancakes. Cliff top walks, beaches and fields to explore – a perfect place.

rooms	4: 3 doubles, 1 twin, all with bath.
room price	£70-£85. Singles, weekdays only, £50.
meals	Breakfast 8.45-9.30am. Dinner, 3 courses, £18.50. Potage supper for late arrivals, £15.50.
closed	October, Christmas & New Year.
directions	From Dorchester A35 for Bridport. After 13 miles 2nd road signed left to Shipton Gorge & Burton Bradstock. 1st left up long drive to farmhouse.

Sydney & Jayne Davies
Innsacre Farmhouse,
Shipton Gorge, Nr Bridport,
Dorset DT6 4LJ
tel   01308 456137
e-mail   innsacre.farmhouse@btinternet.com
web   www.innsacre.com

DORSET

DORSET

The house is set in a maze of paths running through ancient wildflower meadows and medieval woodland. The views from the ramparts of Eggardon's hill fort are superb: from here you can gaze down on the soft stone farmhouse and the sleepy flower-decked lanes. This former shooting lodge has enormous flagstones, stripped floors, chunky studded doors and exposed beams. Rosie's vibrant paintings adorn the walls of the peaceful bedrooms and good bathrooms. Explore the secret valleys and bumpety hills of West Dorset or the spectacular World Heritage coast. Enchanting seclusion.

Quiet seclusion among birds, badgers and wildflowers. The 1806 keeper's cottage sits in its own 12 acres in deepest Dorset and lovely walks lead in all directions. A pretty garden, a sheltered, wisteria-fringed terrace and two cosy guestrooms with lace bedspreads, garden views and a little cream sofa in the twin. It is all thoroughly comforting and welcoming, and your kind, wildlife-loving hosts rustle up fine breakfasts of Beaminster bangers and honey from their bees. Hone your croquet skills and your tennis: the Major is a coach so why not book a lesson?

rooms	2: 1 double/family with bath/shower; 1 twin with bath.
room price	From £56. Singles £40.
meals	Breakfast 7-9.30am. Pub 3-mile easy drive.
closed	Rarely.
directions	On A37, then A356 from D'chester, left at 1st sign for Toller Porcorum. Through village & up hill for 1 mile. At x-roads, right for Powerstock, under bridge. Track 0.5 miles on left, opp. white post by lane. At end, on left.

rooms	2: 1 double with bath & shower; 1 twin with basin & private bath/shower.
room price	£70-£80. Singles from £40.
meals	Excellent inn 500 yds.
closed	Christmas.
directions	Leave Yeovil on A37 to Dorchester. After 1 mile, right for Sutton, Bingham, Halstock, Corscombe. 6 miles to Corscombe; then left after village sign down Norwood Lane; 300 yds, 1st white gate on right.

Rosie & Roger Britton
Gray's Farmhouse,
Toller Porcorum, Dorchester,
Dorset DT2 0EJ
tel 01308 485574
e-mail rosieroger@farmhousebnb.co.uk
web www.farmhousebnb.co.uk

Mrs Valdes-Scott
Woodwalls House,
Corscombe, Dorchester,
Dorset DT2 0NT
tel 01935 891477
fax 01935 891477

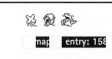

map entry 5

map entry: 158

The well-travelled Jackie and David make light of the practicalities of B&B; they and their 200-year-old cottage have much character and charm. Breakfast in the large, stone-tiled, beamed kitchen, or in the walled courtyard in summer. The twin bedroom, with garden access, is immaculate in fresh white and blue checks, and the sitting room cosy with comfy sofas and pretty coral-checked cushions, inglenook fireplace and window seats. The River Frome – a chalk stream favoured by local fishermen – is within 150 yards of the grounds; you can fish here for £20 a day. Convenient for the A35, yet peaceful.

Solid, Elizabethan grandeur in this magnificent 1590s Grade I-listed manor. Something to delight at every turn: huge, impressive carved antique beds, enormous staircases, beautiful rugs on stone and wooden floors, fabrics to suit the period, fine lake views. Pevsner described the Manor as being "refined to a point of perfection". Mullioned windows, Jacobean fireplaces… the splendours are varied and the grounds live up to the house. Andrew and Mulu will pamper you in great style; Mulu can even give you a massage/beauty treatment in the salon. *Children by arrangement.*

rooms	3: 1 twin with downstairs shower; 1 twin with private bath. 1 single also available.
room price	£50-£54. Singles £35.
meals	Pub/restaurant 1.25 miles.
closed	Easter & Christmas.
directions	From r'bout at top of Dorchester, west on B3150 for 100 yds. Right onto Poundbury Rd (before museum). 1 mile on, over another road, then 2nd concrete track on right beyond Whitfield Farmhouse sign. Cottage set back from road.

rooms	3: 1 four-poster, 1 twin, both with bath; 1 double, with shower &/or with private bath.
room price	£90-£110. Singles £60-£70.
meals	Dinner, 4 courses, £25.
closed	Mid-December-February.
directions	At r'bout on A35, 1 mile NE of Dorchester, follow sign to Kingston Maurward gardens & animal park. In grounds, follow signs to house.

Jackie & David Charles
Whitfield Farm Cottage,
Poundbury Road, Nr Dorchester,
Dorset DT2 9SL
tel 01305 260233
fax 01305 260233
e-mail dc.whitfield@clara.net
web www.dc.whitfield.clara.net

Andrew & Mulu Thomson
The Old Manor,
Kingston Maurward, Dorchester,
Dorset DT2 8PX
tel 01305 261110
fax 01305 263734
e-mail thomson@kingston-maurward.co.uk
web www.kingston-maurward.co.uk

An impossibly pretty English cottage that's 400 years old with a stream to cross and a garden filled with flowers. The village is delightful with fields and hills all around. Nicky, independent, enthusiastic and knowledgeable about walks and visits in Hardy Country, will leave you to your own devices once you are properly advised. Inside, a stone-flagged hall and bedrooms with lathe and plaster ceilings and chalk/limestone walls – unmistakably cottagey. Full of character, and there are home-made jams and free-range eggs for breakfast. *Children over eight welcome. Self-catering available. See back of book.*

The oldest house in the village (1622) in the beautiful Piddle valley; wild deer frolic on the hillside, ducks splash in the village stream. Robin and Liz are the friendliest of hosts and keen to do a good job of caring for you; they have renovated their home and stable block with enormous care. One bedroom is in the house, simple and charming with low-beamed ceilings and white walls; the rooms in the old stables are more modern, and equally comfortable. Breakfast is served round a gleaming mahogany table in a flagstoned, Indian-rugged dining room. The Cerne Abbas Giant, cut into the chalk hillside, beckons.

rooms	3: 2 doubles (1 with room for extra bed), 1 twin, all with basins, sharing 2 baths.
room price	£44. Singles £27.
meals	Breakfast until 9.30am. Good food available locally.
closed	Rarely.
directions	From Dorchester, A37 north. After 5 miles, in Grimstone, right under r'way bridge to Sydling St Nicholas. Lamperts 1st thatched cottage on right, in village.

rooms	5: House: 1 twin with bath. Stables: 3 twins/doubles with bath/shower; 1 twin/double with shower.
room price	From £55. Singles £37.50.
meals	Breakfast until 9.30am. Packed lunch from £3. Pubs/restaurants short walk.
closed	Christmas & New Year.
directions	From Dorchester, A35 for Bere Regis for 1 mile. B3143 left to Piddlehinton. Through village. On left 100 yds after Thimble pub.

Nicky Willis
Lamperts Cottage,
Sydling St Nicholas, Dorchester,
Dorset DT2 9NU
tel 01300 341659
fax 01300 341699
e-mail nickywillis@tesco.net

Robin & Liz Adeney
Whites Dairy House,
Piddlehinton, Dorchester,
Dorset DT2 7TD
tel 01300 348386
e-mail robin.adeney@care4free.net
web www.whitesdairyhouse.co.uk

Pass under a pair of antlers in the stone porch to reach the hall, where fresh flowers and hunting top-hats greet you (and tiger heads stare at you from beneath the table). This mellow, beautiful Victorian mansion was built by Radcliffe in 1887 and its rooms are full of paintings and antiques. Large, generously-equipped bedrooms overlook three acres of garden – nurse a glass of whisky from the decanter in your room as you take in the view: it's worth lingering over. The gardens are truly wonderful, created by Major Barne's father and set in a peaceful 90-acre estate, replete with deer, pheasant and trout.

Smart, spruce, country-style décor – windy corridors, sloping floors and the odd wonky wall. It's a listed farmhouse of two halves, the front 100 years younger than the back. Bedrooms are generous, particularly the cream suite, which has a very pretty bathroom, dressing room and views of garden and paddock; all have mineral water, good mattresses, thick towels. Lisa and Tim are utterly at ease with guests and serve delicious, locally sourced breakfasts. The place hums with birdsong and the garden is lovely. You are only five minutes from Dorchester and, yes, there are Thomas Hardy connections – he used to visit the church next door.

rooms	3: 1 double with bath; 1 double, 1 twin/double with bath & shower.
room price	£70. Singles £45.
meals	Dinner, 3 courses, £20. B.Y.O.
closed	Rarely.
directions	From Bere Regis, 1.4 miles on Wool road; left signed Clueaze & 'Lane End'. After 400 yds T-junc.; right, then left down drive leading to white bungalow on right.

rooms	3: 1 triple with bath; 1 triple with private bath; 1 twin/double with private bath.
room price	£56-£64. Singles £32.
meals	Breakfast 8-9am. Packed lunch £3.50. Pub/restaurant 2.5 miles.
closed	Rarely.
directions	From Dorchester bypass A354 to Weymouth. 1st left to Winterbourne Herringston; at T-junc. right, on for 1 mile; look out for golf course, next left to house.

Major C M Barne
Clueaze,
Wareham, Dorset BH20 7NR
tel   01929 471344
fax   01929 472221
e-mail   majorbarne@ukonline.co.uk

Lisa Bowden
Higher Came Farmhouse,
Higher Came, Dorchester,
Dorset DT2 8AP
tel   01305 268908
fax   01305 268908
e-mail   highercame@eurolink.ltd.net
web   www.highercame.co.uk

DORSET

Thomas Hardy and his brother were so taken by the neighbouring 12th-century church that they helped restore it; Hardy's home, Max Gate, is nearby. This 300-year-old thatched cottage hugs the church boundary and has been carefully and delightfully restored. Sink into comfortable mattresses on king-size beds; bedrooms are simple, serene and softly lit. The village is genuinely quaint and there's a local pub that does excellent food a short stroll away. Good breakfasts with local, free-range eggs, honey, home-made yogurt and preserves. Renée also offers reflexology.

rooms	2: 1 twin/double, 1 double, both with bath/shower.
room price	£55–£65. Singles by arrangement.
meals	Breakfast until 9.30am. Good pub 500 yds.
closed	Christmas & New Year.
directions	A352 Wareham road from Dorchester bypass. Left at sign to West Knighton, or on to Broadmayne & left for West Knighton at x-roads. On for 0.5 miles; cottage just after church.

Peter & Renée East
Church Cottage,
West Knighton, Dorchester,
Dorset DT2 8PF
tel   01305 852243
e-mail   info@church-cottage.com
web   www.church-cottage.com

map: 3 entry: 165

DORSET

The mood is of restrained luxury and uncluttered, often beautiful, good taste. Bedrooms are cream with mahogany furniture, sloping ceilings, beams, armchairs, a radio. There's a large drawing room and good paintings are all around. The Hipwells are delightful; the house, and the garden, are a refuge. Views are soft and lush yet you are in the main square of this attractive town; the house was rebuilt in 1762 after a great fire, on the foundations of a 13th-century goldsmith's house. *Children over 10 welcome.*

rooms	3 twins/doubles, all with private bath.
room price	£50–£55. Singles £30–£35.
meals	Dinner £12, available in winter. Good restaurants 50 yds.
closed	Christmas & New Year.
directions	From A35, A351 to Wareham. Follow signs to town centre. In North St, over lights into South St. 1st left into St John's Hill; house on far right-hand corner of square.

Anthea & Michael Hipwell
Gold Court House,
St John's Hill, Wareham,
Dorset BH20 4LZ
tel   01929 553320
fax   01929 553320

map: 3 entry: 166

DORSET

Halfway between Corfe Castle and Kingston, minutes from the coastal path, the 'Isle of Purbeck' is a glorious area. Here is an 18th-century wisteria-strewn house — actually two cottages that have grown together — which demands that you unwind. Bedrooms are comforting, full of pictures, old pieces and country prints; the double is homely with a fine Victorian button armchair and a mahogany dressing table. There is also a small, pretty twin. Breakfast — fresh from the Aga — is served at tables overlooking courtyard and garden. If you spot wild deer munching on the roses, tell Bron.

rooms	2: 1 double with private bath/shower; 1 twin with shower.
room price	£50. Singles £32.50.
meals	Breakfast 8-9.30am. Good inns 0.5 miles.
closed	Christmas & New Year.
directions	A351 from Wareham to Corfe Castle. At end of village fork right on B3069 for Kingston. Left in 0.5 miles down track; signed.

Bron & Nick Burt
Lower Lynch House,
Kingston Hill, Corfe Castle,
Dorset BH20 5LG
tel   01929 480089

DORSET

The views of Poole Harbour and yachts are delicious; the sumptuousness of bedrooms and bathrooms the icing on the cake. Choose from a harbour-facing suite with its own balcony or a double garden room. In your room there are robes, sweets, sherry, fruit, every bathroom treat — "more luxury than many a five-star hotel," says our inspector. Renate wants your stay to be memorable; breakfasts are served on Spode china — outside, maybe, among the birds, the flowers, the sea breeze — and there's fresh fruit, Parma ham, smoked salmon, kedgeree. A truly spoiling place.

rooms	2 twins/doubles, both with bath & shower.
room price	£58-£70. Singles by arrangement.
meals	Pub 400 yds, restaurants 1 mile.
closed	Rarely.
directions	From A350 Upton crossroads, Blandford Road south for Poole. After 1.5 miles, right at Red Lion pub into Lake Road. Under narrow bridge towards water's edge, then left down Branksea Avenue; last on left.

Renate & John Wadham
53 Branksea Avenue,
Poole, Dorset BH15 4DP
tel   01202 673419
fax   01202 667260
e-mail   johnrenate@lineone.net

A large house kept in pristine condition by Sara and John – the huge and enchanting garden comes in for the same careful treatment, too. Furnishings are sedate, and some newer pieces are well mixed with family antiques. The twin, with patterned carpet, has a good collection of books and the double has views from both windows. Sara pays great attention to detail: a new toothbrush for the forgetful, linen table napkins, a choice of teas. Every view is onto green Hardy Country… or the lovely garden. Bring your racquets – there's a tennis court.

Terrific to have a place in the centre of town… and what a place. Elegant, but the feel is more country house than townhouse and the views beyond the ha-ha are purest Dorset. Lexi is a stickler when it comes to detail and your rooms verge on the sybaritic: fine linen on ornately carved, blue-grey French beds, huge white bath sheets in panelled bathrooms, hand-painted Regency-striped wallpaper, big flowers. Delicious breakfasts include two-tone home-made bread, half white, half brown. But late sleepers beware: to ensure rooms are perfect for the next guests, Alexis kindly asks you to be out of yours by 10am.

rooms	3: 1 double, 1 twin, 1 single sharing 2 baths. Possible use of private bath.
room price	From £46. Singles from £23.
meals	Breakfast 7.30-9.30am. Pub/restaurant 400 yds.
closed	Rarely.
directions	From Wimborne B3078 to Cranborne. Right to Holt. After 2 miles Thornhill on right, 200 yds beyond Old Inn.

rooms	3: 1 double, 1 four-poster & 1 twin, all with baths.
room price	From £65. Singles £45.
meals	Good pubs nearby.
closed	Christmas.
directions	A354 from Salisbury, enter Blandford one-way system. Right after market place, left at fork, then immed. left; cottage at end, 2nd entrance on left.

John & Sara Turnbull
Thornhill,
Holt, Wimborne, Dorset BH21 7DJ
tel   01202 889434
e-mail   scturnbull@lineone.net

Lexi Cook
Bryanston Cottage,
Bryanston Street, Blandford Forum,
Dorset DT11 7AZ
tel   01258 452746
e-mail   jcook@longulf.co.uk

DORSET

DORSET

Below is the River Stour which winds through the valley and under the medieval, nine-arched bridge; above is an Iron Age hill fort; between is Crawford House. It's a Georgian home, soft and pretty, with an old-fashioned air. Bedroom colours are neutral and calm, offsetting floral curtains; one room has four-poster twin beds with chintz drapes. The sun streams through the floor-to-ceiling windows of the downstairs rooms, and charming 18th- and 19th-century oil paintings grace the pale green dining room where Andrea brings you breakfast. Poole ferries are 25 minutes away.

An encapsulation of much that is charming about Dorset... a soft, delightful thatched cottage in an enviably rural setting. Sandy and Paul have poured love into this Grade II-listed farmhouse and garden, the latter bursting with lupins, poppies, foxgloves, clematis, delphiniums. Sandy is extremely welcoming; Paul, brought up in South America, is fluent in Spanish, Portuguese and French and full of stories. Excellent bedrooms with good prints, pretty bedheads and lovely pieces of furniture. The garden room with exposed flintstone walls has its own door to the garden. Special indeed. *Children over 10 welcome.*

rooms	3: 1 twin/double with bath; 2 twins sharing bath.
room price	£50. Singles £25.
meals	Pub in village, 0.5 miles.
closed	Mid-October-mid-April.
directions	1st gateway immed. on left after crossroads (B3075) on A350 going north after entering Spetisbury.

rooms	3: 2 doubles, 1 ground-floor twin, all with shower.
room price	£50-£60. Singles from £30.
meals	Pub in village.
closed	Christmas & New Year.
directions	Leave Blandford for SW, cross river Stour. Hard right after Bryanston school, for W. Stickland (4.5 miles). There, down North St, right signed W. Houghton. House 150 yds on left with 5-bar gate.

Andrea Lea
Crawford House,
Spetisbury, Blandford,
Dorset DT11 9DP

tel 01258 857338
fax 01258 858152

Sandy & Paul Crofton-Atkins
Stickland Farmhouse,
Winterborne Stickland,
Blandford Forum, Dorset DT11 0NT

tel 01258 880119
fax 01258 880119
e-mail sticklandfarmhouse@sticklanddorset.fsnet.co.uk

Breakfast by a log fire in the elegant dining room in winter – a feast of free-range eggs, home-made jams and marmalades. All the rooms in this Victorian house are stylish and very well decorated, with lovely prints, many lamps and stunning views; bedrooms are full of light. After a day out or a good walk, sit beside the fire in the big drawing room with a pile of the family's books. This is a fabulous old house, comfortable and easy and on a quiet road. Its walled half-acre garden with herbaceous borders is Tia's passion. She is welcoming – as are her two little terriers – and is happy to babysit.

The Benjamins worked in the States and have imported that country's high standard of B&B. Bedrooms are more 'grand luxe' than cottagey and the beds are big and of the finest quality; the four-poster has steps up to it. Lovely *toile de Jouy* curtains and an opulent feel throughout: state-of-the-art bathroom fittings, power showers (of course) and fluffy towels. The garden, with Dorset views all around, was professionally designed; they have space for wedding party marquees, too. Sylvia has a passion for antiques – you can buy some of her finds if you wish – and they run bridge, art and pampering weekends.

rooms	3: 1 double with bath/shower; 1 twin/double with shower; 1 single with private bath.
room price	£54. Singles £25.
meals	Breakfast until 9am. Supper tray £8 on first night. Pub 600 yds.
closed	Christmas.
directions	From Dorchester, B3143 into Buckland Newton over x-roads; Holyleas on right opp. village cricket pitch.

rooms	6: 4 doubles, 2 twins, all with bath. Also 1 studio: double, campbeds, cot, kitchenette & shower.
room price	£72–£90. Singles £42–£52. B&B in studio £75–£85; extra beds £15 each.
meals	Good pub within walking distance.
closed	Rarely.
directions	From Sherborne follow signs to A3030, then to Alweston, 2 miles. Past Post Office on right, parking sign on left, next left into Munden Lane. House behind Oxford Bakery.

Tia Bunkall
Holyleas House,
Buckland Newton, Dorchester,
Dorset DT2 7DP
tel 01300 345214
fax 01305 264488
e-mail tiabunkall@holyleas.fsnet.co.uk
web www.holyleashouse.co.uk

Sylvia & Joe Benjamin
Munden House,
Alweston, Sherborne,
Dorset DT9 5HU
tel 01963 23150
fax 01963 23153
e-mail sylvia@mundenhouse.demon.co.uk
web www.mundenhouse.demon.co.uk

map: 3 entry: 173

map: 3 entry: 174

Deep in the Wessex countryside, where Ancient Britons sleep, lies Stourton Caundle and, standing off the road, Golden Hill Cottage. Gaze out of your bedroom window onto flowers and fields, descend to platefuls of local bacon and sausage, and more of home-made jams and Dorset honey; then step outside and immerse yourself in the past – to Sherborne, Kingston Lacy, Badbury Rings. Unwind in the sitting room, elegant with piano and open fire – all yours – at the end of the day. When hunger strikes you are spoilt for choice: the Modern Britons who run the pubs have kept the age-old charm. *Babes in arms welcome.*

Across the road the water meadows descend to the river that winds round Sturminster Newton. Australian Margie is fun and easy-going and the house is reassuringly homely, with some attractive, convivial clutter. In the huge hall fireplace logs burn in winter. There's also a fire in the snug sitting room with its matted carpet and jolly rugs. Bedrooms are big, spotless and attractive with plain Wilton carpets; one of the bathrooms has pretty handmade tiles. Breakfasts, served from the vast and friendly kitchen, are feasts of local sausage, home-made marmalade and fruit salad. A wonderful place.

rooms	1 twin with shower.
room price	£50. Singles £25.
meals	Good pubs/restaurants within 3 miles.
closed	Rarely.
directions	From Sherborne, A352 to Dorchester; after 1 mile, left onto A3030; on to far end of Bishops Caundle, left to Stourton Caundle; after sharp left into village street, house 200 yds on right.

rooms	4: 1 double with bath; 1 double with private bath; 1 twin, 2 singles sharing bath & wc.
room price	From £50. Singles from £27.50.
meals	Packed lunch from £3. Good pub within walking distance.
closed	Christmas.
directions	On A357 Sherborne to Blandford road. House 0.25 miles west of Sturminster Newton bridge, on south side of road. Drive at eastern end of house.

Andrew & Anna Oliver
Golden Hill Cottage,
Stourton Caundle,
Sturminster Newton,
Dorset DT10 2JW

tel	01963 362109
fax	01963 364205
e-mail	anna@goldenhillcottage.co.uk
web	www.goldenhillcottage.co.uk

Charles & Margie Fraser
Newton House,
Sturminster Newton,
Dorset DT10 2DQ

tel	01258 472783
fax	01258 473235
e-mail	carolinepass@lineone.net

Complete peace: the garden runs down to the River Stour and has uninterrupted views over the water meadows. The millhouse, 16th-century and Grade I-listed, is a beautifully maintained place with a unique history. Inside: an original moulded plaster ceiling and half-tester bed in one room, a real four-poster in another, rich colours and impressive pictures. Your hosts have great knowledge of the area; Stourhead and Sherbourne are nearby. There is no sitting room for guests, but the rooms are big and no matter, for the house is magnificent.

The house, named after the 16th-century farmer who built it, has masses of old-style charm. A low-beamed sitting room, comfortably stylish and softly lit, has a big old fender across the fire. Honeysuckle hugs the window of the twin, with its own little door to the garden; the double, with books and big brass bed, looks to the hills. A delightful home, thanks to Sally, who loves to bring guests together over supper and fills the house with flowers. Recline in the hammock as your children help collect eggs for breakfast (a feast of local and organic produce), then stride off into in the green Dorset hills.

rooms	3: 1 double with bath; 1 double, 1 four-poster sharing bath.
room price	£45–£60. Singles from £30.
meals	Breakfast 7-9am. Pub/restaurant 5-minute walk.
closed	Rarely.
directions	On A357 between Sturminster Newton & Blandford. Look for well-marked turning on north side between S. Newton & Fiddleford.

rooms	2: 1 twin with bath/shower; 1 double with private bath/shower.
room price	£52–£60. Singles £30.
meals	Picnic £8. Dinner, from £15.50.
closed	Rarely.
directions	A30 Shaftesbury-Blandford. After 6 miles, right to Sutton Waldron; at T-junc., left; at 2nd T-junc, left. Over little bridge; road curves right; opp. chapel, take road to left; follow to end.

Mr & Mrs A & J Ingleton
Fiddleford Mill,
Fiddleford, Sturminster Newton,
Dorset DT10 2BX
tel   01258 472786

Sally Weldon
Strouds House,
Farringdon, Nr Blandford Forum,
Dorset DT11 8RA
tel   01747 811412
e-mail   sallyweldon@hotmail.com

Tim and Lucy are tangibly happy in this beautifully restored forge. It was built in the 1700s and the wheelwright and carriage-builder from the local estate used to work here. Tim is a classic car restorer and has rebuilt a 1934 Lagonda; Lucy rides long-distance on her Arab horse. The attic bedrooms are snug, with Lucy's quilts, country antiques and sparkling bathrooms. Breakfasts include freshly-squeezed apple juice, organic sausages and bacon and eggs from the Kerridges' free-ranging chickens and ducks. The Downs beckon walkers; warm corners invite readers. Utterly genuine. *Self-catering available. See back of book.*

A new house softening with age, and Ella has great plans for the garden, including a breakfast terrace. In the dining room there's a large collection of books, along with dining chairs decorated with Ella's tapestry work, designed to match the curtains. Thoughtful extras in the simple bedroom – spring water and fresh flowers – and an antique mahogany chair and towel rail. This is a quiet spot for a sedate get-away-from-it-all break, perfect for countryside lovers; you're in an AONB and there are a pub and a church in the charming village. *Children over 10 welcome.*

rooms	3: 1 double/family with shower; 1 double, 1 single sharing bath, only let to same party.
room price	£50–£75. Singles £40.
meals	Breakfast 8-9.30am. Pub/restaurant 4 miles.
closed	Rarely.
directions	From Shaftesbury, A350 to Compton Abbas. House 1st on left before Compton Abbas sign. Left; entrance on left.

rooms	1 twin with private bath.
room price	£50. Singles from £35.
meals	Breakfast until 9.30am. Excellent pub 3-minute walk.
closed	Rarely.
directions	From Shaftesbury, A30 east. Through Ludwell, then left at bottom of hill signed The Donheads. At T-junc. towards Donhead. Pass Foresters Inn on right, fork left after 150 yds. House on right after 300 yds.

Tim & Lucy Kerridge
The Old Forge, Fanners Yard,
Compton Abbas, Shaftesbury,
Dorset SP7 0NQ
tel	01747 811881
fax	01747 811881
e-mail	theoldforge@hotmail.com

Ella Humphreys
Oakdale House,
Donhead St Andrew, Shaftesbury,
Dorset SP7 9EG
tel	01747 828767
e-mail	ella@oakdalehouse.co.uk
web	www.oakdalehouse.co.uk

It's a short stroll into the centre of Shaftesbury, yet this lovely Regency house with its enchanting, one-acre walled garden is so peaceful. Arrive to tea among the roses, then settle into the house. Bedrooms are stylish and comfortable – one looks across to the church and Melbury Hill, the other faces the garden and has a large and luxurious bathroom. The drawing room is elegant in cream, white and gold. Breakfast is superb: the full English variety, with black pudding, kippers, haddock, home-made jams, fresh fruit, eggs every way. A delightful place to stay in a historic little town.

Altogether a surprising house – the austere Gothic exterior doesn't prepare you for the exuberance of within. It's a pleasant surprise: mixtures of fabrics and furniture that blend east and west. Anthony, from Hong Kong, is an excellent chef; he cooks at weekends, so do eat in. Much of his food is Mediterranean with an oriental influence – Thai crabmeat cake with stir-fried veg, wild sea bass with shitake mushrooms. The Chinese bedroom is wonderfully showy with its black and gold lacquer half-tester bed and matching furniture. The views are splendid, too. *Children over five welcome.*

rooms	2 twins, both with bath.
room price	£65. Singles £45.
meals	Breakfast until 9.30am. Good restaurants locally.
closed	January–February.
directions	From Shaftesbury, B3091 for Sturminster Newton. After 0.25 miles down St John's Hill, house 1st on right, parking next to garage.

rooms	6: 3 doubles, 3 family, all with bath/shower.
room price	£58–£100. Singles £45–£73.
meals	Breakfast until 9.30am. Dinner £20–£26, Fri & Sat only. Pub/restaurant 200 yds.
closed	January.
directions	From Sherborne A30 to Milborne Port. House 2nd on right on entering village.

Diana Pow
Cliff House,
Breach Lane, Shaftesbury,
Dorset SP7 8LF

tel	01747 852548
fax	01747 852548
e-mail	dianaepow@aol.com
web	www.cliff-house.co.uk

Mr Anthony Ma & Jorgen Kunath
The Old Vicarage,
Milborne Port, Sherborne,
Dorset DT9 5AT

tel	01963 251117
fax	01963 251515
e-mail	theoldvicarage@milborneport.freeserve.co.uk
web	www.milborneport.freeserve.co.uk

DORSET

The rambling, rose-clad Georgian farmhouse is English to the core. Rooms are stylishly cluttered with lovely old pieces, paintings and prints; there are books, delightful objects and flowers at every turn. Bedrooms under the eaves are deliciously cosy and chic, with curtains and bedheads in creamy chintz. Breakfast is served in the farmhouse kitchen amid copper pans and colourful plates picked up on Richard & Jenny's travels – or under the vine-strewn loggia in summer. The garden overflows with honeysuckle and roses: it is a Dorsetshire dream.

rooms	2: 1 double, 1 twin with private bath, only let to same party.
room price	£55. Singles £35.
meals	Breakfast until 9.30am. Packed lunch £3. Dinner £15-£20.
closed	Christmas.
directions	From Wincanton, A357 for Templecombe. Take 2nd signed turning to Stowell on right opp. entrance to Horsington House. Down hill past church. 0.5 miles on. House on left after phone box.

Richard & Jenny Gold
Windrush Farm,
Stowell, Sherborne, Dorset DT9 4PD
tel   01963 370799
e-mail   jennygold@amserve.com

DORSET

Sit in the beautiful garden with its views to Sherborne Castle Hill – the feel is rural, yet the town is at your door. The interior of this quiet Victorian townhouse is light and airy, its palette off-white and soft green: wonderfully English in feel. Bedrooms are deeply comfortable and inviting; bathrooms white with a touch of chintz. Pamela is courteous and kind, an interior designer who has decorated with a confident hand. You have the best of farm produce at breakfast, and the delights of Sherborne a stroll away: shops restaurants, tea rooms, farmers' market, abbey. *Children over 12 welcome.*

rooms	2: 1 twin/double with bath; 1 double with private bath.
room price	£65. Singles from £32.50.
meals	Good pubs and restaurants within walking distance.
closed	December & January.
directions	From A30, left into North Rd; left at first crossroads into Newlands, then sharp right at Castletown x-roads into Long St; house on left, 150 yds from crossroads.

Mrs Pamela Rae
Tudor Lodge,
Long Street, Sherbourne,
Dorset DT9 3ED
tel   01935 813970

DURHAM

We loved this place – the cobbled courtyard that evokes memories of its days as a coaching inn (Dickens stayed here), the river running through the estate, the garden and potager, the fine breakfasts and home-grown produce. And Peter and Mary, your kind, unstuffy hosts who have three adorable, beautifully-behaved dogs. Every creature comfort has been attended to in this cosy, stylish house: crisp linen, soft lights and embroidered pillows in the bedrooms; big soft towels and heated rails in the bathrooms; a log fire in the drawing room. A perfect stepping stone to Scotland – or the south.

rooms	2: 1 twin/double with bath/shower; 1 twin/double with private bath.
room price	£70. Singles £45.
meals	Dinner, 3 courses, £22.50. Good pubs & restaurants nearby.
closed	Rarely.
directions	A1(M) to Scotch Corner. A66 west until Greta Bridge turn-off. House on left just before bridge.

Peter & Mary Gilbertson
The Coach House,
Greta Bridge, Barnard Castle,
Durham DL12 9SD
tel   01833 627201
e-mail   info@coachhousegreta.co.uk
web   www.coachhousegreta.co.uk

DURHAM

This Georgian townhouse stands impressively horizontal on The Bank in 'Barney'. There you meet Digby, Eva, Ian and George – in that order. Digby's an Old English sheepdog and George is the resident ghost whose manners are unfailingly polite; Eva and Ian merely run the place. Ian cooks the breakfasts and Eva arranges them artistically because that's her thing. They love their guests, provide beautiful rooms – what more could you ask? After the meal stagger forth to see the rest of Barney on the Tees: the castle, the antique shops and the restaurant next door where Cromwell really stayed.

rooms	2: 1 twin with private bath; 1 double with bath/shower.
room price	From £50. Singles from £35.
meals	Good pubs/restaurants 50 yds.
closed	Rarely.
directions	At A1 Scotch Corner, A66 west for 7 miles. Then 1st dual carriageway; right for Barnard Castle. At lights right over bridge, left at T-junc. to Butter Market. Left down bank, house on left.

Ian & Eva Reid
34 The Bank,
Barnard Castle, Durham DL12 8PN
tel   01833 631304
fax   01833 631304

DURHAM

The renovation of the 1825 Regency villa was an enormous task and Sarah-Jane has tackled it with good humour and energy. It's a fine country home – close to so many of the delights of Barnard Castle – that has come alive since Sarah-Jane took over. The guests' sitting room is huge, with comfy sofas and a fire that's lit on chilly evenings. Bedrooms are freshly and simply decorated and have good views. Mature grounds with a beautiful walled rose garden – breakfast here in summer – envelop the big house and merge with a buttercup field. Explore the rolling dales and purple-clad moors.

rooms	3: 1 double with shower; 2 twins, 1 with bath, 1 with private bath.
room price	£55-£65. Singles from £37.50.
meals	Breakfast until 9.30am. Dinner, 3 courses, £22.50.
closed	Christmas & New Year.
directions	From A1, at Scotch Corner, A66 for B. Castle. 7 miles on, approaching 1st section of dual c'way, 1st right for B. Castle to lights. Right over bridge. At T-junc. left for B. Castle Town. Pass school & museum, through gates on left.

Sarah-Jane Ormston
Spring Lodge,
Newgate, Barnard Castle,
Durham DL12 8NW

tel   01833 638110
fax   01833 630389
e-mail   ormston@telinco.co.uk

map: 14 entry: 187

DURHAM

A walker's paradise, with pure air, deer and woodpeckers. The Georgian shooting lodge is in an open glade with views of the moors – you drive for two miles through the forest to get to 5,000 acres of woodland, moors, becks, rivers and ancient trees. The Art Nouveau furniture and fittings make a refreshing change from traditional furnishings and there are some dramatic touches, such as the shocking pink bathroom. Big downstairs rooms, small bedrooms, open fires and books. Helene is an exceptional cook and has lived here all her life. *Children over eight welcome.*

rooms	3: 2 doubles, both with bath/shower; 1 twin with shower.
room price	£53-£65. Singles £36.50-£42.50.
meals	Packed lunch £4. Dinner £22.50.
closed	20 December-3 January.
directions	A68 from Darlington, left to Hamsterley. On for 2 miles (ignore forest signs) into village, then right, signed The Grove, then left. Right (signed), after 3 miles, over stone bridge, house opposite.

Helene Close
Grove House,
Hamsterley Forest,
Bishop Auckland, Durham DL13 3NL

tel   01388 488203
fax   01388 488174
e-mail   xov47@dial.pipex.com
web   www.grovehouse.ws

map: 14 entry: 188

DURHAM

DURHAM

The present façade is Georgian, but medieval vaults and the remains of a moat hint at a more ancient history. The house has been in the family for decades and Jill and Christopher are modestly proud. They have redecorated beautifully, Jill making the soft furnishings herself... sink into a sofa in the sitting room and enjoy a video, retreat to the pretty summer house with a book. Bedrooms are large enough to lounge in; one has a window seat for sunsets, another a canopied oak bed and a view onto the garden pond – spot herons in summer. A fascinating place with a big heart, on the edge of the lovely Pennine hills.

For lovers of horses this is irresistible – there are over 40 of them, the Booths are mad about them and you can learn to ride (or to do so more elegantly). Once a hunting lodge, Ivesley stands at the end of an avenue of beech trees planted in the 1350s to commemorate the end of the Black Death. Half the house is new, discreetly so; the floorboards that creak are in the old part. Big bedrooms are very much 'country house' with antiques, and the grandeur of the dining room and drawing room belies their recent birth. Only 15 minutes from the centre of Durham. *Children over eight welcome.*

rooms	3: 1 double with shower; 1 double, 1 twin, both with bath.
room price	£65. Singles £32.50.
meals	Good pubs/restaurants 2-4 miles.
closed	Christmas.
directions	A689 west from A68 for 2 miles towards Wolsingham. Hall on north side of A689 up walled drive; signed.

rooms	5: 3 twins/doubles, all with bath or shower; 2 singles, sharing bath & shower.
room price	£64. Singles from £37.
meals	Breakfast until 9am. Dinner £24.
closed	Christmas Day.
directions	A1, then A68 to Tow Law. Right onto B6301, signed Lanchester. After 3.7 miles, right at sign. Avenue 0.7 miles up hill on left.

Christopher & Jill Stephenson
Bradley Hall,
Wolsingham, Bishop Auckland,
Durham DL13 3JH

tel	01388 527280
fax	0870 137 4975
e-mail	stay@bradleyhall.net
web	www.bradleyhall.net

Roger & Pauline Booth
Ivesley Equestrian Centre,
Waterhouses, Durham DH7 9HB

tel	0191 3734324
fax	0191 3734757
e-mail	ivesley@msn.com
web	www.ridingholidays-ivesley.co.uk

map: 19 entry: 189

map: 19 entry: 190

BATHROOMS

We don't like or use the term 'en suite' in the book, so...

"WITH bath" or "WITH shower" = en suite.

"With PRIVATE" or "with SHARED bath" means the bathroom is separate (the former you will have to yourself; the latter will be shared with the owner or other guests).

PRICES

We give the price PER ROOM. If you are travelling alone, sadly, you should expect to pay a supplement for using a room for two people. At the back of the book we list places that have a single room or charge no single supplement.

QUICK REFERENCE INDICES

At the back of the book find places where:-

• there are facilities for those in wheelchairs

• rooms for two are available for under £50

• owners will collect you from public transport

• you can stable your horse

• there is a pool or a tennis court

• there are ground-floor bathrooms and bedrooms

The house is minutes from wild walking; the island of Mersea is secluded, surprising; the sea murmurs across the saltings where the Brent geese wheel and the great Constable skies stretch. The house began in 1343 – nearly as old as the exquisite church. The Georgians added their bit, but the venerable beams and uneven old construction shine through. It is a sunny, comfortable, beautiful house. There is a snug, book-filled sitting room, a terracotta-floored conservatory and much wood and soft colours. It is a privilege to stay here, with such agreeable hosts.

Floors slant and the old elm creaks – this timber-framed, 13th-century, Grade II*-listed Essex hall house is tangibly ancient. You have your own drawing room with stunning silk curtains and can be a cherished only guest – or things can be moved around to accommodate a larger group. Strong Designer's Guild colours in the twin bedroom and fresh blues and white in the large double. Stansted airport is 20 minutes away, Chelmsford 12, yet this is very rural: the tennis court is hard by open fields and there are ponds, an island and tame ducks.

rooms	2: 1 double, 1 twin, both with private bath.
room price	£56-£70. Singles £30.
meals	Restaurant 1 mile; pub within walking distance.
closed	Rarely.
directions	From Colchester B1025, over causeway, then bear left. After 3 miles, pass Dog & Pheasant pub. Take 2nd right into Bromans Lane. House first on left.

rooms	2: 1 double, 1 twin, sharing private bath.
room price	£60-£74. Singles £30-£37.
meals	Breakfast 6-10am. Dinner £22.50.
closed	Rarely.
directions	From Stansted, A120 east, then right onto A130. After Ford End, right at r'bout to Gt. Waltham. There, right at Beehive Pub into Barrack Lane. 1.3 miles on, right down track between cottages. Left through gate before barn.

Ruth Dence
Bromans Farm,
East Mersea, Essex CO5 8UE
tel 01206 383235
fax 01206 383235
e-mail bromansfarm@btopenworld.com

Mrs Roslyn Renwick
Fitzjohns Farmhouse,
Mashbury Road, Great Waltham,
Chelmsford, Essex CM3 1EJ
tel 01245 360204
fax 01245 361724
e-mail rosrenwick@aol.com

ESSEX

An Elizabethan jewel in a superb rural setting. Exposed timber ceilings, open fireplaces, nooks and crannies: the 'farmhouse' trumpets its history at every turn. The two-acre garden has old-fashioned roses and a pond that attracts many birds. The Wordsworths (yes, they are related to the poet) are engaging and solicitous people who delight in their guests. Anne, an excellent cook, serves home-grown organic vegetables with dinner, and the hens and bantams provide organic eggs for breakfast served in the Aga-warm kitchen. The perfect retreat from London and so close to Stansted airport, Cambridge and Duxford.

rooms	2: 1 double with bath/shower; 1 twin with private bath.
room price	£80. Singles £50.
meals	Supper/dinner £18-£25. B.Y.O.
closed	Rarely.
directions	From S. Walden B1053 (George St) to Radwinter. Right at church & 1st left after 1 mile, at grass triangle on sharp right-hand bend. Signed.

Antony & Anne Wordsworth
Little Brockholds Farm,
Radwinter, Saffron Walden,
Essex CB10 2TF

tel	01799 599458
fax	01799 599458
e-mail	as@brockholds99.freeserve.co.uk
web	www.brockholds.co.uk

map: 10 entry: 193

GLOUCESTERSHIRE

Everything you could want from a glorious English country house. The splendid Georgian manor sits in acres of landscaped grounds (National Gardens Scheme) with a two-acre lake alive with wildfowl. Bring friends for a house party, get married, or just bring one special other. Antique furniture, sumptuous four-poster beds, kind hosts – perfection – and you can play tennis, croquet, billiards, swim in the outdoor pool, hill-walk, ride or clay-pigeon shoot on Bredon Hill. Groups can book dinner or, if you prefer, there is a good pub in the village. *Min. stay two nights weekends, unless late booking. Self-catering available. See back of book.*

rooms	5: 3 four-posters, 1 twin/double, 1 twin, all with bath.
room price	£95-£120. Singles £75.
meals	Breakfast served in bed at no extra cost! Dinner, for parties only, £20-£35. Pubs/restaurants 3-minute walk.
closed	Christmas. Self-catering always open.
directions	From Cheltenham, A435 north, then B4079. About 1 mile after A438 x-roads, right to Kemerton. Leave road at War Memorial. House behind church.

Bill & Diana Herford
Upper Court,
Kemerton, Tewkesbury,
Gloucestershire GL20 7HY

tel	01386 725351
fax	01386 725472
e-mail	diana@uppercourt.co.uk
web	www.uppercourt.co.uk

map: 9 entry: 194

GLOUCESTERSHIRE

GLOUCESTERSHIRE

Ample space for everyone to feel at ease – and you do so in luxury and style. You are on the site of an extinct medieval village, mentioned in the Domesday Book... until 1610 this was the village church. The ground floor is stone-flagged, with rugs for colour and delightful touches of exotica everywhere; one bedroom is massive and the whole house is a treasure trove of things to look at and read. The gardens, set in 37 acres, are beautiful, with sweeping views, trout lake, tennis court and pool. John and Camilla are wickedly funny and easy-going; you won't want to leave. *Children over seven welcome.*

Astonishing! It feels palpably Elizabethan, with superb mullioned windows, gables and great expanses of stoned, slated and thatched roofs with those unexpected corners which make old buildings so fascinating. Yet, unbelievably, it was started in 1951. Retired builder Cecil and his family have opened their home to guests (and prize-winning gardens) with generosity and bonhomie. There's an outdoor swimming pool flanked by a folly, an all-weather tennis court, croquet, a snooker/billiard room, and an arboretum with almost 300 species of trees. It's immaculate and sumptuous, but fun and special.

rooms	3: 2 doubles, both with bath; 1 single with private bath.
room price	£48-£85.
meals	Supper £24. Excellent pub & restaurant nearby.
closed	Christmas.
directions	4 miles north of Moreton-in-Marsh on A429, left to Aston Magna. At 1st building, immed. right. House 0.75 miles on right, up drive.

rooms	3: 1 double, 1 twin, both with bath; 1 double with private bath.
room price	From £80. Singles from £60.
meals	Excellent pub/restaurant 100 yds.
closed	Rarely.
directions	A424 from Stow for 2 miles to Coach & Horses pub. Opposite, turn right by postbox down single-track lane. Entrance 100 yds on left.

John & Camilla Playfair
Neighbrook Manor,
Nr Aston Magna,
Moreton-in-Marsh,
Gloucestershire GL56 9QP

tel	01386 593232
fax	01386 593500
e-mail	info@neighbrookmanor.com
web	www.neighbrookmanor.com

C J Williams
Windy Ridge,
Longborough, Moreton-in-Marsh,
Gloucestershire GL56 0QY

tel	01451 832328/830465
fax	01451 831489
e-mail	cjw@windy-ridge.co.uk
web	www.windy-ridge.co.uk

Rex and Julia "understand" horses – bring yours and it might not want to leave! There's an honest decency about the Bovills, who are passionate about farming and the rural environment. The Cotswold-stone farmhouse stands in an AONB with views to the hills above Stow; paddocks, stables and 180 acres are home to a suckler herd of Limousin cattle. Rex serves up breakfast eggs from their Sussex hens with Gloucestershire Old Spot sausages and bacon; marmalade is home-made. A wide oak staircase leads to a twin and a double; both rooms are warm, quiet and homely, and the pink bath is huge. Good walks abound.

The part-Tudor, part-Georgian house is named after the little river flowing through its back garden. Sudeley Castle is next door – just pass through the kissing gate into the glorious grounds. David (an organic grain merchant) and Felicity are gentle-mannered and easy and treat you to breakfasts of home-made and local produce. One bedroom has an ornately carved, comfortable four-poster; the twin, under the eaves, its own sun terrace. In the drawing room: oils on walls, antiques, an honesty bar and open fire. Winchcombe is such a satisfying little town, with useful shops, buzzing inns and a real sense of community.

rooms	2: 1 double, 1 twin sharing bath/shower.
room price	£60. Singles from £30.
meals	Dinner occasionally available. Good food nearby.
closed	Rarely.
directions	From Stow-on-the-Wold, B4077 towards Tewkesbury. After 6 miles, left to Temple Guiting. Through village, right at T-junc. opp. Schoolhouse. 1 mile on left on upper side of road.

rooms	3: 1 double with shower; 1 twin with private shower; 1 four-poster with bath/shower.
room price	£65-£85. Singles £45-£60.
meals	Breakfast 8-9.30am. Excellent pubs/restaurants 2-5 minute walk.
closed	Christmas & possibly Easter.
directions	Winchcombe on B4632 between Cheltenham & Broadway. Turn into Castle St by White Hart in centre of village. On left at bottom of steep hill.

Rex & Julia Bovill
Hyde Farm,
Temple Guiting, Nr Cheltenham,
Gloucestershire GL54 5RT

tel 01451 850665
fax 01451 850665
e-mail rajsbovill@hotmail.com

Felicity & David King
Isbourne Manor House,
Castle Street, Winchcombe,
Cheltenham,
Gloucestershire GL54 5JA

tel 01242 602281
fax 01242 602281
e-mail felicity@isbourne-manor.co.uk
web www.isbourne-manor.co.uk

Susie is a bundle of energy, looking after children, horses and B&B with good humour; now and then you may see her riding off into the distance. The house sits on the scarp of the Cotswolds above Sudeley Castle; all bedrooms look west to long views. Colours, fabrics and furniture are in perfect harmony, beds and linen are luxurious and there's a big, curvy claw-foot bath. The easy mix of elegant living and family bustle is delightful, and the sloping garden is lush and colourful, with a grand ornamental pond. Further afield lie plenty of walks – and the mystical ruins of 13th-century Hailes Abbey.

rooms	3: 1 double with bath & shower; 2 twins/doubles, both with bath/shower.
room price	From £70. Singles £45.
meals	Dinner available.
closed	December-January.
directions	From Abbey Sq, Winchcombe, travel north. After 50 metres turn right into Castle St. Follow for 1 mile. After farm buidings, turn right (signed Sudeley Lodge). Follow for 600 yds. On right - first oak door.

Susie & Jim Wilson
Westward,
Sudeley Lodge, Winchcombe,
Cheltenham,
Gloucestershire GL54 5JB
tel   01242 604372
fax   01242 604640
e-mail   jimw@haldon.co.uk
web   www.westward-sudeley.co.uk

Cardinal Wolsey allegedly owned Rectory Farmhouse, then Henry VIII took it from him and gave it to Christ Church College, Oxford. Such is its charm, it has had only two private owners since. Passing a development of converted farm buildings to reach the warm Cotswold stones of this place makes the discovery doubly exciting. More glory within: Sybil, an interior decorator, has created something immaculate, cool and beautiful. Bed linen is white, walls cream; the huge enamel bath has a stunning pink exterior. Sybil used to own a restaurant; breakfast, next to the Aga, is a treat.

rooms	3: 1 double with bath/shower; 1 double with bath; 1 suite with sitting room & shower.
room price	From £70. Singles £50.
meals	Pub/restaurant 1 mile.
closed	Christmas & New Year.
directions	B4068 from Stow to Lower Swell, left just before Golden Ball Inn. Far end of gravel drive on right.

Sybil Gisby
Rectory Farmhouse,
Lower Swell, Stow-on-the-Wold,
Gloucestershire GL54 1LH
tel   01451 832351
e-mail   rectory.farmhouse@cw-warwick.co.uk

GLOUCESTERSHIRE

Gaze over the garden wall as you breakfast on home-laid eggs and home-made jams; dream on those glorious views. The garden, too, is special: it has featured in magazines and James and Karin are passionate about it. The stunning 16th-century manor has three-foot-thick walls, a flagstoned hall, vast fireplaces, sit-in inglenooks and stone mullioned windows. One of the bedrooms has a secret door that leads to a unexpectedly fuchsia-pink bathroom; the other, smaller, has wonderful garden views. A lovely, easy-going house with a family, and dogs, to match – worth a weekend stay.

rooms	2: 1 double with bath/shower; 1 twin/double with bath.
room price	From £80. Singles £60.
meals	Breakfast usually 8-9.30am. Pub/restaurants 5-15-minute drive.
closed	Christmas & New Year.
directions	From Cirencester, A429 for Stow. Right at Bourton Lodge, signed Clapton. Follow signs. In village, pass triangular green on left. House straight ahead on left on corner.

Karin & James Bolton
Clapton Manor,
Clapton-on-the-Hill,
Nr Bourton-on-the-Water,
Gloucestershire GL54 2LG
tel   01451 810202
fax   01451 821804
e-mail bandb@claptonmanor.co.uk
web   www.claptonmanor.co.uk

GLOUCESTERSHIRE

Masses of charm and style here – the 1789 Cotswold farmhouse is clearly much loved, and is a restful place to stay. Outbuildings, courtyards and granary are in the same warm stone as the house, and your hosts are friendly, fun and terrific cooks. Angela is Cordon Bleu trained. Breakfasts and dinners are served in the oak-beamed dining room, where lovely oils complement the beams and flagged floors. Country bedrooms are stylish with curtains in Colefax florals and there are robes in the bathrooms. Walking and riding all around, a good village pub and a pool for summer swims.

rooms	3: 1 double, 1 double with extra single, 1 twin, all with bath.
room price	£70-£80. Singles £35-£40.
meals	Breakfast until 9.30am. Dinner £25. Excellent pub within walking distance.
closed	Christmas.
directions	In middle of village, past Plough Inn on left; look for gates on right.

Angela Storey
Grove Farm House,
Cold Aston, Cheltenham,
Gloucestershire GL54 3BJ
tel   01451 821801
fax   01451 821108
e-mail angela@cotswoldbedandbreakfast.com
web   www.cotswoldbedandbreakfast.com

GLOUCESTERSHIRE

A very special place: good taste, good value, warmth, peace, undaunting luxuriousness… and a total lack of pretension. Bridget, too, is delightful. The house has been here in the appropriately named hamlet of Calmsden ('place of calm') for 500 years and little has changed. There's a lovely drawing room, wonky floors, beams that go the wrong way, ceilings that need ducking, exceptional views. The double bedroom is gloriously sunny and light; unwind amid fat pillows and magazines. The smell of home-baked bread lures you to the wood-panelled dining room for breakfast. *Children by arrangement.*

rooms	3: 1 twin/double with bath/shower; 1 double with shower; 1 twin with private bath.
room price	£60–£75. Singles £35–£40.
meals	Breakfast 8–9am. Excellent pub 1.5 miles.
closed	December–February.
directions	From Cirencester A429 north. After 5 miles, 2nd left for Calmsden, just before Hare & Hounds pub. On for 1.5 miles. 3rd house on right.

Bridget Baxter
The Old House,
Calmsden, Nr Cirencester,
Gloucestershire GL7 5ET

tel	01285 831240
fax	01285 831240
e-mail	baxter@calmsden.freeserve.co.uk

GLOUCESTERSHIRE

English to the core – and to the bottom of its lovely garden where there are many delightful places to sit. Steep honey-coloured gables, mullioned windows and weathered stone tiles enclose this lovely 17th-century house on a quiet village lane. Caroline is a calmly competent hostess with a talent for understated interior décor. You may sit in the large dining room for a quiet read; the two ample, airy bedrooms are furnished with antiques and have either a *chaise longue* or easy chairs. Caroline can organise hire bikes to be delivered to the door.

rooms	2: 1 double, 1 twin, both with bath/shower.
room price	From £66. Singles £43.
meals	Excellent pub within walking distance.
closed	December–January.
directions	South through village from A417. Right after Masons Arms. House 200 yds on left.

Roger & Caroline Carne
The Old Rectory,
Meysey Hampton, Nr Cirencester,
Gloucestershire GL7 5JX

tel	01285 851200
fax	01285 850452
e-mail	caroline.carne@lineone.net

Chickens strut on the lawn – and what a manicured lawn for a working farm! Your charming hosts built the honey-stone house 20 years ago and have kept it immaculately. Light pours into perfectly proportioned rooms through windows hung with velvet and chintz; china sits in alcoves on both sides of the fireplace. Bedrooms, with lovely views, feel just right. After your expertly cooked breakfast – with eggs from those happy hens – you'll be ready for a swim or a game of tennis. Jeanie and James can organise fishing locally, and watersports, cycling and golf, too.

You feel the energy of a new start in old surroundings: here is a home created from a barn that just over 10 years ago was derelict. The décor is fresh – so are the flowers – and the furniture and books old; all is bright and the conservatory looks over the garden that the Barrys have created. The charming owners are happy and proud to have you in their home. Beds are incredibly comfortable with excellent sheets and pillows; there is fine furniture and lovely paintings. This is unspoilt Cotswolds and this delightful house sits in splendid, peaceful isolation.

rooms	2: 1 twin with bath; 1 twin/double with private bath.
room price	£60. Singles £40.
meals	Pubs/restaurants 1-4 miles.
closed	Christmas & New Year.
directions	A417 Cirencester-Fairford road. Pass Meysey Hampton sign & entrance on right opp. sign for Waitenhill & Cherry Tree House. Approx 1 mile from Meysey Hampton, 0.5 miles from Fairford.

rooms	3: 1 double with bath; 1 double, 1 twin, sharing bath/shower.
room price	£68. Singles by arrangement.
meals	Breakfast 8-9am. Excellent pubs & restaurants within 5-10 minutes.
closed	Christmas & New Year.
directions	From Cirencester A417 for Lechlade. At Meysey Hampton crossroads left to Sun Hill. After 1 mile left at cottage. House 400 yds down drive.

Jeanie Keyser
Lady Lamb Farm,
Meysey Hampton, Cirencester,
Gloucestershire GL7 5LH
tel 01285 712206
fax 01285 712206
e-mail jekeyser1@aol.com

Richard & Jill Barry
Hampton Fields,
Meysey Hampton, Cirencester,
Gloucestershire GL7 5JL
tel 01285 850070
fax 01285 850993
e-mail richard@hampflds.fsnet.co.uk

Old-fashioned authenticity here in historic Rodmarton, and much well-worn dignity. Mary is efficient and quietly kind; John is a mediator and works from home. Beamed guestrooms lie on the older, 16th-century side of the house; they have wicker or padded headboards, coloured bathroom suites, formica-surround basins, mahogany chests, framed landscapes on walls. The staircase is listed in its own right, there are some excellent charcoal drawings by John's mother and a striking bust of Mary's uncle in the racing-green dining room. Roman history and good walks abound.

A plum Cotswolds position, a striking garden, stylish decor, exceptional linen – there's masses to recommend Lodge Farm. And then there are your hosts, who can throw a house party, help wedding groups, give you supper *en famille* next to the Aga, arrange dinners in the dining room with crystal and silver. The guest sitting room is inviting with fresh, elegant flowers, family photographs and lots of magazines; throughout are flagstones, Bath stone and wood. Home-produced (Hebridean) lamb for dinner, maybe, and excellent coffee at breakfast. The Salmons breed thoroughbreds and can stable your horse.

rooms	3: 2 doubles, both with bath; 1 twin with private shower.
room price	£60. Singles from £35.
meals	Dinner, 2-3 courses, £14-£17.50. B.Y.O.
closed	Christmas & New Year.
directions	From Cirencester, A433 towards Tetbury. After 6 miles, right, signed Rodmarton. 2nd right into village; house 3rd on right.

rooms	3: 1 twin/double with bath & shower; 1 twin/double with private bath & separate wc; 1 family with private bath.
room price	£50-£60. Family room £75. Singles from £40.
meals	Lunch from £8.50. Packed lunch £8.50. Dinner £12.50, 3 courses, £15.50.
closed	Rarely.
directions	From Cirencester A433 to Tetbury, left onto B4014. After 250yds, left onto Chavenage Lane. Lodge Farm approx. 1 mile on right; dowwn drive, keep to left of barn.

Mary FitzGerald
The Old Rectory,
Rodmarton, Cirencester,
Gloucestershire GL7 6PE

tel	01285 841246
fax	01285 841246
e-mail	jfitz@globalnet.co.uk
web	www.rodmarton.com

Mrs Nicola Salmon
Lodge Farm,
Chavenage, Tetbury,
Gloucestershire GL8 8XW

tel	01666 505339
fax	01666 505346
e-mail	nicky@lodgefarm.u-net.com
web	www.lodgefarm.co.uk

Mike and Carolyn are inspiring – they've opened a fully organic restaurant above which sits an equally charming B&B. "We do it for spirit, not money," says Carolyn, and it's a place with heart that we are delighted to include. Your bedroom may share a bathroom but each room is delightful – huge, like a studio, with oak floors or seagrass matting and lovely art on the walls. They've used local craftsmen to make the beds, light fittings, fire baskets, tables and crockery and you have your own entrance opposite the Herb Wheel. *Children by arrangement.*

Country roads swoop through soft countryside and into honey-coloured villages full of tempting shops and inns; neighbouring Nailsworth has stacks of good restaurants. At the Mill your surroundings are bucolic and the large lake at the side of the house is at windowsill level, giving you a strange feeling of being underwater! The lake, the mill race and Judy – genuinely friendly – make this place special. Guests are in their own wing with separate entrance and sitting room. Bedrooms are fresh and simple. Bring the family and climb the hills.

rooms	3: 1 double with shower; 1 double, 1 twin sharing bath.
room price	£60. Singles £35.
meals	Fully organic restaurant.
closed	Rarely.
directions	M5, junc. 13, A419 to Stroud, then A46 south to Nailsworth. Right at r'bout & immed. left; restaurant & house are opp. Britannia Pub.

rooms	2: 1 twin/double, 1 twin both with shower.
room price	£54-£60. Singles £35.
meals	Several pubs close by.
closed	Rarely.
directions	From Stroud, A46 for Bath. After 2 miles right to North Woodchester then 2nd left, down hill, sharp right up short drive.

Carolyn & Mike Findlay
Heaven's Above at The Mad Hatters
3 Cossack Square, Nailsworth,
Gloucestershire GL6 0DB

tel	01453 832615
fax	01453 832615
e-mail	mafindlay@waitrose.com

Mrs Judy Sutch
Southfield Mill,
Southfield Road, Woodchester,
Stroud, Gloucestershire GL5 5PA

tel	01453 872896
fax	01452 872896
e-mail	judysutch@hotmail.com

map: 9 entry: 209

map: 9 entry: 210

Deep authenticity in this magnificent, Grade-I listed house in a fascinating village. The family has lived here since the 11th century but has 'installed' a housekeeper who looks after guests. Exquisite examples of carved wood, and in the hall, an impressive Doric frieze. One bedroom has a Flemish tapestry and a four-poster with hand-embroidered curtains; others have lovely views, antiques and panelling. Heating is by old-fashioned radiator and bathrooms are delectably antiquated. Dutch ornamental canal, lake, old-master views and an architectural masterpiece... very special.

A perfect English scene... a late 18th-century house tucked down a lane off the country's longest village green. It's a wonderful house and Carol wants you to treat it as home. When we visited, the Aga was being nurtured back to optimum health, there was a jigsaw puzzle that invited a challenge, dogs and cats happily co-existed; the visitors' book was inscribed: "We'll be back" (and return they do). There are lovely gardens with orchards, hens for breakfast eggs, elegant china, and Carol has decorated big bedrooms in muted yellows and rich velvety plums. *Children over 10 welcome.*

rooms	3: 1 four-poster with dressing room with single bed & private bath; 1 twin with bath; 1 double with bath.
room price	£90–£100. Singles, £45–£50.
meals	Breakfast 8.30–10am. Dinner £17.50.
closed	Rarely.
directions	From M5 junc. 13 west, then B4071. Left down village green, then just look to left! Entrance between 2 chestnut trees. 2nd turning left, approx. 400 yds.

rooms	2: 1 twin/double, 1 twin, both with bath/shower.
room price	£60. Singles £30.
meals	Pubs in village. Excellent restaurant 5 miles.
closed	Christmas & New Year.
directions	A38 for Bristol, west onto B4071. 1st left & drive length of village green. 300 yds after end, right into Whittles Lane. House last on right. 3 miles fom junc. 13 on M5.

Rollo & Janie Clifford
Frampton Court,
Frampton-on-Severn,
Gloucestershire GL2 7EU

tel	01452 740267
fax	01452 740698
e-mail	clifford.fce@farming.co.uk
web	www.framptoncourtestate.uk.com

Carol Alexander
The Old School House,
Whittles Lane,
Frampton-on-Severn,
Gloucestershire GL2 7EB

tel	01452 740457
fax	01452 741721
e-mail	bedandbreakfast@f-o-s.freeserve.co.uk
web	www.the-oldschoolhouse.co.uk

Boards creak and you duck – it is a farmhouse of the best kind: simple, small-roomed, stone-flagged, beamed, delightful. The walls are white, the furniture is good and there are pictures everywhere. In spite of great age (16th century), it's light, with lots of windows. You get a great breakfast, too; the 400 acres are farmed organically (cows and sheep). Bring your horse – some of the forest pubs have hitching posts outside. There are stupendous views across the Severn estuary to the Cotswolds, and woodland walks, carpeted with spring flowers. And there is simply no noise – unless the guinea fowl are in good voice.

rooms	2: 1 twin/double with private bath, 1 double with shower.
room price	£60-£70. Singles £30.
meals	Breakfast 7-10.30am, or earlier by arrangement. Packed lunch £3.50. Pub 2 miles.
closed	Rarely.
directions	2 miles south of Newnham on A48, opp. turn for Bullo Pill, large 'pull-in' with phone box on right; turn here; follow farm track to end.

Penny & David Hill
Grove Farm,
Bullo Pill, Newnham,
Gloucestershire GL14 1DZ
tel 01594 516304
fax 01594 516304
e-mail davidandpennyhill@btopenworld.com

Come in spring and the nightingale's song is the only sound that could disturb your slumber; but this is a year-round, soothing retreat, a hunting lodge with views over the rolling Cotswold Hills. You enter an enchanted wood surrounded by a RSPB sanctuary and a pine arboretum planted by Thomas Gambier Parry in 1844. Carol and David are friendly, unobtrusive hosts and are knowledgeable about organic gardening, as reflected in the 13-acre grounds. The bedrooms with new beds and bathrooms have the most wonderful garden views.

rooms	2: 1 twin/double with bath; 1 twin/double with shower.
room price	£50-£60. Singles £30-£35.
meals	Dinner £21.50. Pub/restaurant 4 miles.
closed	Rarely.
directions	From Gloucester A40/A48 r'bout follow A40 (Ross) for 0.7 miles. At brow of hill right up drive of black & white cottage; follow track for 0.75 miles into woods. House at top through iron gates. Drive round to front door.

David & Carol Wilkin
The Pinetum Lodge,
Churcham,
Gloucestershire GL2 8AD
tel 01452 750554
fax 01452 750402
e-mail carol@igeek.co.uk
web www.pinetumlodge.ik.com

GLOUCESTERSHIRE

Petrina is a natural and imaginative cook – a eulogy from a French chef in the visitors' book endorses this – and both she and James thrive on the bustle and conversation of guests; the place is an oasis of comfort and ease. There's plenty of space for everyone (and very early risers may help themselves to tea and coffee in the kitchen). Pastel bedrooms are large and airy, bathrooms good and the beds emperor-size, no less. The elegant drawing room looks over the large gardens and has sweeping views of May Hill and the Malverns. An attractive house to which the Pughs bring a real sense of fun.

rooms	3: 1 double with private shower; 2 twins/doubles with bath/shower.
room price	£60. Singles £30.
meals	Dinner £17.50. Gourmet dinner £22.50.
closed	Rarely.
directions	A40 from Gloucester for Ross-on-Wye, then B4215 (for Newent/Highnam). Whitehall Lane 2 miles on left. House approx. 0.75 miles down lane, on right, behind laurel hedge.

James & Petrina Pugh
Whitelands,
Whitehall Lane, Rudford,
Gloucestershire GL2 8ED

tel	01452 790406
fax	01452 790676
e-mail	pughwhitelands@yahoo.co.uk

GLOUCESTERSHIRE

Utterly delightful people with wide-ranging interests (ex-British Council and college lecturing; arts, travel, gardening...) in a manor-type house full of beautiful furniture. A treat. The house was born of the Arts & Crafts movement and remains fascinating: wood panels painted green, a log-fired drawing-room for guests, quarry tiles on window sills, handsome old furniture, comfortable proportions... elegant but human. The garden's massive clipped hedges and great lawn are impressive, as is the whole place. Refined but nevertheless easy.

rooms	3: 1 double, 2 twins, 1 with private bath/shower, 2 with shared bath.
room price	£68. Singles £44.
meals	Breakfast until 9.15am. Dinner £22. B.Y.O.
closed	December-January.
directions	B4060 from Stinchcombe to Wotton-under-Edge. 0.25 miles up long hill, house at top on left; gateway marked.

Hugh & Crystal St John Mildmay
Drakestone House,
Stinchcombe, Dursley,
Gloucestershire GL11 6AS

tel	01453 542140
fax	01453 542140

GLOUCESTERSHIRE

GLOUCESTERSHIRE

A magnolia rambles around the wooden mullioned windows and an old oak door admits you to the handsome, 16th-century farmhouse. Stone flags, Georgian panelling and polished wooden stairs are softened by pale fabrics, comfortable sofas, books and flowers. The effect is simple, uncluttered, pleasing. The bedrooms are delightful, too, one with an original Thirties' bathroom. John and Sally are inspired gardeners in their Italianate two acres: orchards, ponds, ha-has, paddocks and canal; breakfast includes stewed fruits from the orchard and home-made jams. The setting is wonderful, the peace a balm.

A glorious, sunny house in the Cotswolds with a park-like setting and large trees – space, peace, seclusion. There are family photographs, lovely furniture, interesting pictures, a grand piano and a musical atmosphere; bedrooms are pale and restful with books and pretty tea trays. Breakfasts of butcher's sausages, home-made bread and marmalade are taken in the formal dining room with views into the garden. There are walks all around this conservation area – Shipton Moyne is an award-winning village with its own famous pub, Westonbirt is next door, and picnics for the Beaufort Polo Club can be arranged.

rooms	2: 1 double, 1 twin, both with bath.
room price	From £70. Singles £35-£40.
meals	Pub with restaurant 3-minute walk.
closed	21 December-2 January.
directions	From M5 junc. 16, A38 for Gloucester. After 6 miles, turn for Tytherington. From north, leave M5 at exit 14 & south on A38 for Bristol. Turn for Tytherington after 3 miles.

rooms	2 doubles, both with bath.
room price	£80. Singles by arrangement.
meals	Dinner, 2 courses, £25.
closed	24 December-1 January.
directions	From Tetbury, A433 for Bath. 1st left to Shipton Moyne. After 1 mile 1st right to Westonbirt. House 0.8 miles on left.

John & Sally Eyre
Boyts Farm,
Tytherington, Wotton-under-Edge,
Gloucestershire GL12 8UG
tel   01454 412220
fax   01454 412220
e-mail   jve@boyts.fsnet.co.uk

Susie & Antony Brassey
Hillcourt,
Shipton Moyne, Tetbury,
Gloucestershire GL8 8QB
tel   01666 880280
fax   01666 880570
e-mail   susieb@dial.pipex.com

GLOUCESTERSHIRE

The Kings have farmed here for 75 years and 40 of those have been shared with B&B guests; Sonja knows her stuff and the whole family is involved in the arable and dairy enterprise. The famous Westonbirt Arboretum – breathtaking whatever the season – is a stroll away across the field; the Kings' fine cedar tree sadly succumbed to the elements but its grand trunk is being planked to make a summer house. Bedheads have drapes that give the impression of a half-tester, and throughout are two generations' worth of fine needlework. An honest, good-value place without pretensions.

rooms	3: 1 double, 1 twin, both with shower; 1 twin with shower & separate wc.
room price	From £50. Singles £30.
meals	Pub 200 yds.
closed	Rarely.
directions	A433 from Tetbury for 5 miles. On entering Knockdown, farm on right before crossroads.

Sonja King
Avenue Farm,
Knockdown, Tetbury,
Gloucestershire GL8 8QY

tel   01454 238207
fax   01454 238033
e-mail   sonjames@breathemail.net

HAMPSHIRE

Super hosts and one of the greatest gardens in the book... seven tended acres sit within 100 acres of woodland. There are Japanese and dahlia gardens, azaleas and camellias, fine specimen trees, a formal terrace and exotica, all managed with flair and imagination. You breakfast in the chinoiserie dining room – the allegorical tableau is charming – and bedrooms are furnished in traditional style and have gorgeous garden views. The tennis court is hidden in the garden among some of the largest Wellingtonia in the country. The perfect country house. *Children over 12 welcome.*

rooms	2: 1 twin with bath; 1 twin with private bath.
room price	From £60. Singles from £40.
meals	Dinner with wine, £20.
closed	Christmas Day.
directions	South on A3 to lights at Hindhead. Straight across & after 400 yds, right onto B3002. On for 3 miles. Entrance (signed) on right in a wood.

Jeremy & Philippa Whitaker
Land of Nod,
Headley, Bordon,
Hampshire GU35 8SJ

tel   01428 713609
fax   01428 717698

A handsome Georgian cottage and a truly comforting place to stay. Chintz at the windows, pictures on the walls, a generous oak dresser lined with blue and white china – hard to believe this was once the village post office. The twin has polished walnut beds and dressing table laid with silver-backed brushes; the smaller double has fresh white walls and a scarlet bedcover. Jollyon dashes off bacon and eggs on the Aga, Ruthie helps run the village shop, source of your fine breakfast jams. The guest sitting room looks onto a colourful garden – it is all wonderfully homely.

Four generations of the family have lived here and much beautiful furniture remains, while wooden and stone floors reflect the light that floods in. Elisabeth is Austrian and an interior designer, and brings together intriguing curios, statues and vases. Carpeted bedrooms have good lamps, generous curtains and a traditional country-house feel. There are mature gardens in which to play tennis or croquet; further afield are many opportunities for fishing, walking and visits to famous and historic attractions. *Babes in arms and children over 12 welcome.*

rooms	2: 1 twin, 1 twin/double sharing bath.
room price	£60. Singles £35.
meals	Packed lunch by arrangement. Good pub next door.
closed	Christmas & New Year.
directions	M3, exit 5 to North Warnbrough & sign to Upton Grey (approx. 3 miles). House on left between pub & duckpond.

rooms	2: 1 twin with bath; 1 twin with basin & private bath.
room price	£70. Singles £45.
meals	Breakfast 7.30-10.30am. Nearest pub 1 mile, restaurant 5 miles.
closed	Rarely.
directions	From Andover, on A303, past petrol station, turn for Longparish. From B3048, 1st right for Forton, then 1st left onto private road.

Jollyon & Ruthie Coombs
The Old Post House,
Upton Grey, Basingstoke,
Hampshire RG25 2RL
tel   01256 862574
fax   01256 862025
e-mail   jcpartnership@btopenworld.com

Bill & Elisabeth Hanbury-Bateman
Forton House,
Long Parish, Andover,
Hampshire SP11 6NN
tel   01264 720236
fax   01264 720885
e-mail   bandbbest@aol.com

Charles Dickens is said to have escaped the helter-skelter of London for the peace of the Test Valley to write at Yew Tree House. The warm red brick was there 200 years before him; the famous, conical-roofed dovecote (to which you may have the key) at the end of the herbaceous border 300 years before that. Here is understated elegance and deep tranquillity: a yellow-ochre bedroom with Descamps bed linen to match, cashmere/silk curtains designed by Philip and Janet's son, a profusion of flowers – the garden is gorgeous. The yew was the symbol of peace and plenty in medieval times; it is a fitting name.

Seagrass matting, Moroccan rugs, antiques and a woodburning stove all contribute to the easy atmosphere in this terrifically light and sunny 200-year-old barn. Lindy, who speaks French and lets out her French holiday home in the Lot, organises garden tours. You can relax on the terrace overlooking her pretty well-tended English garden with cornfields beyond, admire the waterfowl on the pond or saunter to the pub past the thatched cottages of this chocolate-box village. Golf, fishing, riding and antique shops nearby. *Children over 10 welcome.*

rooms	2: 1 double with private bath; 1 twin with shower.
room price	£54. Singles £32.
meals	Good pubs in village; restaurants 5 miles.
closed	Rarely.
directions	From A30 travelling west of Stockbridge for 1.5 miles, left at minor x-roads. After 2 miles left at T-junc. House on left at next junction opposite Greyhound pub.

rooms	3: 1 double with shower; 1 twin with private bath; 1 studio double across courtyard with shower & own front door.
room price	£55-£75. Singles from £35.
meals	Excellent pub in village.
closed	Christmas & New Year.
directions	From Salisbury, A354 for Blandford, through Coombe Bissett. After 1.5 miles, left on bend to Rockbourne. Through village, 200 yds after 30mph zone, house signed on left. After 50 yds, gravel drive on right.

Philip & Janet Mutton
Yew Tree House,
Broughton, Stockbridge,
Hampshire SO20 8AA
tel   01794 301227

Lindy & Tony Ball
Marsh Barn,
Rockbourne, Fordingbridge,
Hampshire SP6 3NF
tel   01725 518768
fax   01725 518380

HAMPSHIRE

A n excellent spot for anyone who enjoys walking, cycling, riding, wildlife and space — you can step straight onto open moorland from this smallholding on the edge of the New Forest. There's plenty of room for wet clothes and muddy boots, and cattle graze within 10 feet of the window. You may hear the call of a nightjar in June; Dartford warblers nest nearby. Sue keeps a few sheep, free-range poultry, a horse and two cats. Guests have their own little sitting room, warm, simple bedrooms, a friendly atmosphere and good home cooking. You can walk to one pub and others are nearby. Uncomplicated country B&B.

rooms	2: 1 double with bath/shower; 1 twin/double with bath.
room price	From £55. Singles from £32.
meals	Breakfast 7-9am. Packed lunch £6. Dinner from £15.
closed	Christmas & New Year.
directions	On A338, 1 mile south of Fordingbridge, at small x-roads, turn for Hyde & Hungerford. Up hill & right at school for Ogdens. Left at next x-roads for Ogdens North. House on right at bottom of hill.

Sue Browne
Sandy Corner,
Ogdens North, Fordingbridge,
Hampshire SP6 2QD
tel   01425 657295

map: 4 entry: 225

HAMPSHIRE

T he herringbone brickwork is just one of the features that grants this unusual house Grade II* listing. It dates from the 13th century — Richard de Ranville sailed here from Normandy with his family. Large beds in big rooms overlook a courtyard of old barns; a further room is in the newer courtyard wing: modern and with level access, it is perfect for the less mobile. Delicious breakfasts are served in the palest grey dining room, grand with long table and paintings. There are five acres of garden, a paddock, lovely prints, lots of books and an easy atmosphere. Bill and Anthea are dynamic and fun.

rooms	3 twins/doubles, all with bath/shower; one could be a family room.
room price	£50-£65. Singles from £35.
meals	Pub/restaurant 1 mile.
closed	Christmas & New Year.
directions	Exit M27 junc. 2; A3090 for Romsey. Climb hill; Gardener's Lane on left; on 100 yds, on south side of dual carriageway; house marked by flagpole. Crossing marked with 2 white posts.

Bill & Anthea Hughes
Ranvilles Farm House,
Romsey, Hampshire SO51 6AA
tel   02380 814481
fax   02380 814481
e-mail   info@ranvilles.com
web   www.ranvilles.com

map: 4 entry: 226

Complete privacy in a B&B is rare. Here you have it, and just a 12-minute walk from the centre of town, cathedral and water meadows. Relax in your own half of a Victorian townhouse beautifully furnished and decorated, and immensely welcoming. Fizzy serves sumptuous breakfasts and fresh flowers abound – guests have been delighted. You are also left with an 'honesty box' so you may help yourselves to drinks. The rooms are small and cosy with lovely big antique mirrors, bedspreads and furniture; there is a log fire in the sitting room and a small garden, too. *Children over seven welcome.*

The best of both worlds: a charming house that sits in its own 15 acres with footpaths to the surrounding countryside, and Winchester minutes away. This is a happy family home and your easy-going and amusing hosts love to share it with you. Georgian in look – rather like an old rectory – it is elegantly decorated, full of antiques, family portraits, landscapes, engravings and watercolours. Some of Sue's work hangs in the bedrooms. Tea in the drawing room; soft colours, pretty chintz and long views from your rooms. The house is on the Millennium Pilgrim's Way so the walking is ready-made. *Children over 10 welcome.*

rooms	2: 1 twin, 1 double, both with shower & bath.
room price	£55-£60. Singles £50-£54.
meals	Dinner available nearby.
closed	Christmas.
directions	Leave M3 at junc. 9 & take A272 Winchester exit, then signs for Winchester Park & Ride. Under m'way, straight on at r'bout signed St Cross. Left at T-junc. St Faith's Road about 100 yds ahead.

rooms	2: 1 twin with bath; 1 twin with private bath.
room price	£55-£65. Singles £35-£40.
meals	Pub/restaurant 250 yds.
closed	Christmas & New Year.
directions	From M3, junc. 9, A272 to W'chester; over next r'bout; left at small r'bout for Morestead, then immed. left; 1 mile after M'stead, right to Owslebury. Through village, left to Whadden Lane; 200 yds down, on left; 1st entrance with white fence.

Guy & Fizzy Warren
Brymer House,
29/30 St Faith's Road, St Cross,
Winchester, Hampshire SO23 9QD

tel	01962 867428
fax	01962 868624
e-mail	brymerhouse@aol.com

Sue & Tim Torrington
Great Hunts Place,
Owslebury, Nr Winchester,
Hampshire SO21 1JL

tel	01962 777234
fax	01962 777242
e-mail	tt@byngs.freeserve.co.uk
web	www.byngs.freeserve.co.uk

Part 18th-century farm cottage, part extended Victorian extension; this is a quirky, friendly house and Felicity loves having guests. She's a china restorer and a keen cook with a burgeoning kitchen garden: plums, peaches, figs, for bottling and jamming. You eat in the dining room; wonderful "everything's local" breakfasts and enticing-sounding dinners. Separate staircases lead to the large twin under the rafters and the smaller cottage double, both with garden views, good furniture, linen, books and paintings. Country walks from the doorstep and a mile to Bishop's Waltham, of William of Wyckham fame.

In the heart of a pretty thatch village with an 11th-century church famous for its font, the house is a beautiful, rambling, red-brick place: three 18th-century cottages knocked into one. The family adore it and it's been their home for years. Your hosts are gentle, thoughtful people who give you full use of the family sitting room – comfortable with rugged parquet floor and several sofas – during your stay. Bedrooms are simple and cosy and can interconnect for families. Bantams roam the five acres of lawns traversed by the river Meon; the glorious South Downs Way is a short walk through fields.

rooms	2: 1 double, 1 triple, both with bath & shower.
room price	£60. Singles £35.
meals	Dinner from £18. Lunch £10. Packed lunch £5. Several pubs/restaurants nearby.
closed	Mid-December-January.
directions	B2177 Winchester to Portsmouth. Just before 40mph sign into Bishop's Waltham, left into Ashton Lane.

rooms	2: 1 twin with private bath/shower; 1 single, with bath.
room price	£56. Singles £28.
meals	Pubs in village.
closed	Christmas & New Year & occasionally,
directions	From Petersfield A272 for Winchester. After 3 miles, left, signed East Meon. There, left after church into The Cross.

Felicity & David Webb-Carter
Little Ashton Farm,
Ashton Lane, Bishop's Waltham,
Hampshire SO32 1FR

tel 01489 894055
fax 01489 894055
e-mail flossywebb@hotmail.com
web www.littleashtonfarm.20m.com

Rachel Mackinlay
Cross Keys,
East Meon, Petersfield,
Hampshire GU32 1NN

tel 01730 823251
fax 01730 823632

HAMPSHIRE

A lovely, beamy, roomy 16th-century farmhouse on a site with a medieval history. Harriet is planning a sculpture garden to add to the magic of the two-acre landscaped gardens – already there is a lake, an upstairs conservatory, a heated covered pool, outdoor chess and a croquet lawn. Splendid breakfasts in the spectacular A-frame dining room; bedrooms are large, comfortable and even dramatic – one has a four-poster and a grand marble bathroom. Harriet and Julian are flexible and kind and will tell you about lovely walks in this designated AONB. *Children over eight welcome.*

rooms	3: 1 double, 1 four-poster, both with bath/shower; 1 twin with bath.
room price	£60-£72. Singles by arrangement.
meals	Breakfast 8-9am. Good pubs within 10-minute drive.
closed	Christmas & New Year.
directions	From A272 at Rogate, turn for Harting & Nyewood. Cross humpback bridge; drive signed to right after 300 yds.

	Harriet & Julian Francis
	Mizzards Farm,
	Rogate, Petersfield,
	Hampshire GU31 5HS
tel	01730 821656
fax	01730 821655
e-mail	julian.francis@hemscott.net

HEREFORDSHIRE

You sleep in the ancient heart of the house, among 12th-century timbers and 18th-century additions. Grove House is warm and cosseting – dark polished wood gleams, large, luxurious rooms glow in the firelight. In the elegant guests' drawing room are books by the fire and plump sofas to sink into; in the bedrooms, window-seats and ornately carved canopied beds, in the dining room, Jacobean panelling. Michael is an excellent cook – they make all their own bread and grow vegetables without chemicals; dinner is a special occasion, so do eat in. You can play tennis, swim in the neighbour's pool or walk the Malvern Hills.

rooms	3: 1 twin/double, 2 four-posters, all with bath/shower.
room price	£73. Singles £51.50.
meals	Dinner £24.
closed	Christmas.
directions	Leave M50 at junc. 2, for Ledbury. 1st left to Bromsberrow Heath. Right by Post Office & up hill. House on right.

	Michael & Ellen Ross
	The Grove House,
	Bromsberrow Heath, Ledbury,
	Herefordshire HR8 1PE
tel	01531 650584
e-mail	ross@the-grovehouse.com
web	www.the-grovehouse.com

Forests must have fallen to build this house; the 1612 barn behind the Georgian façade is a soaring tangle of timbers, a paean to carpentry. The hall, open to the roof, is beautiful, with Chippendale panels in the staircase; oak beams and timber crucks are on bold display. Guests have a sitting room; breakfast is served in the beamed dining room. The bedrooms are comfortable; in some Judi provides towelling robes for the quick flit to the antique bath. A delightfully unexpected house with a charming hostess, and there is a lovely walled garden, too... all in the centre of Ledbury.

An honest, authentic farmhouse with livestock, an assortment of farm buildings and a deep sense of rural peace. Elizabeth, a busy farmer's wife, manages it all efficiently with husband Peter – they were lambing when we were there. This is a traditional livestock and hop farm which still dries its own hops; in September you can watch their oast house at work. You will eat home-produced meat, preserves and vegetables – Elizabeth is a fine cook. The buildings, about 500 years old, ramble and enfold both gardens and guests. Bedrooms are timber-framed with bright fabrics.

rooms	3: 1 double with shower; 1 double, 1 twin, both with basin, sharing bath.
room price	£68-£75. Singles £52.
meals	Good selection of pubs/restaurants, 50 yds.
closed	Christmas & New Year.
directions	From Ledbury bypass, A449 for Worcester & town centre. House on left just past Somerfield but before central town crossroads.

rooms	3: 2 twins, 1 double, all with shower.
room price	£40-£50. Singles £28.
meals	Dinner, 3 courses, £15.
closed	Rarely.
directions	From Hereford, east on A438. A417 into Stretton Grandison. 1st right past village sign, through Holmend Park. Bear left past phone box. House on left.

Judi Holland
The Barn House,
New Street, Ledbury,
Herefordshire HR8 2DX
tel   01531 632825
e-mail barnhouseledbury@lineone.net
web   www.thebarnhouse.net

Elizabeth & Peter Godsall
Moor Court Farm,
Stretton Grandison, Nr Ledbury,
Herefordshire HR8 2TP
tel   01531 670408
fax   01531 670408

HEREFORDSHIRE

HEREFORDSHIRE

Super people – natural hosts – and an easy atmosphere. This is an exceptional B&B and good value, too. There's much of architectural interest: a copse of 17th-century oak beams and timbers above, and masses of light. Judy, an artist, has created a beautiful conversion, then decorated with style. Bedrooms are simple and charming, with fresh flowers, good soaps, books, magazines, electric blankets to ensure the deepest sleep. Breakfasts are lavish and include home-made bread and jams. There's the freshest produce for dinner, and you can also eat at the local pub – Judy or Roger will happily ferry you.

What a treat to stay in a 17th-century farmhouse high on a sheep-strewn hill – views reach to the Cotswolds on a fine day. This is an attractive, listed house on a working farm, with tennis court, croquet lawn, stables, gardens and wonderful walks. Inside: more character than luxury with big old fireplaces and beams, comfortable sofas and wonky floors that squeak. Bertie is a dab hand at breakfast, using home-produced free-range eggs, while Caroline cooks a delicious dinner; both work in the wine trade. Bedrooms are engagingly timeworn, with good carpets and fine old family pieces. Utterly peaceful – and fun.

rooms	2: 1 double with bath/shower; 1 twin/double with private bath & shower. 1 single also available for groups/children.
room price	£55. Singles £35.
meals	Dinner, 3 courses, £18.50. B.Y.O. Pub 1 mile.
closed	Rarely.
directions	At Burley Gate r'bout on A417, A465 for Bromyard. At Stoke Lacy church, on right, right, then 2nd right to entrance.

rooms	2: 1 twin with private bath; 1 further twin/double let to members of same party.
room price	£50. Singles £30.
meals	Dinner, 2 courses, £14; 3 courses, £20, with wine.
closed	Rarely.
directions	From Bromyard Post Office, 3 miles on B4203 for Great Witley. Pass Saltmarsh Castle on left. 60 yds on right; next drive with double wooden gates.

Roger & Judy Young
Dovecote Barn,
Stoke Lacy, Herefordshire HR7 4HJ
tel	01432 820968
fax	01432 820969
e-mail	dovecotebarn@mail.com
web	www.dovecotebarn.co.uk

Bertie & Caroline Cotterell
Upper Norton,
Tedstone Wafre, Bromyard,
Herefordshire HR7 4PN
tel	01885 483141
fax	01885 488710
e-mail	bertie@woodenconcepts.plus.com

If you enjoy the luxuries of space and tranquillity, this immaculate house, full of old paintings and fine furniture, will make your heart sing. There are 11 fireplaces in the part-17th-, part-19th-century house, and bedrooms are large and airy, with perfect white linen and carpets soft underfoot; the double is fit for a king. Bathrooms are lavish. In the grounds, handsome lawns, mature trees and two kitchen gardens: Guy not only makes bread but also grows fruit and vegetables. Share them with your kind and considerate hosts at the grand dining table: Amanda loves to entertain.

At Lower Bache a sense of honest industry pervades. The Wiles have created a B&B that introduces you to all that they – and we – hold dear: they smoke their own meat and fish, bake bread daily and have a fully organic wine list. It's a fascinating place – a 17th-century farmhouse with cider house, dairy, butterfly house and 14-acre nature reserve; perched at the top of a small valley the views are tremendous. You stay in private suites, one across the courtyard, the others in the granary annexe – all timber-framed, snug and with their own sitting rooms. Breakfasts are superb. *Children over eight welcome.*

rooms	2: 1 twin with bath; 1 double with bath/shower.
room price	£70. Singles £45.
meals	Packed lunch from £5. Dinner, 3 courses, £25, with wine & pre-dinner drink.
closed	Rarely.
directions	From Tenbury Wells to Leysters, on A4112, left at crossroads in village. Ignore sign to Leysters church. House on left, with wooden gate (after postbox in wall).

rooms	4 suites, all with private bath/shower & sitting room.
room price	£67. Singles £43.50.
meals	Breakfast until 9.30am. Dinner £16.50–£24.50.
closed	Rarely.
directions	From Leominster, A49 north but turning right onto A4112, signed Leysters. Lower Bache then signed after village of Kimbolton. Look out for white butterfly sign.

Guy & Amanda Griffiths
The Old Vicarage,
Leysters, Leominster,
Herefordshire HR6 0HS

tel   01568 750208
fax   01568 750208
e-mail   guy.griffiths@virgin.net
web   www.oldvicar.co.uk

Rose & Leslie Wiles
Lower Bache House,
Kimbolton, Nr Leominster,
Herefordshire HR6 0ER

tel   01568 750304
e-mail   leslie.wiles@care4free.net

Quintessentially English but with wonderful views to the Welsh hills. This is country house living at its most delightful – grand yet cosy; it is relaxed and entirely without pretence. Set in parkland, high above the River Lugg, this fine Regency house was a virtual wreck when James and Henrietta bought it. It's now a family home (housing a charming family), full of light, colour and big log fires. Furnished traditionally and well, there are lots of interesting pictures and prints, and some unusual touches; Henrietta's handmade wallpaper is superb. Breakfast is special, too. *Children over five welcome.*

The timbers of the medieval, cruck-framed, house – and there are many – are probably 1,000 years old. Little of the structure has ever been altered and it is an absolute delight: stone floors, warm yellow paint, paned windows, fireplaces everywhere, wooden stairs, a piano, comfortable chairs. The countryside is 'pure', too, with 1,500 acres of National Trust land five miles away. The bedrooms are small – this was a yeoman's house – but no matter. One is Berrington Hall blue with white bedcovers, so cosy and with a fireplace in its bathroom. Anita is easy-going and good company. Just mind your head.

rooms	3: 2 doubles, 1 twin, all with bath.
room price	£60. Singles £40.
meals	Dinner, 3 courses, £20.
closed	Christmas & Easter.
directions	From Leominster B4361 north; 0.5 miles on, left for Eyton; 1.5 miles on, left for Kingsland. House 0.5 miles on right.

rooms	4: 1 twin with bath; 1 double, 2 singles, sharing bath, for family group.
room price	£60. Singles £27.
meals	Dinner £20.
closed	Rarely.
directions	From Leominster, A49 towards Ludlow. After approx. 4 miles, in village of Ashton, left & house on right behind postbox after 1 mile.

James & Henrietta Varley
Eyton Old Hall,
Eyton, Leominster,
Herefordshire HR6 0AQ
tel   01568 612551
fax   01568 616100
e-mail   varleyeoh@hotmail.com
web   www.eytonoldhall.fsnet.co.uk

Mrs Anita Syers-Gibson
Bunns Croft,
Moreton Eye, Leominster,
Herefordshire HR6 0DP
tel   01568 615836
fax   01568 610620

map: 8 entry: 239

map: 8 entry: 240

Pink fir-apple potatoes and orchard fruit often end up on the dinner table: food is taken seriously here (they've won awards) and dinner is a four-course banquet. Panache in the décor, too: luxurious drapes and medieval-style high-backed chairs in the dining room, leather sofas and oak floorboards in the sitting room. Bedrooms are fresh and bright; bathrooms are seductive (there's a *chaise longue* in one), candlelit and rather magical. The old farmhouse is perfectly quiet at night and Steve and Jill are warm and well-travelled. You'll feel at home. *Children over 10 welcome.*

Well-proportioned rooms and fine furniture here in this Georgian rectory. It is a house that matches its owners, traditional and country-loving. A wooden staircase leads to peaceful bedrooms with comfortable beds: the blue room looks onto garden and church, the white has gorgeous soft furnishings. Rosie and Richard are talented cooks and you eat in the new kitchen *en famille*, or in the big dining room with chandelier. You will feel as well tended as the three-acre garden, perfect with tennis court and pool. The highest 18-hole golf course in England is at Kington, near Offa's Dyke.

rooms	3: 1 double with private bath; 1 twin, 1 double, both with shower.
room price	From £80. Singles £45.
meals	Dinner £25.
closed	Rarely.
directions	A4110 north to Wigmore. At 'Welcome' sign on for 150 yds, then right. Drive 1st on left.

rooms	2: 1 double with bath; 1 twin/double with bath/shower.
room price	From £58. Singles £36.
meals	Dinner, 2-3 courses, £15-£20.
closed	Rarely.
directions	A44 Leominster-Pembridge; right to Shobdon. After 0.5 miles, left to Staunton-on-Arrow; at x-roads, over into village. House opposite church, with black wrought-iron gates.

Steve Dawson & Jill Fieldhouse
Pear Tree Farm,
Wigmore, Herefordshire HR6 9UR
tel   01568 770140
fax   01568 770141
e-mail jill@ptf.me.uk
web   www.peartreefarmco.freeserve.co.uk

Rosie & Richard Bowen
Staunton House,
Staunton-on-Arrow, Pembridge,
Nr Leominster,
Herefordshire HR6 9HR
tel   01544 388313
fax   01544 388313
e-mail rbowen1061@aol.com

This is more like staying in a home than a B&B. Your hosts are delightful: she is a concert singer and he is a wine merchant (and will sell you some excellent wines). You have all the advantages of being in a small, rural town: on one side the church and on the other, a garden that disappears into the rolling hills. Bedrooms are prettily wallpapered, carpeted and cosy and share an attractive bathroom with roll-top bath. You breakfast at a mahogany table in the Georgian, shuttered dining room on Andrew's excellent marmalades and jams. A charming place to stay with superb walking country all around.

A cosy and unpretentious house in a wonderful setting. The sitting room is snug with woodburner and sofas, but the kitchen is the hub of the place, where breakfast and dinner are cooked on the Aga. Grace, chatty and easy-going, obviously enjoys living in her modernised mill house. Rooms are small, with exposed beams and slate window sills; only the old mill interrupts the far-reaching, all-green views. Drift off to sleep to the sound of the Arrow river burbling nearby – a tonic for frenzied city-dwellers. Excellent value. *Children over four welcome.*

rooms	2: 1 double, 1 twin with basin, sharing bath.
room price	£50. Singles £30.
meals	Breakfast 6-10am. Pubs/restaurants 400 yds.
closed	Christmas & New Year.
directions	Coming into Kington, follow signs for centre. Through middle of town & up long steady hill to St Mary's church. House on left opposite.

rooms	3: 1 double with shower; 1 double, 1 twin, sharing bath & wc.
room price	£36-£44. Singles £18-£22.
meals	Dinner from £15.
closed	Christmas.
directions	A438 from Hereford. After Winforton, Whitney-on-Wye & toll bridge on left, sharp right for Brilley. Left fork to Huntington, over x-roads & next right to Huntington. Next right into 'No through' road, then 1st right.

Andrew & Lis Darwin
Church House,
Church Road, Kington,
Herefordshire HR5 3AG
tel   01544 230534
fax   01544 231100
e-mail   darwin@kc3.co.uk
web   www.churchhousekington.co.uk

Grace Watson
Hall's Mill House,
Huntington, Kington,
Herefordshire HR5 3QA
tel   01497 831409

Floorboards squeak and creak in this lovely 17th-century grain barn. There's a conservatory in an old cattle byre and you eat above the vast, open threshing bay. A sense of timelessness prevails: dining in the evening you spot nothing other than the odd light in a distant farmhouse. The shower room (a quick trot downstairs for those in the family room) is very pretty, the bedrooms feel functional with simple, modern furniture, the views are superb. Honest value and a wonderful hostess; peace-seekers and hill-walkers will adore the setting. Ann's lovely and she makes her own bread and preserves.

The house's views alone might earn it a place in this book. But there's much more... a beautifully furnished interior and an interesting four-acre garden with perfumed rose walk. Stephanie and John, who work unobtrusively to make your stay relaxing and enjoyable, are natural hosts and great company. The gracious rooms are large and bright and Stephanie has cleverly combined elegance with vibrant colours and fine furniture and paintings. From your exceptionally comfortable bedroom gaze across the Wye Valley to the Malvern Hills and west to the Black Mountains – glorious. Stephanie's cooking is worth a detour.

rooms	2: 1 family (double & single), 1 twin, sharing shower & wc.
room price	£44. Singles £22. Under 12s, £16.
meals	Breakfast about 8.30am. Packed lunch from £3. Dinner £16. B.Y.O.
closed	Rarely.
directions	From Hay, B4350 to Clifford. Pass castle & right to Bredwardine. Third left at top of hill, for Priory Wood. Pass between chapel & small fenced playing field. Ahead on right.

rooms	2: 1 twin with bath; 1 double with private bath.
room price	From £60.
meals	Packed lunch from £3.50. Dinner from £16.
closed	Rarely.
directions	From A438 Hereford & Brecon road, for Kington on A4111 through Eardisley. House 2 miles up hill on left, behind long line of conifers.

Ann Tong
Castleton Barn,
Priory Wood, Clifford,
Nr Hay-on-Wye,
Herefordshire HR3 5HF
tel   01497 831690
fax   01497 831296

Stephanie & John Grant
Bollingham House,
Eardisley,
Herefordshire HR5 3LE
tel   01544 327326
fax   01544 327880
e-mail   grant@bollinghamhouse.com
web   www.bollinghamhouse.com

map: 8 entry: 245

map: 8 entry: 246

History comes alive at this gracious 16th-century manor house: Wordsworth visited and King Charles II danced on the landing. The house is in a charming black and white village, and is surrounded by beautiful gardens that open for the National Gardens Scheme. The ornate gates, dating from 1720, were admired by Pevsner. There are period furnishings throughout and you sleep in high brass beds with linen sheets. Bathrooms are large and comfortable; you have your own sunny sitting room with a door to the garden. A fire blazes in the flagstoned hall in winter, and in summer you can sit out by the pool.

Escape to some peace and quiet in the Welsh mountains, where the only man-made noise is a passing tractor. The good life is here, presided over by intelligent, humorous and unfussy people who have got their priorities right. The feel is homely, the furniture antique, the atmosphere natural. After a relaxing dinner, ascend the picture-lined stairs to carpeted bedrooms with comfy beds, pale colours, good chintz. Local sausages and bacon for breakfast and a garden to explore – the variety and colour of the springtime flowers is astonishing, and the clematis wonderful.

rooms	2: 1 twin with bath & shower; 1 double with private bath & shower.
room price	From £60. Singles £30.
meals	Dinner from £18.50. Good pubs/restaurants 3 miles.
closed	Rarely.
directions	From Leominster, A44 & follow signs for Brecon. After 6 miles, left into Dilwyn. Round 3 sharp bends. House set back on right behind stone gate piers & wrought-iron railings.

rooms	2: 1 double with private bath; 1 twin sharing bath.
room price	£60. Singles £30.
meals	Dinner £15.
closed	Rarely.
directions	A480 from Hereford, after 10 miles right onto B4230 for Weobley. After 1.75 miles, right; house 2nd on left over cattle grid.

Tom & Jane Hawksley
The Great House,
Dilwyn, Hereford,
Herefordshire HR4 8HX
tel   01544 318007

Dawn & Michael MacLeod
Garnstone House,
Weobley, Herefordshire HR4 8QP
tel   01544 318943
fax   01544 318197

HEREFORDSHIRE

D ating from 1500 and breathtaking in its ancient dignity – undulating floors, great oak beams, thick walls. It is a light, airy, colourful home with exceptional timber-framed bedrooms; the four-poster has an Indian-style bathroom with huge roll-top bath, the suite a sitting area with two sofas. There are a guest sitting room and a small library, too. Yours hosts are delightful and spoil you with decanters of sherry and wine, or chocolates for special occasions. Walk down to the Wye or relax in the garden in summer, fragrant with herbs and flowers. *Self-catering available. See back of book.*

rooms	3: 1 double, 1 four-poster, 1 four-poster suite, all with bath.
room price	£58-£76. Singles from £43.
meals	Pubs 2-minute walk.
closed	Christmas.
directions	From Hereford, A438 into village. House on left with a green sign & iron gates.

Jackie Kingdon
Winforton Court,
Winforton, Herefordshire HR3 6EA
tel   01544 328498
fax   01544 328498

HEREFORDSHIRE

Y ou couldn't be nearer Offa's Dyke: out of the door, onto the bridge and you're there. Helen and Tom love their old cottage – an erstwhile river crossing inn – and give you an easy welcome and a warm bedroom under the eaves. Fat white duvets on antique beds, a dressing table, a sofa, and a fresh, azure-and-white bathroom with sloping ceiling and gilded mirror. Recline in the sitting room, quietly elegant with its old Broadwood square piano and lovely paintings. You have a cottage garden to the front, a terrace for river sunsets to the rear, three friendly dogs and a private beach for hired canoes.

rooms	1 twin with private bath (extra bed on request).
room price	£50-£60. Singles £30-£35.
meals	Pub 0.25 miles.
closed	Rarely.
directions	A438 Brecon; after 6 miles, Nelson pub & garage on right; at next x-roads left to Madley & Preston-on-Wye. Over cattle grid on right before bridge, down drive.

Tom & Helen Cotterell
The Salmon,
Bridge Sollers,
Herefordshire HR4 7JH
tel   01981 590605
fax   01981 590605
e-mail helencotterell@easynet.co.uk

HEREFORDSHIRE

HEREFORDSHIRE

Amid acres of ancient pasture with breathtaking views, in countryside where hills are dotted with castles built to defend the English from attacks from the west, the 16th-century house has been sensitively restored. Wattle and daub and stone remain and everything new has been matched with original materials. There's oak above, around and below, then huge comfort with a four-poster or canopied bed, pretty fabrics, good furniture and lovely bathrooms. Open the French windows, sit on the terrace and watch the evening sun drop behind the Black Mountains. Locally-smoked kippers for breakfast if you want. *Children over 10 welcome*

An ecclesiastic entrance hall sweeps you into this imposing former Victorian vicarage built for a 'gentleman' priest. The stunning carved staircase leads to a galleried landing where light and well-proportioned bedrooms have been well and traditionally decorated. You'll find period furniture, good fabrics and attractive, plain colours. The Gallimores enjoy entertaining and there's a sitting room for guests to relax in; there's also a super garden with Wellingtonia, potager and hedges of laurel and yew. Come for peace and elegance in a rural setting – and exceptional views to Hay and the Radnor Hills.

rooms	3: 1 four-poster, with shower; 1 double, 1 twin, sharing bath (let to members of same party).
room price	£50-£60. Singles from £25.
meals	Dinner from £16.
closed	Rarely.
directions	Leave A465 just before Wormbridge towards Orcop; right at T-junction, pass 3 bungalows on left; left by old stone barn into farmyard; on for 300 yds to house.

rooms	2: 1 double with bath & shower; 1 twin with private bath/shower.
room price	From £50. Singles by arrangement.
meals	Breakfast until 9.30am. Dinner from £18.50. Packed lunch from £3.50. Pub 5 miles.
closed	Christmas.
directions	A438 from Hereford, A480 to Stretton Sugwas. After 10 miles from Hereford, left to Norton Wood & church. House 1st on right.

Charles & Sarah Drury
Skyrrid Farm,
Pontrilas, Hereford,
Herefordshire HR2 0BW

tel	01981 240367
fax	01981 240327
e-mail	sarahjdrury@amserve.com

Jill & Julian Gallimore
The Old Vicarage,
Norton Canon, Hereford,
Herefordshire HR4 7BQ

| tel | 01544 318146 |
| e-mail | galli@gallimore.me.uk |

HEREFORDSHIRE

Jamie is a salmon-smoker so breakfast may be even better than you imagined. Eggs are free-range, sausages are local, china is of fine bone, and beds are huge with sheets of Egyptian cotton… comfort at every turn. It is a handsome house slap in the middle of town, a few paces from the town hall and, of course, the cathedral, traditionally furnished and full of kind touches such as a tea tray with organic shortbread and proper coffee. There is no sitting room, but there's so much right on the doorstep that you won't mind.

HERTFORDSHIRE

Old-fashioned roses, pelargoniums, a willow tunnel and 40 thriving varieties of clematis – a horticultural haven amid open fields. Sue, relaxed and friendly, will point you towards rare wildflower sites in this remote spot. Her green fingers have been at work in the pretty conservatory too, where you eat breakfast – local sausages and home-made muffins – surrounded by greenery and memorable views. Bedrooms are cottagey: we liked the double with its white and brass bed. The peachy guest sitting room is elegant and has doors that open onto the garden, and the setting is simply superb.

rooms	2 doubles, both with bath/shower.
room price	From £60. Singles £45.
meals	Packed lunch from £5. Pub/restaurant 5-minute walk.
closed	Rarely.
directions	In centre of Hereford, beside Town Hall in St Owen Street, on right-hand side. More detailed instructions given on booking.

rooms	3: 1 double with shower; 1 twin, 1 single, both with private bath.
room price	From £55. Singles from £35.
meals	Pub 0.5 miles.
closed	Christmas & New Year.
directions	South on A413 from Wendover. Pass Jet station, left to Kings Ash. 2 miles on, left at x-roads to Old Swan pub. Pass pub. 0.5 miles on, ignore sharp right, but go sharp left onto bridlepath. 2nd gate along.

Jamie & Elizabeth Forbes
Montgomery House,
12 St Owen Street, Hereford,
Herefordshire HR1 2PL

tel	01432 351454
fax	01432 344463
e-mail	lizforbes@lineone.net
web	www.montgomeryhousehereford.com

Mike & Sue Jepson
Field Cottage,
St Leonards, Nr Tring,
Hertfordshire HP23 6NS

tel	01494 837602
fax	01494 837137
e-mail	michael.jepson@lineone.net

Lutyens built this wonderful 1901 house for his mother-in-law, Lady Lytton. It is set down a long drive in six acres of beautiful gardens and fields, and each elevation is different. Architectural peculiarities — such as internal, octagonal windows — abound, and Samantha has applied her considerable artistic skills to the interior. The downstairs rooms are particularly elegant and formal. Unusual colour schemes offset magnificent antiques, tapestries and chinoiserie. The family are happy to share their home, can converse in a clutch of languages and will book tables and taxis if required.

A handsome Grade II-listed rectory in the village where George Bernard Shaw lived — his house is now owned by the National Trust. Relax on the sun-drenched terrace for breakfast or settle by the log fire in the 17th-century dining room. The bedrooms are reached through a flower-filled, cobbled courtyard and there's an ivy-clad squash court in the garden. Helen and Dick are kind and relaxed; they will tell you of wonderful walks and bike rides and introduce you to their enchanting local inn. You'd never guess you were only 35 minutes from London. *Children by arrangement.*

rooms	3: 1 double with shower; 1 family suite (1 double, 1 twin) with bath; 1 double with private shower sometimes available.
room price	£70. Singles £45. Family suite £70–£100.
meals	Breakfast from 7.15am. Pub 15-minute drive.
closed	20 December–3 January.
directions	Into Knebworth on B197, turn into Station Rd which becomes Park Lane. 300 yds after crossing m'way bridge, left into public footpath. After 300 yds, bear left through lodge gates. House at end.

rooms	3 twins/doubles all with bath.
room price	£85. Singles by arrangement.
meals	Light supper trays or dinner, £8–£20.
closed	Christmas.
directions	Exit A1 at junc. 4. Follow signs to B653, towards Wheathamstead. At r'bout on to B653; 1st right for Codicote & Ayot St Lawrence. Left up Bride Hall Lane, signed Shaws Corner. Right into drive before red phone box in village.

Samantha Pollock-Hill
Homewood,
Knebworth, Hertfordshire SG3 6PP
tel   01438 812105
fax   01438 812572
e-mail   sami@pollock-hill.fsnet.co.uk
web   www.homewood-bb.co.uk

Helen & Dick Dunn
The Old Rectory,
Ayot St Lawrence, Welwyn,
Hertfordshire AL6 9BT
tel   01438 820429
fax   01438 821844
e-mail   ayotbandb@aol.com

map: 10 entry: 255

map: 10 entry: 256

ISLE OF WIGHT

The Harrisons bought this glorious Jacobean house for its matchless gardens: 15 acres of pathed terraced gardens, exotica and subtropical flowers. The house is magnificent with 80 rooms; large and comfortable bedrooms are in two wings. The library houses a full-size snooker table (yes, you may use it) and the vast music room a grand piano (yours to play). The dining room has separate tables and delightful Nina Campbell wallpaper. Step back in time – in a quiet, untouristy village in lovely downland this massive house, very much a family home, has softly-spoken, intelligent hosts and acres of space.

rooms	6: 3 doubles, 3 twins, all with bath/shower, in two separate wings.
room price	£54-£65. Singles £37-£45.
meals	Breakfast 8-9.15am. Light meals sometimes available. Pub 3-minute walk through gardens.
closed	Christmas.
directions	From Newport, drive into Shorwell, down a steep hill, under a rustic bridge & right opp. thatched cottage. Signed.

John & Christine Harrison
North Court,
Shorwell, Isle of Wight PO30 3JG
tel   01983 740415
fax   01983 740409
e-mail   bbb@northcourt.info
web   www.northcourt.info

map: 4 entry: 257

ISLE OF WIGHT

Ancient peace – miles from the beaten track, bordered by beautiful stone barns – and stylishness too. There's a refreshing simplicity to this unique 'first-floor' Saxon house where living space was above and downstairs was reserved for storage. Bedrooms are stunning with limewashed walls, polished wooden floors, A-frame beams and sofas; one is up a steep open stairs. You sleep on a French rosewood bed, and there's a huge cast-iron bath in each room – wallow by candlelight with a glass of wine. The secluded garden bursts with shrubs and magnificent fruit trees; breakfasts include smoked salmon and smoothies – superb.

rooms	2: 1 double with bath; 1 double with bath/shower.
room price	£60-£80. Singles by arrangement.
meals	Good pub 1.5 mile.
closed	Rarely.
directions	0.5 miles south of Chale Green on B3399; after village, left at Gotten Lane; house at end of lane.

Caroline Smith
Gotten Manor,
Gotten Lane, Chale,
Isle of Wight PO38 2HQ
tel   01983 551368
fax   0870 1369453
e-mail   b&b@gottenmanor.co.uk
web   www.gottenmanor.co.uk

map: 4 entry: 258

ISLE OF WIGHT

French windows look centrally onto the sheltered garden making it feel like an extra room. Then the lawns fall away as sea views to the south rise up. An infinity garden! It's one of the warmest spots in the UK and plant life revels in the knowledge that the north winds never make it to this clearing in the cliff. The house is small but big on comfort: huge brass bed, power shower and table set just for you in the slate-floored conservatory. Your hosts are easy going, artistic and generous. Scramble on the multi-coloured cliffs, explore the coves, delight in the Ventnor Botanical Gardens.

rooms	1 double with private bath/shower.
room price	£53. Singles £30.
meals	Breakfast until 9.30am. Dinner from £12.50.
closed	Christmas & New Year.
directions	Leave Ventor on A3055 westwards. Past St Lawrence Inn & 1st left into Old Park Rd. 1st right into Hunts Rd (private road); entrance halfway along on right.

Ann Godfrey-Faussett
Hillside Cottage,
The Under Cliff, St Lawrence,
Isle of Wight PO38 1XX
tel   01983 853141

KENT

Sue is a gifted garden designer and bursting with ideas for making her three acres even more special: this year she is creating a 'planet' garden with sparkling surprises. Not many gardens have mown worples to tread: the ancient, wave-like ridge-and-furrows are a most unusual feature in Kent. All the rooms in this wonderfully traditional house are light, airy and comfortable, towels are soft, colours restful and the rooms that share the bathroom have bucolic views. Play tennis or croquet; stroll into historic Westerham. Sue, full of fun and sparkle, knows how to spoil.

rooms	3: 1 twin, 1 double, both with basin, sharing bath; 1 double with private bath.
room price	£50. Singles £40.
meals	Breakfast 7-9am or by arrangement. Excellent places for dinner nearby.
closed	Rarely.
directions	From M25 junc. 6 to Westerham (A25). After town sign & 30mph sign, 1st left into Farley Lane. After approx. 200 yds, left at top, then left again.

Sue & Alastair Marr
Worples Field,
Farley Common, Westerham,
Kent TN16 1UB
tel   01959 562869
e-mail   marr@worplesfield.com
web   www.worplesfield.com

KENT

The 1750 brick farmhouse is home to a charming family – you'll love it here. Guests share a beamed sitting room in the old Bake House with piano and TV. Ample bedrooms are simple but fresh, with country views; one is a feast of oak beams, another has its own stair. Nicholas and Ginny enjoy the buzz of guest company – but understand the need for privacy too. Make the most of their knowledge of the historic houses and gardens of Kent: much lies within a 20-minute drive. Breakfast is a happy affair with heaps of home-made bread and free-range eggs and you can come and go as you please.

rooms	3: 1 twin with shower; 1 twin with bath; 1 twin with private bath.
room price	£50. Singles £35.
meals	Breakfast 7.30-9.30am. Excellent pub 5 minutes' walk.
closed	Christmas Day & very occasionally.
directions	B2027 0.5 miles north of Chiddingstone Causeway. Equidistant between Tonbridge, Sevenoaks & Edenbridge.

Nicholas & Ginny Morris
Charcott Farmhouse,
Charcott, Leigh, Tonbridge,
Kent TN11 8LG
tel   01892 870024
fax   01892 870158
e-mail   nicholasmorris@charcott.freeserve.co.uk

map: 5 entry: 261

KENT

The Wettons are smiley and easy, and their house enchanting. The small manor in this beautiful conservation village was built in the 1600s by a wealthy wool merchant as a place for storage and display. It's a delightfully artistic, beamed home whose character and architectural details have survived intact. Bedrooms are charming, simply furnished with slopey ceilings. A grand piano, an open fire and heaps of books in the guests' drawing room, a flower-filled conservatory for breakfast and a country garden to explore. The resident alpacas do most of the 'mowing'. *Self-catering available. See back of book.*

rooms	3: 1 twin with bath; 1 twin with bath/shower; 1 double with shower.
room price	£56-£66. Singles £28-£33.
meals	Restaurants 2-5 miles.
closed	Christmas & New Year.
directions	A229 Maidstone/Hastings. At lights at Linton x-roads, turn for Coxheath & through village. 1st left down Hunton Hill. Pass church, park & school, then right into Grove Lane.

Gavin & Anne Wetton
The Woolhouse,
Grove Lane, Hunton,
Kent ME15 0SE
tel   01622 820778
fax   01622 820645
web   www.wetton.info

map: 6 entry: 262

Fresh raspberries for breakfast at this 200-acre fruit farm in the Kentish Weald. Antonia and Brian are elegant hosts with a lively sense of humour and a Grade II-listed house. Painted in warm colours, filled with portraits and family antiques, it is a wonderfully comfortable place to stay. Your bedrooms are in their own wing: a twin, deliciously cosy; a double with an extra room for a child and views onto paddock and fields. There are dogs, chickens, a tennis court and a pool, and the apple blossom is a joy in spring. Two minutes from a good pub, 20 from Sissinghurst, and not much further for a trip to France.

Annie goes the extra mile – breakfasts, especially, are a treat and the extras are home-made compotes and jams, locally-baked croissants and brioches. It's friendly, fun and informal and the Parkers have a good sense of humour and hospitality. The bedrooms in this Edwardian house are in the low, more modern wing with easy garden access; both are light and bright and there are treats on the tea tray. The drawing room where you have breakfast was once the house library. It's a splendid room, huge, with ribbon-and-wreath cornicing and a panelled ceiling. *Children over five welcome.*

rooms	2: 1 twin with bath; 1 twin/double with private bath/shower.
room price	From £56. Singles £28.
meals	Pub 15-minute walk.
closed	Christmas & New Year.
directions	From Maidstone, A229 towards Hastings. After 4.5 miles, right at lights onto B2163 Coxheath. After 0.5 miles, drive on left; house at top of drive.

rooms	2: 1 double with private bath; 1 twin with shower.
room price	From £60. Singles from £40.
meals	Good pubs within 2-mile radius.
closed	Christmas & New Year.
directions	A262 to Goudhurst. There, B2079 to Marden. House 2 miles from village, on left.

Brian & Antonia Allfrey
Clock House,
Linton, Maidstone, Kent ME17 4PG
tel   01622 743679
fax   01622 743899
e–mail   antonia@allfrey.net

Annie Parker
West Winchet,
Winchet Hill, Goudhurst, Cranbrook,
Kent TN17 1JX
tel   01580 212024
fax   01580 212250
e–mail   jeremyparker@jpa-ltd.co.uk

KENT

The exterior is remarkable: history, ancient beauty and stunning architecture combine. The house twists, turns, rises and falls, its old stone and wood captivates. It is part-Edwardian, part-Tudor and the Streatfeilds have been in Chiddingstone for centuries, but carry their history lightly. Bedrooms, huge, have a hotchpotch of furniture; one, with bunks, cot and toys would be great for families. Views are wonderful – over the gardens to grazing sheep and hills. In May the sight and scent of the wild azalea garden are intoxicating. *Minimum stay two nights at weekends.*

rooms	3: 1 twin, 1 family, sharing bath; 1 double with private bath.
room price	£55–£60. Singles £30–£40.
meals	Breakfast 7-9am. Light supper & dinner £12.50–£20.
closed	Christmas & New Year.
directions	From A21, Hildenborough exit. Follow signs to Penshurst Place, then to vineyard. Pass it. Right at T-junc. for Edenbridge. Through village, bear left, for Edenbridge. House 0.5 miles on left.

Mr & Mrs Mervyn Streatfeild
Hoath House,
Chiddingstone Hoath,
Nr Edenbridge, Kent TN8 7DB
tel	01342 850362
fax	01342 841066
e-mail	jstreatfeild@hoath-house.freeserve.co.uk

KENT

A proper country house: 16th century and listed, it is full of aromatic log fires and beams to duck. A small flock of sheep and two horses graze the 20 acres; there are dogs, cats and chickens too (and fresh eggs for breakfast). Such entertaining hosts... the Carrells' children were raised and married from here and happy family vibes remain. Bedrooms are light and airy with pastel colours, floral curtains and fresh flowers. You can use the drawing room, and there's a terrace for tea. Carolyn is a mine of information on historic houses in which this lovely area abounds. Great value. *Children over 10 welcome.*

rooms	3: 1 twin with private bath; 2 singles, both with basins, sharing bath & wc.
room price	£50–£56. Singles £27.50–£30.
meals	2 pubs in village, 1 mile.
closed	November-March.
directions	4 miles south of Tunbridge Wells on A267. 1 mile south of Frant, on left. Sign on fence at bottom of drive.

Mrs Carolyn Carrell
Rowden House Farm,
Frant, Tunbridge Wells,
Kent TN3 9HS
| tel | 01892 750259 |

The views from the doorstep are glorious – you won't want to move. There's neither road nor railway line within sight of this working farm, which has been in the family since the year dot – 900, to be exact. Its exterior is handsome and imposing while, inside, comfort and elegance go hand-in-hand. Dining and drawing rooms have high ceilings and beautiful mahogany furniture. Rosemary, kindness itself, looks after guests well, and everyone comments on the peacefulness. Bedrooms – huge, light, unfussy – have large bathrooms to match… and those views!

You are right on Romney Marsh which begs to be explored. A pretty home: roses and climbers decorate the pink and blue brickwork, and gabled windows look onto the marsh. Inside is homely: books, paintings, photos, two little dogs… the garden is peaceful with birdsong. The double bedroom has pink and white *fleur-de-lys* wallpaper while the secluded stable twin is very popular with guests: it's private with its own terrace and sitting room. Adele is lovely – warm and down-to-earth and you can come and go as you like. *Children over 10 welcome.*

rooms	3: 1 twin with bath; 1 twin, 1 double, both with private bath.
room price	£55-£64. Singles by arrangement.
meals	Breakfast until 9am; until 9.30am Sun. Dinner from £12.50.
closed	December-January.
directions	At lights in centre of Hawkhurst, A268 for Rye. 1.5 miles after lights, first turning on right, then immed. right into Conghurst Lane. Driveway signed after 1.25 miles on left.

rooms	3: 1 twin in stable with sitting room & bath; 1 double with bath; 1 twin with private bath.
room price	£50-£70. Singles from £30.
meals	Excellent pub 1.5 miles.
closed	Rarely.
directions	M20, exit 10 for Brenzett. A2070 for approx. 6 miles. Right for Hamstreet, & immed. left. In Hamstreet, right onto B2067, left for Warehorne church. Through Warehorne to level crossing. House 1 mile on, on right.

Rosemary Piper
Conghurst Farm,
Hawkhurst, Kent TN18 4RW
tel   01580 753331
fax   01580 754579
e-mail   rosa@conghurst.co.uk

Adele Sherston
Terry House,
Warehorne, Ashford, Kent TN26 2LS
tel   01233 732443
fax   01233 732443
e-mail   jsherston@ukonline.co.uk

Lord (Bob) Boothby once occupied the timber-framed Wealden house; the snug double above the study was his bedroom. So robust is the building that it survived intact when it slid 50 feet down the escarpment in a dramatic subsidence in 1726. A striking entrance leads straight to the huge sitting room, with massive fireplace and panelled oak staircase. Everywhere 18th- and 19th-century paintings gaze down (some are for sale). Bedrooms are suitably simple and all have 40-gallon iron bathtubs and panoramic views. On a fine day you can see France; the Shuttle terminal and Dover are only minutes away: perfect for wine runs.

Not only are you in the depths of the country but you feel wonderfully private too: your ground-floor bedroom is reached via a corner of the garden all your own. Step past greenery to the breakfast room, cosy with old pine table, dresser and flowers, for your bacon and eggs; if you don't feel like emerging Sarah will happily bring breakfast to your room. You can eat dinner here, too. This is a good stopover point for the Channel – and you're no more than a 15-minute drive from Canterbury and its glorious cathedral. *Babies welcome.*

rooms	3: 2 doubles, both with bath/shower, 1 with adjoining twin for children.
room price	£60. Singles £35.
meals	Breakfast until 9.30am. Restaurants 10 minutes' drive.
closed	Christmas & New Year.
directions	From M20 at junc. 11, A20 south, then B2068 (Stone St), to Lympne. Approx. 0.25 miles on is County Members pub, & school sign on right. Left opp. convex mirror. House at end of lane.

rooms	1 double with bath/shower.
room price	£60. Singles £30.
meals	Breakfast until 9.30am. Packed lunch £5. Dinner, 3 courses, £20.
closed	Rarely.
directions	From A2, 2nd exit to Canterbury. Follow ring road & B2068 for Hythe. Over A2, through Lower Hardres, past Granville pub. Right for Petham & Waltham. 1.5 miles after Waltham, right into Hassell Street. 4th on left.

Peter & Matty Gaston
The French House,
Lympne, Nr Hythe, Kent CT21 4PA
tel   01303 265974
fax   01303 262545
e-mail   gastons@frenchhouse.freeserve.co.uk
web   www.frenchhouse.freeserve.co.uk

Sarah Rainbird
Woodmans,
Hassell Street, Hastingleigh,
Nr Ashford, Kent TN25 5JE
tel   01233 750250

The Lathams are well-travelled, friendly and active, yet firmly attached to their home and its surrounding 200 acres. The house has an interesting mix of styles: Tudor, Georgian and modern co-exist in harmony. High ceilings and a conservatory with terracotta-tiled floor, brimming with greenery, conjure up images of the decadent Twenties. You'll find good furniture, yet the house is homely; bedrooms are comfortable with traditional bathrooms. Guests have their own log-fired drawing room with wonderful views of all that countryside. Only 10 minutes from the Chunnel. *Children over 10 welcome.*

Peter and Mary make a happy team and their conversation is informed and easy. Anthony Eden stayed here during the Second World War to be close to the Channel defences; today you may stay for Chunnel convenience. Downstairs are many beams, large leather Chesterfield sofas, a polished dining table, wooden floors. And there's much magic outside: a wisteria-smothered façade, a croquet lawn, a tennis court and sheep happy to keep the field clipped. Food is excellent. And the bedrooms? One has a Delft-tiled fireplace, one is half-timbered, and the single has a wonderful pink marble sink.

rooms	3: 2 twins, both with bath/shower; 1 double sharing bath/shower, only let to same party.
room price	From £55. Singles £35.
meals	Breakfast until 9.30am. Dinner £20–£25.
closed	Christmas & New Year.
directions	From M20 junc. 11, B2068 north. After 4.6 miles, left opp. Jet garage. House at bottom of hill on left, after 1.7 miles. Left into drive.

rooms	3: 1 double, 1 single, both with bath/shower; 1 twin, with private bath/shower.
room price	£54–£60. Singles £30.
meals	Dinner £20. Good pubs & restaurants 1 mile.
closed	Christmas.
directions	A2 Canterbury to Dover road; Barham exit. Through Barham to Elham. After Elham sign 1st right signed Park Gate 0.75 miles. Over brow of hill; house on left.

Richard & Virginia Latham
Stowting Hill House,
Stowting, Nr Ashford,
Kent TN25 6BE
tel   01303 862881
fax   01303 863433
e-mail   vjlatham@hotmail.com

Peter & Mary Morgan
Park Gate,
Elham, Nr Canterbury,
Kent CT4 6NE
tel   01303 840304
fax   01227 450498

map: 6 entry: 271

map: 6 entry: 272

Rolling hills and woodland, long views over luscious Kent and a lovely garden that Alison has created herself. This is a modern bungalow, a rare phenomenon in this book, a Scandia house built from a Swedish kit. It is brilliant for wheelchair users and altogether easy and comfortable to be in, with floral-covered sofas and chairs and plain reproduction furniture. Alison is sweet, very much a 'coper' who once lived here with her disabled father. The house is so close to Dover that it is worth staying the night before embarking on the ferry fray.

An unusually stylish revival of a Georgian country house. Three perfect cushions on a bamboo bed, an immaculate shower with a stone-mosaic floor, a rococo mirror on a Regency wall… Yet the mood is down-to-earth, and your hosts brim with warmth and good humour. Wooden-floored rooms are chic and serene, embellished with contemporary art and oriental touches; those at the front have stunning views to hills and valley. Madeleine cooks beautifully: be sustained by Whitstable fish and all that the Garden of England has to offer. *Children under 5 free, sharing parents' room.*

rooms	2: 1 double with bath/shower; 1 twin with private bath/shower.
room price	£70. Singles £35.
meals	Dinner occasionally available. Pubs within walking distance.
closed	Christmas.
directions	From A2 Canterbury-Dover, Barham & Kingston sign. Right at bottom of hill by bus shelter, into The Street, Kingston to top of hill & right fork. 1st left on sharp right bend. 100 yds left into farm keeping right of barn.

rooms	4 doubles, all with shower.
room price	£90. Singles £60.
meals	Dinner, 3 courses, £23.95.
closed	Rarely.
directions	A2 towards Dover; turn off Barham; there, past Black Robin Pub; first left; 500 yds on, past 3 houses, drive on right.

Alison Crawley
Hornbeams,
Jesses Hill, Kingston, Canterbury,
Kent CT4 6JD
tel   01227 830119
fax   01227 830119
e-mail   alison@hornbeams.co.uk
web   www.hornbeams.co.uk

Madeleine & Philip Edwards
Elmstone Court,
Out Elmstead lane, Barham,
Kent CT4 6PH
tel   01227 830433
fax   01227 832403
e-mail   enquiries@elmstonecourt.com
web   www.elmstonecourt.com

Charming, compact, this Regency house was built by a Sandwich brewer of ginger beer. Katie has decorated, sponged and stencilled to perfection; the rooms are gorgeous, spotless, dotted with much-loved antiques, fresh with flowers. Bathrooms are warm and well-equipped; one big, cast-iron bath has great taps that fill it in seconds. There are rare and spectacular oriental plane trees on either side of the main gate and stunning hedges and lawns. The area hums with history and Katie and Neil – who runs an Audio Book Library from the converted stables – are enchanting. *Children over eight welcome.*

The value is terrific and the feel is of a busy family home; Jac and Chris work, but nevertheless manage guests with helpful efficiency. Jac can drive you into Canterbury, babysit and prepare simple suppers. There's a guest sitting room and you feel private in your bit of the house. Chris, an umpire, runs a hockey and cricket shop and the two grown-up boys play county/national level sport. Breakfasts, cooked by Chris, are very good, bedrooms are spotless and fresh with floral borders, and bathrooms are modern. *Bookings not accepted from smokers.*

rooms	2 twins/doubles, both with bath/shower.
room price	£85. Singles £57.50.
meals	Dinner £27.50. Light suppers on request.
closed	Christmas & New Year.
directions	From Canterbury A257 for Sandwich. On approach to Ash, stay on A257 (do not enter village), then 3rd left at sign to Weddington. House 200 yds down on left.

rooms	3: 1 double, 1 twin/double, both with shower; 1 double with adjoining twin, with bath, only let to same party.
room price	From £45. Singles by arrangement. Children £5-£15.
meals	Breakfast until 9am; until noon weekends & holidays. Lunch £5. Dinner £10.
closed	Rarely.
directions	From M20 exit 11, B2068 for Canterbury. After crossing A2, house, with postbox in wall, is 100 yds on right. (Head for county cricket ground to phone if lost.)

Katie & Neil Gunn
Great Weddington,
Ash, Nr Canterbury, Kent CT3 2AR
tel   01304 813407
fax   01304 812531
e-mail   traveltale@aol.com
web   www.greatweddington.co.uk

Chris & Jac Bray
Sylvan Cottage,
Nackington Road, Canterbury,
Kent CT4 7AY
tel   01227 765307
e-mail   jac@sylvan5.fsnet.co.uk

All is reassuringly traditional and peaceful in this lovely corner of Kent. The small Georgian house next to the huge mulberry tree has extremely neat outer and walled gardens with fine delphiniums and climbing roses, and well-travelled hosts who clearly care about their guests. Cosy, comfortable bedrooms with touches of chintz and frill and the most inviting beds; a handsome, formal dining room; beamed ceilings, antiques, plump sofas, gilt-framed portraits and pretty flower arrangements set the scene. Golf at Royal St George's and other courses can be arranged. *10 minutes from Canterbury, 30 from ferries and tunnel.*

Eight immaculate acres of garden with pond, obelisk and orchards. Magnificent views, too – this is an AONB – and a very pretty indoor pool that is heated all year round. The house is large, traditional, luxurious. Bold fabrics and vividly coloured walls make a fine background for antiques; a Chinese carpet and oriental pictures hang in the hall. There's a music room with an organ, too: Markham occasionally gives concerts for charity and you are welcome to attend. He and Susan enjoy meeting new people and are lovely hosts. Canterbury and Leeds Castle are easily reached.

rooms	2: 1 double with shower; 1 twin with bath.
room price	£70. Singles £43.50.
meals	Dinner occasionally. Pubs & restaurants nearby.
closed	Christmas & Easter.
directions	A28 Canterbury to Ashford. Left to Shalmsford Street; right imm. after Post Office at Bobbin Lodge Hill. Road bends left, then turn right at T-junc.; 2nd drive on left by Mystole Lane sign.

rooms	3: 1 double, 1 twin, 1 four-poster, all with shower.
room price	£64-£70. Singles £38-£41.
meals	Breakfast until 9.15am. Dinner, 2 courses, £17.50.
closed	Christmas.
directions	From A2 at Faversham, Brogdale road to Eastling. 1.5 miles past Carpenters Arms, right (by postbox). House 0.5 miles on right.

Hugh & Patricia Tennent
Little Mystole,
Mystole Park, Canterbury,
Kent CT4 7DB
tel 01227 738210
fax 01227 738210
e-mail little_mystole@yahoo.co.uk

Susan & Markham Chesterfield
Frith Farm House,
Otterden, Faversham,
Kent ME13 0DD
tel 01795 890701
fax 01795 890009
e-mail enquiries@frithfarmhouse.co.uk
web www.frithfarmhouse.co.uk

This listed dower house has two winding stairs: two Tudor cottages were joined to make one. Amanda enthuses about art history and her rare-breed hens… your breakfast eggs are the best. There's good local produce for dinner, too, served in the dining room on polished mahogany. Bedrooms have patterned fabrics, firm beds and flowers, bathrooms are delightful – one heavily beamed with a claw-foot bath, the other blue-and-white-tiled. Ancient trees in the walled garden, orchards and fields all around, and Doddington Place with its gardens (and opera in summer) a five-minute drive. *Children over four welcome*

This beautiful, porticoed, brick house has a gorgeous drawing room, fabulous antiques and family portraits. There's a secret garden within the grounds and an arbour and a pond. The large front bedroom is tremendous, more like a suite, with good furniture, fine views and an open fire in winter – a rare treat. Bathrooms have towelling robes, shower caps and other comforts. John is unflappable and a touch mischievous, Gillian welcomes you with well-judged humour and easy charm – you'll like them. *Children over 12 welcome.*

rooms	2: 1 double with private bath; 1 twin with bath.
room price	£65–£75. Singles £40.
meals	Breakfast until 9.30am. Light snacks £7.50. Dinner, 3 courses, £20.
closed	Rarely.
directions	M20 junc. 8, then east on A20; left in Lenham towards Doddington. At The Chequers in Doddington, left; house 1.7 miles on left before Lynsted.

rooms	3: 1 double with bath; 2 doubles, both with private bath.
room price	From £70. Singles £40.
meals	Breakfast until noon. Dinner £25.
closed	Christmas & New Year.
directions	From Dover, M2 to Medway Services. Into station, on past pumps. Ignore exit signs. Left at T-junc., 1st left & on for 2 miles. Left at next T-junc. House 3rd on left.

	Amanda Strevens
	Dadmans,
	Lynsted, Sittingbourne,
	Kent ME9 0JJ
tel	01795 521293
e–mail	amanda.strevens@btopenworld.com

	Gillian & John Yerburgh
	Hartlip Place,
	Place Lane, Nr Sittingbourne,
	Kent ME9 7TR
tel	01795 842583
fax	01795 842763
e–mail	jyerburgh@aol.com

LANCASHIRE

Wild deer roam – this is the Ribble Valley, an AONB that feels like a time-locked land. In this former 18th-century tithe barn, where old church rafters support the guest sitting room, you settle in among plump sofas and antiques. Guest bedrooms and sitting room are on the top floor, so have a private feel; bathrooms are huge. The Smiths couldn't be more helpful and breakfast is a feast: jams and muesli are home-made, stewed fruits are from the lovely gardens. Step outside to see Jean's creation – she transformed a field into a riot of colour and scent; a stream meanders through conifers and lawn and water lilies bask in still pools.

rooms	3: 1 double with bath/shower; 1 double with private bath; 1 twin/double with shower.
room price	From £52. Singles £32.
meals	Breakfast 7-9.30am. Good restaurants 1.5 miles.
closed	Christmas & New Year.
directions	M6 junc. 31, A59 to Skipton, left to Clitheroe. Through Clitheroe & Waddington, on for 0.5 miles, left along Cross Lane. 0.75 miles on, past Colthurst Hall, house on left.

Jean & Gordon Smith
Peter Barn Country House,
Cross Lane/Rabbit Lane,
Waddington, Clitheroe,
Lancashire BB7 3JH

| tel | 01200 428585 |
| e-mail | jean@peterbarn.co.uk |

map: 13 entry: 281

LEICESTERSHIRE

Passing traffic is less frequent than passing horses. The lasting impression of this 17th-century cottage is of lightness and brightness; the house is filled with laughter and the Cowdells are terrific hosts. There's a fine collection of paintings and furniture, double oak doors lead from the dining room to the guest sitting room. Bedrooms are restful and fresh; one has three-way views. The garden was designed by Bunny Guinness, the stables accommodate up to six horses and the village of Grimston is delightful. An excellent base if travelling from East Midlands airport.

rooms	3: 1 twin/double with bath & extra single bed; 1 twin/double with shower; 1 ground-floor family with bath & shower.
room price	From £45. Singles £27.50.
meals	Packed lunch £3. Good pub 100 yds.
closed	Rarely.
directions	From A46 Newark-Leicester, onto B676 for Melton. At staggered x-roads, straight for Grimston. 1 mile on, right to Grimston. There, up hill, past church. House on left, just after right-hand bend at top.

Mr & Mrs R L Cowdell
The Gorse House,
33, Main Street, Grimston,
Melton Mowbray,
Leicestershire LE14 3BZ

tel	01664 813537
fax	01664 813537
e-mail	cowdell@gorsehouse.co.uk
web	www.gorsehouse.co.uk

map: 10 entry: 282

LEICESTERSHIRE

There's something to delight everyone at this 1860 traditional farmhouse: a games room for the children, an indoor pool, a newly-laid tennis court, a pond to picnic by, 850 acres to roam and stabling for your horse. Luxurious bathrooms encourage hot soaks, big, comfortable bedrooms have sweeping views. The house is an Aladdin's cave of special things: antique clocks, oriental rugs, tapestry cushions, rich drapes, paintings old and new. Nicky splits her time between Market Harborough and London, leaving her efficient housekeeper to look after you. *Children over 12 welcome.*

rooms	3: 1 double with bath & shower; 1 twin with private bath; 1 double with bath.
room price	£60–£70. Singles £30.
meals	Pubs/restaurants nearby.
closed	Rarely.
directions	From A427 (Market Harborough to Corby) follow sign for East Carlton. House last on left in village.

Nicky Chaplin
Littlefield Farm,
East Carlton, Market Harborough,
Leicestershire LE16 8YA
tel   07860 201395
fax   0207 228 1009

LINCOLNSHIRE

The chaps who serviced Model T-4s here in the 1920s would be amazed at the transformation: the 1760s cottage with its limestone extension is awash with comfort. Family memorabilia in the sitting room, a piano in the dining room, and floral themes in the bedrooms with their brand new beds and pristine tiled bathrooms. Veronica, who couldn't be more helpful and is happy to chat, grows fruit and vegetables for the table; in winter Bob can arrange hunting and beagling parties followed by candle-lit dinner. Two acres of paddock are home to the providers of breakfast eggs, and the fenced-off lawn is perfect for small children.

rooms	3: 1 double with shower; 1 twin with extra sofabed with bath & shower; 1 twin with private bath.
room price	£50–£65. Singles £35.
meals	Dinner, 2–3 courses, £15–£20, by arrangement. Pub within walking distance.
closed	Rarely.
directions	A1 exit South Witham & continue for 0.75 miles. Second cottage on left-hand side.

Veronica & Bob Van Kimmenade
Rose Cottage,
7 High Street, South Witham,
Lincolnshire NG33 5QB
tel   01572 767757
fax   01572 767199
e-mail   veronica@rosecottage-southwitham.co.uk
web   www.rosecottage-southwitham.co.uk

Drift off to sleep on a cloud of rose scent: Ozric makes the only genuine English rose oil and water, distilled here in an outbuilding. Outside your bedroom: three and a half acres of roses – magical. The house is full of intriguing features such as two boat-shaped windows that open onto the garden and a vast studio/sitting room built in the 1900s by Gardner of the RA, filled with paintings and African carvings. There are some fearsome fish on the Portuguese tiles around the claw-footed bath, but Ozric and Chantal are extremely friendly and warm.

Simon and Jane have created a series of soft and restful spaces in their brand-new sympathetic barn conversion. Old beams marry well with new walls, floors, windows and pine. A large, brick-flanked fireplace promises a glowing welcome in winter, French windows pull in the light, sitting and dining rooms are huge. The double bedroom is bright and roomy and looks onto sheep-dotted fields; the single, with a crisp, modern feel, is more separate. The gentle Wrights, new to B&B, have farmed for 30 years and give you home-made sausages for breakfast and eggs from Legbar hens.

rooms	3: 1 double with bath; 1 twin, 1 double, both with private shower.
room price	From £60. Singles £35.
meals	Pub/restaurant 1 mile.
closed	Christmas & New Year.
directions	From Bourne, A15 north for Sleaford, 1st hamlet on left signed to Cawthorpe. House last on right before road becomes track.

rooms	2: 1 twin/double with shower; 1 single with private bath/shower.
room price	£50. Singles £25.
meals	Supper, 2 courses, £12.50. Dinner, 3 courses, £20.
closed	Rarely.
directions	Midway between Lincoln & Peterborough. A15 through Folkingham; turn into Spring Lane next to village hall; 200 yds on right.

Ozric & Chantal Armstrong
Cawthorpe Hall,
Bourne, Lincolnshire PE10 0AB
tel   01778 423830
fax   01778 426620
e-mail   bandb@rosewater.co.uk
web   www.rosewater.co.uk

Mrs Jane Wright
The Barn,
Spring Lane, Folkingham,
Lincolnshire NG34 0SJ
tel   01529 497199
fax   01529 497199
e-mail   sjwright@farming.co.uk

LINCOLNSHIRE

LINCOLNSHIRE

Just nine miles from Boston 'Stump' – Britain's largest parish church. Michael, ex-MP, ex-Navy, was active in the quest to illuminate the church's glories at night; you can see it for miles around. The Brothertons are smashing people, interesting and easy; both enjoy cooking and tending their huge fruit and vegetable garden. The impressive Queen Anne vicarage was built in 1707 with local handmade bricks which have mellowed gloriously. The typical square Lincolnshire hall has stone flags leading to a red-pine-panelled staircase. The guest bedrooms is large, light and charming.

The single-storey house was built in the Sixties and its interior has more character than that of many period homes: Bridget is an interior decorator and her talent shows. There's a conservatory feel to the light-filled, stone-floored dining room with its French windows: the garden, a tranquil spot, is absolutely gorgeous in summer. Checked curtains, matching padded headboards and a delightful, gilt-trimmed copy of a Louis XIV chair in the bedroom; a full-height mirror in the bathroom with deep, cast-iron bath. Bridget is charming company and looking after guests comes easily.

rooms	1 double with private bath.
room price	£45–£55. Singles £32.50–£37.50.
meals	Packed lunch £4.50. Dinner with drinks, £24.50.
closed	Christmas & Boxing Day.
directions	Wrangle 9 miles north of Boston on A52. In village follow signs to Angel Inn. House opp. church by War Memorial.

rooms	1 twin with private bath across hall.
room price	£39.50. Singles £30.
meals	Dinner from £14. Excellent pubs/restaurants nearby.
closed	Christmas & New Year.
directions	A607 Grantham to Lincoln road. On reaching Carlton Scroop 1st left for Hough Lane. Last house on left.

Michael & Julia Brotherton
The Old Vicarage,
Wrangle, Boston,
Lincolnshire PE22 9EP

tel	01205 870688
fax	01205 871857
e-mail	jb141@aol.com

Mrs Bridget Hankinson
Churchfield House,
Carlton Scroop, Grantham,
Lincolnshire NG32 3BA

tel	01400 250387
fax	01400 250241
e-mail	bridget@hankinson30.fslife.co.uk

map: 10 entry: 287

map: 10 entry: 288

LINCOLNSHIRE

One guest's summing up reads: "Absolutely perfect – hostess, house, garden and marmalade." Ann loves having people to stay and makes you feel very much at home. You have the run of downstairs: neat and traditionally smart, with elegant family antiques, parquet and chintz, flowers and space. Dreamy views of the gardens and small lake, and divine dinners, too: game casserole, ginger and meringue bombe… Perfect stillness at the base of the Lincolnshire Wolds and a lovely one-mile walk along the line of the old railway that starts from the door. Very special.

rooms	2: 1 twin with shower; 1 double with bath.
room price	£50. Singles by arrangement.
meals	Dinner £15. B.Y.O. Pub 0.75 miles.
closed	Christmas.
directions	From Wragby A157 for Louth. After approx. 2 miles, at triple road sign, right. Red postbox & bus shelter at drive entrance, before graveyard.

Ann Hobbins
The Manor House,
West Barkwith,
Lincolnshire LN8 5LF
tel   01673 858253
fax   01673 858253

LINCOLNSHIRE

Wide open Lincolnshire farmland on the edge of the Wolds – you'll love your bedroom views. This immaculately kept farm has been in the family for five generations and an award-winning farm trail helps you explore. Or maybe you want to watch the sunset by the trout lake… or sink into squashy leather sofas after supper in front of the fire. Sarah is young, energetic and welcoming and brings you delicious home-made cake on arrival. Bedrooms have dark wooden beds; bathrooms are spick and span. Donkeys graze in the paddock in the winter, and your horse is welcome, too.

rooms	2: 1 double with bath; 1 double with shower.
room price	£48. Singles £32.
meals	Packed lunch £5. Supper from £10. Dinner, 3 courses, from £15. B.Y.O. No meals at harvest time.
closed	Christmas & New Year.
directions	Exit A157 in East Barkwith at War Memorial, into Torrington Lane. House 0.75 miles on right after sharp right-hand bend.

Sarah & Jonathan Stamp
The Grange,
Torrington Lane, East Barkwith,
Lincolnshire LN8 5RY
tel   01673 858670
e-mail   jonathanstamp@farmersweekly.net

Don't expect the ordinary – this house is as flamboyant as your hostess. Sally has a natural eye for lush fabrics and rich detail: swathes of curtain in the pretty, lower-ground bedroom; in the one upstairs, an ornate gilt mirror above a white bed (and your private, pink bathroom is down one flight). The yellow drawing room has sliding windows for summer breakfasts *en plein air*; the dining/kitchen room is charming, with blue damask-patterned walls, pink napkins and fresh flowers. Cream carpeting runs warmly throughout. Sally, much-travelled, organises heritage tours of Britain, so is full of ideas.

Just around the corner from the New King's Road, Amanda's home has indisputable comfort, while the attention to detail and her happy way of doing things make the place special. Harrods' jams and pancakes for breakfast, either in the kitchen or the garden; candles everywhere; and Huggy the dog, an erstwhile star of the silver screen, who turned down the movies in the USA and the promise of a chauffeured limousine for the quiet life in Fulham. The downstairs bedroom is lovely: big and bright, warm and airy and excellent for longer stays; the Italian-tiled bathroom just the ticket. *Children over 12 welcome.*

rooms	1 double with bath; 1 double with private bath (downstairs).
room price	£60–£80.
meals	Continental breakfast included; cooked breakfast ocassionally available. Many restaurants nearby.
closed	Rarely.
directions	From Fulham Broadway tube, walk down Harwood Road, directly ahead. At T-junc. right into New Kings Rd. 2nd left into Wandsworth Bridge Rd. No.34 a few houses along on right. (5-minute walk.) Parking 5pm–8am free.

rooms	3: 1 twin/double with bath; 1 twin/double, 1 single, both with private bath.
room price	£80. Singles £55.
meals	Extensive continental breakfast. Good restaurants nearby.
closed	Rarely.
directions	3 mins from Parsons Green tube (District Line, Wimbledon branch). Over green, keeping White Horse on left; Bradbourne St is over King's Rd, ahead. House on left. Parking free 5pm–9am & all Sunday; otherwise Pay & Display.

	Sally Usher
	34 Wandsworth Bridge Road, London SW6 2TH
tel	020 7731 2805
fax	020 7731 2805

	Mrs Amanda Turner
	3 Bradbourne Street, Fulham, London SW6 3TF
tel	020 7736 7284
e-mail	info@luxuryinlondon.clara.co.uk
web	www.luxuryinlondon.co.uk

LONDON

Caroline mixes the sophistication of the city with the human warmth of the countryside and her lovely big kitchen is clearly the engine-room of the house. It leads through to a light breakfast room with doors onto a pretty brick garden with chairs and table – hope for fine days. The house is long and thin – Fulham style – and reaches up to the guest room in the eaves, which needs no more explanation than the picture below. A really warm place to stay in an accessible part of the metropolis. *Near to King's Road antique shops.*

rooms	1 twin/double with shower & private bath.
room price	£80-£90. Singles £75.
meals	Continental breakfast only, 8.30-9.30am Mon-Fri; 8.30-10am Sat & Sun. Pubs/restaurants nearby.
closed	Rarely.
directions	Public transport: 4-minute walk to Parsons Green tube. Parking: £9.60 per day in street.

Caroline Docker
8 Parthenia Road,
Fulham, London SW6 4BD
tel   020 7384 1165
fax   020 7371 8819
e-mail carolined@angelwings.co.uk

LONDON

Rachel is generous and kind and thinks nothing of it. Her house glows warm gold as you enter, courtesy of Osborne & Little on the walls and excellent lighting – the moment you enter you know you've chosen well. Upstairs, an exceptionally pretty double with pink checks, garden views, fresh flowers and a bathroom that sparkles. But the hub of the house is down in the kitchen... relax on the sofa, open the French windows and enjoy the serenity of a small London garden. The street runs down to the Fulham Road and far too many irresistible shops and restaurants. *Children over 10 welcome.*

rooms	2: 1 double with bath/shower; 1 single with private bath.
room price	£75-£85. Singles from £45.
meals	Continental breakfast until 9.30am. Choice of pubs/restaurants within walking distance.
closed	Rarely.
directions	Public transport: 2 minutes from Parsons Green tube (District Line, Wimbledon branch). Bus 14 to Knightsbridge. Parking in street all day (with charge).

Rachel Wilson
29 Winchendon Road,
London SW6 5DH
tel   020 7731 3901
e-mail rachel.k.wilson@talk21.com

The highlight of this Victorian terraced house is its choice of gardens: small but decidedly pretty. One is in the tiny courtyard (marble-topped table, French café chairs), the other at the back of the house (benches and wooden table). In good weather sit surrounded by hostas, ferns or elegant bay tree and breakfast in style: a huge bowl of tropical fruit salad, croissants and yogurt, juice, even smoothies – Margot is from Melbourne. Up a spiral staircase you find a smallish double (pure cotton linen, a quilted throw), a three-quarter bath and views of cherry blossom, clematis and trailing roses.

Charlotte has travelled the world and is full of good advice on making the most out of your stay in London. In the summer you'll breakfast on the roof terrace among the treetops. In winter, breakfast next to the grand piano; twist Charlotte's arm and she'll play a bit of Cole Porter for you. She's generous, too, and gives you your own sitting room with open fire. The bedroom in this 1872 house is smallish but well laid out with William Morris fabrics. Waffle cotton bathrobes, Molton Brown soaps, a lovely library-like bathroom and a deep bath. An easy-going place and a great city find.

rooms	1 double with bath.
room price	£80. Singles £55.
meals	Continental breakfast included. Great restaurants on Fulham Road and King's Road.
closed	Rarely.
directions	Turn left outside West Brompton tube (District Line); cont. 0.75 miles; left into Rylston Rd; Delaford St 1st right. Parking free eves/weekends; otherwise Pay & Display.

rooms	1 double, with private bathroom. Single available on request.
room price	£80; singles £65.
meals	Continental breakfast included. Restaurants - good value to five star - nearby.
closed	Occasionally.
directions	From Fulham Broadway tube, turn right into Effie Road, then right into Barclay road. Parking free 8-89am and all Sunday. 9am-8pm Pay and Display.

Margot Woods
15 Delaford Street,
London SW6 7LT

tel	020 7385 9671
fax	020 7385 9671
e-mail	margotwoods@telco4u.net

Charlotte Dexter
21 Barclay Road,
Fulham, London SW6 1EJ

tel	020 7384 3390
fax	020 7610 6851
e-mail	info@barclayhouselondon.com
web	www.barclayhouselondon.com

A great find – a charming 1857 house at the end of a cul-de-sac just off the Kings Road. It's also one of those London streets where residents paint their houses in pastel colours, thus creating an architectural rainbow. The loveliest shops and restaurants are a step away, yet here birds sing and peace prevails. Perfect. Your bedroom is extremely light, bright and fun with checks and a wrought-iron bed; the shower room is compact and sparkling. You eat continental breakfast in the wooden-floored conservatory, is bathed in morning sun. Richard and Caroline are extremely welcoming and happy to share all the local secrets.

All the personality, charm and individual attention of a private house – in the heart of London, too. But also a huge canopied four-poster bed, telephone, fax and laundry facilities, a great bathroom, and use of the sitting room – deliciously luxurious. Continental breakfast, with newspaper, is excellent, and everything is prepared by Jenny the housekeeper; oranges are freshly squeezed, jams home-made. You will not find better comfort in central London at these prices, and Pimlico is charming. *Close to Westminster Abbey, Tate Gallery, Buckingham Palace. Good shopping in Knightsbridge & Sloane Square.*

rooms	1 double with private shower.
room price	£90. Singles £60.
meals	Continental breakfast until 9.30am. Excellent pubs/restaurants nearby.
closed	Christmas.
directions	From Sloane Square tube, down King's Road. Bywater St 500 yds along on right. House at end. House outside congestion charge zone. Parking £25 per 24 hours.

rooms	1 four-poster with bath.
room price	£110-£120. Singles £100.
meals	Breakfast 8-9am, continental included, full English £8. Excellent local restaurants.
closed	Christmas.
directions	1 min from Pimlico tube (Rampayne St exit), or 5 mins from Victoria Station. Best bus, 24 to Trafalgar Sq. Parking: NCP or 2-hour meters.

Caroline & Richard Heaton-Watson
20 Bywater Street,
London SW3 4XD

tel   020 7581 2222
fax   020 7581 2222
e-mail   caheatonw@aol.com

Mrs Helen Douglas
Number Ninety-Six,
96 Tachbrook Street,
London SW1V 2NB

tel   020 7932 0969
fax   020 7821 5454
e-mail   helen@numberninety-six.co.uk
web   www.numberninety-six.co.uk

LONDON

This little 1840s terraced house is in the chic hub of Hillgate village. Sunny and quiet, it's just three minutes' walk from Notting Hill Gate tube station, with masses of good restaurants close by. Behind the demure facade lies a seductive mix of exotic textiles and interesting paintings – many by Hilary, a lawyer turned artist. Your cream and white ground-floor bedroom has splashes of colour from cushions, hangings and Indian sofa. Breakfast is in the bright basement dining room, which opens onto a tiny but lush courtyard garden. A rare and unexpected treat in the middle of London.

rooms	1 double with bath/shower.
room price	£80. Singles £60.
meals	Dutch/continental breakfast. Pubs/restaurants nearby.
closed	Rarely.
directions	At Coronet Cinema on south side of Notting Hill Gate turn into Hillgate Street; at 2nd junction, right into Hillgate Place; no. 26 next to Hillgate pub.

Hilary Dunne
26 Hillgate Place,
Notting Hill Gate, London W8 7ST
tel   020 7727 7717
fax   020 7727 7827
e-mail   hilary.dunne@virgin.net

map: 5 entry: 299

LONDON

You are in the middle of Kensington yet utterly quiet; the 1860s townhouse makes a charming central London base. The three rooms are on the garden floor which is light and bright, giving you privacy and your own entrance. The rest of the house is still the family home. Breakfast is served upstairs in the dining room overlooking the pretty, secluded garden. There's an easy formality here: mahogany table and dresser, antique chairs, floral fabrics... and Nanette, who really enjoys people. *Near Kensington Gardens, Holland Park, High Street Kensington. Children over 12 welcome.*

rooms	3: 2 twins, both with bath/shower; 1 double with shower.
room price	£85-£95. Singles £70.
meals	Cooked breakfast 8.30-9am (Mon-Fri), 9-9.30am (Sat-Sun). Pubs/restaurants nearby.
closed	Rarely.
directions	Left out of Earl's Court tube, over Cromwell Road, left into Pembroke Road. Warwick Gardens 3rd on right. Parking £10 per day next door. Public transport: High Street Kensington/Earl's Court tube (8-minute walk).

Nanette Stylianou
47 Warwick Gardens,
London W14 8PL
tel   020 7603 7614
fax   020 7602 5473
e-mail   nanette@stylianou.fsnet.co.uk

map: 5 entry: 300

LONDON

The area is one of London's most sought-after and Sunny's gorgeous family home is right opposite the park – perfectly placed for Kensington High St, Notting Hill and Olympia. The whole top floor is generally given over to guests. Bedrooms are in gentle yellows and greens, with pale carpets, white duvets, pelmeted windows, big porcelain table lights, treetop views. The bathroom is marble-tiled and sky-lit, with a cast-iron bath and shower. Near to Kensington Gardens, and the Number 9 or Number 10 bus will drop you off at the Albert Hall, Knightsbridge or Piccadilly. *Children over 10 welcome.*

rooms	2: 1 double, 1 single, sharing bath.
room price	£90–£100. Singles from £45.
meals	Continental breakfast included. Lots of places to eat nearby.
closed	Rarely.
directions	Public transport: nearest tube Holland Park, 7-minute walk, or High St Kensington. Best buses, 9 & 10 to Knightsbridge. Off-street parking sometimes available.

Sunny Murray
101 Abbotsbury Road,
London W14 8EP
tel   020 7602 0179
fax   020 7602 1036
e-mail   sunny@101abb.freeserve.co.uk

LONDON

In the heart of vibrant Camden Town, well set back in a quiet, wide, tree-lined street, moments from Regent's Park, a superb central London base. The large and stylish kitchen where you breakfast was designed by Peter (an architect and lighting specialist) and every room in the modernist house has had the best brought out of it – small rooms have been cleverly planned and there's a really super large double. All is distinctive and understated with cool colours and fresh flowers. The Bells run this established B&B with a cool professionalism. *Near to Camden Lock and Camden market.*

rooms	3: 1 small double with shower; 1 twin with bunks, 1 twin/double sharing bath.
room price	£90–£100. Singles £45–£60.
meals	Continental breakfast 7-10am. Pubs/restaurants nearby.
closed	Rarely.
directions	From Camden Town tube (Northern Line), up Parkway. Albert St 2nd on left. House on left. Parking free Sunday; otherwise meters.

Joanna & Peter Bell
78 Albert Street,
London NW1 7NR
tel   020 7387 6813
fax   020 7387 1704
e-mail   joanna@peterbellarchitects.co.uk

A modern walled and tranquil home made of African teak and glass. The open-plan living area makes fabulous use of space and is decorated with ethnic ornaments from far-flung travels. It opens to a courtyard garden; halogen lights and a pyramid of glass on the roof brighten still further. Climb the wooden stair to find special bedrooms decorated in Japanese style with low platform beds and modern chairs; the double has two walls of glass. A famous market and lots of good places to eat are close by. Rodger and Sue are a delight and Peckham the parrot completes the picture. *Children by arrangement.*

There's a dramatic vibrancy to Valerie's home, just off Upper Street with its restaurants, and right by the Almeida and Sadler's Wells. She has many artists and actors to stay and has a theatre background herself. The Victorian house is stuffed with oriental, French and Italian pieces, and your basement bedroom is filled with light and character. Walls, doors and much of the furniture are ragged, sponged and stencilled in the colourful style of the Bloomsbury set; the theatrical mood continues in the conservatory, crammed with tropical plants, ferns, seashells and candles. An inspiring place to stay.

rooms	2: 1 double, 1 single, sharing bath, only let only to same party.
room price	£90. Singles from £45.
meals	Extensive continental breakfast 7.30–10am. Pubs/restaurants nearby.
closed	Rarely.
directions	From Camden Town tube, take Camden Rd towards Holloway. Pass Camden Rd BR station & 4th right into Murray St. House on corner of Murray St & Camden Mews. Parking free at weekends; meters during week.

rooms	1 double with private shower.
room price	£85. Singles £65–£70.
meals	Breakfast 8–9am; extensive continental only.
closed	Rarely.
directions	From Highbury & Islington tube, right out of station. Down Upper Street, past Town Hall. Left immed. before Shell garage. Free overnight & weekend parking (Sat 6.30pm on); otherwise meters & car parks.

Sue & Rodger Davis
66 Camden Square,
London NW1 9XD
tel 020 7485 4622
fax 020 7485 4622
e–mail rodgerdavis@btopenworld.com

Valerie Rossmore
26 Florence Street,
Islington, London N1 2FW
tel 020 7359 5293
e–mail valerie.rossmore@virgin.net

The downstairs room is worthy of a top hotel: crisp linen, bamboo blinds, Chinese screens, a marble bathroom. Anne is originally from Borneo; Tim was 'our man in East Malaysia' some 35 years ago. They have travelled widely, are full of life, and now live on the side of a hill above a carpet of London lights. Hats on the hat stand, old maps on the walls, everything sparkles. Two more bedrooms upstairs, one in country house style, the other in contemporary yellow. Anne will do you a steaming hot oriental cooked breakfast or the 'full English'. It's a short walk downhill to buses, tubes and trains.

Not a hard house to find – just knock at the door of the wildest pad on the street. Beatrice is an artist and her 1860s home is an extension of both work and self – funky, easy-going, welcoming. There are big, light-swamped rooms, polished wood floors and bright colours – 21st-century B&B. The hub is the kitchen with its farmhouse table for continental breakfasts and a glass wall that gives onto the garden. Beatrice's other half, James, is a Kiwi garden designer – one of London's best; wander at will and find old dock timbers, a sari-shaded Mexican hammock, willowy grasses and a water garden.

rooms	3: 1 double, 1 twin/double, both with bath/shower; 1 twin with private bath.
room price	£90–£100. Singles from £45.
meals	Dinner £26. B.Y.O.
closed	Rarely.
directions	From Elephant & Castle r'bout, A2 (New Kent, Old Kent, New Cross Rd) to junc. with Queens Rd. Right for Queens Rd. 1st left into Erlanger Rd, left into Sherwin Rd. Right into Pepys Rd up hill. House opposite Telegraph Hill Park.

rooms	1 twin with shower.
room price	£70–£80. Singles £50.
meals	Continental breakfast. Pubs/restaurants 5-minute walk.
closed	Rarely.
directions	From Brockley station, cross Brockley Rd & up Cranfield Rd; cross at church & cont. to Breakspears Rd. Free parking. Trains: Brockley to London Bridge. Buses: 171 & 36 to centre.

Mrs A Marten
113 Pepys Road,
London SE14 5SE

tel	020 7639 1060
fax	020 7639 8780
e-mail	annemarten@pepysroad.com
web	www.pepysroad.com

Beatrice Fraser
57 Breakspears Road,
London SE4 1XR

tel	020 8469 3162
e-mail	bunzl@btinternet.com

Bedrooms here will have you writing home – Indian wall hangings, gold silky bedspreads, rag-rolled walls, rugs on stripped floors, plates of fruit with napkins and knives. A glass of wine or beer from Penny on arrival, a good, big open-plan kitchen/dining room and a different cooked dish every morning. Dinners are delicious, too: fish soup, rack of lamb, chocolate pud. There's a grand piano which you're welcome to play, three dogs and Brian to chauffeur you around London (or Britain) in his 1954 Citröen; station pick-ups and drop-offs, too. You are a mile from the unmissable Dulwich Picture Gallery.

Peace and undemanding luxury: the 1890 Victorian cottage with delightful courtyard garden is a perfect antidote to the rigours of city life. You breakfast in the dining room – the full English works (unusual for London); across the hall, the sitting room, with gilt-framed mirrors, wooden blinds, a plump-cushioned sofa and a piano you are welcome to play. Upstairs, very comfortable bedrooms have pretty linen, books and guides. The next-door bathroom is fabulous with porthole windows and a radio to entertain you as you soak. *Convenient for Chelsea Flower Show, Battersea Park and the South Bank.*

rooms	6: 1 double with bath; 2 doubles, 1 twin, sharing 2 private bath/shower rooms.
room price	£60-£70. Singles £50.
meals	European/cooked breakfast included. Supper tray £10. Dinner, 3 courses with wine, £25.
closed	Rarely.
directions	On A205 east on South Circular. Turn into Woodvale to end. Left then immediately right.

rooms	2: 1 double with private bath/shower; 1 double sharing bath/shower, only let to same party.
room price	£70-£80. Singles £50-£60.
meals	Breakfast until 9am; until 9.30am Sat & Sun. Good restaurants 200 yds.
closed	Rarely.
directions	Please call for directions. Nearby r'way stations (6 mins Waterloo/3 mins Victoria) or 137 bus (Sloane Square 10 mins). Parking £4 per day, 9.30-5.30 Mon-Fri; otherwise free.

Penny & Brian Shepherd
Shepherd's,
39 Marmora Road, East Dulwich,
London SE22 0RX
tel   020 8693 4355
fax   020 8693 7954
e-mail   dulwichdragon@hotmail.com
web   www.shepherdslondon.com

Barbara Graham
20 St Philip Street,
Battersea, London SW8 3SL
tel   020 7498 9967
fax   020 7498 9967
e-mail   stay@bed-breakfast-battersea.co.uk
web   www.bed-breakfast-battersea.co.uk

LONDON

A smart 1880s family home in a leafy conservation area. There's a snug library with club fenders round the fire, a stylish dining room flanked by *trompe l'oeil* pillars and an elegant sitting room with antique furniture which opens to a secluded garden. Big bedrooms have comfy mahogany furniture, pretty fabrics, tartan blankets. Best of all is the huge room at the top: it has two sofas with masses of space all around, and twin beds hidden up in the eaves – perfect for families. Viveka does excellent Swedish breakfasts with marvellous coffee. She will also take you and your luggage to and from the station.

rooms	3: 1 double with bath; 1 family suite (double & twin) with private shower.
room price	£60. Singles £45. Family suite by arrangement.
meals	Continental breakfast 8-9am. Restaurants & pubs 5-10-minute walk.
closed	Rarely.
directions	Ring on arrival at Tooting Bec tube (Northern Line) & you'll be collected. Free off-road parking. 20 minutes by tube to central London.

Viveka & Chris Collingwood
34 Ambleside Ave,
London SW16 1QP

tel	020 8769 2742
fax	020 8677 3023
e-mail	info@bednbrek.com
web	www.bednbrek.com

map: 5 entry: 309

LONDON

This Art Deco mansion block (marble stairs, chrome banister rails, trim carpets) is rather like a 1920s P&O steamer: quietly grand. This delectable bolthole has been refurbished by Mary in great style: Zoffany wallpaper, a marble fireplace and a beautiful Regency rosewood table for breakfast with views onto the small garden. The bedroom is equally pretty (a Louis XIV sofa, big porcelain bedside lamps) and has French windows that open onto a tiny balcony. Very little noise – this is a cul-de-sac – with Hyde Park at the top of the road and Harrods a five-minute walk. A perfect place. *Children over 10 by arrangement.*

rooms	1 double with bath/shower.
room price	£80-£90. Singles £60.
meals	Continental breakfast. Dinner £25. Restaurants nearby.
closed	Rarely.
directions	Directions given on booking. Parking meters (free 6.30pm - 8.30am & Sunday); car park £1.50 hour. Knightsbridge tube. Buses: 9, 10, 52.

Mrs Mary Williams
Knightsbridge, London

tel	020 7581 0395
fax	020 7581 0395
e-mail	bivvywilliams@hotmail.com

map: 5 entry: 310

LONDON

P rivacy is the key element here. You have exclusive use of your own Coach House, separated from your hosts' home by a stylish terracotta-potted courtyard. Breakfast in your own sunny kitchen, or let the gracious Meena treat you to an all-organic full English in hers (she's a whizz at porridge, too). The big but cosy main attic bedroom has *toile de Jouy* bedcovers, cream curtains, rugs on dark polished floors; the brick-walled ground-floor twin is pleasant, light and airy. An exceptionally quiet south London B&B. *Minimum stay three nights; two nights in January/February.*

rooms	2: 1 twin with private shower; 1 family with bath & shower. Only let to same party.
room price	£75-£165.
meals	Breakfast until 9am. Dinner, 4-5 courses, £45. Pub/restaurant 200 yds.
closed	Rarely.
directions	From r'bout on south side of Wandsworth Bridge, head south down Trinity Rd on A214. At 3rd set of traffic lights, 1.7 miles on, left into Upper Tooting Park. 4th left into Marius Rd, then 3rd left.

Meena & Harley Nott
The Coach House,
2 Tunley Road, London SW17 7QJ
tel   020 8772 1939
fax   0870 133 4957
e-mail coachhouse@chslondon.com
web   www.coachhouse.chslondon.com

map: 5 entry: 311

LONDON

I t's a handsome house in a conservation area that manages to be both elegant and cosy. The cream-coloured double bedroom has an armchair, a writing desk, delightful curtains and a big, comfy walnut bed; the en suite is light and airy. A restful dining room overlooks a secluded terrace and garden and there are newspapers at breakfast; eat in in the evening and David, who works in wine, puts a bottle on the table. A friendly, relaxing city base on a quiet, tree-lined street – maximum comfort and good value for London. *Minimum stay two nights.*

rooms	1 double with bath.
room price	£65-£75. Singles £55-£65.
meals	Breakfast 8-9.30am; 10am Sat & Sun. Dinner, 3 courses, £25. Good restaurants nearby.
closed	Rarely.
directions	From Tooting Bec tube, along Balham High Rd towards Balham. 3rd road on right. 7-minute walk from tube. Free parking weekends, otherwise meters or daily rate £2.50.

Mary & David Hodges
108 Streathbourne Road,
London SW17 8QY
tel   020 8767 6931
fax   020 8672 8839
e-mail mary.hodges@virgin.net
web   www.streathbourneroad.com

map: 5 entry: 312

Barnes is London's loveliest village: ducks still live on the village pond opposite a pub where cricketers meet to quench a collective thirst. Helen's immaculate home has boundless style: plantation shutters in the large sitting room, a shiny wooden floor in the big, bright kitchen, doors that open to a sweet garden (perfect for summer breakfasts). Bedrooms have big beds, Australian damask cotton sheets, all the spoiling extras. The top room has skylights – stargaze from bed – and a crisp elegance; the grander double, an Edwardian *bergère* sofa and a purple claw-foot bath in a divine en suite.

The two acres of formal rose beds, borders, lawns and orchards sweep down to the Thames – a magical, secluded London base. This exceptional Palladian house has fine moulded ceilings, portraits, books and fresh flowers; bedrooms are sumptuous with fine fabrics, exquisite furniture and lovely views. Sonia serves delicious home-cooking including a fine repertoire of Jewish and continental recipes. For garden lovers, Hampton Court Palace (home to the International Flower Show) is next door and Windsor, Wisley and Kew a short drive away. *French and Italian spoken. Minimum stay two nights.*

rooms	2: 1 double, with bath; 1 double with private bath.
room price	From £70. Singles £45.
meals	Breakfast until 9.30am. Pubs/restaurants 500 yds.
closed	Christmas & New Year.
directions	From Great West Rd, Hammersmith Bridge to Barnes. At lights by Browns Restaurant, right along Lonsdale Rd for just over 1 mile. Left into Gerard Rd & 1st left into Charlotte Rd. House 1st on left. Free parking.

rooms	2: 1 double with bath/shower; 1 double with private bath.
room price	£90–£100. Singles by arrangement.
meals	Continental breakfast until 9am. Dinner £25.
closed	Rarely.
directions	From Hampton Court r'bout, A308, west, for 300 yds. Hampton Court station 5 minutes; 30 minutes Waterloo.

Helen Smith
1 Charlotte Road,
Barnes, London SW13 9QJ
tel   020 8741 5504
fax   020 8741 5504

Dr Louis & Sonia Marks
Paddock Lodge,
The Green, Hampton Court,
London KT8 9BW
tel   020 8979 5254
e-mail 101723.1100@compuserve.com

This house is just like its farming owners – delightfully warm and natural. Easy-going, comfortable and lived-in, it has touches of real elegance: the drawing room has a grand piano and gilt cornicing. Bedrooms are neither designery nor lavish, but homely and generous with towels, bathrobes, hot water bottles and other indulging extras, even a fridge and sofa. Two are vast and high-ceilinged, with chairs to relax in and good views from long windows. The garden is lovely and there are dogs and horses galore (stabling available); the walls bear the proof of success at point-to-points and shows. Breakfasts are lavish.

A perfectly shaped 18th-century house – its setting is utterly rural and the large grounds deserve exploration. You can cross the bridged pond to an enchanting island, play tennis, swim in the heated outdoor pool, shelter under an arbour. This is a very traditional house with displays of china, an oval oak dining table that seats 12 and antique furniture. The bedroom and sitting room are tucked away in a wing of their own – delightfully private. It's a place of peace and fine views; shooting parties, painting courses and beauty therapies can be arranged, and Sandringham, sailing, golf and beaches are all close by.

rooms	3: 1 double with shower, 1 double with bath/shower; 1 twin with private bath & wc.
room price	£40–£56. Singles £25–£35.
meals	Pub/restaurant 800 yds.
closed	Rarely.
directions	From Kings Lynn, A148 for Cromer. 3 miles after Hillington, 2nd of 2 turnings right to Harpley (no signpost) opp. Houghton Hall sign. 200 yds on, over x-roads & house 400 yds on left.

rooms	1 twin/double with bath.
room price	£70–£75. Singles £50.
meals	Dinner, 2–3 courses, £21.50–£25.
closed	Christmas.
directions	From Kings Lynn A47 for Swaffham. 4 miles on, left at Middleton, by church & left again into Hill Rd. Right into drive (opp. Paul Drive).

Amanda Case
Lower Farm,
Harpley, Nr Kings Lynn,
Norfolk PE31 6TU
tel   01485 520240
fax   01485 520240

Mrs C Knight
The Old Hall,
Middleton, Kings Lynn,
Norfolk PE32 1RW
tel   01553 840490
fax   01553 840708
e-mail   emidas@talk21.com

map: 11 entry: 315

map: 11 entry: 316

NORFOLK

NORFOLK

Vibrant and fresh – this is a living, bustling household. The laid-back, family feel is enhanced by a great sense of colour and style and much that is wooden has been painted; in the homely kitchen, jade woodwork, white walls, an old, cream Aga, a riot of bright china. The rose-pink sitting room has white-painted beams, deep sofas, a log burner and a wooden floor. Upstairs are fresh flowers, faded carpets, good sheets, a lovely bathroom and A-frame ceilings. You can have a real fire in one bedroom – Mary will light it if you ask. Breakfast on local organic produce, home-made bread and jams.

Extraordinarily kind and generous hosts – a guest wrote to tell us so – and they really enjoy having people in their 200-year-old converted barn/smithy, with its wildflower garden and farmland views. It's light and open, with a large kitchen where candles are suspended above the table and dried flowers hang from the beams. There are bees, free-range hens and home-grown organic vegetables and fruit; Jane's an imaginative cook and gives you fresh juice before breakfast. One bedroom is carpeted; the other has seagrass matting. Walsingham is close by and there's plenty to inspire artists. Jane paints and can organise trips.

rooms	2: 1 double with bath; 1 double with private shower. Cot & fold-up bed available.
room price	£50-£60. Singles £27.50-£32.50.
meals	Good pub 3-minute walk.
closed	Christmas.
directions	A148 King's Lynn to Cromer, left onto B1355 just before Fakenham. 6.5 miles to North Creake. Right after phone box, then 300 yds. House on right.

rooms	2: 1 twin/double with private bath; 1 twin/double with private shower.
room price	£45. Singles from £22.50.
meals	Dinner, 3 courses, £15. B.Y.O wine.
closed	Christmas.
directions	From A148 Fakenham for Kings Lynn, then left for Dunton. Straight through Dunton. Keep on main country lane. Barn on left before phone box.

Mary & Jeremy Brettingham
Glebe Farmhouse,
Wells Road, North Creake,
Fakenham, Norfolk NR21 9LG
tel 01328 730133
fax 01328 730444
e-mail info@eastnortheast.co.uk
web www.glebe-farmhouse.co.uk

Michael & Jane Davidson-Houston
Manor Farm Barn,
Tatterford, Nr Fakenham,
Norfolk NR21 7AZ
tel 01485 528393

map: 11 entry: 317
map: 11 entry: 318

A conservation-award-winning farm tucked away in the heart of rural Norfolk; you are next door to a tiny 13th-century church and within lovely gardens (the coast is only 20 minutes away). The two guest rooms, with large sitting room and small kitchen, are in the converted stables – which are beautiful. Antiques, lovely rugs, cushions and artefacts add to the luxury. Breakfast is delicious, with home eggs, bacon and sausages and is served in the dining room of the main house. Libby and Robin have created something special. Kennel and stable available. *Children over 10 welcome.*

For the whole of the 19th century this was Litcham's doctor's house and today, over 200 years after it was built, the red-brick Hall remains at the centre of the community. This is a thoroughly English home with elegant proportions; the hall, drawing room and dining room are gracious and beautifully furnished. There are good reading lights and books by the beds and the big-windowed guest rooms look onto the garden; church fêtes are held in its wonderful three acres. John and Hermione are friendly and most helpful. *Children and dogs by arrangement; use of pool similarly.*

rooms	2: 1 double, 1 twin in stable annexe, both with bath.
room price	£60–£70. Singles £40–£45.
meals	Breakfast until 9.30am or by arrangement. Pub 1.5 miles.
closed	Rarely.
directions	A1065 Swaffham/Fakenham road. 6 miles on, through Weasenham. After 1 mile, right for Wellingham. There, on left, next to church.

rooms	2 twins, both with private bath. Sitting room available. Extra room available occasionally.
room price	£50–£65. Singles by arrangement.
meals	Dinner £20.
closed	Christmas.
directions	From Swaffham, A1065; right to Litcham after 5 miles. House on left on entering village. Georgian red brick with stone balls on gatepost.

	Elisabeth Ellis
	Manor House Farm,
	Wellingham, Nr Fakenham,
	Kings Lynn, Norfolk PE32 2TH
tel	01328 838227
fax	01328 838348
e-mail	l.ellis@farming.co.uk

	John & Hermione Birkbeck
	Litcham Hall,
	Litcham, Nr Kings Lynn,
	Norfolk PE32 2QQ
tel	01328 701389
fax	01328 701164
e-mail	j.birkbeck@amserve.com

Elizabeth is capable and funny – a winning combination. She got the local church bells ringing again after years of silence (tractor grease did the trick). Reached by a bumpy lane and wonderfully quiet, this is a mainly arable farm, with hens, geese and horses, yet the house is unusually elegant. Antiques, silver, porcelain and paintings abound. There's a shared guest sitting room and the bedrooms have high ceilings and pretty details: hand-painted tiles above the basins, padded headboards, lovely prints. Own Soil Association-approved farm eggs for breakfast and Elizabeth's excellent lemon cake for tea.

The luxury of a hotel combined with the friendliness of a B&B – such a gem. Tucked into a hollow, enfolded by gardens, the 18th-century barn has been decorated in style. You have floor-to-ceiling windows in the lofty suite with mezzanine bedroom, and solid, white-painted stone walls, rugs, books, even a grand piano. Allan, a trained chef, welcomes you with tea and scones fresh from the Aga. Breakfasts are special – home-made breads and preserves, fresh stewed fruits, local kippers, eggs from next door. Dinner is served at the mahogany table and Allan spoils you from start to finish – he'll even do your laundry.

rooms	3: 1 double, 1 twin, sharing bath; 1 twin with bath.
room price	£44–£56. Singles in high season, £35–£40.
meals	Breakfast 8–9.30am. Dinner, 3 courses, £15.
closed	Christmas & New Year.
directions	From Fakenham B1146 for East Dereham. After 2 miles, left to Gt. Ryburgh. In village, 2nd left up Highfield Lane opp. pink cottage & on for 0.5 miles; house on right.

rooms	3: 1 suite with bath; 1 twin, 1 single, both with private bath/shower.
room price	£80. Singles £40.
meals	Breakfast 7.30–9.30am. Dinner £20.
closed	Rarely.
directions	From A1067 south of Fakenham towards Stibbard. There right into Wood Norton Rd, then left split (not to Guist); Tylers Barn signed 2nd on left after split.

Elizabeth Savory
Highfield Farm,
Great Ryburgh, Fakenham,
Norfolk NR21 7AL
tel	01328 829249
fax	01328 829422
web	www.broadland.com/highfield

Allan Urquhart
Tylers Barn,
Wood Norton Road, Stibbard,
Fakenham, Norfolk NR21 0EX
tel	01328 829260
fax	01328 829260
e-mail	allanurquhart@freenet.co.uk

Norfolk at its best… huge skies, views that go on forever and absolute peace in this fine Georgian vicarage. An elegant staircase springs from the flagstoned inner hall lit by a glass pyramid high above. Two delightful bedrooms (one capturing sunsets) have good furniture, books, china and pictures. Breakfast in the sunlit dining room on home-made bread and eggs from the home flock and for dinner let Rosie treat you to mussels, crab and game in season. You're just five miles from the coast – sail, walk, cycle, visit the seals… and close to five National Trust properties. *Use of grass tennis court by arrangement. French spoken.*

A fairy-tale house – you almost expect Hansel and Gretel to come skipping out from the woods. (Charcoal used to be burnt here, hence the name, Smokers Hole.) Mary has brought style and luxury to this historic former gamekeeper's flint lodge. There are two private guest suites, each with their own entrance, sitting room, double room and bathroom; the beds are brass and king-size, mattresses are the best, lovely old maps line the walls. Mary, an art historian, wants you to feel cosseted and you will. Here are bird-watching reserves, sandy beaches, salt marshes and vast Norfolk skies – wonderful.

rooms	2: 1 double with private bath; 1 twin/double with bath.
room price	From £55. Ask about singles & children's rates.
meals	Dinner, 3 courses, £20. Supper, 2 courses, £16.50. B.Y.O.
closed	Christmas & New Year.
directions	From Fakenham to Cromer for 6 miles. Left at Crawfish pub into Hindringham, down hill & left, before church, into Blacksmith's Lane. Follow lane, bear right, house on left at top of hill, flinted entrances.

rooms	2 double suites, each with private sitting room and bath/shower.
room price	£85-£100. Singles £90.
meals	Excellent pubs & restaurants within 3 miles.
closed	Christmas.
directions	Off A148 onto B1156 for Blakeney. At x-roads, straight over (pass sign to Saxlingham). Approx. 0.5 miles on, house on right with gravel drive & lamp post.

Rosie & Robin Waters
The Old Vicarage,
Blacksmith's Lane, Hindringham,
Norfolk NR21 0QA
tel 01328 878223
e-mail watersrobin@hotmail.com

Mary Alexander
The Map House,
Smokers Hole, Saxlingham, Holt,
Norfolk NR25 7JU
tel 01263 741304
e-mail enquiries@maphouse.net
web www.maphouse.net

Everything in this unique place is of hotel-like perfection – breakfast, coffee, beds, furnishings – yet the level of care here is personal. The river laps at the walls of the 18th-century windmill and a magnificent sitting room overlooks the marshes; some bedrooms take in the endless seascape and one has a walk-around balcony. Jeremy took over the Mill in 1998, having fallen in love with it as a guest. He upped sticks from his Battersea restaurant and now cooks with the freshest local ingredients: caught-that-day fish or the delicious seamarsh samphire. Don't forget the binoculars. *Self-catering available. See back of book.*

The Americans were out to impress when they created this. Children can play hide-and-seek in the miles of disused tunnels and the lucky few may even find a forgotten missile or two, while adults can relax soaking up the the gamma rays. Sit in comfort in the large underground control room, decorated with red telephones and a large red button (which you are advised not to press). There are extra facilities to die for, such as a private runway (eat your heart out Richard Branson). May suit those with an interest in military history. No need to bring a torch as the walls glow at night. Pick your own room; there's a wide choice.

rooms	7: 3 twins/doubles, 4 doubles, all with bath.
room price	£74–£112. Singles by arrangement.
meals	Breakfast 8.30–9am. Dinner £17.50.
closed	Rarely.
directions	From Holt take Cley Road, through only street in Cley. Mill signed on left. Over bridge to car park.

rooms	846 dormitories, all with bath.
room price	10,000 Air Miles + £50
meals	Dinner, 3 courses, military ration packs.
closed	At one end.
directions	From Moscow, follow the disused missile run to the A33339 Norfolk. Hang a right at barbed wire fence.

Jeremy Bolam
Cley Mill,
Cley-next-the-Sea, Holt,
Norfolk NR25 7RP
tel	01263 740209
fax	01263 740209
web	www.cleymill.co.uk

Ray D O'Active
Blueham Common Airbase,
Norfolk
tel	Armagedden 999
e-mail	glowwalls@secretmission.ru
web	www.dontpressthebutton.ru

NORFOLK

NORFOLK

Play croquet, find a cosy spot to read, or just doze – we applaud Clare's ease and willingness to share her home. The house has a contemporary barn feel and, with clever use of space, light and aspect, several seating areas have been created throughout the open-plan ground floor. Bedrooms are stylish and large; in one there is a double brass bedstead, a striking vine-patterned fabric and a coir-covered floor. Wood everywhere and lovely stone, a formal garden, ponds, a summer house and two self-catering barns. Two National Trust houses are nearby and the coast – thousands of acres of sea, sand and sky.

Arrive on a summer afternoon to find the Norfolk longhouse bathed in sunlight; the welcome from the Heals will be just as warm. The Grade II-listed house is all that remains of the old village of Burgh Parva: it was deserted in 1668 after the Great Plague. The Hall is a handsome and cosy house, whose large bedrooms face west, ensuring views of wonderful sunsets in vast Norfolk skies. Old furniture, rugs and pictures give a feeling of unpretentious ease. The breakfast eggs are fresh from the garden hens, the vegetables are home-grown and there is plenty of game in season.

rooms	3: 1 double with shower; 1 double, 1 twin, both with bath/shower.
room price	£70–£80. Singles from £40.
meals	Dinner, 2 courses, £12.50; 3 courses, £19.50.
closed	Rarely.
directions	From Norwich, A140. On entering Roughton, left into Back Lane. After 0.75 miles, pass cottage on left. Grove Farm 30 yds on right.

rooms	2: 1 twin with private bath; 1 double with private bath/shower.
room price	From £50. Singles from £30.
meals	Breakfast until 9.30am. Dinner £20.
closed	Rarely.
directions	Fakenham A148 for Cromer. At Thursford B1354 for Aylsham. Just before Melton, speed bumps, left immed. before bus shelter; 1st house on right after farmyard.

Clare Wilson
Grove Farm,
Back Lane, Roughton,
Norfolk NR11 8QR
tel   01263 761594
fax   01263 761605
e-mail grovefarm@homestay.co.uk
web   www.grove-farm.com

Judy & William Heal
Burgh Parva Hall,
Melton Constable,
Norfolk NR24 2PU
tel   01263 862569
fax   01263 862569
e-mail judy.heal@btinternet.com

The garden was alive with spring bulbs when we visited and a squadron of white ducks joined in the welcome. They give lovely eggs, says Jo, but do trample the tulips! This big 17th-century rectory is beautiful inside – a relaxed, attractive mix of traditional and contemporary, with lots of interesting pieces, a large, jolly dining room and a delectable double bedroom with canopied brass bedstead. Play croquet in the garden or enjoy the nearby coast. Jo and Giles are keen sailors; she's also an enthusiastic local and architectural historian. Children more than welcome. *All-weather tennis court available by arrangement.*

A gorgeous and incredibly peaceful setting. Sarah has opened up the Georgian Old Laundry beside Heydon Hall, one of Norfolk's finest Grade I-listed Elizabethan houses. The white walls, scrubbed tables and stone flags are still in place but much luxury has been added. Bedrooms have pretty fabrics at the windows and on the headboards; one has a bathroom with a fireplace and free-standing bath. Breakfast downstairs in the sunny guest dining/sitting room with cream furniture and a mellow stone floor. With a private courtyard, it's all beautifully self-contained – and there's a swimming pool that you can use if you ask.

rooms	2: 1 double with bath; 1 twin with private bath, shower & wc.
room price	From £55. Singles £37.50.
meals	Dinner £15. B.Y.O.
closed	Christmas & New Year.
directions	From Fakenham A1067 for Norwich. At Guist clock tower, left; 2nd of 2 turnings to Wood Norton. House on right after 100 yds, through overgrown entrance, over 2 cattle grids.

rooms	2: 1 twin/double with bath; 1 twin/double with private bath.
room price	From £60. Singles in high season, £40.
meals	Dinner, 3 courses, £18. Good pub 0.5 miles, restaurant 5 miles.
closed	Christmas. Self-catering never.
directions	From Norwich, B1149 for 10 miles. 2nd left after bridge, for Heydon. After 1.5 miles, right into village, straight into park, over cattle grid, past Hall to left & follow signs.

Jo & Giles Winter
The Old Rectory,
Wood Norton,
Norfolk NR20 5AZ
tel   01362 683785

Sarah Bulwer-Long
The Old Laundry,
Heydon Hall, Heydon,
Norfolk NR11 6RE
tel   01263 587343
fax   01263 587805

Conservation farmland all around, and acres of wild heathland busy with woodpeckers and owls a stride from the door. Family life in this 17th-century farmhouse revolves around the great kitchen and the draw of the Aga is irresistible on Fiona's bread-baking days. Good, traditional bedrooms are cosy with rugs and *objets* from diplomatic postings abroad, and have farmyard and garden views. Much space and light and, when the teenage children are at home, family chatter. There may be Norfolk kippers for breakfast, along with home-grown eggs, bacon and real marmalade. A tennis court is available for guests' use.

The best of both worlds: a lovely family buzz in the farmhouse where you breakfast, privacy in the stylish 16th-century barn where you stay. All rooms lead off its beautifully vaulted sitting room. A bedroom and a kitchen on the ground floor, then up a little stair to more bedrooms – small but lofty with a delicious, tucked-up-in-the-roof feel (and views to Happisburgh's red and white striped lighthouse). A courtyard garden, billiards in the stable, lovely hosts, and you may come and go as you please. A place for friends or family, with a fresh, contemporary feel. *Children over seven welcome.*

rooms	2: 1 double with bath; 1 double with private bath & shower.
room price	£50. Singles £30.
meals	Dinner from £12.50. Good pubs 2 miles.
closed	Rarely.
directions	A1151 from Norwich for Stalham. Just before Stalham, left to Happisburgh. Left at T-junc. On for 3 miles then 2nd left after East Ruston church, signed by-way to Foxhill. Right at x-roads signed Ridlington. House 1 mile on right.

rooms	3: 2 doubles, both with bath/shower; 1 twin/double with bath.
room price	From £44. Singles by arrangement.
meals	Dinner, 3 courses, from £15.
closed	Christmas & New Year.
directions	From Norwich, A1151/A149 almost to Stalham. Left, for Walcott. At T-junc. left again. 1 mile on, right for H'burgh. Next T-junc., right. Next T-junc., left. Past houses & fields. Road bends right, look for house sign by fence.

Peter & Fiona Black
The Old Rectory,
Ridlington, Norfolk NR28 9NZ
tel   01692 650247
fax   0870 1335719
e-mail   blacks7@email.com

David & Rosie Eldridge
Manor Farmhouse,
Happisburgh, Norfolk NR12 0SA
tel   01692 651262
fax   01692 650220
e-mail   manorathappisburgh@hotmail.com
web   www.northnorfolk.co.uk/manorbarn

NORFOLK

Elegance and prettiness in equal measure. Light, airy, stylish rooms with long Georgian windows dressed in beautiful fabrics – checks, *toile de Jouy* and ochre stripes. The bedrooms are most attractive, too (the family room is one of the best we've seen and opens onto a delightful sleeping area for children, with toys and books). Bibby, a Cordon Bleu cook, uses local produce and vegetables from the walled kitchen garden. There's also a large heated pool. Worstead, the birthplace of worsted cloth, is charming – only a stroll away. Come at the end of July and you can join in the fun of the village festival.

rooms	2: 1 double/family with bath; 1 twin/double with basin & private shower.
room price	£50-£60. Singles £35-£40.
meals	Packed lunch available. Dinner, 2 courses, £14.50; 3 courses, £18. Pub in village.
closed	Christmas & New Year.
directions	From Norwich, B1150 (N. Walsham road). At Westwick, right for Worstead. Under railway bridge. On entering village, left at Manor House, on to school on left. House on right opp. pond.

Michael & Bibby Horwood
Holly Grove,
Worstead, North Walsham,
Norfolk NR28 9RQ
tel   01692 535546
e-mail   stay@hollygrovehouse.co.uk
web   www.hollygrovehouse.co.uk

map: 11 entry: 333

NORFOLK

Peace, tradition and unassuming good taste in this gentle, dignified old house. A large tapestry hangs in the stairwell and foot-square stone slabs make up the ground floor, softened by rugs from Persia and the East. In the sitting room, a beautiful grand piano, which musical guests are welcome to play; in the garden a gazebo, a delightful place to relax with a book. The bedrooms are simple, and the double and one twin can make a self-contained flat, with own sitting room and kitchen. Bramerton is a conservation village on the edge of the Broads. Kind hosts, marvellous value, and home-grown eggs for breakfast.

rooms	3: 1 double with bath; 2 twins, both with private bath.
room price	£50. Singles by arrangement.
meals	Breakfast until 9.30am. Supper £15. B.Y.O.
closed	Rarely.
directions	10-15 minute drive from Norwich and the University. Bramerton signed from A146, 1st left (Norwich-Lowestoft Rd). House opp. church, with white 5-bar gate.

Elizabeth Perowne
The White House,
Bramerton, Norwich,
Norfolk NR14 7DW
tel   01508 538673
e-mail   e.perowne@amserve.net

map: 11 entry: 334

A house on a hill – unusual for East Anglia; the lawns fall away and views stretch out over farmland. Richard and Patricia are utterly charming and so easy to talk to; their respective passions are fishing and gardening and the garden is superb. In the house: fresh flowers, family photographs, agricultural prints, a feeling of light and space. The guest sitting room is generously furnished and Patricia will light a fire for you. The double, predominantly green bedroom is the biggest; all have thick carpets and a quiet Victorian elegance. *Second room let to same party willing to share bathroom.*

So many interesting objects it takes time to absorb the splendour; in the drawing room, gorgeous prints and paintings, unusual furniture, decorative lamps... Caroline has a fine eye for detail. The guest room has a Regency-style canopied king-size bed and decoration to suit the era of the house (1850). The large garden is just as fascinating, with 'rooms' and a huge, jungly pond that slinks between the trees. You can eat in the courtyard or the conservatory; Caroline prepares lovely dinners using much local produce. *Children over nine welcome.*

rooms	2: 1 twin/double, 1 double sharing bath. Extra wc & basin available.
room price	From £50. Singles £30.
meals	Pub/restaurant 1 mile.
closed	Rarely.
directions	A143 Diss/Yarmouth for 9 miles. At r'bout left for Harleston, then immed. left to Starston. Over x-roads, into village, over bridge, immed. right. After 0.5 miles, drive on left by white railings.

rooms	2: 1 double, 1 single, both with private bath.
room price	£50. Singles £25.
meals	Packed lunch £5. Lunch £10. Dinner from £15.
closed	Christmas & New Year.
directions	A11 Attleborough-Wymondham. Take Spooner Row sign. Over x-roads by Three Boars pub. At T-junc. left to Wymondham. 1 mile on, look for rusty barrel on left. Turn into farm track.

Mrs Patricia Lombe Taylor
Conifer Hill,
Low Road, Starston, Harleston,
Norfolk IP20 9NT
tel   01379 852393
fax   01379 852393
e-mail richard.taylor55@virgin.net

Caroline Musker
Sallowfield Cottage,
Wattlefield, Wymondham,
Norfolk NR18 9PA
tel   01953 605086
e-mail caroline.musker@tesco.net

Mrs Garnier has become a legend among B&B-ers – she has done it for so long and looks after her stupendous Grade II*-listed house single-handedly. She tells colourful stories of the house and her family's long local history: from 1349 until the Dissolution of the Monasteries, it was a college of priests; later, it was saved from ruin and brought back to life. It has a stunning panelled dining room, big bedrooms (the sky-blue one is particularly pretty) and great views. Incredible value for such a special house. *Children over seven welcome.*

A thatched, self-contained, octagonal former dairy which makes a perfect retreat. Built on the Berry Hall Estate which is designated as being of national, historic and scenic importance, it has been beautifully restored by the very best craftsmen. There are 126 acres to roam, half of which are woodland but you may be tempted to stay in and finish that book! There's a little kitchen with fridge stocked with delicious things for a continental breakfast, your own terracotta-tiled sitting room, with a luxurious sofabed… or a magical mezzanine bedroom, reached by a steep staircase. There's even a private sun terrace. A real indulgence.

rooms	3: 1 double with private bath; 1 twin, 1 twin/double, both with bath. Also extra shower & wc.
room price	From £50. Singles £25.
meals	Afternoon tea included. Pub 1 mile.
closed	Rarely.
directions	From Thetford A1075 north for Watton. After 9 miles, left to Thompson. After 0.5 miles 2nd left at red postbox on corner. Left again, house at dead end.

rooms	1 double with jacuzzi; mezzanine bed also available.
room price	£65.
meals	Pubs/restaurants nearby.
closed	Rarely.
directions	From A47 Barnham Broom/Weston Longville x-roads, south towards Barnham Broom. After 150 yds, 1st drive on right. Left at T-junc., left again, house on left.

Mrs Garnier
College Farm,
Thompson, Thetford,
Norfolk IP24 1QG
tel   01953 483318
fax   01953 483318
e-mail collegefarm@amserve.net

Deborah Meynell
The Buttery,
Berry Hall, Honingham, Norwich,
Norfolk NR9 5AX
tel   01603 880541
fax   01603 880887
e-mail thebuttery@paston.co.uk

A big, rambling, Regency house on the border of the ancient county of Rutland; its 10 acres are home to all sorts of animals including horses and chickens. It is unsmart, deliciously eccentric and you may get up and go to bed when you please. Dogs jump on sofas, there's croquet on the lawn and their own herbal healthcare by the bed. Your hosts are irresistible – David opens wine on your arrival, Susan supports Compassion in World Farming and both are amusing company. A haphazard collection of furniture, fine paintings in gilded frames, oddities at every turn, and Susan to cook you generous organic breakfasts on the Aga.

The 1970s exterior belies the comfort and elegance within. Tessa's family once owned a house near this site and much of the antique furniture lives on here; her ancestors include a lover of Elizabeth, Empress of Austria, hence the imperial memorabilia on display. Tessa and her ex-Army husband, David, have lived all over the world and the warm domesticity of the house reflects their desire to "come home to roost". You are given a charming welcome and a delicious breakfast with eggs from the chickens and other fowl that wander the garden.

rooms	3: 1 twin, 1 double, both with private bath; 1 family with shower.
room price	£47. Singles £25.
meals	Pubs/restaurants nearby.
closed	Rarely.
directions	From Corby to Stamford, left to Laxton (1 mile); with the Green on right, house on left up drive.

rooms	2: 1 twin, 1 double, both with basin, sharing bath.
room price	£70. Singles £40.
meals	Breakfast 7-10am. Packed lunch £5. Dinner £25. Good pubs locally.
closed	Rarely.
directions	From A14, A508 for Northampton, 1st right to Haselbech. At sharp r-h bend, left to Cottesbrooke, 0.25 miles. Left between 2 red cottages; 1st right between fields. Tarmac drive to house.

Susan Hill-Brookes
Old Vicarage,
Laxton, Nr Corby,
Northamptonshire NN17 3AT
tel   01780 450248
fax   01780 450259
e-mail   susan@marthahill.co.uk
web   www.old-vicarage-laxton.co.uk

Tessa Le Sueur
Haselbech House,
Haselbech Hill, Northampton,
Northamptonshire NN6 9LL
tel   01604 686266
e-mail   lesueur@haselbech.freeserve.co.uk
web   www.haselbechhousefarm.co.uk

A grand avenue of limes leads to this former farmhouse, built in the 1840s and part of the Althorp estate. Valerie and Ian, who know all about the area, are great company and welcome guests with afternoon tea and cakes; they collect and sell Staffordshire pottery. Meals are enjoyed by a log-burning stove in the deep-blue dining room in winter, and on the terrace on warm summer nights. Bedrooms are large and simple, with sofas and armchairs. The garden reveals traces of medieval ridge-and-furrow farming, the views of the countryside are magnificent and it's a great area for riding – livery is available.

Liz clearly derives great pleasure from sharing with guests her 300-year-old stone thatched cottage, heavenly garden, pretty conservatory and converted barn. There are wonderful pictures and furniture wherever you turn: a Jacobean trunk, a Bechstein piano, a beautiful bureau in the bathroom... Beds are hugely comfortable, and Cordon Bleu dinners are elegant affairs, and fun and jolly, too – Liz has a lovely sense of humour. Previous guests have said that staying here is like "staying with a good friend". The conservation village of Staverton is delightful. *Children over eight and babes in arms welcome.*

rooms	3: 1 double with bath, 1 extra twin let only to members of same party; 1 twin with private bath.
room price	£55-£65. Singles £35.
meals	Dinner £17.50. B.Y.O wine.
closed	Rarely.
directions	From N'hampton, A45 for Daventry. After approx. 1.5 miles, 3rd exit at r'bout for Althorp. After 1 mile, 1st exit at r'bout for Nobottle. House just beyond Nobottle on left, on brow of hill.

rooms	4: 2 doubles, 1 twin, all with bath/shower; 1 single with bath.
room price	£82. Singles £52.
meals	Dinner, 3 courses, £26.50.
closed	Christmas & New Year.
directions	From Daventry, A425 to Leamington Spa. 100 yds past Staverton Park Conference Centre, right into village, then 1st right. Keep left, & at 'Give Way' sign, sharp left. House immed. on right.

Valerie Cocks
Nobottle Grange,
Nobottle, Northampton,
Northamptonshire NN7 4HJ
tel   01604 759494
fax   01604 590799
e-mail   stay@nobottlegrange.co.uk
web   www.nobottlegrange.co.uk

Liz Jarrett
Colledges House,
Oakham Lane, Staverton, Daventry,
Northamptonshire NN11 6JQ
tel   01327 702737
fax   01327 300851
e-mail   lizjarrett@colledgeshouse.fsnet.co.uk

Eileen and Clive fell in love with the place the moment they saw the valley from the top of the hill. They are the friendliest hosts and have created splendid comfort; large bedrooms have exposed beams and dreamy views. Built as a coach house in the 1850s, it adjoins the site of a former priory founded in 1175. The garden is gorgeous – watch the ducks, or fish, on the small lake. Open countryside and the Jurassic Way beckon walkers, west-facing terraces catch sunsets, there may be apricot cake on your return... A rural idyll only 15 minutes from the M1 and M40 – but so peaceful you'd never know.

In this wonderful corner of England you're immersed in a restorative peace. The church and the listed vicarage have sat side by side since the 18th century; birdsong and the sound of tennis being played on the grass court add to the Englishness of it all. Inside are winding stairways and warm, homely bedrooms with green views; a rose peeps in at the bathroom window and the Aga-warmed double is in its own wing. Lots of choice for breakfast and your favourite newspaper can be waiting on the table. Your hosts are country people who love horses and dogs – they could not be more kind. *Children by arrangement.*

rooms	2: 1 double with private bath/shower; 1 twin with shower.
room price	£70. Singles £45.
meals	Pub 1 mile; restaurants within 5 miles.
closed	Rarely.
directions	At Staverton on A425 Daventry to Leamington Spa; take road to Catesby opp. Countryman pub for 2 miles. 200 yds after sharp bend right to Lower Catesby. House to left of clock at foot of hill.

rooms	2: 1 double with shower; 1 twin with private bath.
room price	From £60. Singles £35.
meals	Packed lunch £3-£5. Dinner £12-£15.
closed	Christmas.
directions	From M40 junc. 11, dual c'way for N'thampton. 0.75 miles on, left at r'bout for N'thampton; left again 2 miles on. Follow signs for Canons Ashby to Moreton Pinkney. There, fork right across green on track. Beside church.

Clive & Eileen Gardiner Wood
The Old Coach House,
Lower Catesby, Daventry,
Northamptonshire NN11 6LF
tel 01327 310390
fax 01327 312220
e-mail coachhouse@lowercatesby.co.uk
web www.lowercatesby.co.uk

Colonel & Mrs T J S Eastwood
The Old Vicarage,
Moreton Pinkney, Daventry,
Northamptonshire NN11 3SQ
tel 01295 760057
fax 01295 760057
e-mail tim@tandjeastwood.fsnet.co.uk
web www.tandjeastwood.fsnet.co.uk

NORTHUMBERLAND

NORTHUMBERLAND

A south-facing Georgian farmhouse overlooking the Tweed with Holy Island in the distance and not a whisper of noise. You know that Berwick is two miles away and Edinburgh and Newcastle only 45 minutes by train, but you can't feel it. There's broad appeal here for sightseers, birdwatchers, anglers, golfers, deerstalkers and country lovers... a drying room for your wet togs and a deep freeze for your catch. The luxury is irresistible: fine fabrics, bedding as soft as the landscape, a log fire in the sitting room grate. Susan, a trained cook, and Richard, a retired wine-shipper, will advise you on the best places to eat.

Livvy greets you with the warmest welcome and the finest modern cooking. The kitchen is the hub of her house – she's a professional cook – and the house, mid-19th-century, is the last in England. The old Union chain bridge over the river Tweed is 100 yards away; anglers fish for salmon and the riverside walks are wonderful. Log fires in the sitting room, cookbooks and guide books in the library, a revolving summer house in the garden and two small but cheerful rooms for you. Breakfasts are delicious: home-cured bacon, hash browns, own jams, local honey. Five acres, and all that other space.

rooms	2: 1 double with bath/shower; 1 twin/double with shower.
room price	£66-£70. Singles from £43.
meals	Breakfast until 9am. Packed lunch available. Good pubs, restaurants & hotels 5-minute drive.
closed	Christmas & New Year.
directions	Travelling north on A1 level with Berwick, cross bridge over River Tweed; after 1.5 miles take 2nd left signed Low Cocklaw. House on left after 0.5 miles.

rooms	2: 1 twin with bath; 1 double with shower.
room price	£50. Singles £33.
meals	Packed lunch £5. Dinner, 3 courses, £15-£20.
closed	Rarely.
directions	A698; exit from A1 at East Ord, west of Berwick. After 1 mile, right for Horncliffe; follow signs for Honey Farm; past farm 200 yds; house on right.

Richard & Susan Persse
High Letham Farmhouse,
by Berwick-upon-Tweed,
Northumberland TD15 1UX
tel   01289 306585
fax   01289 304194
e-mail   hlfs@fantasyprints.co.uk

Livvy Cawthorn
Chain Bridge House,
Horncliffe, Berwick-upon-Tweed,
Northumberland TD15 2XT
tel   01289 386259
fax   01289 386259
e-mail   info@chainbridgehouse.co.uk
web   www.chainbridgehouse.co.uk

NORTHUMBERLAND

NORTHUMBERLAND

A totally surprising one-storey house, full of beautiful things. It is an Aladdin's cave, larger than you could imagine. The garden/breakfast room is its hub and has a country cottage feel; enjoy locally-smoked kippers here, award-winning 'Bamburgh Bangers' and home-cured bacon from the village butcher. There's also a sun-trapping courtyard full of colourful pots for breakfasts in the sun. Guests have a cheerful sitting/dining room and bedrooms have fresh flowers and good books. Mary is welcoming, amusing and has stacks of local knowledge.

Sylvia is a doyenne of farmhouse B&B, with 25 years' experience under her belt. She received an MBE for her Household and Farming Museum and is justly proud of her gong. She has a wonderful sense of community and Charlie, even if he's been up since dawn with his sheep, will come and chat over breakfast. It's warm, cosy and comfortable – big fires, lots of family furniture, knick-knacks and photos. Breakfasts are as generous as you'd expect, and there are fresh flowers everywhere. Bedrooms are large, with long views, fine cotton sheets and patchwork quilts. True farmhouse B&B. *Children over 10 welcome.*

rooms	2: 1 double, 1 twin, sharing private bath.
room price	£50-£60. Singles £36-£40.
meals	Dinner, 2 courses £15; 3 courses, £20.
closed	Rarely.
directions	From Newcastle north on A1, then right for Bamburgh on B1341. To village, pass 30mph sign & hotel, then 1st right. 400 yds on right.

rooms	3: 2 doubles, both with shower; 1 twin with private bath.
room price	£60. Singles £40.
meals	Breakfast 7.30-9am. Restaurants 4 miles.
closed	Christmas & New Year.
directions	6 miles north of Alnwick on A1, left on reaching dual carriageway, for North Charlton. House 300 yds up on left through trees.

Mary Dixon
Broome,
22 Ingram Road, Bamburgh,
Northumberland NE69 7BT
tel 01668 214287
e-mail mdixon4394@aol.com

Charles & Sylvia Armstrong
North Charlton Farm,
Chathill, Alnwick,
Northumberland NE67 5HP
tel 01665 579443
fax 01665 579407
e-mail ncharlton1@agriplus.net
web www.northcharlton.com

map: 19 entry: 347

map: 19 entry: 348

The Jacksons know every inch of the countryside and coast that surrounds their 1715 home. It's a pretty spot. They farm 400 acres of mixed arable land that sweeps down to the coast yet find time to greet and get to know their guests. Dorothy takes pride in creating an easy and sociable atmosphere – three couples who met here one weekend returned for a reunion! The bedrooms are large, bright and well-furnished; there is a conservatory at the back where you can have tea on arrival, an airy guests' sitting room and splendid views to the sea. *Self-catering available. See back of book.*

In blissful countryside west of Alnwick, with fabulous walking in the Cheviot Hills to the west again, Lyn has created the friendliest B&B. She's also a masseuse and aromatherapist – do book a session. There's a nice garden, a drying room for wet togs and all is pristine indoors, so take off your shoes and settle in for a relaxing time. Bedrooms are uncluttered and serene with blending pale colours and good bathrooms, one with painted floorboards, all with thick towels. Choose from scores of books in the sitting/dining room and make the most of meals; much of the food will be organic, and local.

rooms	3: 2 doubles, 1 twin, all with shower. Bath also available.
room price	£54. Singles £27-£37.
meals	Packed lunches from £3.50. Dinner £15.50.
closed	Christmas & New Year.
directions	From Alnwick, A1068 to Alnmouth. At Hipsburn r'bout follow signs to station & cross bridge. 1st lane to left, approx. 0.5 miles down drive.

rooms	3: 1 double, 1 twin/double, both with bath/shower; 1 double with private bath.
room price	£50-£60.
meals	Dinner £17.50, weekdays only. B.Y.O.
closed	Rarely.
directions	A697 north of Morpeth; take road opp. the Bridge of Aln Hotel, signed Whittingham & Callaly. In Whittingham, 1st left, on for 1.5 miles; cottage on left.

Brian & Dorothy Jackson
Bilton Barns,
Alnmouth, Alnwick,
Northumberland NE66 2TB
tel 01665 830427
fax 01665 830909
e-mail dorothy@biltonbarns.com
web www.biltonbarns.com

Lyn Watson
Callaly Cottage,
Callaly, Alnwick,
Northumberland NE66 4TA
tel 01665 574684
e-mail callaly@alnwick.org.uk
web www.callaly.alnwick.org.uk

map: 19 entry: 349

map: 19 entry: 350

Farmhouse B&B at its traditional best: pine furniture, flowery curtains, big duvets, plain walls. It is cosy and friendly, your hosts are kind and the countryside will be a wild surprise if you don't yet know it. The views are spectacular. Be there at the right time and see fields full of gamboling lambs; revel in the way the salmon and trout on the River Coquet fight for a place on your hook. The National Park is all around you, as are more castles and fortifications than in any other county. Breakfasts are good with fresh Craster kippers, fruit, yogurts and local produce.

Enid thrives on hard work and company, and that combination makes the perfect B&B hostess — you couldn't meet a nicer woman. Choose any of her five large homely bedrooms and stay a week — they are awash with comfort, old paintings, silk fabrics, crisp white linen. There's masses to eat and drink and the views stretch to the horizon. But if you do stray downstairs — past the log fire and the groaning table (dinner is excellent value) — there are 600 acres of farmland to discover and a few million more of the Cheviots beyond that. Wonderful hosts, house and region.

rooms	3: 2 doubles, both with bath/shower; 1 twin with shower.
room price	£55. Singles £35.
meals	Good pubs/restaurants 2-6 miles.
closed	Christmas & New Year.
directions	Left in Rothbury along Bridge St; 1st immed. right over bridge, follow B&B signs for Great Tosson, approximately 2 miles.

rooms	5: 4 doubles, 1 twin, all with bath/shower.
room price	£50. Singles £35.
meals	Breakfast 7.30-9.30am. Dinner, 3 courses, £14.
closed	Christmas.
directions	Leave A1 for A697 for Coldstream & Longhorsley; 2 miles past Longhorsley, left at Todburn sign; 1 mile to x-roads, then right; on 1 mile over white bridge; 1st right, right again, over cattle grid.

John & Ann Foggin
Tosson Tower Farm,
Great Tosson, Rothbury,
Northumberland NE65 7NW
tel 01669 620228
fax 01669 620228
e-mail ann@tossontowerfarm.com
web www.tossontowerfarm.com

Henry & Enid Nelless
Thistleyhaugh,
Longhorsley, Morpeth,
Northumberland NE65 8RG
tel 01665 570629
fax 01665 570629
web www.thistleyhaugh.co.uk

map: 19 entry: 351

map: 19 entry: 352

An important estate, village and 17th-century house 20 minutes from Newcastle, surrounded by medieval woods, deer, badgers, bats and red squirrels. Ho and Margaret are devoted conservationists and have worked hard to restore the listed Palladian Hall, rescuing the fabulous ceramic floor, working shutters, rare staircase and stained-glass window designed by William Morris. Bedrooms and bathrooms are swish with a contemporary touch; views of the walled garden and Victorian fernery from the back windows are glorious. Superb food, fine fabrics, fresh flowers – magnificent.

Guests stay in recently converted farm buildings round a courtyard and each suite is named after the wood used within: Stephen makes and restores antique furniture and there's an example of his artistry at every turn. Bedrooms are compact but guests share a sitting room and a beautiful library within the courtyard, while meals are taken in the oak-beamed main house (once the home of Capability Brown's family). Celia is a friendly, attentive hostess who loves cooking – many ingredients are home-grown; Stephen tops up your drinks from the bar. There's a small but varied wine list, too. A super place.

rooms	6: 3 doubles, 1 twin, all with bath/shower; 1 double with bath; 1 single with private bath.
room price	£97. Singles £55.
meals	Packed lunch £10. Dinner, 3 courses, £25.
closed	22 December–5 January.
directions	Turn east off A1, 6 miles north of Morpeth & 8 miles south of Alnwick, at Eshott signpost. Hall gates approx. 1 mile down lane.

rooms	3: 1 four-poster, 1 double, 1 twin, all with bath/shower.
room price	£58–£70. Singles £40.
meals	Dinner, 4 courses, £20. Good pub 6 miles.
closed	Rarely.
directions	From Newcastle A696 (for Jedburgh). 5 miles north of Belsay, right onto B6342. House on left after 300 yds.

Ho & Margaret Sanderson
Eshott Hall,
Morpeth,
Northumberland NE65 9EP

tel	01670 787777
fax	01670 787999
e-mail	thehall@eshott.com
web	www.eshott.com

Celia & Stephen Robinson–Gay
Shieldhall,
Wallington, Morpeth,
Northumberland NE61 4AQ

tel	01830 540387
fax	01830 540490
e-mail	robinson.gay@btinternet.com
web	www.shieldhallguesthouse.co.uk

map: 19 entry: 353

map: 19 entry: 354

A magical setting, just three miles from Hadrian's Wall. The house is at the end of a long drive – over the burn and an old stone bridge, surrounded by ancient woodland and birdsong. This is an elegant and comfortable home, with large and delightful guest bedrooms furnished with antiques and lovely prints. There is a walled garden, too, and breakfasts, which are delicious, can be served on the terrace. Katie grew up in this lovely house and can tell you all about the area; many guests write to tell us how well they have been looked after. *Children over seven and babes in arms welcome.*

Serene and beautiful now, this mansion once figured in the Jacobite Rebellion. (It was here, in 1715, that the Earl of Derwentwater went into hiding before the Battle of Preston.) A river flows through the parkland surrounding the honey-coloured, Grade-II listed house, and a ha-ha keeps deer out of the gardens. Drawing and dining rooms are big, handsome and furnished with some fine antiques – as are the bedrooms. One has a Victorian four-poster bed, and all are superbly equipped. Pattie is a delightful hostess and a trained Cordon Bleu cook – there's delicious home-made bread and preserves for breakfast.

rooms	3: 1 double, 1 twin, both with bath; 1 twin with private bath.
room price	£70. Singles £45.
meals	Breakfast 7.30-9am. 3 good eating pubs locally.
closed	October-February.
directions	7 miles north of Corbridge on A68. Left on A6079 & after 1 mile, right through Lodge gates with arch. House 0.5 miles down drive.

rooms	3: 1 four-poster, with bath/shower; 1 double with bath/shower; 1 twin/double with shower.
room price	£90. Singles £45.
meals	Dinner, 4 courses, £25.
closed	Christmas & New Year.
directions	From A69 two miles west of Hexham turn off bypass signed Fourstones & Newbrough. On 6 miles to Newbrough; pass Red Lion pub on right. Newbrough Park 200 yds on left.

Simon & Katie Stewart
The Hermitage,
Swinburne, Nr Hexham,
Northumberland NE48 4DG
tel   01434 681248
fax   01434 681110
e-mail   katie.stewart@themeet.co.uk

Mrs Pattie Wilson
Newbrough Park,
Newbrough, Hexham,
Northumberland NE47 5AR
tel   01434 674545
fax   01434 674544
e-mail   newbroughpark@aol.com

Lynne has made many improvements to this 18th-century gentleman's residence and continues to do so. Bedrooms have original Georgian shutters; some have waxed floors with rugs. Guests love the comfy beds. Substantial breakfasts are served in the delightful dining room with its antique oak dresser and other good pieces. All rooms have exceptional views of the Northumberland countryside which beckons the walker, the naturalist, the stressed city soul. A pretty garden, a newly-built stable block, an outdoor arena set in five acres and a big family welcome.

The topiary is magnificent! And the old dovecote fascinates foreigners. This is a solid, Victorian house set in expansive, breathtaking Northumbrian scenery – a magnet for walkers and nature lovers. Your gentle, hospitable hostess welcomes families now that her children have flown the nest, though their Beatrix Potter books and little knick-knacks remain. Lots of photographs, too, mostly of the family on horseback. Twin bedrooms are straightforward but large and perfectly adequate, and all have wonderful views.

rooms	3: 2 doubles, both with shower; 1 family room with bath.
room price	£55. Singles £35.
meals	Restaurants within short drive.
closed	December–January.
directions	A69 signed Ovington, on left if travelling to Hexham. Through Ovington. House signed on left, after sharp corner.

rooms	3 twins (2 with basin) sharing 2 baths.
room price	£50. Singles from £30.
meals	Breakfast from 7am. Dinner from £20.
closed	Rarely.
directions	From A68, south of Tyne at r'bout, east for Stocksfield. B6309 right, signed Hindley. 1st left, then biggest house at end.

Lynne Moffitt
Ovington House,
Ovington, Prudhoe,
Northumberland NE42 6DH
tel   01661 832442
fax   01661 832442
e-mail   lynne.moffitt@btopenworld.com

Mrs J Aldridge
Old Ridley Hall,
Stocksfield,
Northumberland NE43 7RU
tel   01661 842816
e-mail   oldridleyhall@talk21.com

From the front bedrooms and the majestic drawing and dining rooms you look beyond the lawns and cherished roses to a sensational view: the Vale of Belvoir at your feet. Belvoir means 'beautiful view' so you can imagine the scene. The house, large and rambling, has been in the family for generations – though there is less family bustle and the bathrooms and bedrooms are a little dated, the grandfather clock and the formal rooms vividly recall a grander age. Use of the swimming pool and tennis court can be arranged. The hill behind is the highest between here and the Urals in Russia. *Horse B&B by arrangement.*

A butter-yellow 30s semi in a quiet, tree-lined street – the perfect city base. Suzanne, an ex-model, much-travelled, is as immediately engaging as her home, and good company, too. Colour schemes are cool with the odd oriental touch. Your bedroom in the loft – a self-contained hideaway with a good, big bed – is carpeted and crisply decorated with fabrics in bold, floral cream-and-green. Eggs and bacon are served on the terrace in fine weather; Suzanne is happy to take guests to and from the station. The city's attractions are only two miles away, the great oaks of Sherwood Forest 12 miles north.

rooms	3: 2 doubles, both with private bath; 1 twin with shower.
room price	£45-£50. Singles £25-£30.
meals	Good pubs 0.5-1 mile.
closed	Christmas.
directions	On A606 between Nottingham (12 miles) & Melton Mowbray (7 miles). Coming north drive to top of hill, then sharp right into Colonel's Lane. Signed.

rooms	1 double with shower.
room price	£50. Singles £30.
meals	Good pubs/restaurants nearby.
closed	Rarely.
directions	From main Mansfield Rd at junc. with Vale Pub going north. Right onto Thackerey's Lane; at r'bout straight on; after 100 yds right into Whernside Rd. Left at x-roads into Littlegreen Rd; house on left.

Hilary Collinson
Sulney Fields,
Colonel's Lane, Upper Broughton,
Melton Mowbray,
Nottinghamshire LE14 3BD
tel   01664 822204
fax   01664 823976
e-mail   hillyc@talk21.com

S Prew-Smith
The Yellow House,
7 Littlegreen Road, Woodthorpe,
Nottingham,
Nottinghamshire NG5 4LE
tel   0115 9262280
fax   0115 9262280

NOTTINGHAMSHIRE

Clematis romps over the walls of this small organic holding with lush views down the Trent Valley. Di is delightful — she's there when you need her yet knows your privacy is precious; you may even use her kitchen to make coffee and tea. Bedrooms are simple yet cosy, with electric underblankets and sheepskin rugs. You have a sitting room upstairs with comfy seating and old pine, and another with beams and log fires. There's a dolls' house, a garden and a rope in the hay barn for children; stewed Bramleys and Di's jams for breakfast, best organic bacon too. Perfect for walkers, fishermen and families in search of peace.

rooms	3: 2 twins, 1 family (double, 2 singles & cot), sharing 2 bathrooms.
room price	£40. Singles £20.
meals	Breakfast 7–9am. Picnic lunch available. Pubs nearby.
closed	Rarely.
directions	From A46 towards Newark to East Bridgford. At village x-roads right into Kneeton Road. 20 yds after Reindeer pub, left up farm track.

Mrs Di Shouls
Barn Farm Cottage,
Kneeton Road, East Bridgford,
Nottinghamshire NG13 8PJ
tel   01949 20196

NOTTINGHAMSHIRE

Jillie's grandmother studied at the Slade and her paintings line the walls; glass and china adorn every surface. The wisteria-clad Victorian vicarage next to the 12th-century church was falling down when the Steeles bought it; now it's an elegant, traditional country home. Long windows are generously draped, bedrooms are large, baths have claw feet and a number of friendly cats and dogs wait to welcome you. Jerry bakes the bread and all the vegetables come from the garden, where you may play tennis or croquet. Mary Queen of Scots is reputed to have stayed at Langford as guest of the Earl of Shrewsbury.

rooms	3: 1 double, 1 twin, both with bath & shower; 1 small double with shower.
room price	£70–£80. Singles £45–£50.
meals	Dinner £20.
closed	Rarely.
directions	From A1, A46 to Lincoln & left onto A1133 for Gainsborough. Through Langford, 1 mile on, & left for Holme. House 100 yds on, on right, by church.

Jerry & Jillie Steele
The Old Vicarage,
Langford, Newark,
Nottinghamshire NG23 7RT
tel   01636 705031
fax   01636 708728
e-mail   jillie.steele@virgin.net

All the nooks, crannies and beams you expect in such an ancient thatched cottage in a Cotswold village… and much more besides: music, fun, laughter and a wealth of inside information about gardens to visit. Judith is a keen gardener who writes books on the subject (her passion for plants is palpable in her own glorious garden) and her style and intelligence are reflected in the house. Pretty, south-facing and full of sunlight, it has an elegant sitting room that opens onto the garden and a terrace to eat out on in summer. Bedrooms are light, charming, cottagey – this is a thoroughly relaxing place to stay.

There's a marvellous glow to this lovingly restored house. A rare, original and fine example of a large 1650s Yeoman farmhouse, it has more than its fair share of oak beams, stone-mullioned windows, big fireplaces and bread ovens. What's more, there are fine antiques, paintings and, in the attic, a games room with a full-size billiard table; beamed bedrooms are large, light and airy, with views to valley or church. This is an exceptionally pretty village with a proper green. Breakfasts are generous, the Hainsworths are excellent hosts, and their two lovely dogs are "weird-haired" pointers, apparently!

rooms	2: 1 double, 1 twin, both with bath.
room price	£70. Singles £45.
meals	Dinner, 4 courses, £25. Excellent restaurant 150 yards.
closed	Christmas & New Year.
directions	Sibford Gower 0.5 miles south off B4035 between Banbury & Chipping Campden. House on Main Street, same side as church & school.

rooms	2: 1 double, 1 twin, both with bath.
room price	From £75. Singles £50.
meals	Excellent pub & restaurant in village.
closed	Rarely.
directions	From A422, 7 miles north-west of Banbury, left down hill through Alkerton, then up hill. 1st left by church. House on right.

Judith Hitching
Gower's Close,
Sibford Gower, Nr Banbury,
Oxfordshire OX15 5RW
tel   01295 780348
e-mail   j.hitching@virgin.net

Keith & Maggie Hainsworth
Mill House,
Shenington, Banbury,
Oxfordshire OX15 6NH
tel   01295 670642

map 9 entry   64

OXFORDSHIRE

Parish records suggest that on the site of the 1760 house there was once a monastic farm where teachers at Oxford would come for enlightenment and inspiration; today you reap the same benefits, and in considerable comfort. Stephen and Sara happily share their books, piano, tennis court, gardens, lake and local knowledge. Sara is an interior designer: cushions, curtains and sofas are made from beautiful fabrics and the colours throughout are excellent. The beds are memorably comfortable, with goose down pillows and duvets. Breakfast is an easy-going affair and there's a guest drawing room with log fire.

rooms	3: 1 twin/double with shower; 1 twin/double with bath; 1 twin/double with bath/shower.
room price	£68. Singles £40.
meals	Dinner £20. Excellent pubs 600 yds.
closed	Rarely.
directions	In Kings Sutton follow signs to Charlton but before leaving Kings S., take last turning right down lane, off Astrop road, opp. tree with a seat around it. At end of lane.

Sara & Stephen Allday
College Farmhouse,
Kings Sutton, Banbury,
Oxfordshire OX17 3PS
tel 01295 811473
fax 01295 812505
e-mail seallday@aol.com
web www.banburytown.co.uk/accom/collegefarm

map: 9 entry: 365

OXFORDSHIRE

Our inspector really loved this place. The Grove-Whites are super and they run their B&B as a team. The house is charming: low ceilings, exposed beams, stone fireplaces and winding stairs; the bedrooms, perched above their own staircases like crows' nests, are decorated with rich, floral fabrics. All rooms are unusual, full of character, old and luxurious; the family's history and travels are evident all over and the barn room has its own entrance. There are two delightful dogs – Ulysses and Goliath – and it's all so easy-going you'll find it hard to leave.

rooms	3: 1 double, 1 twin/double, both with bath/shower; 1 twin/double with private bath.
room price	£70. Singles £45.
meals	Breakfast 8-9am. Dinner £24. Supper £16.
closed	Christmas.
directions	From M40, junc. 10, A43 for Northampton. After 5 miles, left to Charlton. There, left & house on left, 100 yds past Rose & Crown.

Col & Mrs Grove-White
Home Farmhouse,
Charlton, Nr Banbury,
Oxfordshire OX17 3DR
tel 01295 811683
fax 01295 811683
e-mail grovewhite@lineone.net
web www.homefarmhouse.co.uk

map: 9 entry: 366

Great natural charm in the 17th-century Old Post House – shiny flagstones, rich dark wood, mullion windows. It looks good inside too: luxurious fabrics, papers, colours and fine furniture. Bedrooms are big, with antique wardrobes, oak headboards and swathes of fabric at windows. The walled gardens are rich with espaliered fruit trees and there's a pool. Christine, a well-travelled ex-pat, has an innate sense of hospitality; her two Springer spaniels welcome you, too. There's morning weekday traffic, but your sleep should be sound, and the village of Deddington is delightful. *Children over 12 welcome.*

Helen and John radiate pleasure and good humour. Blenheim Park is a short walk down the lane and this soft old stone house is perfect for any delusions of grandeur: good prints and paintings, venerable furniture, gentle fabrics – nothing is cluttered or overdone. Shallow, curvy, 18th-century stairs lead past grandfather's bronze bust to the splendid double; the tiny twin beyond the fine green shower room has its own challenging spiral stair down to the cobbled courtyard. Breakfast is by the rough-hewn fireplace and the ancient dresser. A delight of a garden and a quiet village complete the picture.

rooms	3: 1 double with private shower; 1 double with bath; 1 twin sharing bath (only let to same party).
room price	£68. Singles £40.
meals	Pubs & restaurants in village.
closed	Christmas & New Year.
directions	A4260 Oxford-Banbury. In Deddington, on right next to cream Georgian house. Park opposite.

rooms	2: 1 double, 1 twin, sharing shower.
room price	£50-£64. Singles from £35.
meals	Pub within walking distance.
closed	Christmas.
directions	A44 north from Oxford's ring road. At r'bout, 1 mile before Woodstock, left onto A4095 into Bladon. Take last left in village. House on 2nd bend in road, with iron railings.

	Christine Blenntoft
	The Old Post House,
	New Street, Deddington,
	Oxfordshire OX15 0SP
tel	01869 338978
fax	01869 337760
e-mail	kblenntoft@aol.com

	Helen Stevenson
	Manor Farmhouse,
	Manor Road, Bladon,
	Nr Woodstock,
	Oxfordshire OX20 1RU
tel	01993 812168
fax	01993 812168
e-mail	helstevenson@hotmail.com
web	www.oxlink.co.uk/woodstock/manor-farmhouse/

Behind the façade of this charming Cotswold stone house – once the village inn – is a delightful family home. The light, white bedroom, simply and exquisitely furnished, has gentle views over the village green; its bathroom is big and beautiful. Take breakfast in the sunny, flower-filled conservatory with glorious, wide-reaching views – on a clear day you can see for over 30 miles. There's a relaxed atmosphere here and your hosts enjoy guests; they are also passionate about rare plants, trees and flowers, and have landscaped and planted a superb garden.

Our inspector called it "a Sawday idyll". Bridget is gracious and elegant, the house and setting intoxicating. This is country elegance with few concessions to modernity: rugs and furniture fit beautifully, the kitchen is stone-flagged and wood-boarded. The Garden House is a wonderful B&B or self-catering hideaway – hunker down with books, play the piano, stroll out into the garden; you have your own bedroom, kitchen, sitting room and log fire. The River Windrush trickles through the garden, the church and the ruins of Minster Lovell Hall sit beside it.

rooms	1 twin with bath.
room price	From £75. Singles £45.
meals	Breakfast until 9.30am.
closed	Christmas.
directions	From Witney, 4 miles for Charlbury on B4022, then left to Leafield. There, pass church & fork left by flagpole & school sign. 100 yds on, house on left, with lawn in front. Turn into gravel drive.

rooms	1 double in Garden House with bath/shower.
room price	£75. Singles £47.50.
meals	Good pubs within walking distance.
closed	Rarely.
directions	From Burford, A40 for Oxford. At next r'bout, left for Minster Lovell, left down hill & across bridge. Through village, house on right before church, in cul-de-sac marked 'Unsuitable for motor vehicles'. Through green gates on right.

Mrs Tania Llewellyn
Old George House,
Leafield, Oxfordshire OX29 9NP
tel   01993 878632
fax   01993 878700

Ms Bridget Geddes
The Old Vicarage,
Minster Lovell,
Oxfordshire OX29 0RR
tel   01993 775630
fax   01993 772534
e-mail ageddes@lix.compulink.co.uk

This beautiful farmhouse was once owned by St John's College, Oxford – the date stone above the entrance reads 1629; parts of the house are even older. There's the happy buzz of family life here: it's relaxed, informal and you settle in easily, welcomed with tea and home-made shortbread by Mary Anne and the equally friendly Robert. Bedrooms are light and airy with small stone-arched and mullioned windows; there are Tudor fireplaces, timbered and exposed walls. The huge twin bedroom has ornate plasterwork and views over the garden and church; the green and peach double is cosier, again with views. *Self-catering available. See back of book.*

Ten acres in which to dream – this 18th-century stone house sits behind a Norman church in a perfect Cotswold hamlet. "England at its most idyllic," said our inspector. The beautifully renovated farmhouse marries character with elegance: a comfortable sitting room, sweet bedrooms (one with its own sitting room), flowers from a garden that is Clare's delight. She and Robin are friendly, vibrant, easy with children – there are children's arts and crafts workshops in the holidays and ponies in the yard which children can ride. The surrounding fields provide glorious views. *Self-catering available. See back of book.*

rooms	2: 1 double, 1 twin, both with shower.
room price	£52–£55. Singles £38–£40.
meals	Breakfast until 9am. Good pub 2-minute walk.
closed	Mid-December–mid-January.
directions	From Oxford, A420 for Swindon for 8 miles & right at r'bout, for Witney (A415). Over 2 bridges, immed. right by pub car park. Right at T-junction; drive on right, past church.

rooms	3: 1 double, 1 twin, both with private bath; 1 twin/double with bath & sitting room.
room price	£58–£80. Singles £44–£55.
meals	Dinner from £20. Good pubs & restaurants in town.
closed	Rarely.
directions	From Burford, A40 for Cheltenham. 1st left, for Westwell. 2 miles to T-junc., then right, through village. Right to Aldsworth then 1st right onto drive. On to end.

Mary Anne & Robert Florey
Rectory Farm,
Northmoor, Nr Witney,
Oxfordshire OX29 5SX
tel   01865 300207
fax   01865 300559
e-mail   pj.florey@farmline.com
web   www.oxtowns.co.uk/rectoryfarm

Clare & Robin Dunipace
The Glebe House,
Westwell, Burford,
Oxfordshire OX18 4JT
tel   01993 822171
fax   01993 824125
e-mail   clare.dunipace@amserve.net
web   www.oxford-cotswold-holidays.com

OXFORDSHIRE

OXFORDSHIRE

Roses and clematis cover this pretty 16th-century, perfectly renovated thatched cottage where breakfast is served around a big pine table in the farmhouse kitchen next to the Welsh dresser. The beamed bedrooms have lovely views; one has a 17th-century four-poster bed with cabbage rose chintz drapes, the Primrose Room with half-tester bed is in the stable annexe and all have hand-embroidered sheets and pillow slips. Sip tea or wine around a winter day's log fire in the beamed sitting room. Daughter Katie makes prize-winning food using as much local produce as possible. Good walks from the doorstep.

Birdsong and sunlight find their way into every room and Margaret, genuinely welcoming, bends to the needs of all guests; one suite, complete with piano, is perfect for wheelchair-users. There are chickens, geese, dogs and, in the lovely garden – a corner of which is Gertrude-Jekyll-inspired – a tennis court and pool. This is a treasured family home, not smart or designery, but with good furniture, masses of books, sparkling bathrooms, a little sitting room… even a kitchen area in which to prepare a snack should you prefer not to walk to the historic village's pubs.

rooms	3: 1 four-poster with bath; 2 doubles with shower.
room price	£75-£90.
meals	Breakfast until 9am. Dinner, 3 courses, £21.
closed	Rarely.
directions	From M4, junc. 14, north on A338. Left onto B4001. Through Lambourn, 1 mile north of village, fork left. 3 miles to Kingston Lisle, left to Uffington. Through village, right after church. House 0.3 miles out, on left.

rooms	5: 1 double with bath/shower; 1 double, 1 twin, both with private bath/shower; 1 twin with private shower; 1 single sharing bath (let to members of same party).
room price	£60-£70. Singles £30-£35.
meals	Packed lunch £5. Pubs in village.
closed	Rarely.
directions	Off A417, 3 miles from Wantage going east. Right into East Hendred; 3rd right into Orchard Lane; past pub; at x-roads, left into Cat St; house behind wall & wooden gates.

Carol Wadsworth
The Craven,
Fernham Road, Uffington,
Oxfordshire SN7 7RD

tel	01367 820449
fax	01367 820351
e-mail	carol@thecraven.co.uk
web	www.thecraven.co.uk

Margaret Bateman
Cowdrays,
Cat Street, East Hendred, Wantage,
Oxford, Oxfordshire OX12 8JT

| tel | 01235 833313 |
| e-mail | cowdrays@virgin.net |

map: 9 entry: 373

map: 9 entry: 374

OXFORDSHIRE

OXFORDSHIRE

Simple comfort and good value. Your functional, no-frills, lemon-yellow rooms are in a detached annexe – a separate garden flat – of this semi-detached worker's cottage; each has its own entrance. Breakfast is in the cosier main house in a pale green dining room lined with country prints. Horse-loving Joanna can advise you on riding and even offers B&B to horses; her husband, a keen rose-grower, may be able to organise rough-shooting, complete with gun dog. If roses, wine, shooting, hunting and stud farms are your thing, you could do no better. Possibly not for *Guardian* readers.

The architecture and the grounds are immediately captivating and the late Georgian interior is impressive in scale, with the light, height and space you expect from this period. The hall is galleried and the staircase, elegantly delicate, sweeps you regally up to the bedrooms. All rooms are large – bathroom suites hark back to the Seventies – and all except one look onto the garden and far beyond. Guests have a large drawing room, woodland to explore, tennis and croquet to play; French windows open onto the grounds. Brian and Wendy are super hosts.

rooms	2 twins in garden flat, both with bath & garden access.
room price	From £45. Singles from £25.
meals	Short drive to restaurants.
closed	Rarely.
directions	Junc. 8/9 M4 to Henley. A4130 to Oxford. Crowmarsh Gifford r'bout, left onto Wallingford bypass. Right at next r'bout, over river, left at 1st of double r'bouts to Moulsford. 1 mile on, right into Caps Lane. Cottage 1st on left.

rooms	5: 2 doubles, 2 twins, 1 single, all with bath.
room price	£65. Singles £45–£55.
meals	Breakfast 7.30-9.45am. Pub 0.5 miles.
closed	Rarely.
directions	From Henley, A4155 for Reading. After 2.5 miles, College on left & pub on right. Before pub turn into Plough Lane. House 1 mile on left.

	Mrs Joanna Alexander
	The Well Cottage,
	Caps Lane, Cholsey,
	Oxfordshire OX10 9HQ
tel	01491 651959
fax	01491 651675
e-mail	joanna@thewellcottage.com
web	www.thewellcottage.com

	Brian & Wendy Talfourd-Cook
	Holmwood,
	Shiplake Row, Binfield Heath,
	Henley, Oxfordshire RG9 4DP
tel	0118 947 8747
fax	0118 947 8637
e-mail	wendy.cook@freenet.co.uk

OXFORDSHIRE

They are efficient and unfussy and the lucky owners of a ravishing house. The décor is oak floors, white walls, wood, antiques, fine prints; there's a minimalist feel, with the odd dash of exotica from much long-haul travel. The drawing room has a vast, magnificent fireplace for winter. Anthea and Stephen are fun – clocks are their main business and the drawing room has a large, projected clock on the wall. Everywhere there is head-clearing simplicity that allows the original features the space to impress.

rooms	3: 1 double with bath; 1 double with private bath; 1 twin/double with shower.
room price	£80.
meals	Pub/restaurant 0.5 miles.
closed	Christmas & New Year.
directions	From M40, A329 for Wallingford. In Stadhampton take lane immed. after mini-r'bout, left across village green. House straight ahead.

Anthea & Stephen Savage
The Manor,
Stadhampton,
Oxfordshire OX44 7UL
tel 01865 891999
fax 01865 891640
e-mail action@timebeam.com

map: 9 entry: 377

OXFORDSHIRE

Marianne has applied talent and her Dutch background to make her 1920s house irresistibly comfortable. There are two sitting rooms, velvet and tapestry sofas, wooden floors, panelling, excellent beds and some lovely Dutch furniture. Big-hearted Marianne imposes few rules, prepares terrific breakfasts and gives lifts in her London cab to Oxford's Park & Ride (so you don't have to worry about your car), to the Ridgeway and to restaurants (she will collect you up until 1am!). Traffic noise from the nearby M40 is constant – loud outside, audible inside – but we defy you not to be charmed.

rooms	4: 2 doubles with private bath/shower; 1 twin sharing bath (let to members of the same party); 1 single with private shower.
room price	From £40-£70. Singles £35.
meals	Packed lunch £3.50. Lunch £5.. Dinner £15.
closed	Rarely.
directions	M40 from London, junc. 7 for Thame, left for Milton Common. Pass Belfry Hotel on right. House on left near end of road.

Mrs M Aben
Langsmeade House,
Milton Common, Thame,
Oxfordshire OX9 2JY
tel 01844 278727
fax 01844 279256
e-mail enquiry@langsmeadehouse.co.uk
web www.langsmeadehouse.co.uk

map: 9 entry: 378

RUTLAND

The stable yard is hung with roses and the delightful garden overlooks the croquet lawn and England's largest lake, Rutland Water (around which you may sail, fish, cycle or ride). Rutland is a mini-Cotswolds of stone villages, gentle hills, market towns and good pubs; historic houses and castles, bird sanctuaries and Georgian Stamford are nearby. Inside the house are high ceilings, stone archways, antique furniture and beds spread with fine linen. Do eat here – Cecilie is a charming hostess and a brilliant cook.

rooms	3: 1 twin, 1 double, both with private bath; 1 single with shared bath.
room price	£70. Singles £35-£45.
meals	Dinner £22.50.
closed	Occasionally.
directions	From A1 Stamford bypass A606 for Oakham for 3 miles. Fork left for Edith Weston. Past village sign take 1st right, Church Lane. Past church right again down hill. House on right on left bend.

Cecilie Ingoldby
Old Hall Coach House,
Edith Weston, Oakham,
Rutland LE15 8HQ

| tel | 01780 721504 |
| e-mail | cecilieingoldby@aol.com |

SHROPSHIRE

A tiny lane leads to Cleeton Court, where Ros greets you with tea and home-made cake. With views over meadows and heathland, the part-14th-century renovated farmhouse feels immersed in countryside – such peace. You have a private entrance to your rooms, and the use of the drawing room, prettily striped in yellow and cream, elegantly comfortable with sofas and log fire. Beamed bedrooms are delightfully furnished, one with a fabulously romantic, chintzy four-poster and a vast bathroom; recline in the cast-iron bath, gaze on views from the west-facing window as you soak. *Children over five welcome.*

rooms	2: 1 twin/double, 1 four-poster, both with bath.
room price	From £60. Singles £40.
meals	Excellent restaurants & pubs 4 miles.
closed	Christmas & New Year.
directions	From Ludlow, A4117 for Kidderminster for 1 mile; left on B4364 for Cleobury North; on for 5 miles. In Wheathill, right for Cleeton St Mary; on for 1.5 miles; house on left.

Rosamond Woodward
Cleeton Court,
Cleeton St Mary, Ludlow,
Shropshire DY14 0QZ

tel	01584 823379
fax	01584 823379
e-mail	kenmorecl@aol.com
web	www.cleetoncourt.co.uk

SHROPSHIRE

Where ancient Shropshire rolls down from Brown Clee to Ludlow, cross the ford (arguably the longest in England) in this tiny stone village and there is Carpenters. The renovation, a mix of high spec modern fittings and antique furniture, is a triumph of character, colour and immaculate taste. Norman is a Michelin *Bib Gourmand* chef and was a director of three excellent London restaurants: you really must eat in. The bedrooms are superbly decorated and filled with light, colour and a peaceful atmosphere. The newly transformed gardens are a mix of formal and natural and a brook runs through. Special indeed.

rooms	2: 1 double with bath/shower; 1 double with shower.
room price	£65. Singles from £40.
meals	Dinner £25. Good pubs & restaurants 5-7 miles.
closed	Rarely.
directions	From A49 at Ludlow, A4117 for Kidderminster. After 0.75 miles fork left onto B4364 for Bridgnorth. After 2.5 miles left to Stoke St Milbrough & Clee St Margaret. There, left through ford, house 2nd on right.

Norman Swallow
Carpenters,
Clee St Margaret, Ludlow,
Shropshire SY7 9DT
tel 01584 823624
fax 01584 823432

map: 8 entry: 381

SHROPSHIRE

Good-sized bedrooms with fine furniture, luxurious beds, excellent linen, bathrobes and bathroom treats — such a generous place. Standing in lush gardens that slope down to a millstream and across meadows to the River Teme, this is a gracious Georgian house with lovely views. It has a millstream and a weir, a motte and bailey castle site, a heronry, a point-to-point course and a ha-ha. Yvonne's reputation for imaginative cooking using local produce is a great attraction for walkers returning from a day in the glorious Welsh Borders. There's an interesting wine list, too. *Children by arrangement.*

rooms	3: 1 double with shower; 2 twins/doubles, both with private bath.
room price	£56-£70. Singles £38-£45.
meals	Dinner £20.
closed	Rarely.
directions	From Ludlow, A49 to Shrewsbury. At Bromfield, A4113. Right in Walford for Buckton, on to 2nd farm on left. Large sign on building.

Hayden & Yvonne Lloyd
Upper Buckton,
Leintwardine, Craven Arms, Ludlow,
Shropshire SY7 0JU
tel 01547 540634
fax 01547 540634

map: 8 entry: 382

Enthusiastic collectors of country artefacts, the Whitfields have filled this Grade II-listed, 16th-century farmhouse with the most eye-catching things. Not every kitchen range has an American cowboy's saddle hanging over it; this one echoes Susan's roots. Floors and doors of oak contrast with brightly coloured walls, and there's a calm, happy atmosphere. Much enthusiasm, too, for the historic village and glorious rolling countryside. Susan will give you full English breakfasts, using local produce; dinners are special, too. Come to walk or cycle or ride – you can even bring your horse.

In a land of fat sheep and ancient hill forts, this 17th-century mill ended Gill and Andrew's search for a refuge from the city. With seclusion and natural beauty, and an absence of fussiness in the house, this is a tranquil retreat. Rooms are comfortable, freshly-decorated and spotless: the double has a Victorian brass bed and newly restored original roll-top bath, and the stone and oak extension blends beautifully and has become a large twin. The River Unk flows through the mill's three acres of meadowland and gardens. *Children over eight welcome. Self-catering available. See back of book.*

rooms	2: 1 double, with extra bunk-bed room, with shower; 1 twin/double with private shower.
room price	£50. Singles by arrangement.
meals	Dinner £15–£17.50. Packed lunch £3.50. Good pubs/restaurants nearby.
closed	Occasionally.
directions	A49 from Ludlow & onto B4368 at Craven Arms, for Clun. In High St on left 0.5 miles from Clun sign.

rooms	3: 1 double with bath; 1 with private bath; 1 twin with bath/shower.
room price	£56–£72. Singles £38–£50.
meals	Breakfast until 9.30am. Dinner £25.
closed	November–February.
directions	From Clun A488 for Bishops Castle. 1st left, for Bicton. There, 2nd left for Mainstone. 1st right after Llananhedric Farm; house by river at bottom of hill.

Anthony & Susan Whitfield
Clun Farm House,
High Street, Clun,
Shropshire SY7 8JB
tel   01588 640432
fax   01588 640432

Gill Della Casa & Andrew Farmer
The Birches Mill,
Clun, Nr Craven Arms,
Shropshire SY7 8NL
tel   01588 640409
fax   01588 640409
e-mail   gill@birchesmill.fsnet.co.uk
web   www.virtual-
          shropshire.co.uk/birchesmill

SHROPSHIRE

M agnificent gardens, a terrific setting and memorable walks all around. Jinlye sits, sheltered, at 1,400 feet surrounded by hills, rare birds, wild ponies and windswept ridges. The skies are infinite and Stretton Hills spring water trickles into the garden. Deep carpets in the bedrooms, horse-brasses on the beams, shining wooden floors in the reading lounge and dining room; the 14-seater Victorian breakfast table is impressive and breakfasts are fun. There is much attention to detail from this mother-and-daughter team and the scent of flowers fills the house in summer. Sleep deeply in big, comfortable beds.

rooms	7: 3 doubles, 2 twins/doubles, 2 twins, all with bath/shower.
room price	£60–£80. Singles £45–£60.
meals	Breakfast 8–9am. Packed lunch available. Excellent pubs & restaurants nearby.
closed	Rarely.
directions	From Shrewsbury, A49 to Church Stretton, past Little Chef & right for All Stretton. Right immed. past phone box & up hill to Jinlye.

Mrs Janet Tory
Jinlye,
Castle Hill, All Stretton,
Church Stretton,
Shropshire SY6 6JP
tel   01694 723243
fax   01694 723243
e-mail   info@jinlye.co.uk
web   www.jinlye.co.uk

map: 8 entry: 385

SHROPSHIRE

A whole mile off the beaten track – a deeply rural spot. Privacy is yours in both the converted dairy and the rustic barn; both lie across a flower-filled yard. Bedrooms have plump beds, sofa, armchairs, good lighting and views of fields that roll towards the setting sun. Feel free to wander in the garden with its border hedges and manicured lawns: Fiona, charming, easy-going and fun, enjoys seeing see the fruits of her labours appreciated. Breakfasts are served in the book-lined dining room of the main house and there's home honey for your bread. A restorative place.

rooms	2 twins, both with bath.
room price	£50. Singles by arrangement.
meals	Pub 1.25 miles, restaurant 4 miles.
closed	Rarely.
directions	From Bridgnorth, A458 to Shrewsbury. 0.5 miles after Morville, right onto stone road & follow signs to farm.

Mrs Fiona Thompson
Hannigans Farm,
Morville, Bridgnorth,
Shropshire WV16 4RN
tel   01746 714332
fax   01746 714332
e-mail   hannigansfarm@btinternet.com

map: 9 entry: 386

From the Gold Room, fine sash windows look across the garden to Acton Burnell Hill, site of England's first parliament. Here are deep beds, soft lights, fine linen, hand-printed wallpaper and English oak in stair, beam and floor. Happy in their role of hosts, the Owens spoil you with afternoon teas before a log fire in the cosy guest sitting room; on warm days, sit outdoors. The two-acre garden hugs the house, a treat with rare plants, croquet lawn and pool for summer. Parts of the house were built in 1660 and the site is mentioned in the Domesday book. Elegant surrounds and lovely people – a restorative place.

A lovely calm sense of the continuity of history and family life emanates from this large, comfortable Victorian home. Jackie and Jim are delightful hosts and great fun. Bedrooms welcome you with flowers, bathrobes, books, duckdown pillows, and stupendous views of the Stretton Hills (even from bed). Tuck into a generous breakfast in the dining room – elegant with family portraits and Bechstein grand piano that you are most welcome to play. Explore the garden with its lupins, sweet peas, delphiniums and 50 types of rose that bloom in profusion. *Children over 12 welcome.*

rooms	3: 1 double, 1 twin/double, both with bath; 1 family (twin/double, 2 singles) with shower.
room price	£65. Singles £35.
meals	Dinner from £15.
closed	Christmas.
directions	From A5 & Shrewsbury, onto A458 for Bridgnorth. Approx. 200 yds on, right to Acton Burnell. Entering Acton Burnell, left to Kenley. 0.5 miles on, left to Acton Pigot. House 1st on left.

rooms	2: 1 double with private bath/shower; 1 twin/double with bath/shower.
room price	£50-£60. Singles £35-£40.
meals	Packed lunch from £2.50. Good pubs & restaurants nearby.
closed	Christmas & New Year.
directions	From Shrewsbury, south on A49. 0.5 miles before Leebotwood, right to Smethcott. Follow signs uphill for two miles & drive on left just before Smethcott.

Hildegard Owen
Acton Pigot,
Acton Burnell, Shrewsbury,
Shropshire SY5 7PH
tel   01694 731209
fax   01694 731399
e-mail   acton@farmline.com
web   www.actonpigot.co.uk

Jackie & Jim Scarratt
Lawley House,
Smethcott, Church Stretton,
Shropshire SY6 6NX
tel   01694 751236
fax   01694 751396
e-mail   lawleyhouse@easicom.com
web   www.lawleyhouse.co.uk

map: 8 entry: 387

map: 8 entry: 388

Jean is immensely kind and has turned her simple Methodist chapel into a warm and homely walker's retreat. Pine furniture, patterned rugs, old wooden floors and a dining/sitting room with a choir gallery, open right to the roof; the effect is impressive. There's a small twin with views and an even smaller (and cosier) single with extra pull-out bed. Tea and cakes by the woodburning stove will be just what you need after a day's trek on the Devil's Chair Ridge. This is a walker's paradise and Jean will transport luggage to your next stop. Simple, small, good value.

rooms	2: 1 twin, 1 single, let only to members of the same party, with private shower.
room price	£44. Singles £24.
meals	Packed lunch available. Pub within walking distance.
closed	Rarely.
directions	From Shrewsbury A488 for Bishop's Castle. Left on edge of Plox Green for Stiperstones. There, left before pub up Perkinsbeach Dingle. Chapel on right.

Jean Lees
The Old Chapel,
Perkinsbeach Dingle, Stiperstones,
Shrewsbury, Shropshire SY5 0PE
tel   01743 791449
e-mail   jean@a-lees.freeserve.co.uk

A heavenly Grade II-listed Georgian house in manicured gardens and a 20-minute stroll from Abbey and town. Joan is a terrific cook — once Aga Cook of the Year, no less — who radiates courtesy and charm; Charles cheerfully assumes the role of 'mine host'. Theirs is an atmospheric home, rich with antiques, polished mahogany and eye-catching wallpapers and fabrics. Home-made biscuits and flowers in every room; we loved the large, sunny double with Victorian painted brass half-tester and *chaise longue*. Summer breakfasts are taken in the conservatory — as is afternoon tea.

rooms	3: 1 double with bath/shower; 1 double with private bath; 1 twin with shower.
room price	From £65. Singles from £49.
meals	Dinner from £25.
closed	Rarely.
directions	A5/A49 junc. (south of bypass) follow signs to centre. Over 1st mini r'bout, 2nd exit at next, past hotel. 2nd left into Upper Rd. 150 yds on at house on bend, left & immed. right into Church Lane. Drive at bottom on left.

Joan Hathaway
Meole Brace Hall,
Shrewsbury, Shropshire SY3 9HF
tel   01743 235566
fax   01743 236886
e-mail   enquiries@meolebracehall.co.uk
web   www.meolebracehall.co.uk

David's family has farmed here for four generations – he tends a 250-acre arable and stock farm. The Breidden Hills and views of the Severn dominate the setting and the simple garden, sensibly, does not try to compete with the scenery. There are three bedrooms in this 1740s border farmhouse: one with Sanderson curtains and borders and a half-tester bed with rope-twist columns, a twin with Victorian wrought-iron bedsteads, and a double with brass bed. Try fresh farm eggs and delicious home-made preserves for breakfast. A smashing place – simple and excellent value.

An atmosphere of life, warmth, elegance and good taste pervades and guests return time after time. Pam – theatrical, laughing, genuine – is just lovely. The house is ancient, magpie-gabled and the church and pound are 800 years old. Beams criss-cross the rooms and vertical framing has been exposed to great effect. There's a grand piano in the drawing room and, on the rambling first floor, bedrooms are pretty and double-glazed. Pam's breakfasts are as generous as her spirit. *Children over 11 welcome.*

rooms	3: 1 double, 1 twin, both with shower; 1 double with bath.
room price	From £45. Singles £30–£45.
meals	Packed lunch £3.50. Good pub 5 miles.
closed	Rarely.
directions	From Shrewsbury A458 Welshpool road. After Ford, right onto B4393. At Crew Green, left for Criggion. House 1st on left after Admiral Rodney pub.

rooms	3: 1 twin, 1 double, both with shower; 1 family (1 double, 2 singles) with bath/shower.
room price	£48–£52. Singles from £30.
meals	Breakfast 7.30–9.30am. Packed lunch available. Good pub within walking distance.
closed	Rarely.
directions	From Shrewsbury, A5 north. Through Nesscliffe & after 2 miles, left to Knockin. Through Knockin, past Bradford Arms. House 150 yds on left.

Liz Dawson
Brimford House,
Criggion, Nr Shrewsbury,
Shropshire SY5 9AU
tel   01938 570235
fax   01938 570235
e-mail   info@brimford.co.uk
web   www.brimford.co.uk

Pam Morrissey
Top Farmhouse,
Knockin, Nr Oswestry,
Shropshire SY10 8HN
tel   01691 682582
fax   01691 682070
e-mail   p.a.m@knockin.freeserve.co.uk
web   www.topfarmknockin.co.uk

SHROPSHIRE

Anyone seeking a second childhood should pay this former pub a visit. All kinds of toys and games add to the attractive clutter, while illustrations from children's books adorn the walls. Bedrooms are charming and homely, with a lived-in feel. But the real joy is Susan herself: generous with her time, spirit and delicious home cooking, she will quickly engage you in lively conversation, her laughter occasionally echoed by Polly the parrot. Other natural sounds are provided by the trickle of the stream which meanders through the enchanting garden where you can picnic by the river. Peaceful, fun, superb value.

rooms	2: 1 double, 1 single, both with private shower. Extra bath available.
room price	£40. Singles £20.
meals	Packed lunch £5. Dinner, 3 courses, from £10. Excellent restaurant 0.5 miles.
closed	Rarely.
directions	From Oswestry, A483 from A5 for Welshpool. 1st left to Maesbury; 3rd right at x-roads with school on corner; 1st house on right.

Mrs Sue Barr
Pinfold Cottage,
Newbridge, Maesbury, Oswestry,
Shropshire SY10 8AY

tel	01691 661192
fax	01691 670563
e-mail	suebarr100@hotmail.com

map: 8 entry: 393

SHROPSHIRE

A Grade II-listed Georgian farmhouse set in five acres of paddock and garden; a real home with a wonderful atmosphere. Animals surround you and reflect the family's interests: three dogs, a cat, two horses and a clutch of hens... game birds grace the walls, glass elephants graze on the mantelpiece. Clare is delightful and gives guests the sort of treatment she loves to receive herself. Your bathroom has exquisite curtains and a lovely roll-top bath, breakfasts are home-grown, and there's a beautiful old stable block for your horse. *Children over 12 welcome. Dogs by arrangement.*

rooms	2: 1 double, 1 twin, sharing bath, let only to same party.
room price	£50. Singles £35.
meals	Packed lunch available. Excellent pubs nearby.
closed	Christmas & New Year.
directions	A528 (north out of Shrewsbury), becomes B5476 at Harmer Hill signed Wem. After 1.25 miles left at x-roads for Myddle. Large red-brick house 150 yds on right on crown of bend.

Clare Sawers
Alderton House,
Harmer Hill, Shrewsbury,
Shropshire SY4 3EL

tel	01939 220324
fax	01939 220324
e-mail	the4sawers@countryside-inter.net

map: 8 entry: 394

Fresh strawberries on Villeroy & Boch plates at breakfast, Egyptian cotton on beds with goosedown duvets as soft as a cloud – just a taste of the perfect attention to detail at this Victorian/Georgian rectory. All is pristine, sparkling, fresh and light and each bedroom has a harmonious blend of furniture, be it rattan, Provençal or classic. Walls are mostly cream, an ideal backdrop for pretty fabrics. Bathrooms have double power showers and the same stylish feel. There is the odd caravan visible but this is a world away from Weston, and with far-reaching views. Jane and Tony are delightful.

rooms	5: 2 doubles, 1 twin, all with bath/shower; 2 doubles, both with shower.
room price	£70. Singles £50.
meals	Good pubs 400 yds.
closed	Rarely.
directions	M5, junc. 21 then follow signs for Kewstoke. After Old Manor Inn on right, left up Anson Rd. At T-junc. right into Kewstoke Rd. Follow road for 1 mile; church on right; drive between church & church hall.

Jane & Tony Chapman
Church House,
27 Kewstoke Road, Kewstoke,
Weston-Super-Mare,
Somerset BS22 9YD
tel   01934 633185
fax   01934 633185
e-mail   chapman1@euphony.net

The Read's converted Victorian grainstore is full of light, good family furniture, portraits and interesting finds. It's down a narrow lane on the Somerset Levels and has a big, Mendip-view garden. They have young grandsons and a black labrador, so are very child- and dog-friendly. Kathlyn is also impressively practical – she took a china restoration diploma to repair the Meissen bird figures they inherited. Two prettily decorated rooms under the eaves and one on the first floor, a lovely sitting room with open fire and a smart dining room. The next door farm is organically run – which the rabbits seem to appreciate!

rooms	3: 1 double with bath/shower; 1 double, 1 twin/family sharing bath/shower.
room price	£50. Singles £32.
meals	Pubs nearby.
closed	Rarely.
directions	M5 junc. 21; north onto A370 towards Bristol. Take 2nd right to Rolstone, then 1st left (unmarked lane). House 3rd & last.

Mrs Read
Rolstone Court Barn,
Rolstone, Hewish,
Weston-super-Mare,
Somerset BS24 6UP
tel   01934 820129
e-mail   read@rolstone-court.co.uk
web   www.rolstone-court.co.uk

The 18th-century farmhouse, with old beams, flagstone floors, pine panelling, country antiques and the friendliest of cats is sunny and delightful. It lies on the southern slopes of the Mendips, with glorious walks to be walked – unless you are tempted to doze under the old apple tree in the garden. Wander among the fine old barns – you might imagine that you've stumbled upon a museum: there's an ancient forge, a cider press, a threshing floor... and Tony's collection of classic cars. Cosy, cottagey rooms have a fresh, cared-for feel and long views to Glastonbury Tor. *Children over 10 welcome.*

Rosalind's enthusiasm for welcoming guests is unstinting; she is cheerful and chatty and, as a geologist and walking enthusiast, is knowledgeable about the area – there are lots of books and maps. Pet sheep, goats, chickens, ducks and friendly cats, too. The large Garden Suite has been adapted for wheelchair users; accessible from its pretty, secluded walled garden and with an inglenook fireplace in its own sitting room, it retains its 17th-century charm. The other rooms are homely with new pine and white units. Lovely views, plentiful breakfasts and you can walk to Wells Cathedral to hear evensong.

rooms	3: 1 double with shower; 1 twin/double with bath; 1 double with private bath.
room price	£54–£60. Singles £36.
meals	Breakfast 8-9am. Good pub 200 yds.
closed	Christmas Day.
directions	From Wells towards Cheddar on A371. At Westbury-sub-Mendip pass Westbury Inn & Post Office Stores on right. House 200 yds on, on left.

rooms	5: 1 suite (twin/double plus extra bed) with shower; 1 double with bath; 1 double with shower; 1 single, 1 twin/double sharing bath/shower & separate wc.
room price	£30–£75.
meals	Packed lunches & light snacks. Good pub food 1 mile.
closed	Rarely.
directions	From Wells, A371 for Shepton Mallet for 1 mile, then left onto B3139. In Dulcote, left at stone fountain. Farmhouse marked, 4th on right after Manor Barn.

Tony & Wendy Thompson
Stoneleigh House,
Westbury-sub-Mendip, Nr Wells,
Somerset BA5 1HF

tel	01749 870668
fax	01749 870668
e-mail	stoneleigh@dial.pipex.com
web	www.stoneleigh.dial.pipex.com

Rosalind Bufton
Manor Farm,
Dulcote, Wells, Somerset BA5 3PZ

tel	01749 672125
fax	01749 672125
e-mail	rosalind.bufton@ntlworld.com
web	www.wells-accommodation.co.uk

The cosiest hillside cottage filled with the prettiest things. French-inspired bedheads and wardrobes made by a local craftsman, antique patchwork quilts and jolly china on the old Welsh dresser in the kitchen. And there's Catherine – warm, spirited, cultured; she'll make you fresh coffee, chat about the area, even give you a guided tour of Wells Cathedral, if you wish. The cottage is set in eight acres, with superb walking country all around. You can play tennis or croquet – and there's your own pretty sitting room with books and magazines. Excellent value.

In the 16th century this beautiful house was a row of weavers' cottages; today it is one thoroughly English home. Savour the interesting furniture, comfortable sofas, beautiful bits and pieces, and paintings with stories to tell. Nunney Castle casts its spells over the house – you can see it from one of the guest bedrooms and the house's huge stone fireplace may have come from there. From the drawing room wander into a garden where birdsong fills the scented air. This is a deeply traditional place to stay, and Jane, charming and flexible, will look after you well. *Cot and highchair available for babies.*

rooms	2: 1 twin/double with bath/shower. Further twin available for members of same party.
room price	£50. Singles £30.
meals	Good pub 0.25 miles.
closed	Christmas & New Year.
directions	From Wells A371 to middle of Croscombe. Right at red phone box & then immed. right into lane. House up on left after 0.25 miles. Drive straight ahead into signed drive.

rooms	3: 1 family, 1 twin, sharing connecting bathroom (separate entrances); 1 double with private bath.
room price	£50. Singles £25.
meals	Good pub yards away.
closed	Christmas.
directions	On A361 out of Frome, right to Nunney. Down hill to market square, left over humpback bridge & immed. left. House 1st on right (2 Horn Street).

Michael & Catherine Hay
Hillview Cottage,
Paradise Lane, Croscombe, Wells,
Somerset BA5 3RL
tel   01749 343526
fax   01749 676134
e-mail cathyhay@yahoo.co.uk

Jane Stagg
The Bell House,
Nunney, Nr Frome,
Somerset BA11 4NP
tel   01373 836309
fax   01373 836309
e-mail janenunney@aol.com
web   www.john-at-nunney.org.uk/Stagg.htm

SOMERSET

An exquisite house: Phoebe, a shepherd, sought the perfect home for her flock and she found it. Terracotta walls, rugs, flagstones and brick – stunning. The antique beds have handmade mattresses, good linen and fat pillows; in the barn you have luxurious privacy. The indoor swimming pool has a breathtaking view through a Gothic, arched window. The house is a treasure box of decorative arts from the carved Dutch fireplaces to the Turkmen rugs, and Phoebe is flexible about arrangements – it's a magnificent place for a house party. *With the cottages (right), 11 bedrooms in all. Babies welcome. Self-catering available. See back of book.*

rooms	6: Barn: 1 double suite with dressing room & kitchen/living area. House: 1 double with bath; 1 double suite with drawing room; 3 singles, usually let to same party.
room price	£100-£180.
meals	Dinner from £25.
closed	Rarely.
directions	From Wells, A39 to Glastonbury. 0.5 miles on left for North Wootton, follow for West Pennard. Right onto A361. 1st left. 1 mile up hill. 1st drive to left at top.

Phoebe Judah
Pennard Hill Farm,
Stickleball Hill, East Pennard,
Shepton Mallet,
Somerset BA4 6UG

tel	01749 890221
fax	01749 890665
e-mail	phebejudah@aol.com
web	www.pennardhillfarm.co.uk

map: 3 entry: 401

SOMERSET

Phoebe has returned these Victorian cottages to the estate – both have been stunningly redesigned. The Golden Fleece has an airy, luxurious living space with a vast kitchen (double Aga, dishwasher, etc) leading to a sunroom and a large drawing room with log fire. The Lamb, with a kitchen/living room and open fire, is a special hideaway for two, a bolthole that you may never want to leave. The views to the Mendips and the utter peace and tranquility are the icing on the cake. *With Pennard Hill Farm (left), there are 11 bedrooms plus the indoor pool. You can self-cater or B&B. See back of book.*

rooms	Fleece: 2 doubles, 1 twin, 1 single with 2 baths. Lamb: 1 double with bath. Both have living rooms & kitchens.
room price	£150-£450.
meals	Dinner from £25.
closed	Very occasionally.
directions	Directions as for Pennard Hill Farm, left. Do not go to hamlet of East Pennard.

Phoebe Judah
Golden Fleece & The Lamb,
Pennard Hill Farm, Stickleball Hill,
East Pennard, Shepton Mallet,
Somerset BA4 6UG

tel	01749 890221
fax	01749 890665
e-mail	phebejudah@aol.com
web	www.pennardhillfarm.co.uk

map: 3 entry: 402

Grand, yes, but without a hint of stuffiness and a terrific place to stay. Pennard has been in Susie's family since the 17th century – the cellars date from then and the superstructure is stately, lofty and Georgian. You have the run of the library, drawing room, magnificent billiard room, 60-acre orchard, meadows, woods, tennis court and six acres of garden with a spring-fed pool where you can swim with the newts. Bedrooms are large and have good views; one is circular with a corner bath in the room. Multi-lingual Martin runs an antiques business from here and he and Susie delight in sharing their house.

rooms	3: 1 twin/double with private bath; 1 double, 1 twin, both with bath/shower.
room price	From £60. Singles by arrangement.
meals	Good pub 2 miles.
closed	Rarely.
directions	From Shepton Mallet south on A37, through Pylle, over hill & next right to East Pennard. After 500 yds, right & on past church to T-junc. at very top. House on left.

Martin & Susie Dearden
Pennard House,
East Pennard, Shepton Mallet,
Somerset BA4 6TP
tel   01749 860266
fax   01749 860732
e-mail susie.d@ukonline.co.uk

The Good Life in the depths of Somerset: organic vegetables on an organic farm, home-made marmalade, own milk and eggs... and a delightful family to boot. The Dowdings used to live in France – they had a Special Place there – and have converted an old stone barn into a self-contained apartment with lime washed walls and *toile de Jouy*. Do your own thing, or have Susie cook breakfast for you. The place has a charmingly French feel, with hens in the orchard and a woodburner in the oak-floored sitting room; Charles grinds their own wheat for daily bread-making. Wonderful Hadspen Garden is a mile away.

rooms	2: 1 double with bath, 1 twin with bath; 2 extra singles available in lounge.
room price	£60-£90.
meals	Breakfast until 9.30am, or you can cook your own. Light supper occasionally available. Pub 0.5 mile.
closed	Rarely.
directions	From A303 at Wincanton, A371 for Castle Cary. Before C. Cary, right on A359 for Bruton. 2nd right for S. Montague. Over x-roads by inn. Round sharp bend, church on left. House on right; right into yard.

Charles & Susie Dowding
Lower Farm,
Shepton Montague, Wincanton,
Somerset BA9 8JG
tel   01749 812253
e-mail lowerfarm@clara.co.uk
web   www.lowerfarm.org.uk

SOMERSET

A mellow Georgian manor surrounded by impressive parkland with formal gardens, rose garden, apple tree pergola and laburnum walk. Your hosts are friendly and kind; she is a needlework expert and her embroideries are everywhere. They are artists and have an eye for detail: fine copies of 18th-century wallpapers, 18th-century fabric around the canopied bed. Something to astound at every turn – one bedroom has Regency striped wallpaper that extends across the entire ceiling giving the effect of a Napoleonic tent. There are elegant antiques, 50s bathrooms, a heated pool. Surprising, unique. *Children over 10 welcome.*

rooms	2: 1 double, 1 twin, both with bath.
room price	£60-£80. Singles £50.
meals	Pubs/restaurants nearby.
closed	Rarely.
directions	From Wincanton, 2nd left on A371, after Holbrook r'bout. Then 3rd right; 1st gate posts on left.

Countess Charles de Salis
Yarlington House,
Nr Wincanton, Somerset BA9 8DY

tel	01963 440344
fax	01963 440335

map: 3 entry: 405

SOMERSET

You may glimpse badgers and kingfishers; you'll certainly see ducks waddling to and from the pond. (There's a outdoor pool for humans, too, sheltered by high garden walls.) The pretty house sits by a river among cherries, magnolias, beeches and chestnuts. Persian rugs sit on warm polished floors, a log fire smoulders in the drawing room, an oak stair leads to the bedrooms. In the easy ambiance of the dining room, under the eye of the rocking horse, Sally serves sumptuous breakfasts of local produce. The family have lived here since 1898 – it's a working farm with 200 acres and a herd of dairy cows.

rooms	3: 1 double, 1 single, both with shower; 1 family/twin with bath/shower.
room price	£50-£60. Singles £25-£30.
meals	Breakfast 8-9am. Good pubs & restaurants 2-4 miles.
closed	Christmas & New Year.
directions	From Wincanton, A371 for Shepton Mallet. After Castle Cary, left on B3153 for Somerton (0.75 miles). Under r'way bridge, white gate & cattle grid immed. on right. Car park up drive, behind house.

Sally Snook
Clanville Manor,
Castle Cary, Somerset BA7 7PJ

tel	01963 350124
fax	01963 350719
e-mail	info@clanvillemanor.co.uk
web	www.clanvillemanor.co.uk

map: 3 entry: 406

You'll be delighted whichever room you choose in this listed Regency house; each is decorated with period furniture, fine bedspreads, elaborate drapes. A flagged hall, high ceilings and long windows give the feel of a small hotel, yet both the grand first-floor rooms and cosier second-floor ones are good value. A stone stair goes right to the top and the Observatory lets in a cascading light. Roy, a jazz musician and wildlife enthusiast, is charming company; he's planted 2,800 trees to attract wildlife and stocked the lake with exotic ducks and black swans. Scrambled eggs at breakfast are excellent.

The harmonious marriage of natural materials with modern and antique furniture makes for a delicious cosiness. The Burnhams — one of whom worked in fashion — have huge flair and the house and garden have been designed with an excellent eye. Coir matting sits happily with dark, antique furniture; a wrought-iron, real-candle chandelier and high-backed chairs lend the dining room an air of warm, pre-Raphaelite Gothic. Bedrooms are uncluttered with crisp linen and soft robes; the twin is the biggest and its bathroom is very close. Superb breakfasts include Heal Farm sausages and bacon. *Children by arrangement.*

rooms	8: 1 four-poster, 1 twin, 1 double, 1 family, all with bath; 1 double with private bath. 1 twin, 2 doubles in converted Coach House.
room price	£49-£85. Singles £45-£60.
meals	Restaurants within walking distance.
closed	Christmas.
directions	From London, M3 junc. 8, A303. At Podimore r'bout A372 to Somerton. House at junction of North Street & Behind Berry.

rooms	2: 1 double with shower; 1 twin with private bath.
room price	£50. Singles £40.
meals	Dinner from £19.
closed	Christmas.
directions	From Somerton Lake B3153 for Langport. Right after 2 miles for Pitney, just before Halfway Inn. Down to bottom of road. Last but one house on right, with dark green railings.

Mr Roy Copeland
The Lynch Country House,
4 Behind Berry, Somerton,
Somerset TA11 7PD
tel   01458 272316
fax   01458 272590
e-mail   the_lynch@talk21.com
web   www.thelynchcountryhouse.co.uk

Peter & Jane Burnham
Estate Farmhouse,
Pitney, Langport,
Somerset TA10 9AL
tel   01458 250210
fax   01458 253227

W ith its thatched roof and Strawberry Hill Gothic windows, The Old Rectory is captivating. You won't find family bustle – the house is run faultlessly and professionally – but there is immense comfort. Soft, large sofas in the sitting room, thick carpeting, easy chairs in the bedrooms and excellent hotel-standard dinners. Carved Tudor oak beams in the sitting room and panelled passages speak of the house's history, and there are French windows from the dining room onto sweeping lawns. In a tiny conservation hamlet surrounded by farmland, the peace is deep.

rooms	5 twins/doubles, all with bath/shower.
room price	From £80. Singles £50.
meals	Dinner, 4 courses, £19.50.
closed	Rarely.
directions	At Horton Cross r'bout (junc. A303/A358) A358 for Chard. After Donyatt, left for Ilminster. After 1 mile, right for Cricket Malherbie. House on left after 1 mile, 200 yds past church.

Michael & Patricia Fry-Foley
The Old Rectory,
Cricket Malherbie, Ilminster,
Somerset TA19 0PW
tel   01460 54364
fax   01460 57374
e-mail theoldrectory@malherbie.freeserve.co.uk
web   www.malherbie.freeserve.co.uk

map: 3 entry: 409

W ith its dignified, creamy Georgian front and smooth lawns, this could easily be formidable. Instead, it's a relaxed and friendly house, full of lovely things. Caryl has a passion for dolls' houses and owns two; Peter is a bookbinder. The dining room is elegant, the bedrooms charming. One is in the main house, with a pretty Victorian bathroom and a big window looking across the gardens to the village. The other, in the Old Coach House across the drive, is delightfully private, with a window seat and wonderful country views. Peter's bookbinding studio is next door and he'll be happy to show you round.

rooms	2: 1 twin with bath; 1 twin with private bath.
room price	£50. Singles £30.
meals	Dinner £14.
closed	Christmas & Boxing Day.
directions	From centre of Crewkerne, B3165 Lyme road & through Clapton. Follow signs to Thorncombe, down steep hill, 1st left into Saddle St; house 2nd on left.

Peter & Caryl Bicknell
Upperfold House,
Thorncombe, Nr Chard,
Somerset TA20 4PY
tel   01460 30209
e-mail pbatupperfold@onetel.net.uk

map: 3 entry: 410

Robert, an ex-restaurateur, is a South African and as easy-going as they so often are; Lesley's cooking gets heaps of praise from guests and she runs cookery courses too. It's a perfect Somerset cottage with an apple orchard and views across fields to the lofty church. The interior is utterly in keeping: pine, coir carpets, wooden beams and a warm sense of fun. Bedrooms are light, restful and simple, with white walls and old pine. Elegance and simplicity, an unobtrusive and delightful family, and easy access to the M5. *Children over 10 welcome.*

So much to delight the eye: elegant Georgian lines, beautiful pictures and Italianate murals, a 19th-century French mirror, French Empire chairs, checks, stripes and *toile de Jouy*... all existing in absolute harmony. The house, 18th century and Grade II-listed, has been renovated by the dedicated Deacons – it is one of the most stylish retreats that you'll find. There's comfort, too: thick bathrobes, warm towels, fat pillows. Elizabeth's cooking is sublime and imaginative, and you are in the heart of the Somerset Levels, surrounded by mystical views and countryside of huge environmental significance.

rooms	2: 1 double with shower; 1 twin with bath.
room price	£50–£56. Singles by arrangement.
meals	Breakfast until 9am. Supper from £15. Dinner from £18.
closed	Christmas.
directions	From M5 junc. 26 take West Buckland road for 0.75 miles. 1st left just before Stone garage. Bear right; 3rd house at end of lane, below church.

rooms	3: 2 doubles, both with private bath; 1 twin with shower.
room price	From £100. Singles £50.
meals	Dinner, 3-4 courses, £20–£25. B.Y.O
closed	Rarely.
directions	From M5, junc. 24; 5 miles via Huntworth to Moorland; 2 miles after Moorland, house on right after sharp right-hand bend.

Lesley & Robert Orr
Causeway Cottage,
West Buckland, Wellington,
Somerset TA21 9JZ
tel   01823 663458
fax   01823 663458
e-mail   orrs@westbuckland.freeserve.co.uk
web   www.welcome.to/causeway-cottage

Crispin & Elizabeth Deacon
Saltmoor House,
Saltmoor, Burrowbridge,
Somerset TA7 0RL
tel   01823 698092
e-mail   saltmoorhouse@aol.com
web   www.saltmoorhouse.co.uk

SOMERSET

SOMERSET

The Ritchies devote a huge amount of energy to their B&B and have done a fine job of renovating this exquisite 17th-century farmhouse in Somerset's lovely Quantock Hills. There's a homely feel with splashes of style where they matter – well-framed prints, good fabrics, comfortable sofas – and they've done everything to make you comfortable. Rooms are pretty, fresh and large and look over the cobbled courtyard or open fields; many look both ways. Breakfast will include home-baked bread and home-made jams. Charles and Jane prepare meals using fresh local ingredients, so eat in.

An exemplary elegance sets off the natural beauty of the 300-year-old farmhouse: handsome furniture and soft colours sit easily with stone flags, beams and wooden panelling. It's a beautiful place, with its own spring, meticulously kept by friendly Pamela who makes all her own jams, marmalade and bread; breakfasts are delicious. Bedrooms and bathrooms are a generous size, attractive and full of character. You are 1,000 feet up on the Quantocks where the views are long and the scenery spectacular; the Smiths' 20 acres of fields and woodland are alive with songbirds. *Children over 10 welcome.*

rooms	3: 1 double with shower; 1 double with private shower; 1 twin with private bath.
room price	£50–£55. Singles £30–£32.50.
meals	Breakfast 8-9am. Dinner £22.50.
closed	Rarely.
directions	From M5 junc. 25. A358 for Minehead. Leave A358 at West Bagborough turning. Through village for 1.5 miles. Farmhouse third on left past pub.

rooms	3: 2 doubles, 1 twin, all with bath/shower.
room price	£50–£55. Singles £30.
meals	Breakfast until 9.30am. Pubs 0.5 miles.
closed	Rarely.
directions	From Taunton, A358 north for Williton. Approximately 7 miles on, right for West Bagborough. Through village, up hill for 0.5 miles. Farm on left.

Charles & Jane Ritchie
Bashfords Farmhouse,
West Bagborough, Taunton,
Somerset TA4 3EF
tel   01823 432015
e-mail   info@bashfordsfarmhouse.co.uk
web   www.bashfordsfarmhouse.co.uk

Mrs Pamela Smith
Tilbury Farm,
Cothelstone, Taunton,
Somerset TA4 3DY
tel   01823 432391

map: 3 entry: 413

map: 3 entry: 414

Fruit from the orchard, vegetables from the walled garden, home-produced bread, eggs and jam, taken in winter beside an open fire. This is an organic smallholding and your enthusiastic hosts have added an easy comfort to their 17th-century rectory farmhouse. Quarry-tiled floors, log fires, books, maps and a piano in the cosy sitting room; American folk art and Susan's pastels add charm. The big bedrooms have fresh flowers and great views (even from the Victorian bath in the en suite). You're surrounded by the beauty of the Quantock hills, with walks starting from the front door. It's a great place for cyclists, too.

Honest country hospitality is yours in the peaceful old house at the end of the lane. Richard and Carol give you good, big bedrooms on the sunny side of the house — warm and homely. Stripped floors and open fireplaces create a turn-of-the-century atmosphere designed to welcome rather than impress, and dinner at the big oak table is a culinary treat — accompanied, in winter, by crackling logs and candlelight. Breakfasts involve local eggs and sausages and superb cappuccino (Richard was in the coffee trade). There's the lovely River Parrett walking trail just outside the door, and the glories of Wells are close by.

rooms	3: 1 double with shower & extra sofabed; 1 twin/double with bath & extra pull-out bed; 1 double with shared bath.
room price	£48–£56. Singles £31–£42.
meals	Dinner, 2-3 courses, £16–£20. Light supper £7.
closed	Christmas.
directions	From Bridgwater, A39 for Minehead. 7 miles on, left at Cottage Inn for Over Stowey. Village 1.8 miles on. House on right after church.

rooms	3: 1 double, 1 twin/family, 1 twin, all with bath/shower.
room price	£60. Singles £40.
meals	Breakfast 7-9.30am. Dinner, 3 courses, £18.
closed	Rarely.
directions	A39 for Minehead. After B'water, 1 mile, pass garage, down hill & at double bend right for Wembdon. Immed. left for Perry Green. After 0.75 miles follow 'No Through Road'; 2nd on left.

Susan Lilienthal
Parsonage Farm,
Over Stowey, Bridgwater,
Somerset TA5 1HA
tel   01278 733237
fax   01278 733511
e-mail suki@parsonfarm.co.uk
web   www.parsonfarm.co.uk

Richard & Carol Wright
Model Farm,
Perry Green, Wembdon, Bridgwater,
Somerset TA5 2BA
tel   01278 433999
e-mail info@modelfarm.com
web   www.modelfarm.com

Massive stone walls, heavy timbers, flagged floors and a lack of fussiness give this Grade I-listed 15th-century farmhouse a real solidity and atmosphere. Don't miss the West Bedroom with its four-poster bed and a ceiling open to the beamed roof – or the oak-panelled Gallery Bedroom where a secret stairway was recently discovered. Feel baronial breakfasting at a 20-foot oak table beside the Great Hall's massive fireplace... There's even a chapel (Ann lets cyclists store their bikes there), a stable room (perfect for wheelchair users) and a barn conversion with six new rooms, including one with a cider press. Wonderful

Coleridge lived just round the corner – you can visit his house, now National Trust. There's a captivating mix of buildings, from medieval on, in this Quantock village; Castle Street is part of the conservation area and is almost film-set perfect. The cottage is 16th century, with fresh, pretty, traditional rooms criss-crossed with beams. The wrought-iron beds are comfortable, sheets and towels are of the finest quality and there are many thoughtful touches: home-made biscuits, spare toothbrushes, mints... It's all wonderfully quiet, too – just the murmuring of the brook to lull you to sleep.

rooms	6: 4 doubles, 1 family, 1 twin, all with bath/shower.
room price	£50–£65. Singles £35–£38.
meals	Breakfast until 9.30am. Pub 500 yds.
closed	Rarely.
directions	From Bridgwater, A39 west around Cannington. After 2nd r'bout, follow signs to Minehead. 1st left after Yeo Valley creamery. Farm 1st house on right.

rooms	3: 1 double with bath & shower; 1 double with bath; 1 twin with shower.
room price	From £48. Singles £28.
meals	Supper £8.50–£10.
closed	Rarely.
directions	A39 to Bridgwater. After 8 miles, left towards Nether Stowey. Left at clock tower into Castle Street; house 100 yds on left.

Ann Dyer
Blackmore Farm,
Cannington, Bridgwater,
Somerset TA5 2NE

tel	01278 653442
fax	01278 653427
e-mail	dyerfarm@aol.com
web	www.dyerfarm.co.uk

Mrs Mark Stacey & Jackie Jones
Stowey Brooke House,
18 Castle Street, Nether Stowey,
Bridgwater, Somerset TA5 1LN

tel	01278 733356
e-mail	marka@stacey77.fsnet.co.uk
web	www.stoweybrookehouse.co.uk

SOMERSET

The Vincents have made the house 'smile' again; charming and Georgian, it overlooks Watchet marina within sight and sound of the sea. Bedrooms are nicely traditional – the pale blue double with pretty drapes looks onto a Mediterranean courtyard; the twin, with chintz valances and curtains, looks out to the Bristol Channel. Expect home-made cakes and generous breakfasts – Susan loves to cook. Relax in the garden amid palm trees, ponds, burgeoning borders and a revolving summer house. The steam railway runs right by and takes you through the Quantock Hills, or to the coast. *Children and dogs by arrangement.*

rooms	2: 1 double with private bath; 1 twin with shower.
room price	From £55. Singles from £28.
meals	Pub/restaurants a short walk.
closed	Christmas.
directions	From railway station & footbridge in Watchet, up South Rd (for Doniford). After 50 yds, left into Beverly Drive. House 50 yds on left with gravel parking area.

Susan & Roger Vincent
Wyndham House,
4 Sea View Terrace, Watchet,
Somerset TA23 0DF
tel   01984 631881
fax   01984 631881
e-mail rhv@dialstart.net

map: 2 entry: 419

SOMERSET

The picture-book, 12th-century priory leans against its church, has a rustic gate, a walled garden, a tumble of flowers. Both house and hostess are elegant, unpretentious and friendly; the old oak tables, flagstones, panelled doors, books and higgledy-piggledy corridors are English through and through. But a perfect English house in a sweet Somerset village needs a touch of pepper and cosmopolitan Jane adds her own special flair with artistic touches here and there. Dunster Castle towers above on the hill, and walks start from the door. *Self-catering available. See back of book.*

rooms	3: 1 double with private shower; 1 twin, 1 four-poster, both with bath.
room price	£65-£75. Singles by arrangement.
meals	Good restaurants & pubs nearby.
closed	Christmas.
directions	From A39 into Dunster, right at blue sign 'unsuitable for goods vehicles'. Follow until church; house adjoined.

Jane Forshaw
The Old Priory,
Dunster, Somerset TA24 6RY
tel   01643 821540

map: 2 entry: 420

A little lane tumbles down to the centre of lovely old Dunster (the village is a two minute-walk) yet up here you have open views of fields, sheep and sea. Exmoor footpaths start behind the house; Janet encourages you to explore, by bike or on foot. Ever helpful and kind, she can assist with luggage and transport. The 1860s house retains its Victorian features, bedrooms are quiet and simple and the double has a view to Blue Anchor Bay, the castle and church. It's very homely, with stripped pine, cream curtains, fresh flowers and garden fruit and home-laid eggs for breakfast. *Children and pets by arrangement.*

Tucked into the folds of Exmoor on the River Quarme, a fascinating white-fronted mill. Step back 200 years: walls twist and curve, and in the breakfast room the spectacular mill machinery is still intact. Bedrooms have stripped floors, Indian rugs, lovely quilts, warm colours, heather from the moor. Outside are lambs, ponies and a special border collie; along the bridle path is a pub. The peace is complete... beyond the gentle splash of water and the chorus of birds. Sally is unflappable and an imaginative cook – relax by the log fire (or river) with a pre-dinner drink and let the evening meal come to you.

rooms	3: 1 double with bath/shower; 2 twins/doubles, both with shower.
room price	£45–£55. Singles £25.
meals	Packed lunch from £3.50. Excellent restaurants a short walk away.
closed	Christmas.
directions	From Williton, A39 for Minehead for 8 miles. Left to Dunster. There, right fork into 'The Ball'. At T-junc. at end of road, right. House 75 yds on right.

rooms	3: 1 double with private bath; 1 double with private shower; 1 twin sharing bath.
room price	£60. Singles £30.
meals	Packed lunch £5. Dinner £17.50–£25. Good pub 1 mile.
closed	Rarely.
directions	Follow A358 from Taunton to Minehead, Raleighs Cross, Wheddon Cross. Straight over x-roads; straight on Exford road, 2 miles. Turn into Luckwell Bridge; house down bridleway on left.

Mrs Janet Lamacraft
Higher Orchard,
30 St George's Street, Dunster,
Somerset TA24 6RS
tel   01643 821915
e-mail   lamacraft@higherorchard.fsnet.co.uk
web   www.higherorchard.fsnet.co.uk

Sally Pearce
West Mill,
Luckwell Bridge, Wheddon Cross,
Somerset TA24 7EH
tel   01643 841896
e-mail   sally.pearce1@btinternet.com

map: 2 entry: 421

map: 2 entry: 422

SOMERSET

Hugo owns the Crown Hotel in Exford and wife Pam's new venture must be the most luxurious B&B on Exmoor. Dark wood Heals' beds have embroidered linen, fat pillows and sumptuous cushions; beside them are big bedside lamps and a tray with bottles of mineral water. Deep luxury. Downstairs – part-14th, part-18th-century – there are real fires everywhere and fine prints and oils. Breakfast is a feast of freshly-squeezed orange juice, fresh fruit salad, butcher's sausages and bacon. The Jeunes have stables and an olympic dressage arena – you can bring your horse – and a lovely, huge, rambling garden.

rooms	3: 1 double, 1 twin, both with shower; 1 suite with bath & shower.
room price	£50-£60. Singles £25-£30.
meals	Dinner, 4 courses, £20-£25.
closed	Rarely.
directions	From Dulverton, pass post office on left & take B3223 (for Exford). Follow wooded road up hill for 2.5 miles. After sharp left bend, house signed on right.

Pam & Hugo Jeune
Highercombe,
Nr Dulverton, Somerset TA22 9PT
tel   01398 323451
fax   01398 323451
e-mail   highercombe@btconnect.com
web   www.highercombe.co.uk

STAFFORDSHIRE

An enchanting, rambling, Jacobean farmhouse, the kind of time capsule you can't simulate: oak timbers and panelling, stone, tapestry drapes, curios, pewter and books galore. There are gorgeous, almost grand, lawned grounds full of birdsong, tennis and croquet and a summer house which sports a turret from Sheffield Infirmary. Rare-breed (Irish Moiled) cattle graze peacefully. Rooms have majestic four-poster beds with good mattresses and great views. Chris and Margaret are busy, informal people and the attitude here is very much 'stay as friends'. You are only two miles from Alton Towers.

rooms	3: 1 double with shower, 2 doubles with baths.
room price	£50-£56. Singles from £30.
meals	Breakfast until 9.30am. Good places to eat within 5 miles.
closed	Christmas.
directions	From Uttoxeter, B5030 for Rocester. Beyond JCB factory, left onto B5031. At T-junc. after church, right onto B5032. 1st left for Prestwood. Farm 0.75 miles on right over crest of hill, through arch.

Chris & Margaret Ball
Manor House,
Prestwood, Nr Denstone, Uttoxeter,
Staffordshire ST14 5DD
tel   01889 590415
fax   01335 342198
e-mail   cm_ball@yahoo.co.uk
web   www.4posteraccom.com

STAFFORDSHIRE

Keen supporters of the countryside, the Balls are restoring wildlife habitats, ponds and hedgerows on their 105-acre farm. Cosy bedrooms are in the cottage and mews and Diana pops round each morning to serve a generous breakfast (free-range eggs, home-made preserves) in the beamed breakfast room at separate tables. For larger parties she cooks dinner, and much of the food is home-produced: the Balls have a big vegetable garden and keep traditional breeds of cattle, sheep and hens. Walk to the 12th-century ruins of Croxden Abbey, or delight the children and spend the day at Alton Towers. *Children over five welcome.*

rooms	5: Farrier's Cottage: 2 doubles, 1 family, all with shower. Mews: 1 double, 1 room with bunks, both with shower.
room price	From £45. Singles £35.
meals	Packed lunch £5. Dinner from £12; minimum 6 people. Good pubs nearby.
closed	Christmas & New Year. Self-catering never closed.
directions	From A50, B5030 at Uttoxeter for Rocester. There, left into Hollington Rd. Nabb Lane 1.5 miles on right.

Diana Ball
Woodhouse Farm,
Nabb Lane, Croxden, Uttoxeter,
Staffordshire ST14 5JB
tel   01889 507507
e-mail ddeb@lineone.net
web   www.alton-towers.glo.cc

STAFFORDSHIRE

Inigo Jones was commissioned to transform the ancient, crumbling castle into a baronial mansion. The 1270 pink-stone crenellated pile retains its guardhouse, moat and turrets; the stunning interior is Jacobean with vast, oak-panelled drawing and dining rooms and massive carved fireplaces. Upstairs, billiards and pool in an immense room. Bedrooms are panelled and regal, bathrooms excellent. Delightful Yvonne has travelled much in China and has furnished her new oriental room with eastern antiques and hand-built Chinese furniture. A glorious place. *Minimum stay two nights. Self-catering available. See back of book.*

rooms	3 four-posters, all with bath/shower.
room price	£85–£95.
meals	Breakfast until 9.30am. Pubs within walking distance.
closed	November-February. Self-catering never.
directions	Caverswall is signed, near Blythe Bridge, just off A50. Take M1 junc. 23A, or M6 junc. 14/15. Entrance between 2 churches in village.

Yvonne Sargent
Caverswall Castle,
Caverswall, Staffordshire ST11 9EA
tel   01782 393239
fax   01782 394590
e-mail yasargent@hotmail.com
web   www.caverswallcastle.co.uk

M ary Queen of Scots was imprisoned in Chartley Castle, opposite this Grade II-listed, half-timbered Elizabethan manor. Push open the studded oak door to discover panelled walls, a terracotta dining room, a wealth of oak beams. In the Sudbury Yellow drawing room are family portraits and exquisite furniture. The bedrooms are large, airy and flower-filled; the four-poster bedroom is oak-panelled and has a secret door to the bathroom. Wonky floors, hearty breakfasts, family silver and lovely parkland – all close to the Peak District, the Potteries and Alton Towers. Jeremy & Sarah are engaging hosts.

rooms	2: 1 four-poster, 1 twin, both with shower.
room price	£60. Singles £35.
meals	Breakfast until 9.30am. Good restaurants/pubs 1 mile.
closed	Christmas & New Year.
directions	Halfway between Stafford & Uttoxeter on A518, just past Chartley Castle ruin on left & at top of hill, on right.

	Jeremy & Sarah Allen
	Chartley Manor Farm,
	Chartley, Nr Stafford/Uttoxeter,
	Staffordshire ST18 0LN
tel	01889 270891
fax	01889 270891
e-mail	jeremy.allen4@btopenworld.com
web	www.chartleymanor.co.uk

map: 9 entry: 427

A 19th-century cottage in a quiet, idyllic setting beside the Shropshire Union Canal – one of England's prettiest. Bedrooms have floral curtains and covers and all is spotless and cosy, with open fires, stripped pine floors, old oak furniture, pretty bathrooms, fresh flowers. Eat outside on the terrace overlooking the canal, or on the narrowboat on an evening cruise – but do book! Diana, who was awarded an MBE for her work with deaf children, makes her own bread, biscuits, cakes and jams; David cuts fresh vegetables and salads from the garden. On a good day for the hens there are home-laid eggs, too.

rooms	2 doubles, both with private bath & shower.
room price	From £55. Singles £35.
meals	Packed lunch £5. Dinner, 4 courses, £17.50. Pub 2 miles.
closed	Christmas & New Year.
directions	From Stafford, A518 for Newport. 4 miles on, left at Haughton (opposite church) for Church Eaton. There, right along Main St. At end of village, left along Little Onn road. Over canal bridge & left after 300 yds. Cottage on left.

	Diana Walkerdine
	Slab Bridge Cottage,
	Little Onn, Church Eaton,
	Staffordshire ST20 0AY
tel	01785 840220
fax	01785 840220
e-mail	daviddiana@walkerdine.com

map: 9 entry: 428

Wild marshes, deserted beaches – the area is silent but for the call of the birds. Steeped in healing tranquillity, the Augustinian monastery has been brought to life by Frances, artist and musician. It is breathtaking and romantic: decorative stonework clasps the windows, the vaulted dining room soars heavenwards. Forty-seven steps lead to cascades of damask, huge stone-arched windows, beautiful beds with goose down duvets and embroidered linen, invigorating power showers. The magic lies in seven acres of gardens, lakeside and wooded grounds. Beyond, fine walks and seafood restaurants.

There's more than a touch of theatre to this beautiful Grade II-listed house. The dining room is opulent red; the drawing room, with its delicately carved mantelpiece and comfortable George Smith sofas, has French doors to the terrace. There's a four-poster in one bedroom, an antique French bed in another and masses of fresh flowers and books. The seven acres of garden include an orchid and wildflower meadow designated a County Wildlife Site. River walks, the Suffolk coast and Sutton Hoo – the Saxon burial site – are close by. Cindy, her delightful three children and their little dog, Snowball, welcome you warmly.

rooms	3: 1 double with shower; 1 double with shower; 1 small double with bath/shower.
room price	£55-£130. Singles by arrangement.
meals	Seafood restaurants & pubs nearby.
closed	Rarely.
directions	From A12 at Woodbridge, B1084 for Orford for 6 miles. Directly after Rendlesham Forest, right at Butley High & Low Corner; on for 0.5 mile; at bottom of hill, drive to right marked 'Private Entrance'.

rooms	3: 1 double, 1 single with basin, sharing private bath; 1 double with bath.
room price	£68-£84. Singles £42-£50. Single room from £28.
meals	Dinner, 1, 2, 3 courses, £10, £20, £27. B.Y.O.
closed	Rarely.
directions	From A12 Woodbridge bypass, exit at r'bout for Melton. Follow for 1 mile to lights; there, right. Immediately on right.

Frances Cavendish
Butley Priory,
Butley, Nr Woodbridge,
Suffolk IP12 3NR

tel	01394 450046
fax	01394 450482
e-mail	cavendish@butleypriory.co.uk
web	www.butleypriory.co.uk

Mrs Lucinda de la Rue
Melton Hall,
Woodbridge, Suffolk IP12 1PF

tel	01394 388138
fax	01394 388982
e-mail	delarue@meltonh.fsnet.co.uk

Wrap-around sea views — you are almost on the beach. Phil, from Zimbabwe, and Juliet are easy-going hosts happy to share this special place. The furniture is Victorian, some mahogany, some walnut; the colours are soft; the bed linen the kind you long to have at home. (White cotton crocheted bedspreads come from the market at Victoria Falls.) Here are old things, good taste, books and magazines galore, rugs on wooden floors, a special light from every window... and fresh milk and home-made biscuits on the bedside coffee/tea tray. You can borrow bikes, play table tennis in the cellar, and sail. Perfect.

A covered terrace leads to a glorious sunroom where you can read, relax and eat; the rest of the house, too, is filled with light. It's an 1860s converted granary at the end of a farm drive. The large bedrooms, with high, beamed ceilings and arched windows, are in the roof — nicely private — and there are lots of thoughtful touches: bath potions, robes, candles, bottled water. All around are medieval churches and the beach is only three miles away — spin off on the bikes with a packed lunch. Carole, gentle and flexible, is involved in the Aldeburgh Festival and the Snape Maltings concerts. Dinners are excellent value.

rooms	2: 1 double with bath; 1 twin with shower.
room price	£65–£75. Singles £55–£65.
meals	Breakfast until 9.30am. Packed lunch £5. Dinner £12.50–£15.
closed	Rarely.
directions	From Ipswich A12 north. Right onto A1094 after 20 miles. House in centre of Aldeburgh seafront, between two lookout towers, with parking outside.

rooms	2: 1 double with private bath; 1 twin with shower.
room price	£53. Singles £26.50.
meals	Packed lunch available. Dinner, 3 courses, from £15.
closed	Rarely.
directions	From A12, B1119. From Saxmundham to Leiston, left onto B1122 for Yoxford. 2 miles on, left at x-roads just before Theberton (30mph sign). 1st left, then right up 1st driveway.

Juliet & Phil Brereton
Ocean House,
25 Crag Path, Aldeburgh,
Suffolk IP15 5BS
tel 01728 452094

Mrs Carole Bidder
The Granary,
Theberton, Nr Leiston,
Suffolk IP16 4RR
tel 01728 831633
fax 01728 831633
e-mail granary-theberton@uku.co.uk
web www.granary-theberton.co.uk

The undisputed charms of this mellow red-brick Georgian townhouse lured the Haddons away from London life. Catherine, an interior designer, has poured her considerable energy and talent into its restoration and with a young family *in situ* the whole place feels alive and loved – elegant yet informal. There are lovely fabrics and beautiful colours everywhere. Breakfast is served in the panelled dining room, and upstairs are a delightful double bedroom, a cottagey twin and, in the attic, a charming family suite. Magnificent gardens, too, with a parterre and rose garden.

Idyllic views of the Alde valley from this deeply comfortable, listed farmhouse. The river borders their 20 acres of meadows, orchard, gardens, ponds and remains of brick-lined moat and the Marshalls encourage wildflowers and wildlife – though the rabbits are less welcome! Sunny Susie's flock of hens and guinea fowl strut freely about. Family antiques and portraits, easy colour schemes, some beams and open fires, home-grown eggs and tomatoes for breakfast and every cosseting thing in the pretty guest bedrooms. Ten miles from the coast, five from Snape Maltings and wonderfully relaxing. *Painting classes possible.*

rooms	3: 1 twin/double with shower; 1 twin, 1 double sharing bath.
room price	From £65. Singles from £35.
meals	Dinner from £15.
closed	Christmas & New Year, unless by arrangement.
directions	Turn off A12 to Saxmundham. Through town & under railway bridge; house 1st on right.

rooms	2: 1 double with shower; 1 twin with private bathroom.
room price	£50-£60. Singles from £40.
meals	Good food available locally.
closed	Rarely.
directions	From A1120, Yoxford to Stowmarket, east to Dennington; take B1120, Framlingham. First left; house 1.5 miles on left.

Catherine & Christopher Haddon
Beech House,
North Entrance, Saxmundham,
Suffolk IP17 1AP
tel 01728 605700
fax 01728 605909
e-mail chris@suncircle.fsnet.co.uk.

Mark & Susie Marshall
Sandpit Farm,
Bruisyard, Framlingham,
Saxmundham, Suffolk IPI7 2EB
tel 01728 663445
e-mail susannemarshall@suffolkonline.net
web www.aldevalleybreaks.co.uk

A dreamy 16th-century Tudor farmhouse, part-moated, with an abundance of beams, original *fleur-de-lys* mouldings, an inglenook fireplace and a thatched summer house. It is a real home, too, full of fun and vitality. Family photographs, seagrass matting, soft colours, fresh flowers, real candles in the candelabra – there's a restrained stylishness throughout. Jane and Peter are delightful and will bring you tea in the drawing room, or a drink if you arrive a bit later. Jane was a professional cook and conjures up inspiring dinners if you book in advance.

The tennis court and garden are surrounded by the 12th-century listed moat – this is a gorgeous old place. Ancient stairs rise and fall all over the 13th-century house, there are sloping floors and raw beams and a dining room that was once the dairy. The family room has a billiard table and toy cupboard; the sitting room is cosy with baby grand, open fire, fresh flowers and lots of books. Elizabeth is delightful and generous, and gives you home-made cake on arrival, and local honey and own bread and marmalade for breakfast. *Children over 10 welcome.*

rooms	2: 1 double, 1 twin, sharing bath.
room price	£60. Singles £40.
meals	Dinner £15-£25.
closed	Christmas & New Year.
directions	From A1120 at Earl Soham, take Kenton road & follow signs to Monk Soham for approx. 2 miles. Right fork at top of hill. House 3rd on right.

rooms	3: 1 double, 2 twins, sharing bath. Extra wc available.
room price	£44. Singles £22. Ask for children's rates.
meals	Good pub within walking distance.
closed	December-February.
directions	A1120 (Yoxford to Stowmarket) to Dennington. B1116 north for approx. 3 miles. Farm on right 0.9 miles north of Owl's Green & red phone box.

Jane & Peter Cazalet
Monk Soham Hall,
Monk Soham, Nr Woodbridge,
Suffolk IP13 7EN
tel   01728 685178
fax   01728 685944
e-mail janecaz860@aol.com

Elizabeth Hickson
Grange Farm,
Dennington, Woodbridge,
Suffolk IP13 8BT
tel   01986 798388
web   www.framlingham.com/grangefarm

map: 11 entry: 435

map: 11 entry: 436

Atmosphere and architecture – it's easy to see what seduced Jackum and David into converting this Grade II-listed Victorian chapel into a home. Your bedrooms are charming – the Stable Room, with access to the courtyard garden, has cream walls, oak floors and wooden beams; the flag-floored Retreat Room has bright rugs and bedcovers from far-flung places. An air of tranquillity pervades, from the wind chimes in the garden to breakfast by the lovely chapel rose window or in the colourful conservatory. Potions and lotions by your bath, books and flowers in every corner, famous bacon from Peasenhall.

You'll love this Georgian vicarage in its tranquil corner with easy access to the heritage coast, and the enchanting Suffolk brick façade hints at the elegance within. Well-proportioned rooms are grand but not too grand – fine old furniture, family portraits in gilded frames, photographs, books – and bedrooms are a treat: four-poster beds, towelling robes and garden views. There is a delightful guest sitting room, too. Paula is good company, loves cooking and keeps the flowers fresh. For breakfast expect the best – local bacon and sausages, marmalade and linen napkins in silver rings.

rooms	2: 1 double with private bath & garden access; 1 twin with shower.
room price	£60–£75. Singles £40–£50.
meals	Good pubs/restaurants within walking distance.
closed	Rarely.
directions	From A12 in Yoxford, A1120 signed Peasenhall & Stowmarket. Chapel 200 yds on right.

rooms	3: 1 double with private bath; 1 double, 1 twin sharing bath.
room price	£50–£70. Singles £35.
meals	Packed lunch £4. Good pubs 3 miles.
closed	Rarely.
directions	From A12, 4 miles north of Yoxford, left for Wenhaston. Pass Star Inn & school on left. After 400 yds, on left, red brick wall around churchyard; drive at far end.

Jackum & David Brown
The Old Methodist Chapel,
High Street, Yoxford,
Suffolk IP17 3EU

tel	01728 668333
e-mail	browns@chapelsuffolk.co.uk
web	www.chapelsuffolk.co.uk

Mrs P Heycock
The Old Vicarage,
Church Corner, Wenhaston,
Southwold, Suffolk IP19 9EG

tel	01502 478339
fax	01502 478068
e-mail	theycock@aol.com
web	www.southwold.blythweb.co.uk/oldvicarage

Pat, kind and immensely caring, is an experienced B&B-er. The attractive modern house has secluded gardens and is close to a large heath — perfect for early-morning walks. Pat has filled her new home with family furniture, pictures and many books; pastel bedrooms are light and comfortable. Peace and quiet, fresh food (much locally produced), a lovely hostess, the charm of Suffolk. The heritage coast, medieval churches and Southwold are merely the icing on the cake. Woottens Nursery is nearby too, popular among serious plant collectors.

The village is enchanting; artists have congregated here for over a century. Ferry House was built in the 1930s for a playwright, using a butterfly design to catch the light — it has Art Deco touches, hand-painted fireplace tiles, simple but pretty rooms, books and bathrobes and fresh flowers everywhere. There's a warm cloakroom for wet birdwatchers' clothes and a welcoming glass of sherry; maybe a blazing log fire on cold mornings. You are only 200 yards from the River Blyth and the sea, and Cathryn and John are delightful. *Children over 10 welcome. Self-catering available. See back of book.*

rooms	2: 1 twin/double with private shower; 1 twin with shower.
room price	£40-£60. Singles £22-£29.
meals	Breakfast 8-9am. Dinner £12. Good inn close by.
closed	Rarely.
directions	From A12, 3.3 miles north of Darsham level crossing, left at x-roads for Wenhaston. Left at Star Inn & immed. right into lane. House 2nd on left.

rooms	3: 1 double with shower; 2 singles sharing bath.
room price	From £50. Singles from £23.
meals	Breakfast until 9.30am. Packed lunch £3.50. Pub/restaurant 150 yds.
closed	Christmas.
directions	From A12, B1387 to Walberswick. House on left at far end of village, near river. Three miles from A12.

Patricia Kemsley
Rowan House,
Hall Road, Wenhaston, Southwold,
Suffolk IP19 9HF
tel   01502 478407
e-mail   rowanhouse@freeuk.com

Cathryn Simpson
Ferry House,
Walberswick, Southwold,
Suffolk IP18 6TH
tel   01502 723384
fax   01502 723384
e-mail   ferryhouse.walberswick@virgin.net
web   www.ferryhouse-walberswick.com

SUFFOLK

SUFFOLK

A lovely, listed Elizabethan farmhouse with Georgian additions, meticulously restored, with ancient and modern character and in a very quiet hamlet with a 12th-century thatched church opposite. Sarah, well-travelled and entertaining, has created a relaxed atmosphere in which you feel entirely at home. She's a terrific cook – why not let her prepare a delicious dinner? The bedrooms have gorgeous fabrics, fresh flowers and cotton sheets; one has a medieval bedstead with carved head- and foot-boards, two have super new bathrooms and all are peaceful. An oft-tinkled Bechstein is there for you to play.

Start the day with a Wissett Sparkler, bubbly from the vineyard that yields a startling variety of wines, all produced using sustainable viticultural methods. The Crafts ran a B&B in the States and though there's a touch of US-style luxury – big beds, good American sheets and excellent bathrooms – but the charm is rooted in Elizabethan England. The Tudor bedroom has five tiny windows and soft pink Suffolk bricks; the exterior has timber, stucco and pantiles. In the Victorian extension, two lofty bedrooms and a sumptuous drawing room where you breakfast and dine overlooking the pretty, tranquil garden.

rooms	3: 1 double, 1 twin, both with bath; 1 single with private bath.
room price	From £65. Singles from £35.
meals	Dinner from £20.
closed	Christmas.
directions	A12 for Wangford. Left signed Uggeshall. Farmhouse 1 mile on left before church.

rooms	3: 2 doubles with shower; 1 double with private bath/shower.
room price	£60–£70. Singles from £40.
meals	Dinner, 3 courses with wine, £20.
closed	Christmas.
directions	From Halesworth, Wissett Road. Through Wissett, towards Rumburgh. Pass church on left & after 0.5 miles turning for Valley Farm on left.

	Sarah Jupp
	Church Farmhouse,
	Uggeshall, Southwold,
	Suffolk NR34 8BD
tel	01502 578532
fax	01953 888306
e-mail	sarah-jupp@lineone.net

	Janet Craft
	Valley Farm Vineyards,
	Wissett, Halesworth,
	Suffolk IP19 0JJ
tel	01986 785535
web	www.valleyfarmvineyards.com

An enchanting, soft, 16th-century Suffolk combination of bricks and beams; enjoy the peace of house and garden throughout the day if you wish. It is friendly and handsome, with antique furniture and William-Morris-style floral sofas and chairs. The fascinating dining room was once a cheese room where 'Suffolk Bang' was made; from here you can wander into the kitchen to chat with Rosemary. You have your own wing – one of the bedrooms is a delightful half-timbered room with sloping ceiling. Four miles away is Wingfield Old College, home of the summer arts festival. *Children over 10 welcome*

A magnificent, Grade I-listed townhouse, beautifully restored with respect and sympathy for original fabric and flavour. Built in the 16th and early 18th centuries, the grand house is a paean to architecture – Tudor, Queen Anne, Georgian and Edwardian – with illustrious touches such as Ionic and Corinthian columns on fireplaces. The large bedrooms have beautiful bathrooms, all with original fittings and luxurious towels and linen. Delicious breakfasts are taken at a round table in the oak-panelled breakfast room overlooking the walled garden. The feel of a country house in a town.

rooms	3: 2 doubles, 1 twin, both with private bath.
room price	From £55. Singles £32.
meals	Good pubs/restaurants 8-minute walk.
closed	Christmas week.
directions	From Scole, A140, right onto A143 for Gt Yarmouth. After 7 miles, right at Harleston. B1116 to Fressingfield. Pass church & Fox & Goose on left. At top of hill, right, then left into Priory Rd.

rooms	3: 1 twin/double, 1 double, 1 four-poster, all with bath/shower.
room price	£90-£110. Singles £55-£65.
meals	Good pubs/restaurants within walking distance.
closed	Christmas & New Year.
directions	From A14, Bury Central exit & follow brown signs for Historic Centre. At r'bout, 1st left into Northgate St. House on right, shortly after lights. Courtyard parking at far end of house.

Stephen & Rosemary Willis
Priory House,
Priory Road, Fressingfield, Eye,
Suffolk IP21 5PH
tel   01379 586254
fax   01379 586254

Joy Fiennes
Northgate House,
Northgate Street, Bury St Edmunds,
Suffolk IP33 1HQ
tel   01284 760469
fax   01284 724008
e-mail   northgate_hse@hotmail.com
web   www.northgatehouse.com

SUFFOLK

Genny's love for her timber-clad home surrounded by flat-racing country is as evident as her enthusiasm for her garden. She has decorated the big, sunny rooms with thought and care, supplying every treat a guest could want, as well as books, magazines and an honesty bar for drinks. As you relax in the drawing room by the log fire you may ask, "Why haven't we organised things like this at home?" That's the cake; the icing is the three-acre garden with its sweeping lawns, herbaceous borders, stream, orchard, lily pond and glorious bulbs in spring. *Children over eight welcome.*

rooms	3: 1 double with shower; 1 twin with private bath; 1 double with bath/shower.
room price	£68. Singles £44.
meals	Breakfast 8-9am. Pubs/restaurants 200 yds-4 miles.
closed	Christmas & New Year.
directions	From A11 (for Thetford & Norwich) B1085 to Red Lodge & Worlington. Right at T-junc. through village; house 200 yds on right.

Genny Jakobson
Brambles,
Worlington, Bury St Edmunds,
Suffolk IP28 8RY
tel   01638 713121
fax   01638 713121
e-mail   genny@trjakobson.freenetname.co.uk

SUFFOLK

A Suffolk classic, just what you'd expect from an old vicarage: a fine Pembroke table in the flagstoned hall, a large open log fire in the sitting/dining room, a long refectory table covered in magazines such as *The Field*, an inviting sofa, a piano, family photos, hunting scenes and silver pheasants. Bedrooms are large, chintzy and handsomely furnished; the double has hill views. Weave your way through the branches of the huge copper beech to the garden that Jane loves; she grows her own vegetables, and keeps hens and house with equal talent. *Children over seven welcome.*

rooms	3: 1 double, 1 twin, both with private bath; 1 single off one of the twins.
room price	From £60. Singles £35.
meals	Breakfast from 7am. Packed lunch £6. Dinner £18. B.Y.O.
closed	Christmas Day.
directions	From Cambridge, A1307 for Haverhill. Left to Withersfield. At T-junc., left. Almost 3 miles on, high yew hedge; at 'Concealed Entrance' sign on left, sharp turn into drive.

Ms Jane Sheppard
The Old Vicarage,
Great Thurlow, Newmarket,
Suffolk CB9 7LE
tel   01440 783209
fax   01638 667270

Breakfast, freshly-squeezed and home-made, is lavish; dinner is a three-course extravaganza. Richard was a yacht skipper, Veronica owned a restaurant in Australia, now they love doing B&B. The house, beamed, thatched and dating from 1550, is enchanting inside and out: logs smoulder in the 'Snug' on wet or wintery days; beds are dressed in crisp cotton and merino wool... there are lotions and potions for your bath, and books and flowers by the bed. Play the Steinway or, more energetically, tennis; sit under the ancient pear trees in summer where you will be brought afternoon tea.

Diana was once a stage manager in the London theatre and it shows: she is outgoing, fun, brilliant with people and has a marvellous sense of style. The bedrooms are perfect, with attractive duvets and curtains, pale walls and garden flowers. On the tea tray are biscuits, proper coffee and a cafetière. The sitting room is a stunning terracotta, a lovely place to be. The garden is surprisingly large, and pretty, with a terrace, fishpond, lawn and borders – sit here awhile and enjoy a glass of wine or a pot of tea while the cats look on as they sun themselves.

rooms	2: 1 twin/double with shower; 1 double with private bath.
room price	From £80. Singles from £50.
meals	Dinner, 3 courses, from £28.
closed	Rarely.
directions	From Bury St Edmunds SW on A143 Haverhill road. Left after 30mph zone, for Whepstead 3 miles (B1066). 2 miles on right at dip in road (signed Rede 3 miles). House 1 mile on, past White Horse Inn, on right.

rooms	3: 2 doubles, 1 twin, all with bath/shower.
room price	From £60. Singles from £45.
meals	Pubs/restaurants a short walk away.
closed	Christmas & January; open New Year.
directions	From Sudbury, B1115 to Lavenham. Pass Swan Hotel on right, next right into Market Lane, cross Market Place, right, then left. House on right next to school.

Veronica & Richard Hayes
Leaf House,
Rede Road, Whepstead,
Bury St Edmunds, Suffolk IP29 4SS
tel   01284 735388
e-mail   mail@leafhouse.co.uk
web   www.leafhouse.co.uk

Diana Schofield
The Red House,
29 Bolton Street, Lavenham,
Suffolk CO10 9RG
tel   01787 248074
web   www.lavenham.co.uk/redhouse

Unwind in front of a huge log fire in the Great Hall and soak up the atmosphere of this fascinating place – a Grade I-listed cloth merchant's house in medieval Lavenham. Gilli and Tim have brought old and new together with flamboyance: timber-framed ceilings perfectly restored, slanting oak floors, flagstones heated underfoot. Richly atmospheric bedrooms have handmade mattresses and hand-crafted beds, sumptuous curtains, flowers, lovely views from mullioned windows. A fabulous house restored to its Elizabethan grandeur, in three acres of grounds in the centre of the village. *Children over 10 welcome.*

This little pink cottage was once a pub, but has been tenderly restored to create a pretty, family house; your room, which is in the converted barn, will appeal to the romantic in you. Sue welcomes you with a glass of Madeira by the enormous inglenook fire, then takes you through the neat little garden – past honeysuckle, aqualegia and Canterbury bells – to the barn. A stable door opens into the primrose-yellow bedroom with exposed beams and soaring rafters. The chintz-headed, king-size bed is covered in cushions, there are fresh flowers on the table and watercolours of Mauritius on the walls. Stunning!

rooms	6: 1 four-poster suite, 1 double, 3 four-posters, all with bath & shower; 1 twin/double with shower.
room price	£85-£136. Singles £60-£85.
meals	Breakfast 8-9am Mon-Fri; 8-9.30am Sat & Sun. Restaurants & pubs within walking distance.
closed	Christmas & New Year.
directions	Turn at The Swan onto Water Street, right after 50 yds into private drive.

rooms	1 double with shower.
room price	£65.
meals	Pubs & restaurants in Lavenham.
closed	Rarely.
directions	From Sudbury, B1115 to Lavenham. Pass Swan Hotel on right, next right into Market Lane. Straight across Market Place into Prentice St. Last on right at bottom of hill.

Tim & Gilli Pitt
Lavenham Priory,
Water Street, Lavenham,
Suffolk CO10 9RW

tel	01787 247404
fax	01787 248102
e-mail	mail@lavenhampriory.co.uk
web	www.lavenhampriory.co.uk

Mrs Sue Wade
Anchor House,
Prentice Street, Lavenham,
Suffolk CO10 9RD

tel	01787 249018
fax	01787 249018
e-mail	suewade1@aol.com
web	www.anchorhouse.co.uk

A lovely address, a lovely house: a 16th-century wool merchant's house on a quiet street close to the centre of medieval Lavenham. Gillian has made it a most delightful and unusual place to stay. The bedrooms are enchanting – white-painted and beamed, with eccentric windows, pretty fabrics, fresh flowers and thoughtful touches. Both rooms have super bathrooms; the twin has its own sitting room, staircase and entrance from the street. Behind the house, unguessed-at from the front, is a lovely, secret garden. Breakfast out here in the summer on local sausages, potato cakes and fresh fruit.

Breakfast on summer mornings on the terrace in the walled garden with home-made marmalade, jams and fruit compotes; in winter, settle beside an arched Tudor brick fireplace in the dining hall. Janus-like, the house looks both ways, Georgian to the front, and richly-beamed, 1485-Tudor behind; Alfred Munnings R.A. was a frequent visitor. The bedrooms, one with flower-patterned paper, the other with pink sponged walls, are elegant and very English: padded bedheads, thick curtains, armchairs, writing desks, candles, standard lamp, books... pretty and full of thoughtful touches.

rooms	2: 1 double, 1 twin both with bath.
room price	£65-£75. Singles £45.
meals	Packed lunches £5. Excellent pubs/restaurants a short walk.
closed	Rarely.
directions	From Swan Hotel in High St, turn into Water St. 3rd left into Shilling Street; long pink house on left.

rooms	2: 1 double with shower; 1 twin with bath & separate wc.
room price	£65. Singles £35.
meals	Breakfast until 9.30am. Dinner £15, if staying more than one night. B.Y.O.
closed	Christmas.
directions	From Sudbury B1115 for Lavenham for 3.5 miles. Right to Little Waldingfield. House on left, 200 yds beyond The Swan.

Bill & Gillian de Lucy
Guinea House,
21 Shilling Street, Lavenham,
Suffolk CO10 9RH

tel	01787 249046
fax	01787 249619
e-mail	gdelucy@aol.com
web	www.guineahouse.co.uk

Mrs Susan T. del C. Nisbett
Wood Hall,
Little Waldingfield, Nr Lavenham,
Suffolk CO10 0SY

tel	01787 247362
fax	01787 248326
e-mail	susan@woodhallbnb.fsnet.co.uk
web	www.thewoodhall.co.uk

The atmosphere is relaxed and easy, and Juliet is full of imaginative ideas for making the most of the countryside, which is wonderful: nature trails, walks, bike rides (borrow a bike), tennis, car-free days out. The house is a glorious, unspoiled, 16th-century hall farmhouse, lived in and loved by the family for 300 years, filled with period furniture and with bedrooms that overlook a wildflower meadow and walled garden. Home-grown bacon, sausages and bantam eggs for breakfast and equally delicious dinners. Juliet is fun, energetic and a keen conservationist. *Gold award for Green Tourism.*

The beautiful drawing room with carved pine mantelpiece and marble hearth faces south with views of the water meadow and the Rivers Brett and Stour. Blue and white Spode china, silver cutlery, embroidered sheets, fresh fruit and flowers and architectural elegance come with a genuine welcoming feel; Meg really enjoys guests of all ages. You can row, canoe or punt to Stratford St Mary for a pub lunch, or you may fish, play tennis or swim in the pool. This Elizabethan jewel sits snug beside an equally lovely 12th-century church.

rooms	3: 1 double/family with basin, 2 twins, all sharing private bath.
room price	£55-£70. Singles from £35.
meals	Occasional supper/dinner from £11.25. B.Y.O. Excellent pub/restaurants 2-3 miles.
closed	Rarely.
directions	From Lavenham, A1141 for Monks Eleigh. After 2 miles, right to Milden. At x-roads, right to Sudbury on B1115. Hall's long drive 0.25 miles on left.

rooms	3: 1 double with bath; 1 twin, 1 family room, both with private bath.
room price	£52-£60. Family room £72. Singles £30-£40.
meals	Excellent places for dinner nearby.
closed	Rarely.
directions	West off A12 at Stratford St Mary. House on left, opp. church sign, 1 mile down Higham road. House has pink timbers & sign on wall.

	Juliet & Christopher Hawkins
	The Hall,
	Milden, Nr Lavenham,
	Suffolk CO10 9NY
tel	01787 247235
fax	01787 247235
e-mail	gjb53@dial.pipex.com
web	www.thehall-milden.co.uk

	Meg Parker
	The Old Vicarage,
	Higham, Nr Colchester,
	Suffolk CO7 6JY
tel	01206 337248
e-mail	oldvic.higham@bushinternet.com

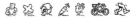

The handsome red-brick house was once the home of children's author Paul Jennings, and sits in an enchanting, part-walled secret garden with views to Dedham Vale. Artist Anne, and Gerald, give you an elegant welcome and a room with a view with crisp linen, gentle colours and a painted brass bed. Though the children have flown, three middle-aged cats remain – guests find it a comforting, welcoming home. Fine breakfasts, delightful people, a special bathroom – and John Constable's village right outside the door.

Your luggage will be carried up an uneven tread in this handsome hall house of 1523 – it was owned by Cardinal Wolsey and has Henry VIII's coat of arms above the fire. It rambles round corners, rich in beams and beloved family pieces; there are two winding stairs. Penny, gentle and well-travelled, gives you tea and cakes in the drawing room, and lights a log fire on chillier days. In the garden: old roses, pear pergola and mulberry tree; in the bedrooms: leaded windows, beamed walls, a good bed. Home-made jam on home-baked bread when you wake, soft robes for the bath before bed.

rooms	2: 1 double with private bath/shower; 1 extra double for members of same party.
room price	From £60. Singles by arrangement.
meals	Good selection of pubs/restaurants locally.
closed	Rarely.
directions	From A12, B1070 to East Bergholt; there, 1st right (Hadleigh Rd), left at T-junc., right at next T-junc.; through village; pass church on left & down hill. House on left, behind yew hedge.

rooms	2: 1 double with private shower; 1 twin with bath/shower.
room price	From £50. Singles £35.
meals	Supper £8.
closed	Rarely.
directions	5 miles west of Ipswich (off A1071). 200 yds after village Post Office Stores; left, next to farmyard.

Gerald & Anne Becker
Hill House,
Rectory Hill, East Bergholt,
Suffolk CO7 6TH

tel	01206 299554
fax	01206 299621
e-mail	geraldannebecker@hotmail.com

Penny Debenham
Mulberry Hall,
Burstall, Nr Ipswich,
Suffolk IP8 3DP

tel	01473 652348
fax	01473 652110
e-mail	pennydebenham@hotmail.com

ORGANIC B&B

To talk of an organic 'revolution' is misleading, for about about three-quarters of organic food is bought by about ten percent of consumers. But it's a start, and the growth is profoundly encouraging. Organic farming (and growing) is the single best solution to our agricultural crisis, but it takes humility for government to recognise this when many billions of pounds have been poured into intensive industrial agriculture and the solving of its attendant crises (Foot and Mouth, BSE etc).

Because so many of our B&Bs are in the countryside we are acutely aware of the need for change. Many owners are working hard to support their communities, buying locally and bringing money into their rural economies. We want to support those efforts, hence our determination to introduce an 'Organic B&B' symbol within the next few years – strange but do-able. We and the Soil Association are working on it and have held our first meeting with a small group of owners. When it happens, you will be able to sleep between organically-grown-cotton sheets, wash with organic soaps and eat eggs and bacon from 'happy' chickens and pigs. We think that this is a target worth aiming for… and it will all be part of a campaign to generate jobs in the countryside – good jobs.

Lovely, interesting people who are helpful and friendly yet never intrusive. Their home, full of happy family memories, is a converted stables and squash court that originally belonged to the next-door manor house; it has a mature charm with lots of trees in the garden, a paddock and a pool. Given the hushed tranquillity you are surprisingly close to the airports and the M25. The bedrooms are small but one has its own entrance, another the use of a sunny sitting room, the third a balcony; there are garden views, too. *Children over eight welcome.*

Such a surprise to bump along a farm track and find 400 acres of farmland so close to London… but this is Surrey, the most densely wooded and rural home-county. The lovely manor — Jacobean at the front, Tudor at the back — has all the features you'd expect. An easy-going John enjoys the higgle and piggle of the old house: all wooden floors and worn rugs, wonky ceilings, window seats and church panel doors. Bedrooms and bathrooms are big, with timbered walls and views to a walled rose garden, two acres of lawn, a tree-lined pond and a hillock on which horses graze.

rooms	3: 1 double with bath & sitting room; 1 twin with shower; 1 twin with private shower.
room price	£75. Singles £45.
meals	Pub/restaurant 0.75 miles.
closed	Rarely.
directions	From M25, exit 11, A319 into Chobham. Left at T-junc.; left at mini-r'bout onto A3046. After 0.9 miles, right between street light & postbox. House 2nd on left.

rooms	2: 1 twin, 1 double, both with bath.
room price	£65. Singles £45.
meals	Supper with wine £25.
closed	Rarely.
directions	From M25/A3. Leave A3 at Guildford, follow signs A323 Aldershot for 2 miles to big black & white r'bout. House 400 yds on left.

Joan & David Carey
Swallow Barn,
Milford Green, Chobham, Woking,
Surrey GU24 8AU

tel	01276 856030
fax	01276 856030
e-mail	swallowbarn@web-hq.com
web	www.swallow-barn.co.uk

John & Pooh Tangye
Littlefield Manor,
Littlefield Common, Guildford,
Surrey GU3 3HJ

tel	01483 233068
fax	01483 233686
e-mail	john.tangye@virgin.net
web	www.littlefieldmanor.co.uk

A homely place with a lovely walled garden and super hosts. Gillian welcomes guests from all over the world (she speaks French, German and Spanish), yet she and David will make you feel like their first ever; their conversation is lively and informed. The house, 16th to 19th century, has exposed timber frames and bold colours: the dining room is red. The guest sitting room, with its log fireplace and piano, is hung with a collection of hats and ethnic treasures. In the walled garden the distant rumble of the A3 reminds you how well placed you are for Gatwick and Heathrow.

People return time and again – the house, the garden, the countryside and the hosts are exceptional. In a vast sitting room, low-slung beams and striking colours jostle for your attention. A sturdy, turning oak staircase leads to the bedrooms; a peek at them all will only confuse you – each one is gorgeous. There's an ornate bedstead in the Chinese room and, in another, an oak bedstead and beams. A further room has a hint of French decadence: golds, magentas and silks. It's enchanting. Sheila knows about antiques and all the local antique shops, too.

rooms	4: 1 twin/double with bath/shower; 1 twin/double with private bath/shower; 2 singles (1 with basin) sharing shower.
room price	£60–£75. Singles £35–£50.
meals	Breakfast 7.30–9am. Good pub 300 yds.
closed	Christmas & New Year.
directions	A3 south. 5 miles after Guildford, Eashing signed left at service station. House 150 yds on left behind white fence.

rooms	3: 1 double with bath; 1 twin, 1 single sharing bath.
room price	£70–£80. Singles from £45.
meals	Breakfast until 9am. Hotel restaurant 0.25 miles.
closed	Rarely.
directions	A3 to Milford, then A283 for Petworth. At Chiddingfold, Pickhurst Rd is off green. House 3rd on left, with large black dovecote.

David & Gillian Swinburn
Lower Eashing Farmhouse,
Eashing, Nr Godalming,
Surrey GU7 2QF
tel   01483 421436
fax   01483 421436
e-mail davidswinburn@hotmail.com

Sheila & John Marsh
Greenaway,
Pickhurst Road, Chiddingfold,
Surrey GU8 4TS
tel   01428 682920
fax   01428 685078
e-mail jfmarsh@nildram.co.uk
web   www.greenaway.nildram.co.uk

SURREY

T his feels as rural as Devon, yet you are almost within walking distance of Guildford. It's a gorgeous 16th-century Grade II-listed farmhouse on a country lane beneath the Pilgrim's Way. Beyond the pretty terraced garden – Michael's passion – views of the North Downs and wooded hills reach out, with hardly a house in sight. Bedrooms have been beautifully furnished by Alison, an interior designer, with lovely fabrics and antique French beds. Log fires are lit in winter when the wind whistles around and there are two friendly dogs to greet you – Herbert and Ha'penny. Perfectly placed for airports and Ascot.

rooms	2 doubles, both with private bath.
room price	£70. Singles £50.
meals	Good pubs/restaurants 2 miles.
closed	Christmas & New Year.
directions	From top of Guildford High St, along Epsom Rd & right into Tangier Rd. At top, bear left into Warren Rd. At sharp r-h bend at top, (One Tree Hill Rd), on for 0.3 miles, bear right into Halfpenny Lane. 0.7 miles down on left.

Michael Bennett
Old Great Halfpenny,
Halfpenny Lane, St Martha,
Guildford, Surrey GU4 8PY
tel 01483 567835
fax 01483 303037
e-mail bennettbird@btopenworld.com

map: 5 entry: 461

SURREY

I t really does ramble – it dates from 1532 and sits in two and a half acres of smooth lawns beyond which lie the village and Surrey hills. Unlike many houses with masses of beams, low ceilings and dark furniture, this one is light and inviting and has the sort of family clutter that makes you feel immediately at home. Patrick is enthusiastic and dynamic, Carol gives you home-made marmalade at breakfast; both leave you plenty of space to unfurl at your own pace. The dining room is stone-flagged and there's a snug study just for guests.

rooms	3: 2 doubles, 1 twin, all sharing bath.
room price	£50-£60. Singles £25-£30.
meals	Breakfast 7-9.30am. Good pubs/restaurants 3-5 miles.
closed	Christmas.
directions	From A3, 1st exit after M25, for Ripley. Through Ripley & West Clandon, over dual carriageway (A246) onto A25. 3rd right to Shere. There, right to Cranleigh. House 5 miles on left, 1 mile past Windmill pub.

Patrick & Carol Franklin Adams
High Edser,
Shere Road, Ewhurst, Cranleigh,
Surrey GU6 7PQ
tel 01483 278214
fax 01483 278200
e-mail franklinadams@highedser.demon.co.uk

map: 5 entry: 462

SURREY

Originally a 16th-century inn, the farmhouse is now a peaceful haven set in five acres with a small lake that once formed part of a moat; a bridge takes you to a little island. Inside, low beams, wattle-and-daub walls, Jacobean-style furniture, antiques, rugs and log fires. One bedroom has a brass bedstead, another a four-poster; the attic bathroom has a whirlpool. At breakfast you can sit in the conservatory overlooking the lake and be entertained by the ducks. Ann and David are relaxed, unpretentious and easy hosts who are happy to ferry airport travellers.

SUSSEX

You have the freedom of the place – a rare treat. Much of it has been here for five centuries, as solid and dependable as your welcome. The silence is filled with birdsong, the lawn gives a feeling of endless space and you are in glorious isolation in three acres of the surrounding AONB – don't be surprised if you see deer and pheasant roaming in the garden. The room in the main house is painted magnolia and has flowery curtains and garden access. The Barn has its own sitting room: wooden-floored, rugged and filled with pine and light. The rooms upstairs are cottage-cosy, floral and deeply traditional.

rooms	3: 1 double, 1 four-poster, both with bath; 1 twin with shower.
room price	£55-£65. Singles £40-£50.
meals	Pub/restaurant 1 mile.
closed	Christmas.
directions	At crossroads in Leigh, follow signs to Charwood. After 1 mile, 1st right (for Herons Head Farm) after sign to Mynthurst. On up drive for 0.5 miles.

rooms	3: 1 double with shower & sitting room; 1 double with bath/shower; 1 twin/double with shower.
room price	£75. Suite £85. Singles £45-£50.
meals	Good pubs/restaurants nearby.
closed	Christmas.
directions	On old A3, north from Petersfield, at hill brow right for Milland, left after 300 yds. Follow lane through woods for 6 miles; right for Midhurst & Redford; cottage on right 150 yds beyond Redford sign & pond.

Ms Ann Dale
Herons Head Farm,
Mynthurst, Leigh, Surrey RH2 8QD

tel   01293 862475
fax   01293 863350
e-mail   heronshead@clara.net
web   www.heronshead.co.uk

Caroline & David Angela
Redford Cottage,
Redford, Midhurst,
Sussex GU29 0QF

tel   01428 741242

map: 5 entry: 463

map: 5 entry: 464

Buried in a birchwood, The Quag feels miles from anywhere, yet Midhurst – "the second most attractive town in England" – is only two miles away. Feel private in your own quarters with bedroom, striking bathroom with chequer-board floor, pine-floored sitting room (big enough for a child's bed) and separate stairs to the garden. You breakfast in the main house at a long wooden table with antique wheatsheaf-back chairs. Views are to the terrace and lawns that run down to Winterbourne stream, then across to the South Downs. Mark works for Christie's, Loveday looks after you. A happy, relaxed atmosphere and good value.

A wooded track leads to the beautiful, mellow, 17th-century farmhouse with tall chimneys and a cluster of overgrown outbuildings. Wood-panelled walls and ancient oak beams, a vast open fireplace, mullioned windows and welcoming sofas create an atmosphere of relaxed, country-house charm. You breakfast in the Aga-warm kitchen; in spring the scent of bluebells wafts through open doors. The large, comfortable, timbered bedrooms – one canopied bed incorporates original oak panelling – overlook fields, rolling lawns and woodland where you can stroll in peace. *Children by arrangement.*

rooms	1 twin with bath/shower.
room price	£60. Singles £35.
meals	Supper £20-£25.
closed	Christmas & occasionally.
directions	A272 Midhurst to Petersfield. 2 miles from Midhurst, left signed Minsted. Count seven telegraph poles, then 1st left. White house 1st on right.

rooms	3: 1 double, 1 twin, sharing bath; 1 double/family with bath.
room price	£50-£70. Singles by arrangement.
meals	Breakfast 8-9.30am or by arrangement. Excellent pubs/restaurants 2-5 miles.
closed	Christmas.
directions	Given on booking.

Loveday & Mark Wrey
The Quag,
Minsted, Nr Midhurst,
Sussex GU29 0JH
tel   01730 813623
fax   01730 817844
e-mail   mwrey@dial1.co.uk

Maggie Paterson
Fitzlea Farmhouse,
Selham, Nr Petworth,
Sussex GU28 0PS
tel   01798 861429

map: 5 entry: 465

map: 5 entry: 466

Deer come to your window and miles of unspoiled woodland walks start from the door. Not really a B&B, more a tranquil hideaway for independent nature lovers – welcoming hosts live in the neighbouring listed cottage and lavishly replenish your refrigerator daily with a choice of bread, hams, cheeses, yogurts, real coffee and much more. There are a kettle and a toaster and all mod cons for self-serve, continental-style breakfast. Annabelle prepares your rooms carefully and the feel is simple country style. You have your own front door and terrace and can come and go as you please – or stay all day.

A house has been here since the Bronze Age and the history of Lordington could fill this book. Jacobean, with numerous modifications, it is vast and impressive, with majestic views past clipped yew, box and walled garden to the valley beyond. The Hamiltons have brought warmth to the house, yet it remains engagingly old-fashioned; the panelled drawing room is lovely. Bedrooms are large and have magnificent views: a floral double, and a twin, with Windsor bedheads and *toile de Jouy* wallpaper up and over wardrobe doors. You are in an area of outstanding natural beauty. *Children over five welcome.*

rooms	2 double studios, both with shower.
room price	From £60. Singles by arrangement.
meals	Pubs within walking distance.
closed	Rarely.
directions	From Midhurst, A286 for Chichester. After Royal Oak pub on left, Greyhound on right, on for 0.5 miles, left to Heyshott. On for 2 miles, do not turn off, look for white posts & house sign on left.

rooms	2: 1 double, 1 twin, both with private bath & shower.
room price	From £60. Singles from £35.
meals	Packed lunch from £5. Dinner £15-£25. Pubs from 1 mile; restaurants 4-8 miles.
closed	Rarely.
directions	Lordington (marked on AA road maps) on west side of B2146 6 miles south of South Harting & 0.5 miles south of Walderton. Enter through white railings by letterbox; fork right after bridge.

Alex & Annabelle Costaras
Amberfold,
Heyshott, Midhurst,
Sussex GU29 0DA
tel   01730 812385
fax   01730 812842

Mr & Mrs John Hamilton
Lordington House,
Lordington, Chichester,
Sussex PO18 9DX
tel   01243 375862
fax   01243 375203
e-mail   audreyhamilton@onetel.net.uk

map: 5 entry: 467

map: 4 entry: 468

Vivien is happy for breakfast to turn into an early-morning house-party in her lovely yellow kitchen; you are spoiled with kippers and porridge and, later, home-made cakes for tea. You are close to Goodwood – husband Tim manages a local stud – and the house, built by Napoleonic prisoners of war, was once part of the Goodwood estate. Bedrooms are in the old cattle byres that were originally converted for the Reads' growing family. They are a good size, attractively furnished and decorated and always have fresh flowers. Lovely views from the garden, and there's a tennis court, too.

This 1810 flint cottage is prettily and traditionally decorated with antiques and chintz. The double room has green views; the small, 'single' room a lovely wrought-iron double bed. Once a dancer, Lesley now performs – with undimmed vivacity – to the whims of her visitors, and loves having people to stay. Breakfast is served exquisitely, with silver and linen and locally sourced food. The outdoor pool is an added bonus. Peace and quiet, Lesley's easy generosity, delectable Bosham with its harbour walks and sailing boats, and the Downs only two miles away… a special place.

rooms	2 doubles/twins, both with bath/shower.
room price	£60-£80. Singles £40.
meals	Excellent pubs in village, 1 mile.
closed	Christmas.
directions	A272 to Midhurst, A286 to Singleton. Left for Goodwood: up over Downs, pass racecourse, next right for Lavant. House 1st on right 0.5 miles on.

rooms	2: 1 double with bath; 1 single, let to members of the same party.
room price	£55-£70. Singles £40-£45.
meals	Breakfast 7.30-9am. Good pubs/restaurants nearby.
closed	Christmas.
directions	From Chichester, A259 west for Bosham; through Fishbourne, past garden centre, left into Walton Lane. After sharp bend, right into Crede Lane; 200 yds to end of drive. On left, with white garage.

Tim & Vivien Read
The Flint House,
East Lavant, Chichester,
Sussex PO18 0AS
tel 01243 773482
e-mail theflinthouse@ukonline.co.uk

Mrs Lesley Hankey
Crede Farmhouse,
Crede Lane, Bosham,
Sussex PO18 8NX
tel 01243 574929
e-mail lesley@credefarmhouse.fsnet.co.uk

SUSSEX

M ary is relaxed and easy and her 16th-century former farmhouse charming. Flagstoned floors, beams, a cosily cluttered drawing room filled with Bechstein piano, cello, double bass... And cats and more cats: some real, others framed or created from wood, metal or stone. The bedrooms have bathrooms with views of Bosham and the whole place has the feel of a lived-in family home – Mary has been here for 30 years. Wide Sussex skies overhead, a short stroll to the water's edge – the Chidham Peninsula is a paradise for birdwatchers – and it's 20 minutes' walk to an excellent pub.

rooms	3: 1 twin, 1 double, sharing bath; 1 double with private bath.
room price	From £48. Singles £34.
meals	Excellent pub in village.
closed	Christmas.
directions	From Chichester towards Portsmouth. Pass Tesco on right. 3rd exit off r'bout, to Bosham & Fishbourne. A259 for 4 miles, pass Saab garage on right. Next left into Chidham Lane. House last on left, 1 mile down.

Mary Hartley
Easton House,
Chidham Lane, Chidham,
Chichester, Sussex PO18 8TF
tel   01243 572514
fax   01243 573084
e-mail   eastonhouse@chidham.fsnet.co.uk

map: 4 entry: 471

SUSSEX

B ees buzz blissfully, water bubbles in the fountain and you may swim in the pool. The Sedgwicks – Nigel is studying History of Art and Juliet has a framing business – have created a mellow retreat. Bedrooms are large and there's a Waring & Gillow bed from which you can gaze across the coastal plain to the South Downs as the sun streams in. This is a sunny spot, hence the many local market gardeners. Juliet frequently travels to London for exhibitions via the excellent rail connection; happily, the three-acre garden and double-glazing shield you from any train noise.

rooms	3: 1 double with bath; 1 double, 1 twin, sharing bath.
room price	£60-£80. Singles £40-£45.
meals	Packed lunch available. Dinner £15-£25.
closed	Christmas.
directions	From Chichester A27 east (or west from Arundel). South on B2132 for Yapton. Right on Lake Lane just before level crossing. House 0.5 miles on right.

Nigel & Juliet Sedgwick
Todhurst Farm,
Lake Lane, Barnham, Arundel,
Sussex PO22 0AL
tel   01243 551959
e-mail   nigelsedg@aol.com

map: 5 entry: 472

Their Cumbrian house was in Special Places; now Mike and Janet have moved to one of Sussex's prettiest villages. Built in 1587, the thatched cottage is so endearing that you wish there were more bedrooms; narrow stairs lead to a small, private sitting room, and your bedroom is beyond. Dramatic beams bisect primrose walls, the ceiling slopes to floor-level windows on either side and an exquisite quilt covers the big white bed. Robes are provided for the trip downstairs to the bathroom. The Wrights really know how to look after people – aromatherapy is on offer and the breakfast menu is out of this world!

It is a 15th-century hall house, once one vast room with a central fireplace venting through the roof. Although a 'guesthouse' it has just two rooms and they are comfortable and woody, with Egyptian cotton, power showers and all mod cons. You'd hesitate to light a match here, lest you set the ancient timbers alight! The double is richly beamed and has a padded headboard and opulent bedspread, the twin has velour-padded headboards and fewer beams, and Joy's numerous paintings are for sale: land, sea, and other scapes. Steyning is an ancient market town with a fine 11th-century church worth visiting.

rooms	1 double with private bath/shower.
room price	From £56. Singles £36.
meals	Excellent pub in village.
closed	Christmas & occasionally.
directions	Off A24 onto A283 for Storrington. There, B2139, then right into village; house on left opp. phone box.

rooms	2: 1 double, 1 twin, both with bath/shower.
room price	£78. Singles £49.
meals	Dinner, 3-4 courses, £15-£24. Good pubs locally.
closed	Rarely.
directions	From A24, A283 for Shoreham. After 4 miles, right for Steyning through High Street & over mini-r'bout. House immed. on left.

Mike & Janet Wright
Stream Cottage,
Church Street, Amberley, Arundel,
Sussex BN18 9ND
tel   01798 831266
fax   01798 831266
e-mail   enquiries@streamcottage.co.uk
web   www.streamcottage.co.uk

Joy & John Turner
30 High Street,
Steyning, Sussex BN44 3GG
tel   01903 815595
fax   01903 816686
e-mail   johnturner57@aol.com
web   www.artyguesthouse.co.uk

SUSSEX

A typical 15th-century Sussex farmhouse with beams and bags of character. Delightful Celia has filled it with fascinating things; she once sold antiques and has an excellent eye. The single rooms are charming and stylish and are furnished with some interesting pieces; the double is equally lovely, light and airy and overlooks this garden. This has received the same lavish attention as the house and has been restored to its original layout with two bridged ponds — you could happily spend a morning wandering among the colours and scents. Excellent pubs are nearby and you are not far from Glyndebourne.

rooms	3: 1 double with private bath; 2 singles sharing bath.
room price	£60. Singles £32.
meals	Breakfast until 9.30am. Good pub 5-minute drive.
closed	Christmas & New Year.
directions	From Uckfield, A26 Lewes road. Right for Isfield & on for 1 mile. Right over level crossing & house on sharp left bend with high fence & gate, approx. 0.5 miles on.

Celia Rigby
The Faulkners,
Isfield, Sussex TN22 5XG
tel   01825 750344
fax   01825 750577

map: 5 entry: 475

SUSSEX

A thoroughly charming, miniature country house, with a courtyard at the front and a walled garden at the back — both are a riot of colour in spring and summer. When you arrive you may join Lucy for tea and cakes round the large oak table in the kitchen: a lovely start. The guest bedroom is bright and fresh, with Egyptian cotton on the beds and home-made biscuits on the tea tray. Lucy fills the house with flowers — you'll feel well looked after. Wander through the garden to woodland behind; only bird ballad disturbs the peace. Handy for opera lovers: Glyndebourne is nearby.

rooms	1 twin/double with bath.
room price	£70. Singles £45.
meals	Packed lunch £5. Good pub 1 mile.
closed	Christmas & New Year.
directions	A26 for Uckfield; straight at Little Horsted r'bout for Ridgewood. 1st right down New Road; at phone box right down concealed drive. Cottage 2nd on left.

Mrs Lucy Ann
Park Cottage,
Ridgewood, Nr Uckfield,
Sussex TN22 5TG
tel   01825 767104
fax   01825 763005
e-mail   l.ann@btinternet.com

map: 5 entry: 476

Sarah has impeccable taste and is constantly striving to make her thoroughly English 17th-century house even more beautiful. Rich colours, well-chosen fabrics, good oil paintings: this would make a perfect escape for cultured sybarites. There's a heated pool, a tennis court and a spectacular garden; she recently planted thousands of Dutch tulip bulbs given to her by a friend. The food is special, too, with an adventurous but always carefully judged menu, and the orange juice for breakfast is freshly squeezed. Sarah will also prepare you a hamper for Glyndebourne, a 10-minute drive away.

A listed 17th-century house beside the church in a tiny village, 10 minutes from Glyndebourne. Alison was chef to the Beatles and will not only give you a delicious hamper, but tables and chairs too. Willie is a former world rackets champion who gives tennis coaching; there's a tennis court in the large, pretty garden, and a swimming pool, too. Relax by the inglenook fire in the drawing room after a walk on the Cuckoo Trail or the South Downs; then settle down to a great supper – local fish, maybe, with home-grown vegetables. This is an easy-going, fun and informal household. *Children over 12 welcome.*

rooms	3: 1 twin with bath; 1 twin with private bath; 1 twin/double with private shower.
room price	£80–£110. Singles by arrangement.
meals	Breakfast until 9.30am. Lunch from £16. Hampers £28. Dinner, 3 courses, £24.
closed	Rarely.
directions	0.5 miles past Halland on A22, south from Uckfield, 1st left off Shaw r'bout towards E. Hoathly, on for 0.5 miles. Drive on left with postbox. Take central gravel drive.

rooms	2: 1 double, 1 single, sharing bath (let only to same party).
room price	£50. Singles £30.
meals	Dinner £20. B.Y.O.
closed	Christmas & Easter.
directions	From Boship r'bout on A22, A267. 1st right to Horsebridge & immed. left to Hellingly. House next to church, in Mill Lane.

	Sarah Burgoyne
	Old Whyly,
	East Hoathly, Sussex BN8 6EL
tel	01825 840216
fax	01825 840738
web	www.oldwhyly.co.uk

	Alison & Willie Boone
	Globe Place,
	Hellingly, Sussex BN27 4EY
tel	01323 844276
fax	01323 844276
e-mail	aliboone@btopenworld.com

SUSSEX

Stacks of woody character, with exposed beams and a woodburning stove in an inglenook in the sitting/dining room. Charming views through the lead-latticed windows in the cosy bedrooms and, from the garden room, you can see "the spot where Harold camped before he got it in the eye in 1066". Breakfast and dinner are taken at separate tables and, afterwards, you can walk through the Collins' 40 acres and see the 500 broadleafed trees they've planted. Chickens and geese and 1,000 acres of woodland add to the rural bliss — and Paul and Pauline are such nice people. A super place.

rooms	3 doubles, all with bath.
room price	From £54. Singles from £33.
meals	Supper around £10.
closed	January.
directions	From Battle on A271, 1st right to Heathfield. After 0.75 miles, right into drive.

Paul & Pauline Collins
Fox Hole Farm,
Kane Hythe Road, Battle,
Sussex TN33 9QU
tel   01424 772053
fax   01424 772053

map: 6 entry: 479

SUSSEX

You may be on a dairy farm in deepest Sussex but it's not Cold Comfort! The pretty Edwardian farmhouse is refreshingly light and comfortable, its owners enlightened and good company. The guest wing's big sitting room has a happy mix of family pieces, a cupboard of cards and games, an open fire and lovely views to lake and woods. French windows open onto a terrace with lavender, roses and herbs — bliss for fine-weather breakfasts; bedrooms are country-style and serene. Battle is just a 20-minute walk on the 1066 footpath; return to one of Penny's delicious, Mediterranean-style dinners.

rooms	2: 1 twin/double with private shower; 1 double, sharing shower (let only to same party).
room price	£40–£60. Singles £25–£40.
meals	Dinner £18.
closed	Christmas & New Year.
directions	A271 from Battle, left onto B2204 for 1 mile. Left after nursery; 0.5 miles down farm track, left at sign.

Penny & John Rodgers
Farthings Farm,
Catsfield, Battle, Sussex TN33 9BA
tel   01424 773107
e-mail   penny.rodgers@btopenworld.com
web   www.farthingsfarm.co.uk

map: 6 entry: 480

SUSSEX

The gorgeous house has been many things – wool store, school and former home of poet Conrad Aiken; hard to believe the deep red dining room, full of busts and paintings, was an old Baptist chapel. Jenny is engagingly easy-going and has created a lovely atmosphere. Rooms are traditionally furnished, with rich drapes, antique four-posters... there's a large attic room with beams, a book-lined honesty bar, a mind-your-head stairway, a small library to keep away the rainy day blues. A smart retreat among Rye's cobbled streets where there's so much to see and do.

rooms	12: 9 doubles, all with bath/shower; 1 single, sharing bath; 2 honeymoon suites with bath.
room price	£35-£112.
meals	Breakfast 8-9.30am; Sunday 8.30-10am. Many local restaurants.
closed	Rarely.
directions	From London, into centre of Rye on A268, left off High St onto West St, then 1st right into Mermaid Street. House on left. Private car park, £3 a day for guests.

Jenny Hadfield
Jeake's House,
Mermaid Street, Rye,
Sussex TN31 7ET
tel   01797 222828
fax   01797 222623
e-mail   jeakeshouse@btinternet.com
web   www.jeakeshouse.com

map: 6 entry: 481

SUSSEX

House and owner have a vibrancy that is unique. Sara has created a special atmosphere in her truly welcoming, rule-free townhouse in lovely history-laden Rye. You'll be enchanted by original art, fine antiques and attention to detail, but masses of books and many personal touches herald the fact that this is a real home. Super, luxurious bedrooms have views of either a quiet cobbled street or the large, quiet garden, complete with a Smuggler's Watchtower. There is a bookroom for rainy days and a sitting room with open fire, too. Breakfasts are generous and organic/free-range.

rooms	2: 1 four-poster with shower; 1 four-poster with bath & shower.
room price	£70-£90. Singles £45-£65.
meals	Breakfast 8-9.30am. Dinner available nearby.
closed	Rarely.
directions	In Rye, follow signs to town centre & enter Old Town through Landgate Arch into High St. West St 3rd on left. House halfway up on left.

Sara Brinkhurst
Little Orchard House,
West Street, Rye, Sussex TN31 7ES
tel   01797 223831
fax   01797 223831
web   www.littleorchardhouse.com

map: 6 entry: 482

All doors lead to the garden, it seems. Wisteria and roses scent the air and you can play croquet amid the beauty; the guest sitting room and the dining room have patios, too. You'll feel nurtured in this large, late-Victorian country house: Norma fills the bedrooms with flowers, the bathrooms with soaps and shampoos, and is happy to make restaurant bookings for you. The pretty twin has matching chintz-skirted dressing-table and curtains, the king-size double comes with dressing-gown and slippers. Fine views to Ashdown Forest, too. *Children over 8 welcome.*

Both Graham and Jennifer have travelled extensively in the Army with The King's Own Scottish Borderers; there is a regimental 'museum' in the downstairs cloakroom. They are kind and dedicated hosts happy to help you plan your day or book a table at the village pub for you. Visitors from 59 nations have enjoyed the comforts of this unspoilt, wisteria-clad 1930s bastion of old-Englishness. The garden is beautiful; the fruit and veg plot big enough to feed an army. Log fires in winter. *Children over 10 welcome.*

rooms	3: 1 double with bath/shower; 1 twin with shower; 1 double with basin, & private bath/shower.
room price	From £50. Singles from £30.
meals	Pubs/restaurants within walking distance.
closed	Occasionally.
directions	A26 from Tunbridge Wells for Uckfield. At Crowborough Cross, take Beacon Rd. 4th right into Warren Rd. Bottom of hill to Rannoch Rd. Right. House on left after 200 yds.

rooms	3: 1 double, 1 twin, both with private bath; second twin available.
room price	From £65. Singles from £43.
meals	Pub in village.
closed	Rarely.
directions	From M25, A22 to Maresfield. At mini-r'bout in centre of village, under stone arch opp. church & pub, & over 5 speed bumps. House 1st on left.

Norma Backhouse
Hope Court,
Rannoch Road, Crowborough,
Sussex TN6 1RA
tel   01892 654017

Graham & Jennifer Allt
South Paddock,
Maresfield Park, Nr Uckfield,
Sussex TN22 2HA
tel   01825 762335

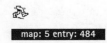

SUSSEX

Just one ground-floor guest room and a huge deal of homely comfort. You are at the opposite end of the house from the owners, so you feel private; your bathroom is a couple of steps from the bedroom door. The softly-lit room has a pine dressing table, rattan chairs, matching curtains and duvet covers, fresh flowers and lovely views of the three-acre garden. The Sussex Archeological Society says the house has Elizabethan origins and some of the smaller, mullioned windows bear this out. Ancient timbers and polished floors in the snug dining room and Jeannie and Nick are charming and easy to talk to.

rooms	1 double with private bath.
room price	£55. Singles £35.
meals	Pubs 2.5 miles.
closed	Rarely.
directions	From Haywards Heath, B2028 to Lindfield. House on left, 1.5 miles after passing church at north end of Lindfield.

Jeannie & Nick Leadsom
Little Lywood,
Ardingly Road, Ardingly, Lindfield,
Sussex RH16 2QX

tel	01444 892571
e-mail	nick@littlelywood.freeserve.co.uk

SUSSEX

Copyhold hides, snugly, behind a 1,000-year-old box hedge, its land delineated by an ancient field boundary. First a farm, then an ale house, the 16th-century building seems small from the outside, but opens into a quirky interior with many exposed timbers. Frances did the renovation herself and landscaped the gardens; nightingales and owls fill the woodland. The guests' dining room and inglenook sitting room are oak-beamed, uncluttered and cheerful; bedrooms are also beamed, with views over meadow and woodland. Your lively, independent-minded hostess will happily find time to chat by the fire.

rooms	3: 1 double, 1 twin, both with shower; 1 single with bath.
room price	From £60. Singles from £40.
meals	Breakfast 8-9am. Pubs/restaurants 2-3 miles.
closed	Rarely.
directions	From Gatwick, M23 south & follow signs to Cuckfield. There, right at 1st mini-roundabout, left at second, right at 3rd. Left at T-junc. Lane 1st on right, after entrance to Borde Hill Gardens.

Frances Druce
Copyhold Hollow,
Copyhold Lane, Borde Hill,
Haywards Heath, Sussex RH16 1XU

tel	01444 413265
e-mail	10@copyholdhollow.freeserve.co.uk
web	www.copyholdhollow.freeserve.co.uk

Beautiful within, solidly handsome without. A flagstoned hallway and an old rocking horse, ticking clocks and the smell of beeswax polish. Jane has a real flair for interior decoration and, thanks to subtle colours, oak beams and beautiful old furniture, has achieved a seductive combination of comfort and style. She and Richard are friendly, easy hosts; she was a ballet dancer, he has green fingers and runs his own fruit farm near by. (The freshly-picked produce appears in pretty bowls on the breakfast table.) Look out across the attractive garden to glorious views of neighbouring farmland.

An 1856 Victorian farmhouse with log fires, old pine and wonderful views to folklore-rich Meon Hill. Stories of witchcraft and other spookery abound. The bedrooms are romantic: a pine box bed and a medieval frieze of flying angels (pure fairy tale), four-posters, antique quilts. Delicious breakfast menus change daily, making imaginative use of home-grown fruits from the orchard. A great start for a day's walking on the Heart of England Way, or a ride on one of the many cycle tracks. Bikes are available and there's a disused railway line which takes you straight into Stratford.

rooms	2: 1 twin/double with bath/shower; 1 twin/double with shower.
room price	£75. Singles £47.50.
meals	Dinner £22.50.
closed	Rarely.
directions	A46 from Evesham or Stratford; exit for Salford Priors. On entering village, right opp. church, for Dunnington. House on right, approx. 1 mile on, after 2nd sign on right for Dunnington.

rooms	3: 2 four-posters, both with shower; 1 twin/family with private bath.
room price	From £65.
meals	Pub 0.5 miles.
closed	Rarely.
directions	From Stratford, A3400 south, then B4632 (for Broadway & Mickleton) for 6 miles. Left for Upper Quinton. 400 yds on left.

Jane Gibson & Richard Beach
Salford Farm House,
Salford Priors, Nr Evesham,
Warwickshire WR11 8XN

tel	01386 870000
fax	01386 870300
e-mail	salfordfarmhouse@aol.com
web	www.salfordfarmhouse.co.uk

Mrs Gail Lyon
Winton House,
The Green, Upper Quinton,
Stratford-upon-Avon,
Warwickshire CV37 8SX

tel	01789 720500
e-mail	gail@wintonhouse.com
web	www.wintonhouse.com

WARWICKSHIRE

Left column

Admire the Wyandotte bantams strutting across the lawns – they are prize-winners; Liz also keeps quails and you can buy their eggs to take home. The garden is pretty with mellow stone, clipped hedges, broad paths and billowing plants. Inside: flagstones, beams, deep fireplaces and mullioned windows. The sitting room has old books and polished furniture; bedrooms are peaceful – two have lovely views. One ground-floor bedroom is ideal for wheelchair users and overlooks the garden. Home-made marmalade for breakfast and home-grown food for supper. *Self-catering available. See back of book.*

rooms	4: 3 twins/doubles, all with bath & shower; 1 single with shower.
room price	From £65. Single from £35.
meals	Breakfast until 9.30am. Supper, 2 courses, £15.50. B.Y.O. Very good pub 1 mile.
closed	Rarely.
directions	From Stratford-upon-Avon, A3400 for Oxford. After 5 miles, right by church in Newbold-on-Stour & follow signs to Blackwell. Fork right on entering Blackwell. Entrance beyond thatched barn.

Liz Vernon Miller
Blackwell Grange,
Blackwell, Shipston-on-Stour,
Warwickshire CV36 4PF

tel	01608 682357
fax	01608 682856
e-mail	sawdays@blackwellgrange.co.uk
web	www.blackwellgrange.co.uk

map: 9 entry: 489

Right column

WARWICKSHIRE

From the upper bedrooms you look onto never-ending green – oaks, fields and meadows… you could almost imagine a Jane Austen heroine riding out for dinner and romance. Here are vast terraces, ancient trees, a formal garden, an 800-acre farm and the only noise that of passing pheasants. Bedrooms and bathrooms are stately, walls are panelled and floors are stripped and shiny, embellished with Turkish rugs. You have a formal dining room and a library littered with armchairs and sofas. Dream of port and cigars – on a pea-green carpet. Kari runs it all without fuss. Unselfconscious and magnificent.

rooms	3: 1 double, 1 single sharing bath (only let to same party); 1 twin with private bath.
room price	£90. Singles by arrangement.
meals	Plenty of pubs & restaurants within 5 miles.
closed	Christmas & New Year.
directions	From Shipston-on-Stour, turn off B3400 north to Honington. In Idlicote, left at pond & through stone gateposts. House on left, after church.

Kari Dill
Idlicote House,
Idlicote, Shipston-on-Stour,
Warwickshire CV36 5DT

tel	01608 661473
fax	01608 661381
e-mail	dill@idlicote.freeserve.co.uk

map: 9 entry: 490

WARWICKSHIRE

WARWICKSHIRE

You'll be in your element if you fish or play tennis. You can do both from these beautiful, landscaped, rose-strewn gardens that slope gently down to the River Stour. Jane, a Cordon Bleu cook, runs her 16th- and 17th-century house with huge energy and friendliness. The A-shaped double in the main part of the house has ancient beams, oak furniture and a lovely bathroom, while a pretty blue twin and a single are in the other wing: private and self-contained, with a large and elegant drawing and dining room for all guests to share. It's seductively easy to relax here; breakfast alone is worth the stay.

Hard to believe the house is so new: with its open-beam ceilings and antiques it has a timeless feel. Posy and Graeme, kind, fun and well-travelled, create a mood of warmth and welcome. Pale-walled bedrooms are cheery and fresh with soft lighting, excellent beds, top-of-the-range bathroom fittings and lovely long views. Find time to ride locally or play tennis – the court is new – or explore the Cotswolds and Shakespeare country... Posy will help you unlock the region's secrets. On summer nights you can watch the setting sun from the patio.

rooms	3: 1 twin with bath; 1 double with private bath. 1 single available.
room price	From £70. Singles from £35.
meals	Dinner from £20. Excellent local restaurants.
closed	Rarely.
directions	From Stratford, A422 for 4 miles for Banbury. After 4 miles, right at r'bout onto A429 for Halford. There, 1st right. House with black & white timbers straight ahead.

rooms	3: 1 double with shower; 1 twin & 1 triple, both with bath.
room price	From £58. Singles from £34.
meals	Dinner from £15. Good local pubs.
closed	Rarely.
directions	A422 from Stratford-on-Avon for Banbury. After 8 miles, right to Oxhill. Last house on right on Whatcote Road.

Jane Pusey
The Old Manor House,
Halford, Shipston-on-Stour,
Warwickshire CV36 5BT
tel   01789 740264
fax   01789 740609
e-mail   wpusey@st-philips.co.uk
web   www.oldmanor-halford.co.uk

Graeme & Posy McDonald
Oxbourne House,
Oxhill, Warwick,
Warwickshire CV35 0RA
tel   01295 688202
e-mail   graememcdonald@msn.com
web   www.oxbournehouse.co.uk

Wonderful to leave the busy world behind and head down the track that leads – eventually – to the barn. Bedrooms have been carefully decorated with seashell stencils, star-painted ceilings and colour-washed walls; wooden-latched doors open to sunny, sky-lit bathrooms. The annexe room has its own entrance and a wrought-iron four-poster. Carolyn and John could not be nicer, and keep horses and poultry – you won't be short of fresh eggs for breakfast. They've set aside 10 acres for nature conservation and will tell you about their nesting barn owls. A secluded retreat. *Children over eight welcome.*

Here's a big house in the country, minus the expected creaks and draughts and plus every comfort and mod con. It almost feels like a small hotel (there's even a helipad). The carpets are opulent and the beds four-poster; there's also a striking 'Oriental' suite. Relax in a leather armchair with a pre-dinner drink in the small, rather nautical sitting room. This is a fully organic, Soil Association registered farm; dinner is organic and the dining table is superb, carved from a single piece of fallen cedar tree. The garden is lush and landscaped, with fields all around – look out for the fat Hebridean sheep.

rooms	3: 1 four-poster with extra single with bath/shower; 1 double with shower; 1 double with bath/shower.
room price	£46–£52. Singles from £30.
meals	Breakfast 7.30–9am. Pubs/restaurants 3 miles.
closed	Christmas.
directions	From Stratford, A422 to Pillerton Priors, then sign to Pillerton Hersey. There, down Oxhill Bridle Rd, opp. phone box. House at very end (1 mile). Or M40 junction 12, 6 miles on B4451.

rooms	4: 3 four-posters, all with bath, 1 with dressing room; 1 double with bath.
room price	£110–£140. Singles from £70.
meals	Dinner, 3 courses, £25.
closed	Rarely.
directions	From Stratford, over Clopton bridge & immed. left onto Tiddington Rd. 1st right onto Loxley Rd. Last on left with white gates.

Carolyn & John Howard
Dockers Barn Farm,
Oxhill Bridle Road, Pillerton Hersey,
Warwick, Warwickshire CV35 0QB
tel 01926 640475
fax 01926 641747

Ms Kate McGovern
Glebe Farm House,
Loxley, Stratford-upon-Avon,
Warwickshire CV35 9JW
tel 01789 842501
fax 01789 841194
e-mail scorpiolimited@msn.com
web www.glebefarmhouse.com

Y ou can get from your bath to your seat in the Stratford theatre in 10 minutes, if you hurry. This is a Grade II-listed thatched house, dated 1501 and set in an extremely pretty garden. Even the barn where you sleep – also thatched, beamed and listed – is 17th century. The Garden Suite has its own gorgeous conservatory – great for watching the wildlife – and the Hayloft has a little sitting room and kitchenette. Both have splendid corner baths. The rooms don't get a great deal of natural light but are comfortably equipped. Breakfast is in the main house and is the time to be sociable with the delightful Anne.

The peace, the views and the greenness will revive flagging spirits and soothe the frazzled; one guest said she'd had "the quietest sleep in years." David and Julia are charming and good-humoured and devoted to their ancient house and garden. Mallards glide over the pond, ducklings visit for breakfast, a stream runs by the 400-year-old yew and there's a pergola and patio in the garden. Inside all is smart and traditional: inglenooks, comfortable sofas and a beamed dining room with chairs embroidered by Julia. Bedrooms are a good size; one has an oak-panelled wall and wonderful views.

rooms	2 doubles, both with bath/shower.
room price	£65–£70. Singles £45.
meals	Pub 3 minute walk.
closed	1 December–7 January.
directions	From Stratford, A422 Banbury road for 4 miles & turn off for Loxley. Through village & left at bottom of hill. 3rd house on right.

rooms	2: 1 double, 1 twin, sharing bath/shower room.
room price	£54. Singles £27.
meals	Restaurant 5-minute walk; 3 pubs 1.5 miles.
closed	Christmas & New Year.
directions	From A423 to Priors Hardwick. 1.8 miles on, left for P. Hardwick. 1st hard left on S-bend ('No Through Rd' sign). Down lane & right onto concrete road. House on right.

Mrs Anne Horton
Loxley Farm,
Loxley, Warwick,
Warwickshire CV35 9JN
tel   01789 840265
fax   01789 840645
e-mail   loxleyfarm@hotmail.com

Julia & David Gaunt
Hollow Meadow House,
Priors Hardwick, Southam,
Warwickshire CV47 7SP
tel   01327 261540
fax   01327 261540

map: 9 entry: 495

map: 9 entry: 496

Kim has the sort of kitchen that city dwellers dream of: big and welcoming and it really is the hub of the house. She and John fizz with good humour and energy and take pride in those times when family and guests feel easy together. You will be offered tea on arrival, home-made jams for breakfast and perhaps even a guided walk round the fascinating, historic village. The house is large with a wonderful garden, tennis court, terrace and croquet lawn. The rooms are big, soft and supremely comfortable with lovely pieces of furniture. A special place and absolutely genuine people.

Hot bedroom colours make a change from the usual creams and chintzes – one is vibrant blue with a red ceiling, another crimson with purple, another burnt orange. The art is contemporary and it's bold and vibrant and fun, just like Prue. She's passionate about good food, too – organic and mostly vegetarian. Expect home-made bread, velvety egg puddings, succulent stuffed mushrooms and a fresh fruit platter drizzled with lime and honey dressing. This substantial blue stone 1850s townhouse is right opposite Warwick's park and less than a mile's riverside walk to the castle.

rooms	2: 1 double, 1 twin/double, both with private bath.
room price	From £54. Singles from £35.
meals	Breakfast from 6.45am. Dinner, for 4 only, £25. Good pub 5-minute walk.
closed	Rarely.
directions	From Banbury, A361 north. At Byfield village sign, left into Twistle Lane, straight on to Priors Marston. 5th on left with cattle grid, after S-bend.

rooms	3: 1 twin with bath/shower; 1 double with shower; 1 double with bath & shower.
room price	£70. Singles £45.
meals	Breakfast 6am-12 noon. Dinner by arrangement. Restaurants/pubs 0.5 miles.
closed	Rarely.
directions	On A445, 500 yds past St John's Museum towards Leamington, directly opp. entrance to St Nicholas' Park.

Kim & John Mahon
Marston House,
Priors Marston, Southam,
Warwickshire CV47 7RP

tel	01327 260297
fax	01327 262846
e-mail	kim@mahonand.co.uk
web	www.ivabestbandb.co.uk

Prue Hardwick
The Hare on the Park,
3 Emscote Road, Warwick,
Warwickshire CV34 4PH

tel	01926 491366
e-mail	prue@thehareonthepark.co.uk
web	www.thehareonthepark.co.uk

map: 9 entry: 497

map: 9 entry: 498

Cathy's sense of humour carries her through each gloriously eventful day. This is fabulous for families, with so much room to play and so much to see: sheep, turkeys, geese, Saddleback pigs. It's a fascinating house, too. Dated 1640, it has low ceilings and steep stairs. Timbered passages lead to large, sunny bedrooms with leaded windows and polished wooden floors. (The family room has everything needed for a baby.) There's a proper farmhouse dining room, where Cathy serves sausages, bacon, pork, game and lamb from the farm. Next door is Big Pool where you may fish with a day ticket.

A theatrical home: dark wood, reds and pinks dominate and, in one bedroom – more theatre – plush velvet curtains open to the bathroom. The conversion of the 1737 barn is immaculate: the kitchen, with Aga and stone floors, gives onto a stunning patio, conservatory and drawing room, and bedrooms and bathrooms are big and plush. Everything is on a grand scale. Denise, cheerful and kind, runs her B&B with careful attention to detail and realises how much guests appreciate comfort. Much rural charm, a large garden, excellent value and close to Birmingham and the NEC. *Advance booking essential.*

rooms	2: 1 double with single & cot, 1 twin, both with bath.
room price	From £50. Singles from £32.50.
meals	Breakfast 7-9am. Packed lunch £3. Children's high tea £3. Dinner from £15.
closed	Christmas & New Year.
directions	From M40, junc. 15, A46 for Coventry. Left onto A4177. 4.5 miles to Five Ways r'bout. 1st left, follow for 0.75 miles; signed opp. Farm Gate Poultry down track on left.

rooms	3: 1 double, 2 twins, all with bath.
room price	£70. Singles £45.
meals	Breakfast until 8.30am. Pub 1 mile.
closed	Rarely.
directions	At M6 junc. 4, A446 for Lichfield. At sign to Coleshill South, get in right lane & turn off. From High St, turn into Maxstoke Lane. After 4 miles, 4th right. 1st drive on left.

Cathy Dodd
Shrewley Pools Farm,
Haseley, Warwick,
Warwickshire CV35 7HB
tel   01926 484315
e-mail cathydodd@hotmail.com

Mrs Denise Owen
Hardingwood House,
Hardingwood Lane, Fillongley,
Nr Coventry, Warwickshire CV7 8EL
tel   01676 542579
fax   01676 541336
e-mail denise@hardingwoodhouse.fsnet.co.uk

Valerie was a student of fashion history and dotted around the Threlfalls' half of the 16th-century manor house are fashion prints, photographs, hatboxes, dressmakers' dummies. There are William Morris fabrics and paper in the dining room, a cosy sitting room for you in the gabled attic and a grand piano in the ballroom, where concerts are held. The good-sized Chinese bedroom has curios brought back from travels; the twin room is smaller. A conservatory looks onto a huge lawn – do seek out the small Victorian vegetable garden with gravel walkways and the thatched Wendy house beneath giant yew trees.

Lots of thoughtful touches – books in the bedroom and roses from the garden, newspapers at breakfast, cosy chairs in the guest sitting room, a winter fire. Helen makes her own bread and jams and serves breakfast in the dining room with views to the garden of sweeping lawns, magnolias, chestnut trees and the lovely high stone walls that abut All Saints Church. There's a tennis court out there, too. Fine flagstoned floors, little window seats and a carved lintel that dates the house as 1703… it is delightful and deeply comfortable.

rooms	2: 1 double with bath; 1 twin with private shower.
room price	£56-£60. Singles £35-£42.
meals	Breakfast until 9.50am. Good pubs in village; excellent restaurants a short drive away.
closed	Christmas & New Year.
directions	From Cirencester, A419 south for 4 miles, leaving dual carriageway on left, for Ashton Keynes. Left immed. after White Hart, 100 yds on, through stone pillars, house on right.

rooms	2: 1 double with bath; 1 double with private bath.
room price	£60. Singles £35.
meals	Dinner £18.50.
closed	Christmas & New Year.
directions	A429 Malmesbury to Cirencester. In Crudwell, at Plough, right for Minety & Oaksey. Straight on, then left between church & tithe barn pillars.

Valerie & Roger Threlfall
1 Cove House,
Ashton Keynes, Wiltshire SN6 6NS
tel   01285 861226
fax   01285 861226
e-mail roger@covehouse.co.uk

Helen & Philip Carter
Manor Farmhouse,
Crudwell, Malmesbury,
Wiltshire SN16 9ER
tel   01666 577375
fax   01666 823523
e-mail user785566@aol.com

Delightful quiet seclusion whatever the season. On colder days, large comfy sofas envelop you and fires warm you; in summer, you eat in the cool shade of the arbour, draped in wisteria and climbing roses. The garden is exceptional, and the bright conservatory with its huge oak table is filled with a profusion of flowers and colour. Garden vegetables and herbs (mostly organic) are used at dinner to magnificent effect. Bedrooms are quiet with lovely country views and Liz and Colin are so easy and flexible that you feel like a visiting friend.

The vine-hung, thyme-carpeted arbour and gazebo are magical in summer and there is much in the deliciously walled garden to hold your attention. Doi is relaxed and friendly and does B&B because she loves it. Breakfast is cooked as you want it, when you want it. Gently-decorated bedrooms have space, views, flowers and old photographs; one has a half-tester bed, all are hugely comfortable. The dark blue dining room has wooden floors and a solid oak table with tapestry chairs while the drawing room has French windows overlooking the garden and an open fire. A lovely place.

rooms	2: 1 twin with bath; 1 twin with private bath.
room price	£65–£70. Singles £37.50–£40.
meals	Breakfast until 9.30am. Dinner, 2-3 courses, £14–£18.
closed	Christmas & Easter.
directions	From A429, B4040 through Charlton, past Horse & Groom pub. 0.5 miles on, left signed 'Bullocks Horn No Through Road'. On to end of lane. Right. 1st on left.

rooms	3: 1 triple with private bath; 1 double with bath; 1 double with private bath & shower.
room price	£50. Singles £30.
meals	Good pubs 1-5 miles.
closed	Christmas.
directions	From Malmesbury B4042 for Wootton Bassett. Left to Lea & Charlton. In Lea, right opp. school. House along drive through fields, 1 mile from road.

Colin & Liz Legge
Bullocks Horn Cottage,
Charlton, Malmesbury,
Wiltshire SN16 9DZ
tel   01666 577600
fax   01666 577905
e-mail   legge@bullockshorn.clara.co.uk

Tony & Doi Newman
Winkworth Farm,
Lea, Nr Malmesbury,
Wiltshire SN16 9NH
tel   01666 823267
e-mail   doinewman@winkworth89.freeserve.co.uk

map: 9 entry: 503

map: 9 entry: 504

Farmyard heaven in the Cotswolds. A 17th-century manor farmhouse in 550 arable acres, with horses in the paddock, dozing dogs in the yard, tumbling blooms outside the door, and a perfectly tended village, with duck pond, a walk away. Here are country antiques and beautiful bedrooms softly lit: colours are muted, linen fine, pillows fat, bathrooms big. At breakfast Victoria treats you to traditional farmhouse fare, or smoked salmon and scrambled eggs, or fresh fruits and home-made breads. A perfect setting, with Castle Combe and Lacock close by, and a tot of whisky before bed. *Children over 12 welcome.*

In an ancient hamlet a few miles north of Bath, an impeccable conversion of an early 19th-century barn. Bedrooms are fresh and cosy with sloping ceilings and the drawing room is elegant with porcelain and chintz, its pale walls the perfect background for striking displays of fresh flowers. Sliding glass doors lead to a south-facing patio... then to a well-groomed croquet lawn bordered by flowers, with vegetable garden, tennis court, woodland and paddock beyond. Helga and David, generous and kind, tell you all you need to know about the region, from the splendours of Bath just below to the golf courses so nearby.

rooms	3: 2 doubles, both with bath; 1 twin with private bath.
room price	£60. Singles £35.
meals	Excellent pubs within walking distance.
closed	Christmas.
directions	From M4 A429 to Cirencester (junc.17). After 200 yds 1st left for Grittleton; there, follow signs to Alderton. Farmhouse near church.

rooms	2: 1 double, 1 twin/double, both with private bath.
room price	£60. Singles £35.
meals	Dinner £15. Also excellent local pubs.
closed	Rarely.
directions	From M4 junc. 17, A429 for Chippenham. A420 to Bristol (East) & Castle Combe. After 6.3 miles, right into Upper Wraxall. Sharp left opposite village green; house at end of drive.

Victoria Lippiatt
Manor Farm,
Alderton, Malmesbury,
Wiltshire SN14 6NL

tel	01666 840271
fax	01666 840271
e-mail	j.lippiatt@farmline.com
web	www.themanorfarm.co.uk

Helga & David Venables
The Coach House,
Upper Wraxall, Nr Bath,
Wiltshire SN14 7AG

tel	01225 891026
fax	01225 892355
e-mail	venables@compuserve.com
web	www.upperwraxallcoachhouse.co.uk

WILTSHIRE

A generous and attractive restoration of a 19th-century cottage, with landscaped garden and views to Spye Park. You are in a peaceful little hamlet yet near Lacock and other national treasures. Ginny radiates charm and spoils you with thoughtful touches: home-made biscuits by the bed, home-made soaps by the bath. The drawing room is vastly comfortable – log fires, coral sofas, choice pieces. Bedrooms are elegant affairs... up past the family portraits to soft eiderdowns and *toile de Jouy*. Birds trill in the garden, the parrot chats by the Aga and there are three guest-loving dogs. *Children over six welcome.*

rooms	3: 1 double, 2 twins, all with private bath.
room price	£50. Singles £30.
meals	Packed lunch £8. Lunch £10. Dinner, 3 courses, £18.
closed	Christmas & New Year.
directions	From Devizes/Chippenham A342. Follow Chittoe & Spye Park. On over cross roads onto narrow lane. House second on left.

Mrs G Scrope
Glebe House,
Chittoe, Chippenham,
Wiltshire SN15 2EL
tel 01380 850864
fax 01380 850189
e-mail gscrope@aol.com
web www.glebehouse-chittoe.co.uk

map: 3 entry: 507

WILTSHIRE

A ccording to our inspector, "splendid, sunny and sumptuous" sums up this house. Richard, a wine enthusiast and Pippa, a skilled cook, cosset you in huge style. The whole early Georgian house is elegantly furnished and decorated, bedrooms are large and luxurious, and from the triple-aspect drawing room you look out through French windows onto perfect lawns bordered by mature trees. There's a superb grass tennis court, magnificent walking and two first-class riding stables nearby. In 1643 the Battle of Roundway was fought on the Downs behind the house. *Children over 12 welcome.*

rooms	3: 1 double with private bath; 2 twins/doubles, both with bath.
room price	£76-£90. Singles £50-£60.
meals	Dinner, for 4 or more, £23.50. Pub/restaurant 300 yds.
closed	Christmas & Easter.
directions	West along A4. Left just before Calne for Heddington; 2 miles to Ivy Inn & left at T-junction. House on left opposite church; white gate & cattle grid.

Richard & Pippa Novis
Heddington Manor,
Heddington, Nr Calne,
Wiltshire SN11 0PN
tel 01380 850240
fax 01380 859176
e-mail richardnovis@compuserve.com

map: 3 entry: 508

A big old farmhouse bang in the middle of crop circle country, close to the bustling market town of Devizes; Janey and Nick, intelligent and fun, help you discover the region. Theirs is a generous and attractive home where parquet and Indian rugs, antiques and chintz create a special feel. Two rooms in the converted red-brick barn welcome you with beams and beautiful views; a cosy sitting room is downstairs. Play tennis, take a sauna, and do eat in – meals are a feast of home-grown produce. A gorgeous place, with only the hum of the grain dryer at harvest to break the peace. *Pets by arrangement.*

Janet – robust and hardworking – is dedicated to hunting and dressage and runs a thriving livery in the grounds. The presence of the horses and the dogs gives a farming feel and you come not to be feted but to join in with it all. The house's origins lie way back in 1189, bits were added in the 16th century and meals are taken around a monastery refectory table that's as old as the house. Downstairs has a homely, natural feel while the bedrooms, perhaps with patterned carpet or kidney-shaped dressing table, are comfortable; the double is the prettier, the twin more traditional and formal.

rooms	3: 1 twin with bath/shower; 1 twin with bath; 1 double with shower.
room price	£60. Singles £35.
meals	Dinner, 2 courses, £12.50, 3 courses, £18. Packed lunch £10.
closed	Christmas.
directions	A361 from Devizes; after police HQ, 2nd left; 1 mile into village. Road bends left at post/phone box, then right bend; house on next right at sharp left bend.

rooms	4: 1 double, 1 twin, both with shower; 2 singles with private bath or shower.
room price	£48–£56.
meals	Breakfast 7.30–9am. Dinner, 4 courses with wine, £20; reduction for 2 courses.
closed	Christmas & New Year.
directions	From Devizes, A360 to Salisbury or A342 to Andover. After 4 miles right on B3098. House 1 mile west of Urchfont.

	Janey Hillier
	Roundway Farmhouse,
	Devizes, Wiltshire SN10 2HZ
tel	01380 723113
fax	01380 723113
e-mail	hillier@roundwayfarm.com
web	mysite.freeserve.com/roundwayfarm_devizes

	Mrs Janet Firth
	Eastcott Manor,
	Easterton, Devizes,
	Wiltshire SN10 4PL
tel	01380 813313
e-mail	janetlnfirth@aol.com

WILTSHIRE

A listed Georgian thatched farmhouse and a stylish B&B – Val and David moved out of London in search of peace and found it in the heart of crop circle and Stonehenge country. Val is a talented interior decorator who specialises in paint finishes and has stamped her elegant mark on every room: a gentle terracotta linen-effect in the guest sitting room; big yellow checks in the bathroom. A tranquil atmosphere pervades this home with its old rugs on wooden floors, log fires, crisp white bed linen and plump pillows. The garden is charming too and contains a 16th-century drover's rest – possibly the grandest-ever garden shed!

rooms	3: 1 double with bath; 1 twin, 1 single, both with private bathrooms.
room price	From £60. Singles from £30.
meals	Dinner £25.
closed	Rarely.
directions	From Marlborough, A345 through Pewsey. 3 miles on, at Woodbridge Inn r'bout, right to Hilcott. House 2nd on left over cattle grid. From M3/A303, Hilcott 11 miles from Amesbury r'bout via Upavon & Woodbridge r'bout.

Val Maclay
Hilcott Farm House,
Hilcott, Marlborough,
Wiltshire SN9 6LE
tel   01672 851372
fax   01672 851192
e-mail beds@hilcott.com

map: 4 entry: 511

WILTSHIRE

An intriguing name, Puckshipton: it means Goblin's Barn. The house sits deep in the lush countryside of the Vale of Pewsey, reached by a long tree-lined drive. Guests stay in the Georgian end, with a private entrance that leads to a Regency-blue hall. Rooms are stylish and uncluttered, an attractive mix of the old and the new. One bedroom has a splendid four-poster, the other has oak beds made by James, who is both forester and fine-furniture-maker. He and Juliette are a friendly and charming young couple with three small children. A relaxed and lovely place to stay.

rooms	2: 1 twin/double with private bath/shower; 1 four-poster with bath & shower.
room price	£65-£75. Singles £40.
meals	Supper £10-£15.
closed	Christmas.
directions	Devizes A342 towards Rushall; left to Chirton, right to Marden & through village. On for 0.25 miles; right into private drive.

Juliette & James Noble
Puckshipton House,
Beechingstoke, Pewsey,
Wiltshire SN9 6HG
tel   01672 851336
e-mail jamesmcc.noble@virgin.net
web   www.puckshipton.co.uk

map: 4 entry: 512

A treat of a 17th-century brick-and-flint manor in a beguiling spot by the river Avon – bring your fishing gear. Isabel is a delight and a great cook (she used to run a chalet in the Swiss Alps), ready for a chat by the Aga as she chops and stirs. She has decorated her beautifully converted home in style: the guests' drawing room is elegantly English with a cosy fire and a touch of the Orient; bedrooms are prettily-papered in pale pink and blue. Mattresses are the best. Breakfast is served at a polished oak table, glazed doors are thrown open to the garden in summer.

You could be a hundred miles from Marlborough, not two. Here is a lovely Queen Anne farmhouse tucked under chalk hills in the middle of the biggest bluebell woods in the country. Elizabeth and Christopher, who have lived here for years, love sharing their home. Bedrooms are fresh, white and cosy, with painted pine furniture and modern patchwork quilts, and guests have their own sitting room. The sun-trap garden is full of roses and lavender and has views of the surrounding 25 rolling acres – this is marvellous walking country. Your horse is welcome, too.

rooms	2 twins/doubles both with bath/shower.
room price	£60. Singles from £35.
meals	Dinner, 3 courses, £20.
closed	Rarely.
directions	From Upavon towards Andover on A342. Manor third house on right & last before bridge.

rooms	3: 1 double with bath; 1 double with private bath; 1 twin for members of same party sharing bath.
room price	From £55. Singles from £35.
meals	Packed lunch £5. Good restaurants/pubs 2-3 miles.
closed	Christmas.
directions	From Marlborough, A4 west for 2 miles. 1st left after end of 40mph limit, for Clatford. Over crossroads, farm 1.5 miles on right through 5-bar gate.

Isabel Green
The Manor,
Upavon, Pewsey, Wiltshire SN9 6EB
tel   01980 635115
e-mail isabelbgreen@hotmail.com

Elizabeth & Christopher Morgan-Smith
Clatford Park Farm,
Marlborough, Wiltshire SN8 4DZ
tel   01672 861646
web   www.clatfordparkfarm.co.uk

In the valley of the Kennet River – which flows briskly past the foot of an immaculate lawn – is this exquisitely decorated home. It looks every inch a doll's house, but Jeremy and Heather, friendly and relaxed, add a deft human touch. The elegance of excellent breakfasts taken in the conservatory is balanced by the comforting hubbub emanating from the family kitchen. There's a sitting room for you with an open fire and, upstairs, the cleverly converted bedrooms are ingeniously clustered around the chimney breast. Time slips by effortlessly here; many people come to visit the crop circles.

A delightful place, with hosts to match: you'll feel wonderfully welcome. Bill – who sculpts and paints – has applied his considerable flair to the renovation and decoration of the 17th-century thatched cottage. The beamed sitting room is as comfy as can be, bedrooms are colourful and charming, there are antique rugs on walls and floors and art everywhere. The garden impresses with its sculpted hedges, clouds of lavender, carp-filled pond and roaming pig. Swim in the pool, shelter under the loggia, book an art class with Bill. The countryside is fabulous, too. *Children by arrangement.*

rooms	3: 1 double with bath; 1 twin, 1 single sharing bath.
room price	£70. Singles £35.
meals	Lunch/packed lunch from £3. Pub 500 yds.
closed	Christmas.
directions	From Hungerford, A4 for Marlborough. After 7 miles, right for Stitchcombe, down hill (bear left at barn) & left at T-junc. On entering village, house 2nd on left.

rooms	3: 1 double with bath; 1 double, 1 twin, sharing bath.
room price	£55-£60. Singles £30-£35.
meals	Dinner £23.
closed	Rarely.
directions	From Marlborough, A346 Salisbury Road south. At roundabout ending Burbage bypass, B3087 Pewsey Road. Right at x-roads 0.3 miles on. 1st house on right.

Jeremy & Heather Coulter
Fisherman's House,
Mildenhall, Nr Marlborough,
Wiltshire SN8 2LZ
tel   01672 515390
fax   01672 519009
e-mail   fishermans.house@virgin.net
web   www.business.virgin.net/neville.burrell/fiishermans.htm

Felicity & Bill Mather
Westcourt Bottom,
165 Westcourt, Burbage,
Wiltshire SN8 3BW
tel   01672 810924
fax   01672 810924
e-mail   westcourt.b-and-b@virgin.net
web   www.westcourtbottom.co.uk

Rozzie and Jonny escaped London to restore a medieval cruck truss hall house (beautifully) and create wildflower meadows, hedgerows and ponds. They are delightful people, new to B&B and eager to welcome guests to their home. Rooms are freshly decorated yet have a lovely old feel: the country furniture is charming, the crucks and trusses a carpenter's delight. Bedrooms have new beds and crisp linen, bathrooms are spot-on, and there's a lovely dining room. Encircled by footpaths and fields, Westcourt is the oldest house in a perfect village, two minutes from the pub.

An impressively handsome medieval manor house. Arched, mullioned windows, jutting gables, tall chimneys and a porticoed entrance raise expectations of an interior that are not disappointed. There's a vast Tudor fireplace (complete with Elizabethan graffiti), a whole gallery of ancestral oil paintings and fascinating historic furniture and artefacts. You dine in spring with the scent of wisteria and lilac wafting through the dining room windows. Bedrooms are plush with big beds, modern touches where they matter and views over the grounds. *Self-catering available. See back of book.*

rooms	2: 1 twin with private bath; 1 double with private shower.
room price	£70. Singles from £40.
meals	Excellent pub/restaurant nearby.
closed	Christmas & New Year.
directions	A338 Hungerford-Salisbury; after 4 miles signed Shalbourne; through village & fork left at pub; 150 yds, 2nd drive on right.

rooms	3: 2 doubles, 1 twin, all with bath/shower.
room price	£90-£100.
meals	Breakfast until 9.30am. Dinner for groups only.
closed	Christmas & New Year.
directions	From Bath A36 Warminster road for 5 miles, left onto B3108, under railway bridge & up hill. 1st right, turn off Winsley bypass into old village, then 1st left, into lane marked 'except for access'.

Jonny & Rozzie Buxton
Westcourt Farm,
Shalbourne, Marlborough,
Wiltshire SN8 3QE

tel	01672 871399
e-mail	info@westcourtfarm.com
web	www.westcourtfarm.com

John & Elizabeth Denning
Burghope Manor,
Winsley, Bradford-on-Avon,
Wiltshire BA15 2LA

tel	01225 723557
fax	01225 723113
e-mail	burghope.manor@virgin.net
web	www.burghope.co.uk

WILTSHIRE

A rare treat to have your milk fresh from the cow – the Helyers have a fine pedigree herd of Holstein Friesians. This rather grand Victorian-gothic farmhouse is on a tenanted arable and dairy farm. The bedrooms are large and pretty with period furniture and crisp linen; there are impressive countryside views, a baby grand and a billiard room. Everything is elegant but cosy at the same time, and the Helyers are immensely friendly. Terrace doors are thrown open for *al fresco* summer breakfasts. The estate is 1,400 acres and SSSI, treasured for its wild flowers and butterflies. *Children by arrangement.*

rooms	3: 1 twin/double & 1 double, both with shower; 1 twin with private shower.
room price	£54–£60. Singles £40–£48.
meals	Pub/restaurant 1.75 miles.
closed	Christmas & New Year.
directions	Exit A303 at junc. with A36 & follow signs for Salisbury. 2 miles on, right for The Langfords. In Steeple Langford, right for Hanging Langford. At T-junc. opposite village hall, left for Little Langford. House 0.25 miles on left.

Patricia Helyer
Little Langford Farmhouse,
Little Langford, Salisbury,
Wiltshire SP3 4NR
tel   01722 790205
fax   01722 790086
e-mail bandb@littlelangford.co.uk
web   www.littlelangford.co.uk

map: 4 entry: 519

WILTSHIRE

Folded into stunning countryside, this Grade II-listed, one-time butcher's shop has been in Darea's family for years. Stylishly cluttered, sparkingly clean, there are beautiful objects and lovely pieces at every turn. Darea's enthusiasm for life and books and travel is infectious: she can identify every rich and rare specimen in her garden, keeps detailed diaries and albums of her many travels and has thrown nothing away. Your chintzy bedrooms are seductively cosy. A fascinating corner of England – and Stonehenge, Longleat and Stourhead beckon.

rooms	2: 1 twin with bath; 1 twin/double with basin & private bath.
room price	£60–£65. Singles from £35.
meals	Breakfast until 9.30am. Excellent pub 50 yds.
closed	Rarely.
directions	Exit A303 at junc. with A36 for Wylye. In village, cross river & round sharp left-hand bend. House 25 yds on right.

Mrs Darea Browne
Perrior House,
Wylye, Warminster,
Wiltshire BA12 0QU
tel   01985 248228
e-mail dareabrowne@aol.com

map: 4 entry: 520

Y ou have your own entrance, parking area, terrace and sitting room, freshly decorated and well thought out. Everything is new and cosy and comfortable and just outside your windows is a cottage garden alive with colour. Your hosts are impressively organised – they run a catering business from home – and breakfasts will set you up for the day. The bathroom is duck-egg-blue, the bedroom ochre. If you long for your own space and the freedom to come and go as you please, you have it. The family has been here for three generations. *Children over 10 welcome.*

I nstantly impressive – the 15th-century honey stone that lights up in sunlight, the soft, particularly English shade of paintwork, the Jacobean 'extension', the wisteria, the solidity... The feel is engagingly chaotic and easy, just the way we like it. If you're travelling with family, or if you want to feel relaxingly away from everybody else, choose the roomy twin that connects with the dear little single; the twin/double, with lily-patterned green-and-white headboard and curtains, is of a good size, too. It's not 'le grand luxe' but there are a pool and a tennis court. A stimulating place.

rooms	1 twin with bath/shower.
room price	£60. Singles £40.
meals	Packed lunch £7. Dinner, 3 courses, £20.
closed	Christmas & New Year.
directions	A303 to Wylye, then for Dinton. After approx. 4 miles left at x-roads, for Wilton & Salisbury. On for 2 miles, down hill, round sharp bend, signed Sandhills Rd. 1st low red brick building on left.

rooms	3: 1 twin/double with private bath; 1 twin/double, 1 single sharing bath.
room price	£60. Singles £38–£40.
meals	Packed lunch £6. Excellent restaurant and good pubs nearby.
closed	December–January.
directions	From Salisbury, A36 to Wilton, then A30 (to Shaftesbury). After 3 miles, in Barford St Martin, right onto B3089; after 2 miles, right to Baverstock; after 0.75 miles stone gateway on right, on S-bend.

Harriet & Peter Combes
The Duck Yard,
Sandhills Road, Dinton, Salisbury,
Wiltshire SP3 5ER
tel   01722 716495
fax   01722 716163

Tim & Belinda Hextall
Baverstock Manor,
Dinton, Salisbury,
Wiltshire SP3 5EN
tel   01722 716206
fax   01722 716510
e-mail   hextallbavers@hotmail.com

map: 4 entry: 521

map: 4 entry: 522

Toast your toes on a warm stone floor in this quadrangle conversion – what were once Victorian agricultural outbuildings are now a harpsichord workshop and a B&B. The geothermal underfloor heating system is just one of the initiatives that has won the Smalleys an environmental award. Bedrooms, which feed off a long corridor, are functionally furnished with matching bedcovers and curtains, and perfectly lit. Walls are white or bare brick, ceilings high and beamy: all is simplicity and calm. You'll want for nothing with Gail in charge (her blueberry pancakes are wonderful) and Peter is charming.

Such attention to detail – you will feel immensely spoiled. Each bedroom is large, light and hugely comfortable with easy chairs and sofas; you could wallow for hours in the roll-top bath in the South Room's oak-panelled bathroom. And there's a cosy guest sitting room down the book-lined hall. Watercolours, rich oils, polished antiques and the charm of your hosts create a special atmosphere in this Queen Anne farmhouse and family home. Explore the magical garden, meander down to the river, stride out across the meadows, fish the farm's lakes – an enchanting place.

rooms	4: 1 double, 1 twin/double, 2 singles, all with shower.
room price	£60-£70. Singles £36-£40.
meals	Breakfast 7.30-9.30am. Good pubs 1 mile.
closed	December-January.
directions	A354 from Salisbury to Blandford. In Coombe Bissett, right to Broadchalke. House signed 1 mile after White Hart on right behind Stoke Manor.

rooms	3: 1 twin/double with bath & shower; 1 twin/double with private bath; 1 double with shower.
room price	£50-£70. Singles £35.
meals	Good pub/restaurant 2 miles.
closed	Christmas.
directions	From Salisbury on A36 for Southampton. After 1 mile right immed. at dual carriageway (no signs). Right at signs to Downton. Farm on right after 2.5 miles.

Gail & Peter Smalley
Ebblesway Courtyard,
High Road, Broadchalke, Salisbury,
Wiltshire SP5 5EF
tel   01722 780182
fax   01722 780482
e-mail enquiries@ebbleswaycourtyard.co.uk
web   www.ebbleswaycourtyard.co.uk

Ian & Annette Fergie-Woods
Witherington Farm,
Nr Downton, Salisbury,
Wiltshire SP5 3QT
tel   01722 710222
e-mail ian@witheringtonfarm.co.uk
web   www.witheringtonfarm.co.uk

map: 4 entry: 523

map: 4 entry: 524

The Grade II*-listed part-timbered house, half-moated, peeps through the trees as you approach – a magical spot. Roger and Anne are the kindest of hosts and spoil you at breakfast with local bacon, orchard fruits and home-made jam. Traditional, elegantly manicured bedrooms have glorious views of the Abberley Hills. The log-fired sitting room is yours to share with other guests, so cosy you won't mind if it rains – just snuggle in for the day. Outside: barns and outbuildings, gorgeous gardens, duck pond, moat, tennis court and, at Great Witley, the finest baroque church in England. *Children over 10 welcome.*

Their cooking, their personality, the welcome and the extensive wine list have guests returning time and time again. Maybe grapefruit, home-made marmalade, kedgeree or devilled kidneys for breakfast and rack of lamb or steak for dinner... do eat in. Walkers, too, love it here – Ann is happy to lend maps from her collection and there is masses of beautiful countryside very near. There are dried flowers, house plants and pastel colours downstairs and, upstairs, large bedrooms are spick and span and have views over the long garden and the Malvern Hills.

rooms	3: 1 twin with bath; 1 twin with private bath; 1 single with private shower.
room price	£50–£60. Singles £25–£40.
meals	Breakfast until 9am. Good pubs 1-5 miles.
closed	Christmas & New Year.
directions	A443 from Worcester; 1st left, B4197 to Martley; after 0.25 miles 1st right on sharp left-hand bend; up hill; 1st house on right.

rooms	3: 1 twin/double, 1 double, both with bath; 1 double with private bath.
room price	£53–£59. Singles £35.
meals	Dinner, 4 courses, £17.70.
closed	Christmas & New Year.
directions	From M50 junc. 1, A38 for Worcester. After 3 miles, left for Upton-upon-Severn & cross River Severn. At T-junc., right onto B4211. Left onto B4209 for Malvern Wells. 3rd house on right.

Roger & Anne Kendrick
Home Farm,
Great Witley, Worcester,
Worcestershire WR6 6JJ
tel 01299 896825
fax 01299 896176
e–mail anniekendrick@hotmail.com
web www.homefarmbandb.com

Ann & Tony Addison
Old Parsonage Farm,
Hanley Castle, Worcester,
Worcestershire WR8 0BU
tel 01684 310124
fax 01684 310124
e–mail opwines@aol.com

WORCESTERSHIRE

A 12th-century timber-frame house that has been smartly dressed in Georgian attire — it wears it well and surprises you with its beamy interior. The house sits at the foot of the majestic Malvern Hills, so there are fine views; all around are the Archers' 26 acres and there's a two-acre trout-stocked lake, too (you may fly-fish). The huge, dazzling black-and-white floored hall leads to antique-filled dining and drawing rooms. Bedrooms are large and country-house traditional and the house Scotch awaits you. Elizabeth breeds and shows miniature horses — fascinating.

rooms	3: 1 twin/double, 1 twin, both with bath/shower; 1 twin with shower.
room price	£80. Singles £50.
meals	Breakfast until 9.30am. Pubs/restaurants 800 yds & 4 miles.
closed	Rarely.
directions	West on A4104 to Upton-upon-Severn. Once there, cross river, left up main street, on for 3 miles until red phone box on left. Left at sign & take left fork.

Philip & Elizabeth Archer
Welland Court,
Upton-upon-Severn,
Worcestershire WR8 0ST
tel   01684 594426
fax   01684 594426
e-mail   archer@wellandcourt.freeserve.co.uk

YORKSHIRE

G ringley Hall, built in the early 1800s by the Duke of Portland, was once a children's home and Dulce and Ian took seven years to restore it. Rooms are large with high ceilings and floral fabrics; bedrooms are big and comfortable with settees and flowers. The bathrooms have 50s suites but are large and the towels generous. The garden is superb — a gardener's dream: two walled, dog-happy acres that include a nursery and potager, bright borders and sweeping lawns. There are a grass tennis court and games room, too. Home-made breads and jams and marmalades for breakfast.

rooms	4: 2 twins/doubles, both with bath/shower; 1 twin with private shower. Family suite on request.
room price	£70-£80. Singles £50.
meals	Breakfast until 9am. Dinner, 4 courses, £27.50.
closed	Rarely.
directions	From Bawtry, east on A631. Approaching Gringley, 1st left after school sign. On for 150 yds. House on left with iron gates.

Ian & Dulce Threlfall
Gringley Hall,
Gringley on the Hill,
Yorkshire DN10 4QT
tel   01777 817262
fax   01777 816824
e-mail   dulce@gringleyhall.fsnet.co.uk
web   www.gringleyhall.co.uk

YORKSHIRE

This modern cottage makes an excellent city alternative to corporate hotels. Both Stephanie's daughters are designers and a sense of style runs in the family. We loved the strong colours – the tiled hall with Chelsea Green walls, the bold yellow drawing room, the Madder Red room that overlooks the garden, the single room, intensely blue, with its patchwork throw made from the daughters' childhood dresses. The Hornbys are easy-going and love good food. A delightful find – and a good place from which to catch daily ferries to the continent. *Children over eight welcome.*

rooms	2: 1 double with private bath; 1 single available to members of same party.
room price	£30–£60.
meals	Supper/dinner £12/£18, with wine.
closed	Rarely.
directions	Where M62 becomes A63, follow Humber Bridge signs. At large r'bout north of bridge, left, A164 to Beverley. 3 miles on, right to Kirk Ella. Pass golf course & immed. after Post Office drive 1st on right after Hogg Lane.

Stephanie & Martin Hornby
Box Cottage,
2 Hogg Lane, Kirk Ella, Hull,
Yorkshire HU10 7NU
tel   01482 658852
e-mail   boxcottage2@aol.com

map: 15 entry: 529

YORKSHIRE

It's English to the core – a solid forme farmhouse in fine Pennine scenery, its stone mullion windows denoting 17th-century origins. Your gentle, gracious hosts offer guests their own, good-sized sitting room – carpeted and cosy, with flowery curtains, good antiques and, on chilly evenings, an open fire. Bedrooms are generous, and cottagey, with old brass beds and fresh flowers. Home-made muffins for breakfast, and good, traditional English dinners, too – just the thing for walkers who've trekked the Calderdale or the Pennine Way. *Children over eight welcome.*

rooms	2: 1 family suite, 1 double, both with shower.
room price	£60. Singles by arrangement.
meals	Packed lunch £4. Dinner £22.
closed	Christmas & New Year.
directions	Ripponden on A58. Right up Royd Lane 100 yds before lights. Right a T-junc. opp. Beehive Inn. On for 1 mile. House on right. Gateway or blind bend: reverse in.

David & Judith Marriott
Thurst House Farm,
Soyland, Ripponden,
Sowerby Bridge, Yorkshire HX6 4NN
tel   01422 822820
e-mail   thursthousefarm@bushinternet.com

map: 14 entry: 530

You are in Brontë country – walkers will be in heaven. Step out of the front door, past the walled garden, through the field (horses, Jacob sheep) straight into open countryside. There are good big bedrooms in the solid, very old listed farmhouse and large bathrooms too, with bright, Seventies' suites full of sudsy things, robes and fluffy towels. Geoff's breakfasts are generous in the finest Yorkshire manner. All is comfortable and homely with open fires and Pat and Geoff enjoy sharing their knowledge of walks, golf courses and local history.

Chris's father loved Canada and built his timber-framed house in the style of a log cabin. No pioneer austerity here, but a deeply comforting place to stay. Honey walls and polished floors give the sitting room a light, airy feel, cheerful throws on squishy sofas make it cosy, and there are fine views of the River Wharfe and Dales Way. Bedrooms are attractive with chintz cushions and fresh flowers; bathrooms are charming. You're superbly well looked after: Pam loves cooking and Chris buys his wines direct from a friend with a French vineyard. Great walking and trout fishing all around, and the solitude a balm.

rooms	3: 1 double with bath/shower; 1 twin with shower; 1 twin with private bath/shower.
room price	£48-£55. Singles £25-£35.
meals	Packed lunch available. Dinner from £10. Pub/restaurant 200 yds.
closed	Rarely.
directions	1 mile from Halifax on A58 Leeds road. Turn between Stump Cross Inn car park & Rosewood Furniture shop. 100 yds to gates.

rooms	3: 2 doubles, 1 twin, all with bath/shower.
room price	£60. Singles £35.
meals	Packed lunch £4. Dinner £20.
closed	January & February.
directions	From Skipton A59 to Bolton Abbey. At r'bout, B6160 for Burnall. 3 miles after Devonshire Arms, right immed. after Barden Tower for Appletreewick. Down hill, over bridge, up hill & on for 0.5 miles. Cross bridge; immed. on left.

Pat & Geoff Horrocks-Taylor
Field House,
Staups Lane, Stump Cross, Halifax,
Yorkshire HX3 6XW
tel 01422 355457
e-mail stayatfieldhouse@yahoo.co.uk
web www.fieldhouse-bb.co.uk

Pam & Chris Knowles-Fitton
Knowles Lodge,
Appletreewick, Nr Skipton,
Yorkshire BD23 6DQ
tel 01756 720228
fax 01756 720381
e-mail pam@knowleslodge.com
web www.knowleslodge.com

An air of quiet decency surrounds 17th-century Scar Lodge, reputed to have been a brewery for monks at Fountains Abbey; it's a restful retreat for those intent on sampling a slower pace. Comfortingly traditional bedrooms have valley views, patchwork quilts, fresh fruit, stitched linen and bathrobes; there's a sitting room, too, and a sunny spot upstairs for reading. Valerie, modest and gentle, is an accomplished artist – she runs courses and holds exhibitions here. Many consider Grassington a jewel in the Dales: cobbled streets, browseable shops and inspiring walks. *Children by arrangement.*

Garden lovers *have* to visit The Old Vicarage. So should hill-walkers. For teddy-bear-collectors it's optional but a good idea. Judi and Steve make you feel that no part of their much-loved home is out of bounds, and have been known to hold *al fresco* Italian suppers in the courtyard. Start the day with breakfast in the cosy, sociable, Aga-warmed kitchen; finish with a soak in a roll-top bath. Over 100 varieties of clematis and rose are to be discovered down cobbled paths past lily pond and willows; trickling waterways, sheep and the odd tractor are all that you hear.

rooms	2: 1 double with bath/shower; 1 double with private bath.
room price	£50–£55. Singles £30–£32.50.
meals	Breakfast from 7am. Packed lunch £3.50. Pubs & restaurants in Grassington.
closed	Rarely.
directions	B6265 Skipton-Grassington; enter 'main street' Grassington & right-hand fork past Grassington House Hotel; right after Folk Museum into Gillsfold; narrow road into Grange; 1st left, lodge on right.

rooms	3: 1 double, 1 twin, sharing bath, only let to same party; 1 double with shower.
room price	£58. Singles £35.
meals	Dinner, 3 courses, £20. B.Y.O.
closed	Rarely.
directions	From Harrogate, A59 (west). Right B6451. Right at Wellington pub. House on right, next to Christ Church.

Valerie Emmerson
Scar Lodge,
Hardy Grange, Grassington, Skipton,
Yorkshire BD23 5AJ

tel	01756 753388
fax	01756 753388
web	www.scarlodge.co.uk

Judi Smith
The Old Vicarage,
Darley, Harrogate,
Yorkshire HG3 2QF

tel	01423 780526
fax	01423 780526
e-mail	judi@darley33.freeserve.co.uk
web	www.darley33.freeserve.co.uk

map: 14 entry: 533

map: 14 entry: 534

Peter and Marion are quiet hosts, concerned for your rest and well-being. Their cottage, part of a 200-year-old mill, looks out over garden and mill stream to open fields. Although just a mile from the centre of Harrogate, it all feels wonderfully rural and there's lots of wildlife. The guest sitting room with coal-effect fire has a breakfast alcove with a vaulted stone ceiling and small library leading off. Bedrooms and bathrooms are modest and cosy. Peter was a professional golfer for 20 years and can arrange for you to play. *Children over 12 welcome.*

Come to be truly spoiled – Nigel and Julia's Grade II-listed townhouse is imbued with comfort and easy style. Beds are generous, mostly six-foot wide, with large enamel baths or astonishingly powerful showers. For breakfast, free-range eggs, handmade sausages, specially smoked bacon and cafetières of steaming fresh coffee. Gleaming dark wood, pretty fabrics, fresh flowers, fluffy towels... All this in the Duchy, Harrogate's most elegant area, just yards from some fine antique shops and the Pump Room Museum. If you decide to be independent, ask about the Garden apartment.

rooms	3: 1 double, 1 twin, both with shower; 1 twin with private bath.
room price	£50. Singles by arrangement.
meals	Breakfast until 9am. Good restaurants 1 mile; pub 0.5 miles.
closed	Rarely.
directions	From Harrogate, A61 towards Killinghall. Knox Mill Lane on right after approx. 0.5 miles.

rooms	3 doubles, all with bath/shower.
room price	£75.
meals	Restaurants within walking distance.
closed	Rarely.
directions	A61 Ripon Road from town centre. Swan Road 1st left. House 150 yds ahead.

Peter & Marion Thomson
Knox Mill House,
Knox Mill Lane, Harrogate,
Yorkshire HG3 2AE
tel   01423 560650
fax   01423 560650

Nigel & Julia Macdonald
Britannia Lodge,
16 Swan Road, Harrogate,
Yorkshire HG1 2SA
tel   01423 508482
fax   01423 526840
e-mail   info@britlodge.co.uk
web   www.britlodge.co.uk

Bring together an interior designer and a keen gardener, give them a Grade II-listed Georgian house in the gateway to the Dales and you have an English idyll. Guests use the South Wing with a separate entrance through the Mediterranean-style courtyard, and dine, deliciously, in the green-painted winter dining room by an open fire... or, in summer, in the cool white dining room overlooking the courtyard. Bedrooms are sumptuously decorated and huge – big enough to lounge in – with long garden views and the Jowitts are super hosts. The house has featured in glossy mags so you'll go home brimming with ideas.

A perfectly proper house run with faultless precision by John and Harriet – former wine importer and interior decorator respectively. The walk to Fountains Abbey and Studley Royal – the most complete remains of a Cistercian abbey in Britain – is a treat; you are spoiled for things to do and see and can consider your options in the manicured garden. Magnificent countryside, with views and deer all around. Two beautifully decorated bedrooms and bathrooms have thoughtful touches such as bathrobes and toiletries. *Golf, riding and clay pigeon shooting can be arranged.*

rooms	2 twins/doubles both with bath & shower.
room price	£80.
meals	Dinner, 3 courses, £25.
closed	Rarely.
directions	From southern end of Ripon bypass, turn to Bishop Monkton. After 0.75 miles, gateway on left turning into wood; signed.

rooms	2: 1 twin/double, 1 twin, both with bath.
room price	£96. Singles £63.
meals	Dinner £28.
closed	Christmas & New Year.
directions	A1 to Ripon. B6265/Pateley Bridge road for 2 miles. Left into Studley Roger. House last on right.

Tommy & Juliet Jowitt
Thorpe Lodge,
Ripon, Yorkshire HG4 3LU
tel   01765 602088
fax   01765 602835
e-mail   jowitt@btinternet.com
web   www.thorpelodge.co.uk

John & Harriet Highley
Lawrence House,
Studley Roger, Ripon,
Yorkshire HG4 3AY
tel   01765 600947
fax   01765 609297
e-mail   john@lawrence-house.co.uk
web   www.lawrence-house.co.uk

It is hard to resist Maggie's home-made jams and marmalade, the local home-cured bacon or the sausages from the farm up the road; harder still to say no to the kedgeree. The rambling 16th-century farmhouse, original fireplaces and shutters intact, is cosily furnished with floral fabrics and country antiques. A wonderfully steep stair leads to the main house bedrooms; others are in a converted outbuilding. Maggie's enthusiasm is infectious and her description of Fountains Abbey means a visit there is a must. Remember, this World Heritage Site was the richest area of England when wool was king.

The welcoming mellow brick façade of this 18th-century farmhouse says it all. This is the friendliest of places, with traditionally elegant rooms enlivened by the odd quirky touch. Only three minutes' walk from the village centre, it is surrounded by 28 acres, bounded by the river Swale and home to ducks, ponies and rare-breed sheep. It's hard to believe that the A1 is just four miles away. You can walk, fish, dally on the croquet lawn or play tennis before a pre-dinner drink on the stone-flagged terrace with glorious views of the Vale of York. Annie's home-made camomile tea helps your deep sleep.

rooms	4: 1 double, 2 twins/doubles, all with shower; 1 double with bath/shower.
room price	£58-£70. Singles from £45.
meals	Breakfast 8.15-9.15am. Good pubs & restaurants nearby.
closed	December & New Year.
directions	B6265 from Ripon for Pateley Bridge. Past entrance to Fountains Abbey. House on right, 2.5 miles from Ripon.

rooms	3: 1 double with bath; 1 twin/double with shower; 1 four-poster with private bath.
room price	£60.
meals	Dinner £25. Good pubs 3-minute walk.
closed	Rarely.
directions	From A1(M), Boroughbridge exit. At north side of B'bridge follow Easingwold/Helperby sign. In Brafferton-Helperby, right at T-junc., right up Hall Lane. Left in front of school.

Maggie Johnson
Mallard Grange,
Aldfield, Nr Fountains Abbey, Ripon,
Yorkshire HG4 3BE

tel	01765 620242
fax	01765 620242
e-mail	maggie@mallardgrange.co.uk
web	www.mallardgrange.co.uk

Sam & Annie Atcherley-Key
Laurel Manor Farm,
Brafferton-Helperby, York,
Yorkshire YO61 2NZ

tel	01423 360436
fax	01423 360437
e-mail	laurelmf@aol.com
web	www.laurelmf.co.uk

Wide windows frame an outstanding view. This spot, on the edge of the North York Moors National Park, was chosen for its outlook and the house designed to make the most of the scenery... views stretch from the Pennines to the Wolds. Big, stylish, modern, the house is set in two acres of hillside garden. Light floods uncluttered, elegant rooms; the drawing room has an open fire in winter; generous bedrooms and bathrooms are attractive and comfortable. Phillip and Anton love what they are doing, so you will be treated like angels and served freshly cooked dinners of outstanding quality. *Children over 12 welcome.*

Drive through a stone archway into an old courtyard; the 17th-century beamed farmhouse, once attached to Rievaulx Abbey, is still very much part of a working farm. Inside, a magnificent grandfather clock and a genuine Yorkshire farming welcome from Andrew and Margaret. The guests' sitting and dining rooms are full of 18th-century antiques and the bedrooms are frilled, flowery and comfortable, with lovely views; the double has a half-tester bedstead with a soaring canopy. A great place to stay, run with graceful efficiency by Margaret. *Children over 10 welcome.*

rooms	3: 2 twins/doubles, both with bath/shower; 1 double with private bath/shower.
room price	£75–£90. Singles £55–£65.
meals	Breakfast 8–9.30am. Dinner, 4 courses, £25.
closed	Rarely.
directions	From Thirsk, A19 south, then 'caravan route' via Coxwold & Byland Abbey. 1st house on left, just before Ampleforth.

rooms	3: 1 twin, 1 double, both with shower; 1 twin with private bath & shower.
room price	£52–£60. Singles £35.
meals	Breakfast 8–9.30am. Excellent pubs & restaurants 1–3 miles.
closed	Christmas & New Year.
directions	From Thirsk A170 for 12 miles. Right onto B1257 1 mile before Helmsley. 50 yds on, left by church. House at end of 'No Through Road'.

Anton van der Horst & Phillip Gill
Shallowdale House,
West End, Ampleforth,
Yorkshire YO62 4DY
tel	01439 788325
fax	01439 788885
e-mail	stay@shallowdalehouse.co.uk
web	www.shallowdalehouse.co.uk

Margaret & Andrew Wainwright
Sproxton Hall,
Sproxton, Helmsley,
Yorkshire YO62 5EQ
tel	01439 770225
fax	01439 771373
e-mail	info@sproxtonhall.demon.co.uk

YORKSHIRE

The moors lie behind this solid, stone farmhouse, five yards from the National Park, in farmland and woodland with fine views... marvellous walking country. The house is full of light and flowers; bedrooms are pretty and not overly grand. The sitting room has deeply comfortable old sofas, armchairs and fine furniture; rich colours and hunting prints give the dining room a warm and cosy feel. The Orr family has poured affection into this house and the result is a home that's happy and remarkably easy to relax in... wonderful.

rooms	2: 1 twin/double with shower; 1 twin/double with private bath.
room price	£70. Singles from £40.
meals	Breakfast until 9.30am. Dinner, 3 courses with wine, from £30.
closed	Rarely.
directions	From A170 Kirkbymoorside/Pickering road, to Sinnington. On village green, keep river on left & fork right between cottages. Up lane, bearing right up hill. House past church.

The Orr Family
Hunters Hill,
Sinnington, York,
Yorkshire YO62 6SF
tel 01751 431196
e-mail ejorr@tiscali.co.uk

map: 14 entry: 543

YORKSHIRE

The Woods have spent much of their lives in the east and it shows: their Grade II-listed Georgian house has a harmonious mix of oriental and fine English furniture, pictures and fabrics. They look after you well, with plump pillows, flowers and magazines, towelling robes and prettily-decorated bedrooms – the simple elegance is striking. Free-range scrambled eggs courtesy of the next-door farm; bread, jams, shortbread and potato scones, all home-made; coffee freshly ground. Colourful lupins stand proud in the garden and masses of roses and dreamy sunsets vie for your attention.

rooms	2: 1 twin, 1 double, sharing private bath.
room price	£60. Singles £30. Dogs £5 per visit.
meals	Breakfast until 9.30am. Packed lunch £5. Dinner, 4 courses, £17.
closed	Rarely.
directions	From Malton, B1257 for Helmsley. Through Amotherby then right to Kirkbymoorside. On for 3.25 miles. At Great Barugh, left at T-junc. House on right, 50 yds past pub.

Janie Wood
Barugh House,
Great Barugh, Malton,
Yorkshire YO17 6UZ
tel 01653 668615
e-mail barughhouse@aol.com

map: 14 entry: 544

An Aga-cooked breakfast and lots of fresh, seasonal fruit ... the Cravens are generous in spirit and are warm and amusing hosts. The High Hall was built in 1767 of mellow York stone and has an air of quiet repose. Furniture is traditional: china in panelled alcoves, old prints and watercolours on the walls, a Delph fire-surround in the drawing room. Bedrooms are snug and comfortable, with proper tea trays and fresh flowers. In wintertime, views reach to Pickering Vale. A newly-built terrace overlooks the garden and makes a perfect place for summer drinks, and Barney the black lab is pure delight.

A gorgeous, working farmhouse in the Yorkshire Wolds, surrounded by a big colourful garden and sloping fields. The house has a well-loved, lived-in patina and rooms are cosily scattered with family pieces, pictures and books. Huge, light-filled guest bedrooms have original cast-iron fireplaces and flowery drapes; pine-floored bathrooms are folksy, not flashy. This is shooting and fishing country, and your hosts are country sports enthusiasts; Jane loves gardens and gardening, too. The countryside is memorable and the unspoilt coast lies six miles away.

rooms	2: 1 twin, 1 double, both with private bath.
room price	£70. Singles £40.
meals	Breakfast 7.30–9am. Two pubs & a bistro in village.
closed	Rarely.
directions	Through Thornton le Dale on A170 for Scarborough. Road rises after village centre. Pass church on left. Hurrell Lane near top of hill on right. House immed. on right.

rooms	2: 1 double, 1 twin, both with private bath.
room price	£50.
meals	Good pubs 0.5 miles.
closed	Rarely.
directions	From A614 at Nafferton, signs to Burton Agnes. At x-roads, follow signs to Lowthorpe; in village, phone box on left opp. 2 white farm cottages; farm drive immed. after through white gate.

Richard & Tuppie Craven
The High Hall,
Hurrell Lane, Thornton le Dale,
Yorkshire YO18 7QR
tel   01751 474371
fax   01751 477701
e-mail   cravengriffin@aol.com

Jane Legard
Well Close Farm,
Lowthorpe, Driffield,
Yorkshire YO25 4AS
tel   01377 254259
e-mail   jameslegard@hotmail.com
web   www.legard.co.uk

A book-filled sitting room with brocade sofas, oak furniture, maple floors, dark green walls, shuttered windows... perhaps a coal fire in your room, or a cast-iron bath with Victorian fittings. This is a solidly traditional house set just inland from the drama of Flamborough Head. Geoffrey is a naval historian and the house is stuffed with his books; Lesley keeps alive the craft of Gansey knitting, selling the intricate fishermen's sweaters, along with antiques, in the converted stable block. Take an atmospheric cliff top walk, or a boat trip to see the puffins.

The Cleveland Way runs along the cliffs a mile off and Christine is happy to help you plan your stay (a trip to the Alan Ayckbourn Theatre, maybe?). Christine loves interior design and bedrooms are carefully co-ordinated: the twin with a pink and green floral theme and the original Victorian fireplace, the double with matching headboard and drapes in blue, gold and rose. Comfort is yours: there are bathrobes in fitted wardrobes and big showers. Big breakfasts — with kippers, if you choose — are served in the sunny conservatory or round the polished mahogany table. There's a billiards table here, too.

rooms	2: 1 double, 1 twin/double, both with bath.
room price	£70-£80. Singles £43.
meals	Breakfast 8.30-9.30am. Dinner £26.
closed	Christmas.
directions	From Bridlington, B1255 to Flamborough. Follow signs to lighthouse, past church on right. House on next corner (Lighthouse Road/Tower Street).

rooms	2: 1 twin with shower; 1 double with private bath & shower.
room price	From £50. Singles from £30.
meals	Pub 600 yds, more within 2-mile radius.
closed	Rarely.
directions	A171 from Scarborough to Whitby; at Scalby crossroads, by tennis courts, take road on right. Signed 500 yds on right.

Lesley Berry & Geoffrey Miller
The Manor House,
Flamborough, Yorkshire YO15 1PD
tel 01262 850943
fax 01262 850943
e-mail gm@flamboroughmanor.co.uk
web www.flamboroughmanor.co.uk

John & Christine Goodall
Holly Croft,
28 Station Road, Scalby,
Scarborough, Yorkshire YO13 0QA
tel 01723 375376
fax 01723 360563
web www.holly-croft.co.uk

A 20-minute stride down the fields to Levisham Station and the start of some wonderful jaunts on the North Yorkshire Moors Steam Railway (you are in the middle of the National Park). Warmth and comfort are the key notes of this family home – log fires on chilly nights, flowers in the rooms, home-made scones for tea. Cheery bedrooms are painted fresh yellow; all are carpeted and cosy. Have a drink at the local pub – a 50-yard stroll – or dine at home on Michael's beef and Yorkshire pudding (Heather does the puds). Superb walks from the doorstep, and excellent riding, too. Very good value.

L ose yourself in the gardens, dangle your feet in Hutton Beck, which runs through it, and feel the history of the place. Settled pre-Roman but rebuilt in Georgian times, the house has a story to tell, having been an 18th-century smithy, a tannery and a fine country house; Kate and Barry have gently coaxed it into a cosseting B&B. Traditional comforts – good beds, fine furniture, log fires, lots of books, deep armchairs – and a modern, multi-cultural twist to the outstanding food, much of which is local or home-grown. The moors and the village – the prettiest in England? – are a fine combination and your hosts great fun.

rooms	3: 1 double, 1 twin/double, both with shower; 1 twin/double with bath/shower.
room price	£46-£56. £270-£290 per week. Singles £24-£28.
meals	Breakfast 8-9.30am. Packed lunch £3-£5. Dinner £10-£12.
closed	Rarely.
directions	From A169 take Lockton/Levisham road. Once through Lockton, look for house sign after 0.75 miles on right, in Levisham.

rooms	3: 1 four-poster with bath/shower; 1 double with shower; 1 twin/double with bath.
room price	£65-£70. Singles £40-£45.
meals	Packed lunches available. Dinner, 3 courses, £18.
closed	Rarely.
directions	A170 for Scarborough. Hutton-le-Hole signed left 1 mile east of Kirkbymoorside; house on left before village hall; signed.

Mrs Heather Holt
Rectory Farmhouse,
Levisham, Pickering,
Yorkshire YO18 7NL
tel   01751 460491
e-mail   stay@levisham.com
web   www.levisham.com

Kate Seekings & Barry Jenkinson
Moorlands of Hutton-le-Hole,
Hutton-le-Hole, York,
Yorkshire YO62 6UA
tel   01751 417548
fax   01751 417760
e-mail   special@moorlandshouse.com
web   www.moorlandshouse.com

Free-range children and dogs scramble and amble around in an atmosphere of happy chaos. Jill is young and energetic and you will immediately warm to her; Andrew is unflappable. You are in a remote valley near the North Yorkshire Moors where the 1800s courtyard is such a rare survivor of local rural architecture that the BBC filmed it for posterity. The rooms, with views to the craggy moor, have been refurbished but this is first and foremost a family home, so don't expect anything designery. Breakfast on home-baked soda bread, farm eggs and proper bacon; for dinner, savour the Kellys' own beef and lamb.

The entrance is dramatic – the Cleveland Hills rise up behind and, all around, there are 164 acres of parkland. The views go on forever, the wildlife comes to you. Footpaths lead from the farm to the moors and take you past wild geese and cantering Soay sheep from the Outer Hebrides. Martin and Margaret are interested, involved people: you feel your presence counts. Inside, china knick-knacks and florals contrast with the bright whiteness of the rooms; views from your bedroom are glorious. Guests must take dinner – there are fine wines and you won't mind in the slightest.

rooms	3: 1 double, 1 family, 1 twin, all with private bath.
room price	£50. Singles £25.
meals	Packed lunch available. Dinner, 3 courses, £15.
closed	Rarely.
directions	From Malton, A170 Pickering road to Cropton. Through Rosedale Abbey & up onto moor & over cattle grid. Approx 1.5 miles on, right for Fryup. After 2 miles, right at T-junc. Farm 1st on left.

rooms	3: 2 doubles, 1 twin, 1 with bath, 2 with private bath/shower.
room price	Half-board £90 per room (£45 p.p.). Singles by arrangement.
meals	Breakfast until 9.30am. Dinner, 5 courses, included.
closed	Christmas.
directions	B1257 south from Stokesley to Great Broughton. Left at village hall onto Ingleby road for 2 miles to church at Ingleby Greenhow. Entrance right after church, through pillars.

Jill Kelly
Stonebeck Gate Farm,
Little Fryup, Danby, Whitby,
Yorkshire YO21 2NS
tel 01287 660363
fax 01287 669010

Margaret & Martin Bloom
Manor House Farm,
Ingleby Greenhow, Great Ayton,
Yorkshire TS9 6RB
tel 01642 722384
e-mail mbloom@globalnet.co.uk

map: 14 entry: 551

map: 14 entry: 552

YORKSHIRE

YORKSHIRE

A peaceful spirit, warmth and friendliness pervade this elegant, bay-windowed farmhouse. Anne goes to great lengths to make you comfortable and her cooking is delicious. The house, which incorporates the former cottage and dairy buildings, has pale, fresh colour schemes, an interesting collection of books and superb views. The pretty guest rooms face south and you will be drawn to explore the gentle, rolling dales, the moors and the coastline. York, Durham and other fascinating historic places are nearby.

Even in the mayhem of the lambing season they greet you with tea, home-made biscuits and a smile – the Pearsons are the nicest, most genuine, farming folk imaginable. Their farmhouse is as unpretentious as they are; one bedroom is in the house and another four in converted outbuildings away from the homely hub. Rooms have a mixture of antique and modern furniture and views of the garden and of the Hambleton Hills. The road that runs past the house is quiet, yet you are well placed for the Dales and the moors. Local sausages, home-made marmalade and home-grown eggs for breakfast.

rooms	2: 1 twin, 1 twin/double, both with private bath.
room price	£76. Singles £48.
meals	Dinner from £25.
closed	December-January.
directions	North on A19 A172 for Stokesley. Pass sign on right to Carlton & Busby. House 0.5 miles further on left, with 2 red triangular reflectors at entrance to tree-lined drive.

rooms	5: 1 family, 1 twin, 1 double, 1 single, all with shower. Gate Cottage: 1 double with bath.
room price	£48-£52. Singles £27-£31. Gate Cottage: £50-£60.
meals	Breakfast until 9.30am. Dinner £16.
closed	December-February.
directions	From Northallerton, A167 north for Darlington for 4 miles. House on right, signed.

	Anne Gloag
	Busby House,
	Stokesley, Yorkshire TS9 5LB
tel	01642 710425
fax	01642 713838

	John & Mary Pearson
	Lovesome Hill Farm,
	Lovesome Hill, Northallerton,
	Yorkshire DL6 2PB
tel	01609 772311
fax	01609 774715
e-mail	pearsonlhf@care4free.net

map: 14 entry: 553

map: 14 entry: 554

A gracious, comfortable house with big, beautiful rooms and approachable, charming owners. The house was a rectory first, then the residence of the Bishops of Whitby. Both J M W Turner and Ruskin stayed here as guests of Reverend William Kingsley, cousin of author Charles. Built of warm brick it's surrounded on three sides by rambling gardens, rare old trees, a tennis court, orchard and croquet lawn. The elegant, deep pink dining room looks south over the garden and guests have use of the superb drawing room with its fine Venetian window and a particularly enticing window-seat. *Children over 10 welcome.*

Oriella goes the extra mile for you and loves having guests. Flamboyant, kind, great fun, she has created a gloriously eclectic mix of styles in a fine Georgian house. There are plenty of delicious corners in which to sit and read or listen to music... feast your eyes on antique tapestries, paintings and oriental pieces. In the big secluded gardens are great copper beeches, formal lawns, enclosed spaces and three big ornamental ponds fed by a natural spring. The generous bedrooms are chintz-paisley and the suite has a seven-foot-square bed with the down of 226 ducks to snuggle under.

rooms	2: 1 twin with wc, basin, private bath & shower; 1 double with private bathroom & dressing room.
room price	From £50. Singles from £30.
meals	Breakfast until 9.30am. Pubs/restaurants nearby.
closed	Rarely.
directions	Take A168 (Northallerton road) off A19; over r'bout; left into village; house opposite pub, next to church.

rooms	3: 1 double, 1 twin, both with bath; 1 suite with bath/shower.
room price	£90–£100. Singles £50-£55.
meals	Dinner, 4 courses, £25. Pub/restaurant a short drive.
closed	Rarely.
directions	From A1 at Leeming Bar, A684 to Bedale. 0.5 miles out of town, turn for Newton-Le-Willows. Right at T-junc., left at Wheatsheaf pub, then immed. right through gates.

Caroline O'Connor-Fenton
The Old Rectory,
South Kilvington, Thirsk,
Yorkshire YO7 2NL
tel   01845 526153
fax   01845 523849

Oriella Featherstone
The Hall,
Newton-Le-Willows, Bedale,
Yorkshire DL8 1SW
tel   01677 450210

To the front, the perfect English country village with close-clipped verges; behind, beyond the ancient apple tree and the garden wall, the Dales. Four 17th-century almshouses have become Rookery Cottage and the oak-panelled dining room was once the village post office. It all feels natural, normal, homely, free of studied co-ordination. And there are plenty of spoiling touches – generous baths, pretty basins, Floris soaps, fine food… Breakfast features home-made jams and marmalades, perhaps kedgeree made from Ronnie's catch of the day. Dine at the pub opposite – one of the north country's finest.

Gerry is the only person to have won the Grand National (1960 on Merryman II), and started it (in 1996). A portrait of the winning pair hangs in the dining/living room; Gerry is a happy man. The bedrooms differ – one is decorated in peppermint and cream; another has a drawn threadwork bedspread. Views are of paddock and moorland. A mecca for real ale enthusiasts, Masham is the home of both Theakston and Black Sheep breweries. It is also boisterous field sports country, so possibly Pasture House is not for objectors.

rooms	2: 1 twin, 1 double, both with basin, sharing bath.
room price	£48–£58. Singles from £34.
meals	Breakfast 8.30–9am. Packed lunch £4.50. Country inn opposite for dinner.
closed	Rarely.
directions	From Masham, A6108. Leyburn 8 miles on. House on left, opp. Blue Lion Country Inn.

rooms	3: 2 doubles, 1 twin with basins, all sharing bath & wc.
room price	£40. Singles £20.
meals	Dinner, 3 courses, £15. B.Y.O.
closed	Christmas Day.
directions	From A6108 (Ripon to Richmond rd), turn off 0.35 miles north of Masham, for Healey. Through Healey to junction for Colsterdale. Take right fork. House 1st on left.

	Mrs Ursula Bussey
	Rookery Cottage,
	East Witton, Leyburn,
	Yorkshire DL8 4SN
tel	01969 622918
fax	01969 622918
e-mail	ursulabussey@aol.com
web	www.rookerycottage.co.uk

	Avril & Gerry Scott
	Pasture House,
	Healey, Masham, Yorkshire HG4 4LJ
tel	01765 689149
fax	01765 689990
e-mail	avril.scott1@tiscali.co.uk

map: 14 entry: 557

map: 14 entry: 558

YORKSHIRE

YORKSHIRE

You feel as if you are caught in a tranquil time-warp; no TV, just utter calm and windows that frame the Wensleydale hills. In the middle of the Yorkshire Dales National Park, it's a superb base for walkers. Gail and Ann bake their own bread and make jams and marmalade, and their delicious dinners are prepared with fresh, local produce. Two bedrooms have four-posters and all have beautiful views. If you're arriving by car, take the 'over-the-top' road from Buckden to Hawes for the stunning countryside. Expect a real welcome from their two labradors. *Minimum stay two nights.*

This will take your breath away. One moment you are on a town pavement facing a somewhat sober Georgian front; the next, in a lofty room, elegant with Adam fireplace, fine mouldings, period furniture. Bedrooms and bathrooms are similarly splendid, with sumptuous beds, cast-iron baths, exquisite Swale valley views... Breakfasts are superb. As if this were not enough, there is the most enchanting walled garden, superbly designed, adorned with hostas, clematis, old roses – a feast for the senses. Tim and Austin are engaging hosts and their house, one of our favourites, continues to captivate.

rooms	4: 1 double, 1 twin, 2 four-posters, all sharing bath or shower.
room price	£40-£42. Singles £25-£29.
meals	Breakfast 8.30am. Dinner, 4 courses, £14.50, not Thurs; good value wine list.
closed	November-mid-February.
directions	Approx. 320 yds off A684, on road north out of Hawes, signed Muker & Hardraw.

rooms	3: 1 double, 1 twin, both with bath/shower; 1 double with private bath/shower & sitting room.
room price	£80. Singles £50.
meals	Breakfast 8.30-9.30am. Pub/restaurant 250 yds.
closed	Rarely.
directions	Next door to Halifax Building Society, opposite side of Barclays at bottom of Market Place. Green front door with small brass plaque.

Gail Ainley & Ann Macdonald
Brandymires,
Muker Road, Hawes,
Yorkshire DL8 3PR
tel   01969 667482

Austin Lynch & Tim Culkin
Millgate House,
Richmond, Yorkshire DL10 4JN
tel   01748 823571
fax   01748 850701
e-mail   oztim@millgatehouse.demon.co.uk
web   www.millgatehouse.com

map: 14 entry: 559

map: 14 entry: 560

The outward look is solid, impressive; the feel is warm, family, comfortable, easy. The house was built in 1929 on the site of an 18th-century house, so... masses of architectural history: folly, icehouse, urns and sundials remain from the original estate. A stalwart oak staircase and an inner hall are lit by a glass dome and portraits line the galleried landing. The scale and colour of the gardens are breathtaking, so are the views. Sarah fills the house with flowers so it's cosy and charming even on the dreariest day; there are lots of games to play and a lovely log fire gives a welcoming glow.

The house was once much bigger and what remains is the Victorian section of a Georgian mansion. Now a manageable size, it's in absolutely tip-top condition and extremely comfortable. A sense of space remains, with high, plaster-worked ceilings and pale bedrooms. Fireplaces everywhere, big baths, high beds, large windows onto the beautiful grounds and a terraced lawn that runs down to the Tees; there's a book-lined study and a sitting room for guests, and you can fish, play tennis or croquet. Grandeur and welcome here – not to be missed.

rooms	2 twins, both with bath.
room price	£70-£80. Singles from £45.
meals	Restaurants/pubs 5 miles.
closed	Rarely.
directions	A1 to Scotch Corner, then A66 for Penrith. House 0.25 miles after lay-by on left, lodge & white posts; through gates.

rooms	2 twins, both with private bath.
room price	£70. Singles £35.
meals	Good pub 1 mile.
closed	10 December-1 January.
directions	From A1, exit onto B6275. North for 4.2 miles. Into drive (on left before Piercebridge); 1st right fork.

Sarah Baker Baker
Sedbury Hall,
Richmond, Yorkshire DL10 5LQ
tel   01748 822722
e-mail   sarahbakerbaker@hotmail.com

Caroline & Richard Wilson
Cliffe Hall,
Piercebridge, Darlington,
Yorkshire DL2 3SR
tel   01325 374322
fax   01325 374947
e-mail   petal@cliffehall.freeserve.co.uk

Books, magazines, bath essences, biscuits by the bed — Christina is lovely and spoils you as she would a friend. Her pretty, listed, limestone farmhouse dates from 1820 and is bigger inside than it looks. Ivory walls are a perfect foil for some good furniture and paintings. Bedrooms, light and airy, are in a suite separated from the house by a latch door — you feel nicely self-contained. Newsham is an AONB and the panoramic views over rolling countryside are superb. Waterfalls, moorland, villages, castles beckon — and this is a handy stopover to and from Scotland.

The views are over Teesdale and the walking is everywhere; the village, tiny and solid in stone, is perfect. A captivating hideaway in the 18th-century coach house is yours up a steep stone stair: a lofty, cross-beamed ceiling, lemon-yellow fabrics against a cream wall, soft lighting, good linen, and Angela's charming watercolours and pottery adding to the fresh, country feel. Inside the rectory, more rooms in which to linger — here the mood is of a classically English country house. Angela can teach you to fish, is a great cook — salmon fishcakes, own eggs at breakfast — and has green fingers too: her garden is glorious.

rooms	2: 1 twin with bath & shower; 1 twin sharing bath, only let to same party.
room price	£55. Singles £27.50.
meals	Dinner, 2-3 courses, £12–£15.
closed	Christmas & New Year.
directions	From Scotch Corner west on A66. Approx. 7 miles on, down hill. Left to Newsham. Through village; 2nd left for Helwith. House on right at top, name on gate.

rooms	3: 1 double with bath/shower; 1 twin with private bath; 1 single sharing bath, let to members of same party.
room price	£70. Singles from £35.
meals	Breakfast from 7am. Dinner or supper available. Pubs & restaurants 3-10 miles.
closed	Christmas & New Year.
directions	South off A66 for Greta Bridge & Barningham, 10 miles west of Scotch Corner. Immed. left for B'ham for 2 miles. Before village, through dry stone walls, house 2nd entrance left after village sign.

Christina Farmer
Hill Top,
Newsham, Richmond,
Yorkshire DL11 7QX
tel   01833 621513
e-mail   cdfarmer@lineone.net

James & Angie Delahooke
The Old Rectory,
Barningham, Nr Richmond,
Yorkshire DL11 7DW
tel   01833 621122
fax   01833 621421
e-mail   jdelahooke@aol.com

www.thirdangle.com

SCOTLAND

Farming runs deep in the blood at Camaloun, home to a farmer's son and a farmer's daughter who met at a farmers' ball. They run sheep and cattle – you'll see them in the yard – but by the look of it they take off shoes at the back door: the place is spotless. The feel is reassuringly traditional though a makeover is on the cards and wallpaper, books and curtain fabrics were brought out for inspection. Simple, homely bedrooms have pretty views across garden and farm. There are fresh flowers, old pine windows, gentle greens and yellows. Fyvie Castle, Haddo Hall and Pitmeddan Gardens are all close.

Veronica's ancestor, William McCombie, lived on the farm and founded the breed, Aberdeen Angus. The handsome farmhouse has been in the family since 1762 and you can roam the surrounding 300 acres of rolling hills. Décor is traditional country house with some lovely family pieces, hunting prints, Colefax fabrics, Farrow & Ball paints. Guests are treated very much as friends and your Cordon-Bleu-trained hostess is delightfully easy-going; dinner can be served either in the dining room or in the Aga-warmed kitchen. So peaceful, and on the Aberdeen 'Castle Trail', too. *Fishing and shooting breaks available.*

rooms	2: 1 double with private bath; 1 twin with bath.
room price	£50. Singles £25-£30.
meals	Breakfast until 8.30am.
closed	Christmas & New Year.
directions	A947 north from Fyvie; house signed left after 2 miles.

rooms	3: 1 twin with bath/shower; 1 twin with bath; 1 double with private bath.
room price	From £60. Singles £40.
meals	Dinner, 3 courses, £25.
closed	Rarely.
directions	20 miles from Aberdeen on A944 (towards Alford); through Tillyfourie, then left for Muir of Fowlis & Tough; after Tough, 2nd farm drive on left, signed.

Mrs Wyness
Meikle Camaloun,
Fyvie, Turriff,
Aberdeenshire AB53 8JY
tel 01651 891319
fax 01651 891319
e-mail w.wyness@btinternet.com
web www.farmhousebandb.co.uk

John & Veronica Evans-Freke
Lynturk Home Farm,
Alford, Aberdeenshire AB33 8DU
tel 01975 562504
fax 01975 563517
e-mail lynturk@hotmail.com

map: 23 entry: 565

map: 23 entry: 566

ABERDEENSHIRE

If the address gives the impression of the metropolis, note that there was no sign of Nos. 1 or 2 and that the only noise comes from the River Don. Candacraig, the erstwhile laundry for this 1520 estate, is a Highland retreat for those who like to mix style with gentle eccentricity. Iain and Mary run an easy-going ship – breakfast times are negotiated and the art of conversation is practised with meandering flair. There's much comfort, too: claw-foot baths, wall-hangings, old pine dressers, cut-velvet curtains, and Nelson the one-eyed deer. Balmoral is down the road. Don't miss Iain's traditional Scottish cooking.

rooms	3: 1 double with shower; 1 double with bath & shower; 1 double with private bath & shower.
room price	£70. Singles from £42.50.
meals	Dinner, 3 courses, £25.
closed	Rarely.
directions	East on A944 towards Strathdon. House signed on right through pillared entrance gates.

Iain & Mary Edgar
No. 3 Candacraig Square,
Strathdon, Aberdeenshire AB36 8XT
tel   01975 651472
fax   020 7681 1218
e-mail   no3@buchanan.co.uk
web   www.candacraig.com

ABERDEENSHIRE

An absolute gem, one of the loveliest places we know. Crystal-clear morning light and views from bedrooms of river, field, forest, hill. Sandpipers and swallows nest, curlew, osprey and lapwing glide. Expect a warm country-house feel and the comfiest beds in Scotland! Your room may be huge – two are – and full of fine furniture, fluffy bathrobes, fresh flowers, maybe even a balcony. Meg picks flowers for your room and her food is delicious; David serves with much good humour. Nearby, golf, hiking, fishing and castles by the hatful. Unmissable.

rooms	3: 1 twin/double with bath/shower; 1 twin/double with balcony & dressing room, with private bath; 1 twin/double with private bath/shower. Extra shower, too.
room price	£60–£80. Singles from £35.
meals	Supper £15–£18. Dinner £25. Local pub/bistro.
closed	Rarely.
directions	From Aboyne, A93 west for Braemar. Just after 50mph sign, left down Rhu-na-Haven Rd. House 400 yds on, 4th gateway on right.

David & Meg White
Lys-na-Greyne House,
Rhu-na-Haven Road, Aboyne,
Aberdeenshire AB34 5JD
tel   01339 887397
fax   01339 886441
e-mail   david@lysnagreyne.freeserve.co.uk

ABERDEENSHIRE

At the foot of Glenesk, this 18th-century house has a gorgeous setting. Your hosts are fun; John has a twinkle in his eye and Valerie, lover of labradors, adores a chat and is charming and kind. Soft sofas, pretty lamps, robes in the bathroom – it's deliciously old-fashioned, stylish and cosy. Family photos sit alongside fine china and prints that hint at John's love of country pursuits. Valerie waves her wand in the kitchen: her fish, meat and game dishes are matched by fine wines (their son is in the trade) served in glasses that sparkle. A delightful place.

rooms	3: 1 twin with shower; 1 twin with private bath; 1 single sharing bath if in same party, otherwise private bath.
room price	£65. Singles £35–£45.
meals	Breakfast until 9.30am. Dinner, 3 courses with wine, £22.
closed	14 December–14 January.
directions	From A90, B966 through Edzell, on towards Fettercairn. House just under 2 miles on, behind a beech hedge; enter 2nd gate on left.

Valerie & John Smart
Woodmyre,
Edzell, Brechin,
Aberdeenshire DD9 7UX

tel	01356 648416
fax	01356 648416
e-mail	smart@woodmyre.freeserve.co.uk

map: 23 entry: 569

ANGUS

Amazing. A listed Peel tower that dates to 1300 and which once was home to the Abbot of Arbroath, murdered in St Andrews on Henry VIII's orders. His private chapel remains, as does his secret stair. As for the rest of the house: turret staircases, a green Art Deco bathroom, a 1500s ceiling in the Great Hall, and a Tudor kitchen with a walk-in fireplace that burns night and day. Kirstin and Adrian are experts at breathing new life into old houses and have already started to reclaim the garden. Lunan Bay, one of Scotland's most beautiful beaches, is at the end of the road. There's a loch too.

rooms	2: 1 double, 1 twin/double, sharing bath/shower.
room price	£75. Singles from £50.
meals	Packed lunch up to £10. Dinner, 4 courses, £28, with wine.
closed	Rarely.
directions	North from Arbroath on A92; through Marywell, then right by Shell garage for Auchmithie; left at T-junc; on for 2 miles; at 90° bend, private road to Ethie Barns; on right.

Mrs Kirstin de Morgan
Ethie Castle,
Inverkeilor, By Arbroath,
Angus DD11 5SP

tel	01241 830434
fax	01241 830432
e-mail	kmydemorgan@aol.com

map: 23 entry: 570

This is the last house on Mull: miss it and you'll end up in the Sound of Iona. Ian used to dive for scallops, now he restores furniture, while Jane is variously an upholsterer, a district nurse and a cook (she was on uninhabited Mingulay cooking for geologists when we visited). Their house looks out onto Fionnphort Bay. The ferry to Iona leaves outside the front door, but stops at six, ensuring a good night's sleep. Pretty bedrooms up in the eaves are cosy, with fresh flowers and piles of books. One has views to Iona, the other looks onto the bay, and you can watch the fishermen land crabs and lobsters.

Barbara and Hew are generous, kind people – they run a 400-acre hill farm but find time for real hospitality and delicious food. This includes home baking and local shellfish. The house is elegantly white, the farm definitely a working one, and the views are stupendous. Wander as you wish and admire; the eye always comes to rest on the water and boats of Loch Craignish and the Sound of Jura. The drawing room is the original 16th-century *bothy* with four-foot-thick walls and log fire. Bedrooms are simple and the downstairs loo doubles as the library.

rooms	2: 1 triple, 1 twin with shared shower.
room price	£36-£44. Singles £31.
meals	Good pub within walking distance.
closed	Occasionally.
directions	A849 west to Fionnphort. Follow road to slipway. House signed on right. Follow road to very end; house on left at top of slipway.

rooms	5: 1 double with bath & sitting room; 1 suite (1 double, 2 singles with sitting room & bath, let to same party).
room price	£68. Singles £34.
meals	Lunch from £10. Dinner £23-£35.
closed	22 December-3 January & 4th week of August.
directions	From A816, B8002 to Ardfern, & through village. 0.75 miles past church, long white house on top of hill on right. Right by Heron's Cottage, up drive to Corranmor.

Ian & Jane Slade
Shore House,
Fionnphort, Isle of Mull,
Argyll & Bute PA66 6BL

tel	01681 700631
fax	01681 700631
e-mail	ian@shorehouse.fsworld.co.uk
web	www.isleofmull-uk.co.uk

Hew & Barbara Service
Corranmor House,
Ardfern, By Lochgilphead,
Argyll & Bute PA31 8QN

tel	01852 500609
fax	01852 500609
e-mail	corranmorhouse@aol.com

A 'Wee Free' church used to stand on the site; Rob and Sheila will tell you all about it – history is their delight. This is a delectable place to stay, a 19th-century manse in acres of peaceful woodland garden on the unspoilt Cowal peninsula, Scotland's first National Park, the Isle of Bute nearby. Bedrooms have old family pieces and fine views: we liked the twin with the pink French wallpaper, antique brass beds and old desk (complete with writing paper). Your hosts are enormous fun – and very good cooks. The wooden-shuttered, book-lined dining room is an intimate setting for memorable meals. What a treat.

The River Awe roars past the foot of the pretty garden; Robert keeps his rods handy and can show you where the salmon leap. The 1960s lodge conceals a rich rococo interior of 18th-century style and comfort; a quick tour of his home will net you six busts in the conservatory and an eccentric collection of bric-a-brac. The dining room walls are sponged a pinkish red – very cosy – and a fire crackles on cold nights. Robert entertains easily, turning his gatherings into house parties. Rooms are simply furnished, light and airy and outside the windows are two munros.

rooms	3: 1 twin with shower; 1 twin, 1 double, sharing bath.
room price	£65. Singles £40.
meals	Packed lunch £5. Dinner, 2 courses, £20; 3 courses, £25. B.Y.O.
closed	Rarely.
directions	From Tarbet A83 to Cairndow. Before village, left on A815 to Strachur, then lochside for Dunoon; entrance 75 yds on right signed 'Free Church'. House on brow of hill.

rooms	3: 2 twins/doubles, 1 twin, all with bath.
room price	£70. Singles by arrangement.
meals	Dinner £25.
closed	Christmas & New Year.
directions	From A85 (Oban road), 23 miles west from Crianlarich. 1.5 miles after Awe Barrage, right signed 'Inverawe Fisheries' just before bridge. 1st on left after high hedge. If you reach Taynuilt you've gone too far!

Sheila & Rob Macpherson
The Old Manse,
Strachur, Argyll & Bute PA27 8DF
tel   01369 860247
e-mail   sheilamacpherson@strachur247.freeserve.co.uk

Robert Knight
Bridge of Awe Lodge,
Taynuilt, Argyll & Bute PA35 1HT
tel   01866 822642
fax   01866 822510

map: 17 entry: 573

map: 21 entry: 574

Twenty paces from the door, past the standing stone, and you're on your own beach with views across Ardmucknish Bay to Mull – a staggering Hebridean landscape. The 1911 house, built by a Glasgow shipping magnate, has been given a 21st-century makeover by these two ex-Edinburgh architects. The result is a cool, calm, minimalist interior: low-slung beds, velvet throws, piles of cushions, luxury bathrooms. If your tastes are modern, you'll be in heaven: CDs, DVDs... this is B&B for the next generation. Breakfast on banana and walnut porridge, eggs en cocotte, the full Scottish works. *Children over 12 welcome.*

The road runs out in half a mile, the hills of Glen Creran cradle you, a private loch laps at the end of the garden – this is heaven. Stella and Earle pamper: tea when you arrive, maybe in the garden; delicious food beautifully presented; beds turned down, curtains drawn, bedside lamps on, carafes of water, Roberts radios, hot water bottles, books and flowers.... Nothing is left to chance, everything is a natural response. Absolute peace – and a great place to recharge city-spent batteries. For the more active, Beinn Sguilard is a three-hour climb; the Broadbent young do it before breakfast!

rooms	7: 4 doubles, 2 twins, all with bath & shower; 1 single with bath/shower.
room price	£64-£80. Singles from £36.
meals	Pubs nearby.
closed	Rarely.
directions	North from Oban on A828; over Connel Bridge; north for two miles; house signed left just after lay-by, before Benderloch village.

rooms	3: 1 twin, 1 double, both with bath; 1 twin with private shower.
room price	£56-£68. Singles £28-£34.
meals	Breakfast 8-9am. Dinner, 4 courses, £24.
closed	Rarely.
directions	14 miles north of Connel Bridge, 20 miles south of Ballachulish on A828 (Oban, Fort William, Glencoe rd). At north r'bout of new bridge follow Invercreran signs for 2 miles, then straight up glen for 1.5 miles. Cottage on right.

Mark McPhillips & Suzanne Pole
Dun Na Mara,
Benderloch, Oban,
Argyll & Bute PA37 1RT
tel   01631 720233
e-mail   stay@dunnamara.com
web   www.dunnamara.com

Earle & Stella Broadbent
Lochside Cottage,
Fasnacloich, Appin,
Argyll & Bute PA38 4BJ
tel   01631 730216
fax   01631 730216
e-mail   broadbent@lochsidecottage.fsnet.co.uk
web   www.lochsidecottage.fsnet.co.uk

ARGYLL & BUTE

W hat views! "The word 'breathtaking' is entirely appropriate," says our inspector. Loch Linnhe is 200 yards away and light floods in; there is wood outside and in, windows everywhere and the walls are white to reflect the sun. Their daughter's modern art hangs above a classical marble fireplace in the sitting room; the dining room is open-plan, with a good, simple, long oak table. Bedrooms are done in fresh apple greens, yellows and white with fresh flowers, books and views. The two-acre garden is 100% organic, fertilised by seaweed, roamed by ponies and free-range chickens.

rooms	3: 1 double with shower; 2 twins sharing bath & shower.
room price	£40–£60. Singles by arrangement.
meals	Breakfast until 9.15am. Pub 1 mile.
closed	Christmas & New Year.
directions	From Oban north on A85, then A828. On to village of Duror, then left, for Cuil. House on left after 0.5 miles.

Bridget & Hugh Allen
Druimgrianach,
Cuil Bay, Duror,
Argyll & Bute PA38 4DA
tel   01631 740286

map: 21 entry: 577

AYRSHIRE

Y ou have the comforts of a country-house hotel yet you are treated as friends. Antique furniture, rich, thick drapes, family photos and everything just so in the Thomsons' unusual and elegant, 1930s-style house. The yellow drawing room with an Adam fireplace is smart and large, the bedrooms are cosy; the twin is burgundy and cream, the double aqua-blue. Felicity, who specialises in Scottish dishes, serves delicious breakfasts at the refectory table in the dark red dining room. A stream runs through the very pretty garden towards 13 acres of woodland and its banks are home to water-loving plants and entertaining ducks.

rooms	4: 3 doubles, all with bath/shower; 1 twin with private bath.
room price	£90. Singles £55.
meals	Excellent pubs 10-minute drive.
closed	Rarely.
directions	From Glasgow, A77 for Ayr. Pass Little Chef, left for Underwood & Ladykirk. Left at T-junc., over bridge, past farm on right, down hill & left. Past gates to Underwood House, then immed. left. House signed. At end of lane.

Felicity & Austin Thomson
Nether Underwood,
By Symington, Kilmarnock,
Ayrshire KA1 5NG
tel   01563 830666
fax   01563 830777
e-mail   netherund@aol.com
web   www.netherunderwood.co.uk

map: 17 entry: 578

AYRSHIRE

Within and without it is delightful and John and Moira are kind, relaxed and interesting; they have an unfussy manner that makes it easy to relax. The atmospheric drawing room is stately and half-panelled. There are bay windows, oak and oils, and bedrooms are done in fresh colours – blues and whites – with good linen and towels, fine furniture, decorative wash bowls, and shutters rather than curtains. It is a fine house, with views to the River Doon which flows through the garden. The sea is only a mile away and Glasgow an hour. *Children over 10 welcome.*

rooms	2: 1 double with private bath; 1 twin with shower.
room price	£70. Singles £40.
meals	Breakfast until 9.30am. Pub/restaurant 25 yds.
closed	Christmas & New Year.
directions	B7024 into Alloway on south side of Ayr. Follow Burns Heritage Centre signs. House on left, opp. Burns Monument & church.

John & Moira Pollok-Morris
Doonbrae,
40 Alloway, Ayr, Ayrshire KA7 4PQ

tel 01292 442511
fax 01292 442511
e-mail doonbrae@aol.com

map: 17 entry: 579

BANFFSHIRE

Great Scottish hospitality from people who care and go the extra mile. Nothing is too much trouble: a superb home-cooked supper, a bottle of wine, delightful conversation and much laughter. Bill gardens and produces much for the table; in summer, they are 95% self-sufficient. Doreen keeps the house spotless and plans culinary feasts for the evening. Bedrooms are delightful, as is the whole house: expect comfy beds, open fires, a baby grand and fine views. Only an hour from Aberdeen airport yet close enough for you to enjoy the little fishing villages of the Moray coast. Exceptional. *Children by arrangement.*

rooms	2: 1 double with shower; 1 twin with bath.
room price	£55-£60. Singles from £30.
meals	Dinner, 3 courses, £20.
closed	Rarely.
directions	From Keith, A95 for Banff. After 3.5 miles, left signed Grange Church. Left again opposite church.

Doreen & Bill Blanche
Grange House,
Grange, Keith, Banffshire AB55 6RY

tel 01542 870206
fax 01542 870206
e-mail wd.blanche@zetnet.co.uk

map: 23 entry: 580

BANFFSHIRE

This is the good life — 30 acres at the end of the track, a field of Highland cattle, a loch that attracts so much bird life a hide is soon to be added, and a burn that tumbles down the hill in the wood, by which you can walk. Hazel and James came here to croft 25 years ago. They renovated crumbling walls, licking them into rather good shape, which is not surprising given that James is a dry-stone waller (though he did use cement on the house). Their B&B is a delight and more impressive than the photo suggests. A cathedral roof, shiny wooden floors, cashmere blankets, sparkling bathrooms and easy-going people make this place special.

rooms	2 twins, both with shower.
room price	£54. Singles £30.
meals	Breakfast until 8.30am. Dinner, 3 courses, £16.
closed	December-February.
directions	North from Aberchirder on B9023. Right at Lootcherbrae (still B9023); 2nd left for Ordiquhill. After 1.7 miles, right at farm track opp. Aulton Farm; last croft up track.

Hazel & James Watt
Balwarren Bed and Breakfast,
Ordiquhill, Cornhill,
Banffshire AB45 2HR
tel   01466 751688
fax   01466 751688
e-mail   balwarren@hotmail.com
web   www.balwarren-bed-and-breakfast.com

BERWICKSHIRE

This is a new venture for Sally and David and much hard work has gone into creating a most attractive place to stay. The house was built in 1767 — as the magnificent Adam-style ceilings and fireplaces attest — with Victorian additions; generous sash windows look south to the Cheviots. Lose yourself in the wooded four acres, with lawns, herbaceous borders, a glass house and a kitchen garden. David is chef and uses home-grown, organic and local produce: speciality sausages and cheeses, Lammermuir lamb, wild Tweed salmon… Sally is a classically trained professional singer and runs residential courses. A charming place.

rooms	3: 1 twin/double with bath; 2 twins/doubles with private bath/shower.
room price	£57-£70. Singles £38.50.
meals	Lunch £6. Dinner, 3 courses, £14.50. Good pubs nearby.
closed	Rarely.
directions	From A1, B6437 to Chimsede. Follow for 1 mile, left at top of hill signed Reston. Fairlaw is signed 400 yds on right, past farm.

David & Sally Price
Fairlaw House,
Fairlaw, Nr. Auchencrow,
Berwickshire TD14 5LN
tel   01890 761724
e-mail   fairlawhouse@btopenworld.com
web   www.fairlawhouse.co.uk

BERWICKSHIRE

Lucy's cooking is mouthwatering: kedgeree and waffles for breakfast, Cordon Bleu dishes by night, delightfully served in an elegant dining room. A sense of solidity pervades this Victorian home, run by the charming Forrest family who have farmed here for years. Bedrooms are bright and comfortable and full of lovely extras like flowers, good books and magazines; big bathrooms have Crabtree & Evelyn soaps. Log fires in winter; lambs and calves in spring; flowers in the garden and antique farm machinery to admire in the yard. Golf, fishing and moorland walks beckon, and Edinburgh is only an hour away.

rooms	3: 1 double, 1 twin, sharing private bath; 1 double with extra single bed, with bath/shower.
room price	From £55. Singles by arrangement.
meals	Dinner from £15. B.Y.O.
closed	Rarely.
directions	From A1 north of Berwick, turn off at Grantshouse; A6112 to Duns for 6 miles to village of Preston. House on right, just after sharp bend into village (B&B sign).

Mrs Lucy Forrest
Preston Farmhouse,
Preston Farm, Preston Duns,
Berwickshire TD11 3TQ
tel   01361 882826
fax   01361 882066
e-mail   lucy@forrest4.freeserve.co.uk
web   www.forrest-preston.co.uk

map: 19 entry: 583

CAITHNESS

A big old country house in 10,000 acres. In the sitting-room hall, fires burn at both ends of the room, while a drawing-room grand stands on the stairs – they hold concerts occasionally. Described by an American guest as "Steamboat Gothic", Thrumster packs quite a punch: the curtains date to 1863, some of the art came out of the Royal Academy and the vaulted wooden ceiling gives the impression of being inside a church. Thrumster is home to The Yarrows Archaeological Trail, one of the most important neolithic settlements in northern Europe. It stretches back 5,800 years.

rooms	2: 1 double with shower; 1 twin with private bath.
room price	£65. Singles £35.
meals	Dinner, 3 courses, £25.
closed	Rarely.
directions	A99 north through Ulbster. After 2 miles, pass church & 'Yarrow Archaeological Trail' sign, then 1st left (200 yds) & up drive to house.

Islay MacLeod
Thrumster House,
Thrumster, Caithness KW1 5TX
tel   01955 651387
fax   01955 651733
e-mail   thrumster@btinternet.com
web   www.thrumster.co.uk

map: 26 entry: 584

An 1800 manse with the village on one side, open country on the other, and the River Esk across the lane. A light and airy home with big rooms, most of which look south to England, two miles away. Drawing room windows frame country views; there are fresh flowers, open fires, rugs on wooden floors and old oils on the walls. Good-sized bedrooms come with crisp linen, patchwork quilts, window seats, maybe a *chaise longue*. Archie and Elisabeth are exceptionally friendly. A three-mile circular walk starts from the door, the local pub does fine food, and Hadrian's Wall beckons. *Children over eight welcome.*

The grandeur may be faded, but this former manse in stunning Border country is holding its own. There's a lovely garden, your own, well lived-in drawing room with old pictures and log fire, comfortable bedrooms and some amazing floral wallpapers. Your hosts, who have been happy here for years, are keen on country sports and, with notice, will be delighted to arrange hunting or fishing for you to give your holiday an extra dimension. This is a smoking household and the bedrooms are only ever let to just you or you and your friends so you can make up your own rules. *Children by arrangement.*

rooms	3: 1 double with bath; 1 twin with bath/shower; 1 twin/double with private bath/shower.
room price	£60-£70. Singles £30-£35.
meals	Good restaurant 2-minute walk.
closed	Rarely.
directions	M6, junc. 44, then A7 12 miles into Canonbie. Over bridge; immed. right & immed. left into yard.

rooms	3: 2 twins, 1 single, sharing private bath.
room price	£60. Singles £30.
meals	Restaurant 1.5 miles.
closed	Rarely.
directions	From M74 junc. 20, B722 to Eaglesfield. 2nd left after 350 yds, for Middlebie. There, house next to church.

Elisabeth & Archie Findlay
Kirklands,
Church Road, Canonbie,
Dumfries & Galloway DG14 0RA
tel 01387 371769
fax 01387 371784
e-mail irvineho@aol.com

R & U Milne Home
Kirkside of Middlebie,
Lockerbie,
Dumfries & Galloway DG11 3JW
tel 01576 300204

map: 18 entry: 585

map: 18 entry: 586

Fabulous Knockhill: stunning place, stunning position, a treasure-trove country house full of busts and screens, oils and mirrors, chests and clocks, rugs and fires. Exquisite 'shabby chic' with a lime green drawing room for tea and drinks, floor-to-ceiling windows… a bohemian feel throughout. Fine stone stairs lead up to country-house bedrooms that are smart yet homely, with great views, loads of books, bathrobes and plush carpets. A grand farming feel, and the Morgans are the easiest and most charming of hosts. "These are top people doing B&B in the very best way," says our inspector.

An old manse at the top of the hill, right next door to the church, with a 12th-century motte. Views from the garden stretch for miles around. The house is light and airy, with the original varnished pine floors, sweeping stairs and a mellow grandeur. Spotless bedrooms have a simple country elegance, nothing to jar the senses: shuttered windows with twin-aspect garden views, pretty florals, crisp linen, an old oak dresser, a deep cast-iron bath. You'll love Jane's cooking: pork with plum and sage marinade, perhaps, or chicken with chicory and crème fraîche. Tawny owls in the garden, so music to fall asleep to.

rooms	2: 1 twin with bath/shower; 1 twin with private bath.
room price	£70–£75. Singles £37.50.
meals	Dinner £23. Good pub 5 miles.
closed	Christmas & New Year.
directions	From M74 junc. 19, B725 for Dalton for 1.2 miles. Right at x-roads to Lockerbie, 1 mile on, right at stone lodge. House at top of long drive.

rooms	3: 1 double with private bath; 2 twins, both with bath/shower.
room price	£72–£76. Singles from £41.
meals	Dinner £24. B.Y.O.
closed	Rarely.
directions	M74 junc. 17 to Lockerbie. B7076 for Johnstonebridge. 1st right after 1.5 miles; after 100 yds left over m'way bridge. After 1 mile, right at T-junc., then 2nd left to church. House next to church.

Yda & Rupert Morgan
Knockhill,
Lockerbie,
Dumfries & Galloway DG11 1AW
tel   01576 300232
fax   01576 300818
e-mail morganbellows@yahoo.co.uk

Frank & Jane Pearson
Applegarth House,
Lockerbie,
Dumfries & Galloway DG11 1SX
tel   01387 810270
fax   01387 811701
e-mail jane@applegarthtown.demon.co.uk

map: 18 entry: 587

map: 18 entry: 588

A 1703 farmhouse set in 700 acres, with the odd free-range pheasant to escort you up the drive. Inside, the farmhouse turns 'country house' with walking sticks and fishing rods and polished wooden floors in the panelled dining room (the table seats 26). There's a fountain in the courtyard, an honesty bar in the snooker room, while themed bedrooms (India, China, Scotland, Africa) might have a brass bed or a free-standing bath. The Pickups farm and provide much for the table (organic lamb, venison, duck and partridge). You may see buzzards or sparrow hawks and can fish, play golf, cycle, sail or ride locally.

Sink into the sofas without worrying about creasing them; this is a beautiful, 18th-century, Scottish, Georgian, family home with not a hint of formality. The sociable Dicksons are at ease and so will you be. The sitting and dining rooms connect through a large arch and there are family pictures and rugs on wooden floors. In the bedrooms: a cast-iron bed, excellent furniture, elegant linen and masses of light and good books – this wonderful house gets better and better. There are 200 acres, a dog, cat, donkeys and free-ranging hens, and you can walk, play golf, sail or cycle in magnificent countryside.

rooms	7: 1 double, 3 twins, all with bath & shower; 1 twin, 1 twin/double, both with bath; 1 twin/double with shower.
room price	£70. Singles £35.
meals	Breakfast 8-9am. Dinner £17.50.
closed	Christmas & New Year.
directions	A75, then north on A712 towards Corsock. After 2 miles, Craigadam signed on right.

rooms	2: 1 twin with private bath/shower 1 double with bath/shower. Cot etc available.
room price	£72. Singles £36.
meals	Supper occasionally available. Pub 1 mile, restaurant 5 miles.
closed	Christmas.
directions	A75 Dumfries ring road for Stranraer. Approx. 15 miles to Springholm & right to Kirkpatrick Durham. Left at crossroads, after 0.8 miles, up drive on right by white lodge.

Mrs Celia Pickup
Craigadam,
Castle Douglas,
Dumfries & Galloway DG7 3HU
tel   01556 650233
e-mail   inquiry@craigadam.com
web   www.craigadam.com

Willie & Catriona Dickson
Chipperkyle,
Kirkpatrick Durham, Castle Douglas
Dumfries & Galloway DG7 3EY
tel   01556 650223
fax   01556 650223
e-mail   dickson@chipperkyle.freeserve.co.uk

DUNBARTONSHIRE

Blairbeich is magnificent – a wonderland in the woods. It is a fusion of Californian and Scandinavian styles and has a mini-loch that laps three feet from its walls. There are light stone floors and cathedral ceilings, and delightful ground-floor bedrooms look onto the loch – an enclave of wilderness that universities come to study. Despite all this it is the interior that knocks you flat: Malla has covered every square inch with something spectacular and the sitting room is a private art gallery. Mosaic showers, Grecian urns, rare orchids and woodpeckers... and curling on the loch in winter. Fantastic.

rooms	2: 1 double with bath & shower; 1 double with shower.
room price	£60-£90. Singles from £45.
meals	Dinner, 4 courses, £30. Lunch £10-£15. Packed lunch £7.50-£10.
closed	Rarely.
directions	From west, A811 into Gartocharn; 1st right (School Road); 1 mile up to T-junction, then left; house on right, signed.

Malla Macdonald
Blairbeich Plantation,
Gartocharn, Loch Lomond,
Dunbartonshire G83 8RR
tel   01389 830257
fax   01389 830752
e-mail macdonald@blairbeich.com
web   www.blairbeich.com

map: 17 entry: 591

DUNBARTONSHIRE

Bertie, a naval man, was based in the Falklands for a year; the whole family went, so good tales get told. It also explains the penguins dotted around the 1730s house. Piles of books in the sitting room, and views out back to the Arrocha Alps rising beyond a hidden Loch Lomond. Bedrooms have brass beds, wooden blinds, tartan carpets, pretty pine furniture, fresh flowers, good linen; bathrooms are spotless. One room has a distant glimpse of the loch, while triple-glazing ensures that the road passes quietly at night. Breakfast? Try porridge, kedgeree, oatcakes, bacon, eggs...

rooms	3: 2 doubles, 1 twin/double, all with shower.
room price	£56-£60. Singles from £38.
meals	Breakfast 8-9.30am. Dinner, 3 courses, £22.
closed	Christmas & New Year.
directions	A82 north from Glasgow, then A811 east at Alexandria. House signed left 0.75 miles east of Gartocharn.

Bertie & Lizzie Armstrong
The Old School House,
Gartocharn, Loch Lomond,
Dunbartonshire G83 8SB
tel   01389 830373
fax   01389 830373
e-mail bertiearmstrong@compuserve.com
web   www.the-old-school-house.co.uk

map: 17 entry: 592

Sophie, Tom, three daughters, cats, dogs and ducks are all delightful and couldn't be more welcoming; they are very happy to share their home and let you to come and go as you please. Bedrooms are downstairs and have huge windows, shutters and wonderfully thick curtains, lashings of hot water, modern floral prints and period paints. Upstairs: wooden floors, enormous ancestral paintings, bold colours, a huge wooden dining table and an antique baby chair. Full Scottish breakfasts set you up for the day; the Aga-cooked porridge is particularly good. A short walk from the city sights.

rooms	2: 1 double, 1 twin, both with bath.
room price	£70-£80. Singles £40.
meals	Excellent restaurants nearby.
closed	Rarely.
directions	From Edinburgh centre, along Princes Street, left down Leith Street. Right fork down Leith Walk; Gayfield Square 2nd on left.

Sophie & Tom Murray
26 Gayfield Square,
Edinburgh EH1 3PA
tel   0131 556 5260

A house of magnificent proportions: a cantilevered staircase with cupola above, lofty ceilings and bedrooms on the expected scale. There are, too, impressive oil paintings, marble mantlepieces, mosaic wall art, elaborate window treatments, antiques and tables set with silver and crystal. You are in New Town, five minutes from the centre, yet rooms at the front overlook acres of private gardens and top-floor rooms at the back have views of the Firth of Forth. Mrs Lloyd is a bright, easy-going hostess and her home one of only 20 complete Georgian houses left in Edinburgh. *Off-street parking available.*

rooms	9: 1 triple, 1 twin, 3 doubles, 3 twins/doubles, 1 single, all with bath/shower.
room price	£90-£100. Singles by arrangement.
meals	Breakfast 8-9am Mon-Fri; until 9.30am Sat/Sun. Restaurants/pubs 2-minute walk.
closed	Rarely.
directions	Abercromby Place lies parallel to Queen Street, 3 streets north of Princes Street in city centre in 'New Town'. Off-street parking.

Eirlys Lloyd
Abercromby House,
17 Abercromby Place,
Edinburgh EH3 6LB
tel   0131 557 8036
fax   0131 558 3453
e-mail   eirlys.lloyd@virgin.net
web   www.abercrombyhouse.com

EDINBURGH & THE LOTHIANS

The house is blessed with fine features: a cantilever staircase and cupola, a bow-walled dining room, spiral stairs down to the basement where the guest rooms are. It's a rare find, too – an entire, undivided Georgian house in a lovely terrace (1821) so close to the city centre. Susie and Andrew have done everything well and the brightly coloured rooms are better kitted out than most poly-starred hotel rooms; the single, however, has no window. But the comfort here comes with a personal touch and with very congenial hosts who can give you inside knowledge of this most beautiful of Scottish cities.

rooms	3: 1 double, 1 twin, both with shower; 1 single with bath.
room price	£70–£110.
meals	Breakfast 8–9am. Many restaurants close by.
closed	Christmas.
directions	Queensferry Rd out of Edinburgh for Forth Road Bridge. Travel 250 yds along Queensferry St. Before Dean Bridge, bear left, down Lynedoch Place (which is also the top of Belford Road)..

Andrew & Susie Hamilton
16 Lynedoch Place,
Edinburgh EH3 7PY
tel 0131 225 5507
fax 0131 226 4185
e-mail susie.lynedoch@btinternet.com
web www.16lynedochplace.co.uk

EDINBURGH & THE LOTHIANS

High on Edinburgh's most exalted Georgian escarpment, this exquisite, light, bright eyrie mixes early 19th-century elegance with Danish and Middle Eastern style. Brass beds, burnished pine floors, a vast hall with a stairway that floats regally above a magnificent sitting room, long views of the Firth of Forth and Fife from the airy twin. Erlend, an award-winning travel writer, creates gourmet feasts at breakfast: Asparagus Apocalypse, *oeufs à la brioche*, Mushroom Taleggio, Pommes Rimbaud... The delightful Cloustons will meet you from the train and help you carry up your bags. It's relaxed, informative, fun.

rooms	2: 1 double with shower; 1 twin with bath & shower.
room price	From £95. Singles from £70.
meals	Many places within walking distance.
closed	Rarely.
directions	Heriot Row is parallel to Princes Street, 3 major blocks north.

Erlend & Hélène Clouston
41 Heriot Row,
Edinburgh EH3 6ES
tel 0131 225 3113
fax 0131 225 3113
e-mail erlendc@blueyonder.co.uk
web www.wwwonderful.net

The slender glass case, reflected in the gilt mirror, holds two white lilies; the sea of stripped pine has just one rug. On each soft yellow wall hang just two pictures, such as the two striking charcoal nudes done by their daughter. Big, pure – an aesthetic delight. Breakfast by the white-shuttered window over the gardened square is a lingering pleasure: organic and/or home-made, an imaginative and delicate feast. Sandra is irresistible; John is laconic and interesting. Both are generous with their huge flat. Cars on cobbles are audible, but guests have slept exceptionally well in the antique Georgian brass bed.

Impressive architectural features – cantilevered staircase, marble fireplaces, double-barrelled cupola and soaring ceilings – coupled with Fiona's professional interior design talents make for a stunning city base. The feel is sumptuous: generous curtains, pretty bedspreads and towels, Crabtree & Evelyn goodies, camellias fresh from the garden. The chandelier has real candles and the beds are four-poster or canopied. Fiona and Colin are lovely, their breakfasts are superb, and you have a fascinating 10-minute stroll through some of Europe's finest classical architecture to the centre of the city.

rooms	1 double with private bath.
room price	£85-£95. Singles £50-£55.
meals	Restaurants 5-10-minute walk.
closed	20-28 December.
directions	North from Prince St., cross George St., & Queen St. to Heriot Row & Abercromby Pl. India St. runs north from west end of Heriot Row.

rooms	3: 2 doubles, 1 single, all with bath.
room price	£100-£120.
meals	Good restaurants 5-minute walk.
closed	Christmas Day.
directions	From Edinburgh, Queensferry Rd for Forth Rd Bridge. 3rd right after Dean Bridge into Dean Park Crescent, then 2nd right into Danube Street.

Sandra & John Keith
50 India Street,
Edinburgh EH3 6HD

tel   0131 225 3340
e-mail   sandrakeith@brilliantbreakfasts.com
web   www.brilliantbreakfasts.com

Fiona Mitchell-Rose
7 Danube Street,
Edinburgh EH4 1NN

tel   0131 332 2755
fax   0131 343 3648
e-mail   seven.danubestreet@virgin.net

EDINBURGH & THE LOTHIANS

Discuss the delights of the city with your friendly, multi-lingual hostess – Gillian is a Blue Badge Guide. Comfortable bedrooms below stairs are attractively decorated in muted pinks, greens and cream; one has a lovely carved wooden bedhead and looks onto the patio garden. Scottish shortbread and books in the bedrooms, local artists' paintings on the walls and, from your breakfast table, a springtime view of crocuses, daffodils and blossom. A seductive city base, with the Meadows park opposite (look upwards to Arthur's Seat) and a short walk from the university, concerts, theatres and museums.

rooms	2: 1 twin with bath/shower; 1 twin (with single room attached) with bath/shower.
room price	£75 (£80-£90 during Edinburgh Festival). Singles from £55.
meals	Breakfast 8-9am. Many pubs/restaurants nearby.
closed	22-27 December.
directions	From centre of Edinburgh (West End), Lothian Rd to Tollcross (clock) & Melville Drive. At 2nd major traffic lights, right into Argyle Place & immed. left into Fingal Place.

Gillian Charlton-Meyrick
2 Fingal Place,
The Meadows, Edinburgh EH9 1JX
tel 0131 667 4436
fax 0131 667 4436
e-mail bleish1936@aol.com

map: 18 entry: 599

Second entry

Both house and garden are an oasis and American Clarissa has lost none of her enthusiasm for her adopted city. From the guest sitting room you look onto pear trees and clematis and, in the distance, the rolling Pentland Hills. Snug up in the winter next to the log fire; in summer, take your morning paper onto the terrace above the south-facing garden. There are books, fresh flowers, interesting art and ceramics and, because you are on an old, quiet street, utter, surprising, peace. One of the bedrooms has a lovely antique American four-poster. Clarissa is involved in the arts and local events and can help plan your day.

rooms	2: 1 double with bath; 1 double sharing bath.
room price	£60-£80. Singles £30-£40.
meals	Good restaurants/pubs nearby.
closed	23-29 December.
directions	From centre of Edinburgh, A702 south, for Peebles. Pass Churchill Theatre (on left), to lights. Albert Terrace 1st right after theatre.

Clarissa Notley
1 Albert Terrace,
Edinburgh EH10 5EA
tel 0131 447 4491
e-mail canotley@aol.com

map: 18 entry: 600

Yellow is the keynote here, lending the rooms – including the newly decorated bathroom – a fresh, light, sunny air. Bedrooms, blissfully quiet, come with books and magazines, garden flowers, good linen, pretty china. In the dining room you are treated to the full Scottish breakfast feast, much of it organic; Iola, who is charming, is also a good cook, and makes her own bread and jam. There's a peaceful garden with a patio that catches the evening sun: perfect for relaxation after a day of city exploration. The pleasures of Edinburgh lie an easy bus ride away.

First and foremost it is a home – this Edwardian townhouse certainly feels friendly and easy – but it's big on comfort, too. Barbara goes the extra mile for you: beds are capacious, bathrobes are large and fluffy, curtains are pelmeted, fireplaces renovated and there's sherry on the dresser. Barbara is super – so is Poppy, the cairn terrier! – and is more than happy to help you plan your stay. For breakfast, local sausages and bacon, Finnan haddock, kippers or omelette. Regular buses run to the city centre and there are eating places within a 10-minute walk.

rooms	2: 1 twin with private bath; 1 double with private shower.
room price	£56-£70. Singles by arrangement.
meals	Restaurants within walking distance, more in city centre.
closed	23-28 December.
directions	Enter Edinburgh on A702. 0.5 miles from bypass, fork right down Braid Rd, after pedestrian crossing. House 0.5 miles on left after mini-r'bout. Free on-street parking.

rooms	3: 2 doubles, both with bath/shower; 1 twin/double with shower.
room price	£75. Singles £50.
meals	Many restaurants within walking distance.
closed	Rarely.
directions	Leave city bypass at Straiton exit & follow A701 for City Centre until 1st r'bout. Take 2nd exit, Craigmiller Park, then 2nd left, Wilton Rd & 2nd right, Granby Rd. Free on-street parking.

	Iola & Michael Fass
	60 Braid Road,
	Morningside, Edinburgh EH10 6AL
tel	0131 446 9356
fax	0131 447 7367
e-mail	iolafass@blueyonder.co.uk
web	www.braidroad.com

	Barbara Kellett
	32 Granby Road,
	Edinburgh EH16 5NL
tel	0131 667 9078
fax	0131 668 1051
e-mail	barbara.kellett@virgin.net
web	www.barbara-kellett.com

EDINBURGH & THE LOTHIANS

EDINBURGH & THE LOTHIANS

Some hosts work hard at giving a big welcome; with the Westmacotts it just happens. They are easy-going, entertaining and energetic. Gather round the fire for a drink before setting off for supper, linger over a hearty breakfast as conversation flows. Family paintings and country views in the dining and drawing rooms, bathrobes and warm comfort in the large bedrooms. Wander through the orchard, pop in and see the working cooperage (barrel-makers). You are a 10-minute drive from Edinburgh airport, and from Dalmeny village there are trains to the city every half hour; Louise can meet you at the station.

rooms	4: 2 twins/doubles, 1 double, 1 single, sharing 2 baths & separate wc.
room price	£56–£64. Singles from £28.
meals	Good pubs/restaurants 2 miles.
closed	Christmas.
directions	From lights in centre of Kirkliston, follow sign for Forth Rd Bridge (A8000) & on at r'bout. Approx. 0.5 miles on, 1st right after Milton Farm. Down lane, over small bridge & right before cottages.

Louise & Michael Westmacott
Craigbrae,
Kirkliston, Edinburgh EH29 9EL
tel 0131 331 1205
fax 0131 319 1476
e-mail louise@craigbrae.com
web www.craigbrae.com

map: 18 entry: 603

Sarah's friendly, relaxed, laid-back, and mixes B&B and a busy family life with humour; she treats you like a friend, too. The house, 1830s Georgian, buzzes with life – it's homely and cluttered in the communal bits, yet your rooms are pristine with comfy chairs, garden views and striking colours. Lots of the decoration is extraordinary, some of it inherited from the previous Italian owner – gold cornicing, murals... unusual, stunning. A cupola lights the stairwell; one bedroom has an enormous bathroom, one a sitting area. No sitting room, but this is Edinburgh and it doesn't matter.

rooms	2: 1 twin/double, 1 double, with shared bath.
room price	£70–£90. Singles £35–£45.
meals	Dinner available locally.
closed	Rarely.
directions	In Edinburgh, 500 yds north of Botanic Gardens.

Sarah Nicholson
44 Inverleith Row,
Edinburgh EH3 5PY
tel 0131 552 8595
fax 0131 551 6675
e-mail inverleithbandb@yahoo.com

map: 18 entry: 604

Catch your breakfast in the river if you will, and Annie will prepare it for you – along with omelettes with fresh herbs, home-made conserves and marmalade: she's a professional cook. Her cosy terraced cottage overlooks the salmon-trout river Esk, and is stylish within. The look is crisp white with dashes of colour: charming. Bedrooms, fresh and airy – and one up narrow stairs – are filled with original paintings, fresh flowers, books and magazines; coir carpeting runs throughout. Annie is a one-off – breezy with a great sense of humour, and a gorgeous retriever to make a fuss of you. *Children over six welcome.*

rooms	2: 1 double with shower; 1 twin with private bath, down narrow stairs.
room price	From £40. Singles £25.
meals	Breakfast 7-9am. Pubs/restaurants 5-minute drive.
closed	Rarely.
directions	From south A1, exit for Musselburgh. Through town & cross bridge. Eskside West 1st left. From Edinburgh, A199 (A1) to Musselburgh bridge. Eskside West on right, just before bridge.

Annie Deacon
53 Eskside West,
Musselburgh,
East Lothian EH21 6RB
tel 0131 665 2875
e-mail anniedeacon@talk21.com

Vast, high-ceilinged public rooms with a hotchpotch of comfortable furniture, patterned carpeting, artificial flowers and two life-size retrievers that stand sentry by the fireplace! This is a musical household; you may accompany chorister daughter Daisy to performances in St Mary's Cathedral (guests do), or play the grand piano. A superb 19th-century tub adorns the bathroom of the master suite and all the rooms are unfussy and on the expected scale. The house was built on a Roman site and guards a 16th-century secret tunnel; Cromwell plotted his siege of Edinburgh Castle from here.

rooms	3: 1 family, 1 double, 1 twin, all with bath.
room price	From £80. Singles £45.
meals	Breakfast 8-9am. Pubs/restaurants nearby.
closed	Rarely.
directions	From Edinburgh, A199 (A1) to Musselburgh. There, follow signs to Inveresk. At top of Inveresk Brae, sharp right into cul-de-sac. 2nd opening on right, opp. gates with GM on them, bear right past cottages to house.

Alice & John Chute
Inveresk House,
3 Inveresk Village, Musselburgh,
East Lothian EH21 7UA
tel 0131 665 5855
fax 0131 665 0578
e-mail chute.inveresk@btinternet.com
web www.btinternet.com/~chute.inveresk

Gwen has lavished a huge amount of time and love on her 1780s Georgian manse – bedrooms are light and airy and hung with generous swathes of fabric; easy chairs have pretty cushions. There are many original features: fireplaces, arched glass, long, Georgian windows. The sea is two minutes from the house and this is heaven for golfers – there are 18 courses within easy reach. There's also a fascinating sea bird centre close by, and you are only a 30-minute drive from Edinburgh. Regular trains will take you to the foot of the castle.

If you rush past, you're missing a treat: this is a lovely 18th-century family house into which the infectiously vibrant Carina and Jim have poured energy, affection and artistic flair. A comforting hubbub comes from the kitchen – Carina is an excellent cook and you'll be chatting easily before you know it. There's table tennis and snooker and peace for those seeking a country retreat with beaches – traditional pan-tiled villages are just a stone's throw away. Bedrooms are well furnished with large, bright and recently decorated bathrooms.

rooms	3: 1 double with shower; 1 twin with private bath; 1 four-poster with bath/shower.
room price	£60-£80. Singles by arrangement.
meals	Restaurants within walking distance.
closed	Christmas & New Year.
directions	From Edinburgh, A1 for Berwick. Left onto A198, follow signs into North Berwick. Right into Station Rd signed 'The Law', to 1st x-roads, left into town centre; house on left behind wall.

rooms	2: 1 double, 1 twin, both with bath/shower.
room price	£70-£90. Singles £45.
meals	Lunch from £20. Dinner with wine, £25.
closed	20 December-6 January.
directions	From Edinburgh A1 for Berwick-upon-Tweed. Left for East Linton, left under railway bridge & through village; 0.5 miles on, left for Markle. First white house on right.

Gwen & Jake Scott
Glebe House,
Law Road, North Berwick,
East Lothian EH39 4PL
tel	01620 892608
fax	01620 893588
e-mail	j.a.scott@tesco.net

Carina & Jim McGuinness
Markle House,
East Linton, East Lothian EH40 3EB
tel	01620 860570
fax	01620 860937
e-mail	mcguinness@marklehouse.fsnet.co.uk

Surrounded by 350 acres of undulating countryside yet so close to Edinburgh! The Georgian farmhouse sits in lovely gardens, its peace interrupted by the odd strutting pheasant. On sunny days you take breakfast in the conservatory, heady with jasmine and climbing geraniums. Smart bedrooms have inspired fabrics and colours, great views and space; the drawing room is delectable with deep coral walls and a log fire. Barbara is a warm and charming hostess. Play tennis or explore the farm – it's won awards for conservation and Michael's commitment to the countryside is wide-ranging and deep.

Susan is genetically predisposed to spoiling people rotten. Her home-baking is sinful (expect a feast for breakfast), her green fingers have teased a garden from an awkward field, and she's hot on Scottish history, so can help you plan your day. Her modern house on the edge of a residential estate has lovely big rooms that swim with light. A smart green dining room, a multi-windowed sitting room, and spotless bedrooms, country-cosy with wicker chairs and crisp linen. The M8 passes within a mile, but triple-glazing soundproofs entirely. Edinburgh and Glasgow are an easy train ride. *Children over 12 welcome.*

rooms	4: 2 doubles, both with bath/shower; 1 twin with shower; 1 single with private bath.
room price	£50–£60. Singles from £25.
meals	Two excellent pubs 1 mile.
closed	Christmas.
directions	From A1 at Haddington B6368 south for Bolton & Humbie. 2.5 miles on through Bolton, at top of hill, fork left for Eaglescairnie. Entrance 0.5 miles on left.

rooms	2: 1 twin with shower; 1 twin with private bath/shower.
room price	£60. Singles £30.
meals	Packed lunch £5. Pub/restaurants 0.5 miles.
closed	Christmas, New Year & occasionally.
directions	M9, junc. 3, then A803 into Linlithgow. There, right onto A706 for Bo'ness & 0.2 miles on left. Follow to very end of road.

Barbara Williams
Eaglescairnie Mains,
Gifford, Haddington,
East Lothian EH41 4HN

tel	01620 810491
fax	01620 810491
e-mail	williams.eagles@btinternet.com
web	www.eaglescairnie.com

Mr & Mrs W Denholm
Lochmill House,
3 Lade Court, Linlithgow,
West Lothian EH49 7QF

| tel | 01506 846682 |
| e-mail | williedenholm@hotmail.com |

Sit on the terrace and listen to numerous songbirds. Surprisingly, you are in the middle of St Andrews, only a 10-minute walk from the Royal and Ancient Golf Club. This tall, terraced house may be grey-stoned and traditional on the outside, but Jill has decorated the interior with a distinctly contemporary flourish. Gorgeous mosaic tables and showers, a stunning turquoise kitchen, and a bright conservatory where breakfast can be served... in the bedrooms, antique bedcovers, lovely linen and chintzes. Enchanting. Jill is easy, really friendly and generous. *Children over 12 welcome.*

An avenue of beech trees patrolled by guinea fowl leads to the house. If the sea views and the salty smack of St Andrew's Bay air don't get you, walk inside and have your senses tickled pink. The double-ended drawing room has two open fires, a grand piano, fine windows and its original pine floor – gorgeous. Great cooking, with maybe crab or pheasant served in the purple dining room; both Sandy and Frippy excel in the kitchen. From the front door head down to the beach, walk the wild coast or jump on a quad in the back field. Exceptional.

rooms	4: 1 twin, 1 double, both with shower; 1 double with bath/shower; 1 double with private bath.
room price	From £70. Singles £42.
meals	Pubs/restaurants nearby.
closed	Rarely.
directions	Into St Andrews on A917. Past Old Course Hotel. Right at 2nd mini r'bout, left through arch at 2nd mini r'bout. 250 yds on, right into Queens Gardens. Right at T-junc. House on left.

rooms	3: 1 twin with bath; 1 twin/double with shower; 1 twin/double with private bath.
room price	£60–£70. Singles from £40.
meals	Dinner £25.
closed	Rarely.
directions	From St Andrews, A917 for 2 miles for Crail. Driveway in 1st line of trees on left after St Andrews.

Jill Hardie
18 Queen's Terrace,
St Andrews, Fife KY16 9QF
tel 01334 478849
fax 01334 470283
e-mail jill_hardie@hotmail.com

Sandy & Frippy Fyfe
Kinkell,
St Andrews, Fife KY16 8PN
tel 01334 472003
fax 01334 475248
e-mail fyfe@kinkell.com
web www.kinkell.com

FIFE

A 1744 smithy – the last horse walked out in the early 1980s – which Keith and Rosie renovated 12 years ago, building the house around Keith's pipe organ. A simple place, rich in spirit, and good value. Rosie makes clothes in the workshop and you're free to wander in. There are home eggs, garden veg, Rosie cooks soups and casseroles and turns berries into jams. The sitting/breakfast room is roomy; smallish bedrooms have comfy beds and pretty florals. Both rooms are roadside, but are double-glazed and the traffic passes quietly at night. There's golf, beach walks and the fishing villages of Crail and Pittenweem to explore.

rooms	2: 1 twin with shower; 1 twin with bath/shower.
room price	£50–£60. Singles £35.
meals	Dinner from £20.
closed	Occasionally.
directions	From St Andrews, A917 for Crail. After 4 miles, ignore turning for Boarhills, & continue to small river. Over bridge; house 2nd on left.

Rosie & Keith Birkinshaw
Falside Smiddy,
Boarhills, St Andrews,
Fife KY16 8PT

tel   01334 880479
e-mail   rosiebirk@whsurf.net

HIGHLANDS

A stupendous, moated house, in the family since 1780. You get columns, a grand piano, big fireplaces, trophies, a snooker table, gilt mirrors, silver candelabras and Elizabeth, who welcomes you in the friendliest way. Beautifully Georgian, the house sits in its own estate; 2.5 lochs to fish, wonderful walks, a boat and 1,000 acres of organically reared cattle. The manor – from the antler-bedecked billiard room to the Italian hand-painted and panelled drawing room to the huge four-poster room with its bearskin – generates a sense of traditional life lived to the full. Superb.

rooms	3: 2 doubles, both with bath/shower; 1 four-poster with shower & private bath.
room price	£70. Singles £35.
meals	Dinner, 3 courses, £22.
closed	Rarely.
directions	From Inverness, A96 for Nairn. After 9.5 miles right on B9090 through Cawdor. B9090 turns left for Nairn, but continue onto B9101. At sign, right up drive.

Elizabeth & Jamie Mackintosh-Walker
Geddes House,
Nairn, Highlands IV12 5QX

tel   01667 452241
fax   01667 456707
e-mail   elizabeth@geddesonline.co.uk
web   www.elizabeth@geddesonline.co.uk

You're in the middle of nowhere, and if you follow the paths you may see wild goats or red kites. Head for the Moray Firth and look back across the water to Inverness, or walk down to Munlochy Bay in search of dolphins. Climbing roses and a remarkable 'Californian Glory' flourish outside; inside are bedrooms decorated in country style and a sitting room with hand-painted floors. There are bowls of fruit, maps and walking sticks, and a garden reclaimed from recalcitrant Black Isle gorse. Gavin runs garden tours and can take you off to Inverewe, Attadale, Cawdor and Dunrobin Castle.

Staggeringly remote, Skiary is the only surviving house of a 1765 crofting and fishing settlement. A 22-mile roller coaster road ends at Loch Hourn where you decant into a boat, or walk the final mile; no roads lead in and the water laps 20 paces from the front door. No electricity, just oil and paraffin lamps, an open fire, a 'greenhouse' dining room and country cooking to write home about, a swimming hole in the burn, tame red deer. There's stupendous walking either side of the loch (John will ferry you), while snug bedrooms come with wild flowers, fruit, torches and hotties. Incomparable.

rooms	2: 1 twin with bath; 1 twin with private shower.
room price	£46–£54. Singles from £25.
meals	2 miles to local pub.
closed	Christmas & New Year.
directions	A9 north over Kessock Bridge. First right (1 mile); then right again (0.25 mile) for Kilmuir. Straight up, follow road left, then straight on. Ignore 'No through road' sign, continue past Drynie Farm, follow road to right; house 1st left.

rooms	3 twins, all sharing bath.
room price	£170 (full-board) for two; £85 p.p.
meals	Breakfast, packed lunch & dinner included. B.Y.O.
closed	October–April.
directions	From Invergarry, A87 north; left after 5 miles to Kinloch Hourn. On for approx. 22 miles to Kinloch Hourn, at end of road; hosts will meet you with boat.

Araminta & Gavin Dallmeyer
Craigiewood,
North Kessock, Inverness,
Highlands IV1 3XG
tel   01463 731628
fax   01463 731628
e-mail   2minty@high-lights.co.uk
web   www.craigiewood.co.uk

John & Christina Everett
Skiary,
Loch Hourn, By Invergarry,
Highlands PH35 4HD
tel   01809 511214

FEEDBACK

Our work would be blossom in the wind if we didn't know what actually happens when you go to one of these places. Most of the letters we get convey tales of kindness and generosity. Occasionally we hear tales of woe — and we always listen carefully to them, and act upon them. We chat to owners about feedback, good and bad, and anonymously inspect if we hear of serious problems. We are also able to amend the write-up where it is necessary as a result of your feedback.

It is sometimes through you that we first hear that owners have handed over to someone else/expanded/cut down/become more or less welcoming. We like you to tell us if people are exceptionally kind or if you got lost following our directions. In other words, you can help keep us up-to-date between our inspections. And it's fun to learn what goes on out there.

Please refer to the report form at the back of the book.

Garramore was one of the headquarters of Special Operations Executive in World War II. Occasionally, large and aged gentlemen turn up and ask odd questions in strange accents, only to be disarmed by Julia. She runs her home in an easy, slightly irreverent style: throws over sofas, rugs, maps, shelves packed with books, walls stuffed with her mother's exceptional art. Big bedrooms come in lilacs, yellows and aquamarines, with tartan woollen blankets on comfy beds. Don't miss the beaches of Morar; when the sun's out you'll think you're in the Caribbean — well, almost!

Joan is lovely, bright and bubbly; she's turned B&B into an art form. Hers is a grand Victorian house, high on the hill with views of Loch Linnhe; whales have been sighted from the breakfast table. Bedrooms are tremendous (Jessica Lange stayed while filming *Rob Roy*): a private terrace, a Louis XV walnut bed, crushed velvet window seats, a *chaise longue*, a marble bathroom with claw-foot bath. Deep greens and reds, decanters of sherry, fresh flowers and an exquisite, carved wood fireplace. Breakfasts are wonderful: build yourself up, then climb Ben Nevis for the best view in Scotland.

rooms	6: 1 family, 1 double, both with bath; 1 twin with private shower; 3 family, sharing separate shower & bath.
room price	£40-£56. Singles £30.
meals	Pubs & restaurants 5 miles.
closed	Rarely.
directions	From Fort William, A830 to Mallaig. Approx. 4 miles past Arisaig & 1 mile before Morar.

rooms	4 doubles, all with bath/shower.
room price	£80-£92. Singles 10% off room rate.
meals	Seafood restaurants 12-minute walk.
closed	Mid-November-Easter.
directions	From Glasgow, A82 to Fort William; there, turn right up Ashburn Lane, next to Ashburn guesthouse. House on left at top.

Julia & Sophie Moore
Garramore House,
South Morar, Nr. Mallaig,
Inverness-shire PH40 4PD
tel   01687 450268
fax   01687 450268

Joan & John Campbell
The Grange,
Grange Road, Fort William,
Inverness-shire PH33 6JF
tel   01397 705516
fax   01397 701595
e-mail   jcampbell@grangefortwilliam.com
web   www.thegrange-scotland.co.uk

map: 21 entry: 617

map: 21 entry: 618

INVERNESS-SHIRE

A peaceful, no-smoking home run by Margaret, a professional musician and James, a retired chemical engineer. It is a converted coach house with stables in the beautiful Great Glen that sits among 50 wild lochside acres of rhododendron, woodland and wonderful trees. Bedrooms are traditional, and there are fabulous views of Loch Lochy and the surrounding mountains from the big picture window in the guest drawing room. Walk to the private shingle beach on the loch, spot the wild roe deer in the grounds. *Children over eight welcome.*

rooms	3: 1 twin with small shower; 1 double with bath/shower; further twin available.
room price	From £52. Singles £30-£35.
meals	Breakfast 8.30am. Good restaurants/bistro 2-5 miles.
closed	Rarely.
directions	From Spean Bridge north on A82. After 5 miles, house signed on left.

Margaret & James Cairns
Invergloy House,
Spean Bridge,
Inverness-shire PH34 4DY
tel 01397 712681
fax 01397 712681
e-mail cairns@invergloy-house.co.uk
web www.invergloy-house.co.uk

INVERNESS-SHIRE

This much loved home, in epic Highland countryside, has been in the Murray family for three generations. The house is comfortable without being imposing, an 1850 original with later add-ons, mostly clad in gleaming white wood. Christina is lively, down-to-earth, a great hostess. Wholesome, whole-hearted hospitality is guaranteed – along with home-produced honey and fruit and veg from the garden. The position is perfect for exploring the Highlands in every direction. Unexpectedly, three llamas add an exotic touch.

rooms	2: 1 double with extra single bed, with bath/shower; 1 twin with shower.
room price	£50. Singles £25.
meals	Breakfast until 9.30am. Dinner £15.
closed	Christmas & New Year.
directions	North of Aviemore for 26 miles, left onto B851 for Fort Augustus. Over bridge, through Inverarnie to Farr & past playground on left. House 2nd gate on left.

James & Christina Murray
Farr Mains,
Farr, Inverness,
Inverness-shire IV2 6XB
tel 01808 521205
fax 01808 521466
e-mail specialplaces@farrmains.freeserve.co.uk

INVERNESS-SHIRE

Pine martins nested in the hedge recently – rare indeed. This former ferryman's house is small, welcoming, homely, delightful, and you are yards from the River Spey with its spectacular mountain views. Explore the wonderful countryside or relax in the garden with a tray of tea and home-made treats. The sitting room is cosy with a woodburning stove and lots of books (no TV). Free-spirit Elizabeth, who lived in the Sudan and is a keen traveller, cooks delicious meals: heathery honeycomb, home-made bread and preserves, herbs from the garden, wild salmon. A superb base for nature lovers and explorers, and good value.

rooms	4: 1 double, 1 twin, 2 singles, sharing 1 bath & 2 wcs.
room price	£44. Singles £22.
meals	Packed lunches £5. Dinner £17. B.Y.O.
closed	Rarely.
directions	From A9, follow main road markings through village, pass golf club & cross river Spey. From B970 to Boat of Garten, house on left, just before river.

Elizabeth Matthews
The Old Ferryman's House,
Boat of Garten,
Inverness-shire PH24 3BY
tel   01479 831370
fax   01479 831370

ISLE OF SKYE

Donald looks after the garden, Rosemary cooks and bakes her own bread, the loch starts at the end of the garden and the mountains rise beyond. This is Clan MacLeod territory: Skye is steeped in inter-clan rivalries stretching back 800 years, and its history is celebrated in poetry, music and song. The house is delightful with comfy beds, fine linen, a country-house feel and tremendously spoiling hosts. Make the most of their deep knowledge of the different parts of this fascinating and varied landscape and its history.

rooms	3: 2 twins/doubles, both with bath/shower; 1 single with private bath/shower.
room price	From £70. Singles from £35.
meals	Breakfast to 9.30am. Dinner, 4 courses, £23.
closed	Christmas & New Year.
directions	From Skye Bridge, follow signs for UIG to Sligachan Hotel. Left fork to Dunvegan (22 miles). There, left (just after Health Centre) for Glendale. White house in trees after 0.75 miles.

Donald & Rosemary MacLeod
Kinlochfollart,
By Dunvegan,
Isle of Skye IV55 8WQ
tel   01470 521470
fax   01470 521740
e-mail   klfskye@tiscali.co.uk
web   www.klfskye.co.uk

ISLE OF SKYE

The sky envelops you, sea, lochs and views surround you, and Linda has created a quietly delightful retreat. The 300-year-old tacksman's house is hidden down a private drive – and with what energy and enthusiasm it has been renovated. Marcus is restoring the walled garden which produces certified organic fruit and veg. Lovely views from your bedroom and the family sitting room, both bathed in an explosion of golden light at sunset; fresh flowers, bathrobes, peace and seclusion. Wander down to the beach through an avenue of oaks, explore the island by pony. *Self-catering available. See back of book.*

rooms	3: 1 double with shower; 1 double with private bath; 1 twin with shared bath, let only to members of the same party.
room price	From £80. Singles £50.
meals	Restaurant 3 miles.
closed	Christmas & New Year.
directions	Cross Skye Bridge; A87 north, through Broadford & Portree. At Borve, A850 (left fork) for Dunvegan. Pass Treaslane river & 2 miles on, gates & Gate Lodge. House 0.5 miles along drive through trees.

Marcus & Linda Ridsdill-Smith
Lyndale House,
Edinbane, Isle of Skye IV51 9PX
tel   01470 582329
e-mail   linda@lyndale.net
web   www.lyndale.net

map: 20 entry: 623

MORAY

The Meiklejohn coat of arms flies from the flag pole, a mere apple's throw from the orchard in which King Malcolm was murdered 1,000 years ago. This is a small country mansion built in 1776, its huge rooms crammed with beautiful things. A grand double-aspect drawing room, a flower-filled dining room and enormous bedrooms with sofas at the foot of four-posters. Blervie is "a restoration in progress", but much has been accomplished. There are original doors and shutters, antiques, antlers, violins; the stone stairs came from Blervie Castle, and there's the sweet smell of burnt beech from the grand marble fireplaces. Magical.

rooms	2: 1 four-poster with single bed & private bath; 1 four-poster with bath.
room price	£60. Singles £30.
meals	Breakfast until 9.30am. Dinner, 4 courses, £22.
closed	Christmas & New Year.
directions	From A96 to Forres. South at clocktower, straight across at r'bout & take B9010. Pass hospital & 1 mile on, left at Mains of Blervie sign. Right at farm.

Paddy & Fiona Meiklejohn
Blervie,
By Forres, Moray IV36 2RH
tel   01309 672358
fax   01309 672358
e-mail   meiklejohn@btinternet.com

map: 22 entry: 624

This is the grand home of an illustrious family: Macleans have lived here since 1862. The carpet in the hall is clan tartan, the solid oak stair is hung with oils, standards and the odd ceremonial sword. John farms 500 acres, Veronica runs a play school and cooks sublimely. You breakfast in the conservatory/kitchen overlooking the walled garden, and dine at night in an immensely grand dining room. A winter fire crackles in the drawing room. Traditional bedrooms have books and lovely views; one is decorated eccentrically in electric pink. The peace is interrupted only by the odd call of the guinea fowl.

Simple but freshly decorated and comfortable bedrooms, crisp, clean air and a silence disturbed only by wildlife… your sleep will be sound. Come if you love space, animals and the values of a hard working farm. The views make the heart soar and there are 1,300 acres to roam with sheep, cattle, horses and wildlife. An excellent place for families with an easy atmosphere – Arran, in spring, encourages children to bottle-feed lambs; she and John are open and friendly. Sit in the walled garden, or set off to explore the nearby Roman encampment, Lyne Fort. Particularly good value.

rooms	3: 1 twin with bath; 1 twin with private bath & shower; 1 single with private bath.
room price	£60-£70. Singles from £30.
meals	Dinner, 3 courses, £20.
closed	Rarely.
directions	From Elgin, A96 west for Forres & Inverness. After 2.5 miles, right onto B9013 for Burghead. After 1 mile, signed right at x-roads. Continue to sign 'Westfield House & office'.

rooms	3: 2 doubles, 1 twin, sharing 2 baths.
room price	£40-£44. Singles £24.
meals	Breakfast 8-9am. Packed lunch £3-£5. Supper £12. Dinner, 4 courses, £24. B.Y.O.
closed	Christmas Day.
directions	4 miles west of Peebles on A72, signed on right-hand side of main road.

John & Veronica Maclean
Westfield House,
Nr. Elgin, Moray IV30 8XL
tel   01343 547308
fax   01343 551340
e-mail veronicamaclean@hotmail.com

Arran & John Waddell
Lyne Farmhouse,
Lyne Farm, Peebles,
Peeblesshire EH45 8NR
tel   01721 740255
fax   01721 740255
e-mail awaddell@farming.co.uk
web   www.lynefarm.co.uk

map: 22 entry: 625

map: 18 entry: 626

In ancient times Rannoch was cattle-rustling country and a hint of Wild West lingers. Surprisingly you could arrive in some style — from Euston on the overnight sleeper; your hosts will pick you up. But any elegance you may experience on board is beaten in spades at the lodge: the house and its position are beyond reproach. Ceiling-to-floor windows in the drawing room look straight down the loch (it starts 30 paces from the fire), tropical ferns flourish in the conservatory, and one of the bedrooms has an 1880s bathroom. Walk through ancient Caledonian pine forest, fish and sail on the loch. A perfect place.

An 18th-century farm building halfway up a mountain: Lindsay has carried out award-winning renovation and is now working on the garden. Inside: patchwork bedspreads, blue-and-white Portuguese tiles, seagrass matting and a woodburning stove. You have your own kitchen, dining and sitting room, so you can self-cater (minimum three days), too. Lindsay is charming and loves nurturing her garden, her pets and her guests. Sit on the patio as you tuck into her fruitcake, gaze at snow-capped mountain-to-loch views. The sunsets and walks are fabulous. *Children over eight welcome.*

rooms	3: 2 twins with bath; 1 twin/double with shower & bath.
room price	£80. Singles £40.
meals	Dinner, 3 courses, £25. Packed lunch £10.
closed	Christmas & occasionally.
directions	Take Calvine turn from A9. After 10 miles right towards Kinloch Rannoch. In main square, left over bridge. First right on South Loch Road. House 10 miles on right, signed.

rooms	2: 1 double, 1 twin, sharing private bath & sitting room. Only let to same party.
room price	£60. Singles £42.
meals	Dinner, 3 courses with wine, £20. Inn 0.75 miles.
closed	Christmas & New Year.
directions	From A9 north of Pitlochry, take Killiecrankie turning. Left onto B8019 for Tummel Bridge & Kinloch Rannoch for 8 miles to Loch Tummel Inn. House up forestry track on right, 0.75 miles on.

Archie & Anne Boyd
Finnart Lodge,
Rannoch, Perth & Kinross PH17 2QF
tel   01882 633366
fax   01882 633232
e-mail   aandaboyd@aol.com
web   www.finnart-lodge.co.uk

Lindsay Morison
Grenich Steading,
Strathtummel, Pitlochry,
Perth & Kinross PH16 5RT
tel   01882 634332

Glenmarkie stands three and a half miles up a track, in a hidden glen; if you are looking for peace and seclusion, you've found it. Luxury, too. Patricia has renovated this shooting lodge with devotion: an 1880 'boudoir grand' in the main hall, three country-house sitting rooms, an enormous oak dining table from Winchester College, and an indoor pool with a sauna. There's a breathtaking, seven-mile view down the glen and a loch in front of the house where red and roe deer stop to drink, a hundred at a time. Bedrooms are delightful. You can stand in front of a fire and listen to the wind roar past outside. Magic.

Ancient, historic and packed with interest, the house was begun as a tower in 1585 and added to until Victorian times and into the present century. Inside it is delightfully old-fashioned, even a little threadbare in places but so much to compensate: beautiful plasterwork, marble busts, antiques, impressive staircase, open fires. Paul is a conservationist and writer and both he and Louise welcome with grace and humour and are generous in a naturally spontaneous way. You can roam freely on the estate with its parkland, woods and heather moorland.

rooms	4: 1 double with bath & shower; 1 double, 1 twin, both with private bath & shower; 1 single with shower.
room price	£80-£100. Singles £40-£50.
meals	Supper £15. Dinner, 4 courses, £28.
closed	Rarely.
directions	B951 east from Kirriemuir. Right 0.5 miles west of Kirkton of Glenisla, following signs for Glenmarkie riding centre. Follow track for 3.5 miles. House visible 1 mile up the track.

rooms	3: 1 double with shared bath; 1 four-poster with private bath; further single available.
room price	£60-£70. Singles £30-£35.
meals	Dinner £15-£20.
closed	Christmas & New Year.
directions	From Blairgowrie, A926 to Kirriemuir. After 5 miles, left to Alyth. Through town on Airlie St. After 2.5 miles, round sharp left bend. Right into drive.

	Patricia & Bernard Dukes
	Glenmarkie Lodge,
	Glen Isla, by Blairgowrie,
	Perth & Kinross PH11 8QB
tel	01575 582343
fax	01575 582343
e-mail	bernard.dukes@btinternet.com
web	www.glenmarkielodge.co.uk

	Paul & Louise Ramsay
	Bamff House,
	Alyth, Blairgowrie,
	Perth & Kinross PH11 8LF
tel	01828 632992
fax	01828 632992
e-mail	louiseramsay@bamff.demon.co.uk
web	www.bamff.co.uk

map: 22 entry: 629

map: 22 entry: 630

The view from the balcony that circles the drawing room is simply stunning, and the deep gorge provides fabulous walks. Nicky and Lachie battle to keep up with the demands of the vast, impressive home – it's been in the family for 500 years; you, too, will forgive it any mustiness or dustiness. Staying here is a memorable experience – nothing contrived, sterile or luxurious, but so much drama and intrigue this could be the setting for a film. Breakfast is served in the 18th-century library, and you have use of the Regency drawing room, too.

Historic, traditional, a country house set in lovely gardens and run by delightful people. The bedrooms are big, utterly charming and among the most comfortable that we have stayed in. There's a 170-acre private loch where birds can be observed and pike fished, a great organ halfway up the main stairs with air pumped from a building in the grounds, and a 16th-century central building with wings added in 1780 to a design filched from Adam. So much of interest. Elegant furniture, lovely pictures, a magnificent setting, wonderful hosts. *Self-catering available. See back of book.*

rooms	2: 1 four-poster with bath; 1 twin with extra single bed & private bath.
room price	£70. Singles £35.
meals	Breakfast 8-9am. Restaurant 3 miles, pub 6 miles.
closed	Christmas & New Year.
directions	From Blairgowrie, A93 for Braemar for 2 miles. Just before end of 30mph limit, sharp right-hand bend, with drive on right. Follow drive for 1 mile.

rooms	3: 1 twin, 1 double, 1 with bath, 1 with bath/shower. Children's twin available, sharing parents' bathroom.
room price	£70-£80. Singles from £40.
meals	Pubs/restaurants 2 miles.
closed	Christmas & New Year.
directions	From Blairgowrie, onto A923 for Dunkeld. Look for sign saying 'Kinloch. Drive safely'. 1st entrance on left after sign.

Nicky & Lachie Rattray
Craighall Castle,
Blairgowrie,
Perth & Kinross PH10 7JB
tel 01250 874749
fax 01250 874749
e-mail lrattray@calinet.co.uk

Kenneth & Nicolette Lumsden
Marlee House,
Kinloch, Blairgowrie,
Perth & Kinross PH10 6SD
tel 01250 884216

A slice of heaven half a mile down the track. Eight acres and three wee lochs cradle these converted cottages. Inside, a warm feel, fresh colours, a tidy home; the bedroom is excellent, with white bathrobes and good linen. Other bounties include free-range organic eggs, an Aga-cooked breakfast, a huge sitting room with an open fire, lovely views towards the Grampians – and Norman, the smiling farmer, who had been playfully banished (unsuccessfully) from his home the afternoon we visited so as not to make the place look untidy. Nicely down-to-earth people with a gentle sense of humour; good value, too.

Expensive, but worth it. Here is huge comfort: generously furnished, elegant bedrooms and bathrooms to expand in, beautiful food served at one large table, house-party style; you will be spoiled. The approach sets the scene – a mile-long drive through wood and rhododendron leads to formal gardens, exotic trees, ferny burn and waterfall. It is a surprising house (built in 1969) and the third to be built on this historic site; you can see the remains of earlier castles. The interiors are magnificent, your hosts are great fun. *Children over 12 welcome.*

rooms	1 twin with bath.
room price	£50-£55. Singles from £25.
meals	Pub/restaurant 3 miles.
closed	Christmas & New Year.
directions	A85 west from Perth. After 6 miles, right for Glenalmond, Harrietfield; after 4 miles, left for Glenalmond; pass G. College, then right, for Mains of Cairnies. Sharp right at white gate; on right.

rooms	3: 2 twins/doubles, both with bath/shower; 1 twin/double with bath.
room price	From £140. Singles from £85.
meals	Breakfast 8-9.30am. Dinner, 3 courses, £30.
closed	Christmas & New Year.
directions	From M90 Broxden r'bout, A93 for Perth for 1 mile, then sharp right onto B9112 for Dunning. After 2.7 miles, wrought-iron gates on right.

Claire Milne
Cairnies Cottage,
Glenalmond,
Perth & Kinross PH1 3SE

tel   01738 880381
fax   01738 880381

Derek & Angela Straker
Dupplin Castle,
By Aberdalgie, Perth,
Perth & Kinross PH2 0PY

tel   01738 623224
fax   01738 444140
e-mail   dupplin@netcomuk.co.uk
web   www.dupplin.co.uk

map: 22 entry: 633

map: 22 entry: 634

Anne clearly has the Midas touch: a traditional Scottish farmhouse outside and, inside, a rainbow of colour and light. Pale wooden floors and heapfuls of flowers, a conservatory/dining room overlooking a wonderful garden, and a gate leading to the hills – the Coronation Way runs through the farm. Big bedrooms are delightful: coral walls, crisp linen, old rugs, masses of space, windows framing country views; bathrooms spoil. Don't miss Anne's food: it, too, is exceptional. Guests love it here, and even though the A90, a half mile away, can be busy by day, it passes quietly at night.

A lovely Georgian manse tragically burnt down in 1996 but rebuilt with taste, elegance and style. Light wood predominates and rooms are warm with cornicing, thick carpets, combed ceilings, traditional bedding and lots of space. Joanna and Duncan clearly enjoy doing B&B and the atmosphere is relaxed and informal. Eat in the wonderful country kitchen or in the conservatory overlooking a pretty walled garden with colourful borders. Under five miles from the motorway and 35 from Edinburgh.

rooms	3: 1 double with bath/shower; 1 twin with bath; 1 twin with shower.
room price	£70–£80. Singles from £45.
meals	Breakfast 7.30–9am. Dinner £25.
closed	Rarely.
directions	From A90 Perth to Dundee road, Kinfauns exit (not Kinfauns Castle). Drive up hill for 0.25 miles, left, & straight up hill to gates on left.

rooms	2: 1 twin with bath/shower; 1 twin with private bath.
room price	£60–£64. Singles £30–£32.
meals	Dinner from £20.
closed	Christmas & New Year.
directions	From Edinburgh, cross Forth Road Bridge. Follow M90 to junc. 8. Through Glenfarg, then 1st right, for Arngask. 1st house on right. From north leave M90 at junc. 9 for Glenfarg, then left to Arngask after approx. 6 miles.

Anne & David MacLehose
Over Kinfauns,
Perth, Perth & Kinross PH2 7LD
tel	01738 860538
fax	01738 860803
e-mail	b&b@overkinfauns.co.uk
web	www.overkinfauns.co.uk

Joanna & Duncan Cameron
The Old Manse,
Arngask, Glenfarg,
Perth & Kinross PH2 9QA
tel	01577 830394
fax	01577 830394
e-mail	duncanandjoanna@aol.com

It is a delight: now lovingly restored and seamlessly extended, the old farmhouse has comfortable cottagey bedrooms, pristine shower rooms and an elegant drawing room with a little tower built especially to take in the view that sweeps down the valley to the 'links' of the Forth. Your hosts are ebullient and enthusiastic – ask Hamish about all things Scottish and try Frances's fragrant jams and jellies. There are books, pictures, family antiques and a very special garden, but a Winnie the Pooh weathervane says it all: this is a fun place to stay, and the Lindsays couldn't be kinder. *Children and dogs by arrangement.*

Once the farmhouse for Drummond Castle, now the B&B for those who wish to visit the castle gardens. Carola and Robert have turned the old dairy into a cosy bolthole, with *toile de Jouy* fabrics, a sparkling white bathroom with lovely red towels, and wicker chairs on your own private terrace. You breakfast in the main house with a 16th-century tapestry on the wall. The formal parterre gardens date from 1630 and are considered to be among the finest in Europe. The castle, too, is magical, and has connections with Robert the Bruce, Mary Queen of Scots, James IV, Bonnie Prince Charlie and Cromwell.

rooms	2: 1 twin, 1 double, both with private shower.
room price	From £50. Singles from £25.
meals	Breakfast 7.30am onwards. Light supper available. Good pub 1 mile.
closed	Rarely.
directions	From M90, junc. 6, then A977 to Kincardine Bridge. 1 mile after The Crook of Devon, right to Rumbling Bridge & Crieff (A823). 1 mile on, house signed to right; at end of lane.

rooms	1 twin with bath/shower.
room price	£60. Singles £35.
meals	Excellent restaurants/pubs nearby.
closed	Rarely.
directions	Off A9 on A822; left after Muthill marked golf course. 1st right past cottage; next left; up drive on right.

Frances & Hamish Lindsay
Caplawhead,
Rumbling Bridge,
By Yetts o' Muckhart, Nr Kinross,
Perth & Kinross KY13 0QD
tel   01259 781556
e-mail   hamish-frances@caplawhead.freeserve.co.uk

Carola & Robert Philippi
Mains of Drummond,
Crieff, Perth & Kinross PH7 4JA
tel   01764 681285

A grand old country pile set in 200 acres, with its own river in which you may spy the odd commuting salmon. In the house, massive rooms, elegantly proportioned, one with an exceptional 1750s plaster-moulded ceiling. Long shuttered windows give big views across the lawn to an ancient plane tree; its much older sibling blew down in 1868 and was turned into furniture, some of which fills the hall. Bedrooms have old rugs, long curtains, beautiful furniture – just what you'd hope for. Chopin dedicated two nocturnes to Jane Stirling, a former daughter of the house, and probably played here.

A 1690 farmhouse full of beautiful pieces: ancient *armoires*, mahogany dressers, creaking floorboards and the biggest beds. Bedrooms have great style. One has a bath in which you can lie and look out on the fields, both have pretty floral fabrics and lots of books. Outside there's a one-acre walled garden and a tennis court. You dine in a conservatory overlooking the garden with views to distant Stirling Castle and the Wallace Monument; dinner may be salmon from the Teith or game from the local hills. Expect to add an ounce or three. *Self-catering available. See back of book.*

rooms	2 twins, both with bath/shower.
room price	£76. Singles from £48.
meals	Dinner £25.
closed	Rarely.
directions	From junc. 11 of M9, B8033 for Dunblane. Get in right hand lane & take 1st right across reservation to lodge. Keep on drive, over bridge, up hill to house.

rooms	2: 1 double, 1 twin/double, both with bath/shower.
room price	£76-£80. Singles £53-£55.
meals	Breakfast 8.30-9am. Dinner £25.
closed	Christmas.
directions	From M9, north, junc. 10 onto A84 for Doune. After 5 miles, left on B826 for Thornhill. Drive on left after 2.2 miles, right off farm drive.

Sue & Patrick Stirling-Aird
Kippenross,
Dunblane,
Perth & Kinross FK15 0LQ
tel   01786 824048
fax   01786 824482
e-mail   kippenross@hotmail.com

Fiona & Colin Graham
Mackeanston House,
Doune, Trossachs,
Perth & Kinross FK16 6AX
tel   01786 850213
fax   01786 850414
e-mail   enquiries@mackeanstonhouse.co.uk
web   www.mackeanstonhouse.co.uk

Culture seekers, sailors, walkers and cyclists will all be happy here. After such activity, the Andersons' substantial Victorian farmhouse is the ideal place for gentle and cosseting recovery. Large, light bedrooms sport traditional furniture and modern paintings; a warm red sitting room has a wood-burning stove and a huge view over Barr Loch and the Renfrewshire Hills. Linger over a 'Slow Food' dinner of home-grown Jacob lamb or Highland beef with vegetables, salad and herbs from the elegant two-acre garden.

A neat, professionally run house and Kate shows much attention to detail and friendliness. Her cooking is good, too: she places importance on presentation and uses whatever is fresh, local and best; everything, including bread and the cake on your tea tray, is home-made. Bed linens and decor are fully co-ordinated and Kate puts fresh flowers in the rooms and smellies in the bathroom. The whitewashed croft was a blacksmith's until the 50s; the views are from the modern conservatory or the terrace, to the distant An Teallach mountain range. The sea and wonderful beaches are close by.

rooms	3: 1 double/family, 1 twin, 1 double, all with shower.
room price	£60-£80. Singles from £45.
meals	Breakfast 7-9am. Packed lunch £7. Dinner £25.
closed	Rarely.
directions	From Glasgow, M8 west to junc. 28a, A737 to Irvine. After 7 miles, right on A760 to Largs. 2 miles past Lochwinnoch under railway bridge, 600 yds on left. Brown tourist signs.

rooms	3: 1 double with shower; 1 double with bath; 1 double with private shower.
room price	£70-£90. Singles £40-£50. Half-board £65-£75 p.p.
meals	Breakfast until 9.30am. Packed lunch £6. Dinner, 4 courses, £25 (not Sundays).
closed	December.
directions	From Inverness on A835 towards Ullapool. Left 12 miles south of Ullapool onto A832 coastal route to Gairloch. 29 miles from this junction, house last on left in Laide.

Janet Anderson
East Lochhead,
Largs Road, Lochwinnoch,
Renfrewshire PA12 4DX

tel	01505 842610
fax	01505 842610
e-mail	admin@eastlochhead.co.uk
web	www.eastlochhead.co.uk

Kate & Steve Macdonald
The Old Smiddy,
Laide, Ross-shire IV22 2NB

tel	01445 731425
fax	01445 731696
e-mail	oldsmiddy@aol.com
web	www.oldsmiddy.co.uk

Windows for walls in this modern, curved, lochside house: a panorama of inspirational views unfolds as you move from room to room. The sitting room welcomes with its grand piano, open fire, books, CDs, games and telescope; bedrooms, one with a balcony, have comfortable beds, wicker chairs, crisp duvets and every little luxury. Anne, good company, is a trained chef who searches out the best local ingredients for her simple, modern cooking. After a perfect breakfast with real orange juice, explore the lush garden, or stroll to your rocky private beach and search for the cave. *4% surcharge for credit cards.*

A delightful house, 15th century at the back, 1870 at the front, with lawns that tumble towards the loch. The interior is equally impressive, with the original tiled floor in the hall, an open fire in the drawing room and Nina Campbell fabric on the dining room wall. Lucinda has redecorated with flair, bringing a bright and breezy county-house elegance to her home. One of the bedrooms comes in lilacs and purples and one of the bathrooms has loch views – spot rare birdlife while you soak. There's a moor out back, a brand new tennis court hidden away at the front, and you can fish on the loch. The views are all you'd hope for.

rooms	3: 1 double, 2 twins, all with bath/shower.
room price	£76-£84. Singles £58-£62.
meals	Packed lunch from £7.50. Dinner, 4 courses, £28.
closed	Christmas & New Year.
directions	On outskirts of Ullapool from Inverness on A835, left immed. after 4th 40mph sign. Take cattle grid on right & left fork down to house.

rooms	3: 1 double with bath & shower; 1 double, 1 twin, with shared bath.
room price	£60-£70. Singles £35.
meals	Dinner, 3 courses, £25.
closed	Occasionally.
directions	A9 for Tain, then B9165 for Fearn. First left for Loandhu, then 1.5 miles & on left.

Anne Holloway
Tanglewood House,
Ullapool, Ross-shire IV26 2TB
tel   01854 612059
fax   01854 612059
e-mail   tanglewoodhouse@ecosse.net
web   www.tanglewoodhouse.co.uk

Lady Poole
Loch Eye House,
Fearn, Ross-shire IV20 1RS
tel   01862 832297
fax   01862 832914
e-mail   loofy@ndirect.co.uk

map: 25 entry: 643

map: 22 entry: 644

ROSS-SHIRE

Braelangwell is a jaw-dropper: a 1790 Georgian mansion set in 77 acres, much of which is ancient woodland. Three cows mow the lawn while Himalayan musk roses climb up one side of the house. Walk through the pillared entrance and you find a hall with an 1840-painted ceiling, a ballroom in Wedgewood blue, a stone-flagged billiard room, and a dining room with painted floorboards and floor-to-ceiling windows. In the bedrooms you may find a brass bed, a slipper bath, *toile de Jouy* fabrics, Farrow & Ball paints; the four-poster Garden Room is well worth the out-splash. Cromarty, as in the shipping forecast, is five miles away.

rooms	3: 1 four-poster with bath; 1 double with private bath; 1 twin with bath & shower.
room price	£70–£100. Singles from £60.
meals	Breakfast until 9am. Pubs/restaurants 5 miles.
closed	December–February.
directions	Through Munlochy; leave A832 for B9160; on for three miles; ignore right turn for Mount High & phone box; on till house signed left, through gates.

Laura & Ronnie Strange
Braelangwell House,
Balblair, Black Isle,
Ross-shire IV7 8LT

tel	01381 610353
fax	01381 610467
e-mail	braelangwell@btinternet.com
web	www.btinternet.com/~braelangwell

ROXBURGHSHIRE

A visiting child was heard to exclaim that she loved this house: "there isn't a modern thing in it!" Sir Walter Scott, who often visited his uncle and aunt here, might well have agreed. But Lessudden, though 16th century with a magnificent 17th-century staircase, does make a few nods to modernity: there's central heating and Angie's excellent food is cooked in a sparkling new kitchen. Bedrooms are comfortable and homely; one overlooks the Cheviots, the other the Eildons. This tower house in the Tweed valley is a warm and attractive family home, with a relaxed atmosphere, assorted animals and a possible ghost or two.

rooms	2: 1 twin with bath; 1 twin with private bath.
room price	£50–£60. Singles £35.
meals	Dinner, 3 courses, £25.
closed	Rarely.
directions	North on A68 to St Boswells. Right opp. Bucclench Arms Hotel, on through village; turn to golf course on left, then left up drive.

Mrs Douglas-Hamilton
Lessudden,
St Boswells,
Roxburghshire TD6 0BH

tel	01835 823244
e-mail	alasdaird@lineone.net

SCOTTISH BORDERS

A 17th-century farmhouse with 1908 restorations and additions and an unusual clapboard extension. The house is imbued with the spirit of the Scottish Arts & Crafts movement: ornate wrought-ironwork and decorative carvings and an amazing 16th-century Florentine ceiling in the drawing room. Great attention to detail here – fruit and flowers in your deeply comfortable rooms, oil lamps on the tables at supper. Bob cooks the freshest ingredients: wild mushrooms, organic hill lamb, garden herbs – all delicious. Sleep soundly beside the green of the Borders' sheep-farming village, awake to stunning views.

rooms	5: 2 doubles, 2 twins/doubles, 1 twin, all with bath/shower.
room price	£80. Singles £50.
meals	Breakfast 8-9.30am. Dinner £25.
closed	Christmas, January & February.
directions	From Biggar, A702 for Edinburgh. Just outside Biggar, right on A72 for Skirling. Big wooden house on right opp. village green.

	Bob & Isobel Hunter
	Skirling House,
	Skirling, By Biggar,
	Scottish Borders ML12 6HD
tel	01899 860274
fax	01899 860255
e-mail	enquiry@skirlinghouse.com
web	www.skirlinghouse.com

map: 18 entry: 647

SCOTTISH BORDERS

The south-facing front bedrooms have the views – be captivated by the tranquil, rolling Borders at their most romantically beautiful. The house is part 18th century and dark heavy furniture adds a solid Victorian feel. Bedspreads are patterned, walls pale pink and beige; there's a big log fire in the sitting room to cheer you on chilly days. Johan will tell you all about the best castles and keeps, gardens, walks and rivers, but don't dash off to explore until you've eaten Jill's sustaining Scottish breakfast with haggis; her smoked salmon and scrambled eggs are equally delicious. *Discounts for longer stays.*

rooms	3: 2 doubles, 1 twin/double, all with bath/shower.
room price	£50-£56. Singles from £37.
meals	Walker's supper from £9. Good food & real ale pub in village.
closed	Christmas.
directions	From Jedburgh, A68 for Edinburgh. Left after 3.5 miles to Ancrum. Fork left to Denholm before village. After 1.75 miles, right, signed Lilliesleaf. Up hill 0.75 miles, then left to house.

	Jill & Johan Hensens
	Ancrum Craig,
	Ancrum, By Jedburgh,
	Scottish Borders TD8 6UN
tel	01835 830280
fax	01835 830259
e-mail	acas@ancrumcraig.clara.net
web	www.ancrumcraig.co.uk

map: 18 entry: 648

COTTISH BORDERS

Highland cattle graze contentedly as you drive up to the early 17th-century laird's house — you are in the magnificent Borders and Bonchester is a pretty village in the middle of the hills. There are over 140 species of wild flowers in the surrounding countryside and 60 acres of woodland and grazing, so you are undisturbed by 21st-century noise. You breakfast in the big kitchen at one large table and there's a sitting room with woodburner for guests; bedrooms are supremely comfortable and the house filled with lovely things. Before dinner relax with your hosts over a drink — they are super people. *Horse stabling available.*

rooms	2: 1 twin, 1 double (with extra bed), both with private bath or shower.
room price	£70-£80. Singles from £35.
meals	Dinner, with drinks, £28.
closed	Rarely.
directions	A68 over Border & 1st left onto B6088 for Chesters. Through Chesters; enter Bonchester down hill towards large bridge. Pass The Horse & Hounds. Over small bridge; drive on left.

Christopher & Jacqui McLean May
Hobsburn,
Bonchester Bridge, Hawick,
Scottish Borders TD9 8JW
tel   01450 860720
fax   01450 860330
e-mail   b+b@mcleanmay.com
web   www.mcleanmay.com

map: 18 entry: 649

SELKIRKSHIRE

A wonderfully peaceful place in the rolling hills of the Scottish Borders, ideal for families or walkers who want to feel at one with nature. This is an organic farm producing milk from British Friesians and meat and wool from Scottish Mule ewes: a real back-to-nature approach. Simple bedrooms are in traditional farmhouse style; all the nooks and crannies you'd expect to find in a 1700s house, but with rooms brightened by big windows. From the family room you can see the old Border keeps and a spider web of stone walls. Sheila and Martyn have detailed walking maps for you and could not be more helpful.

rooms	2: 1 double with shower; 1 family with private bath.
room price	£46. Singles £28. Family room £55.
meals	Breakfast usually 8.30am. Packed lunch from £4. Dinner from £12.
closed	Rarely.
directions	North from Galashiels, A7 past Torwoodlea golf course & right to Langshaw. After 2 miles, right at T-junc., then left at Earlston sign in Langshaw. White house, in trees, signed at farm road.

Sheila & Martyn Bergius
Over Langshaw Farm,
Galashiels, Selkirkshire TD1 2PE
tel   01896 860244
fax   01896 860244
e-mail   bergius@overlangshaw.fsnet.co.uk

map: 18 entry: 650

STIRLING

A Grade II-listed Georgian country house standing in 28 acres; roe deer 'prune' the roses, pheasants roam, wild flowers flourish. George Buchanan, tutor to James VI of Scotland, was born here. Walking sticks and the bell of HMS Tempest in the porch, long rugs and wooden floors in the hall, an open fire and bay windows in the drawing room. At breakfast, sit at the big oak dining room table and gaze out across open country to the local distillery in the distance. Big bedrooms are excellent: crisp linen, electric blankets, pristine bathrooms, fresh flowers – and a piano on the landing.

rooms	3: 1 twin with bath; 2 doubles, sharing bath. Doubles only let to members of same party.
room price	£60. Singles £30.
meals	Good pubs/restaurants within 2 miles.
closed	Rarely.
directions	4 miles west of Blanefield. Left off A81 opp. Cairn Conservatories. After 300 yds, house 1st entrance on left after bridge.

Rozie Parker
The Moss,
Killearn, Stirling G63 9LJ

tel	01360 550053
fax	01360 550053
e-mail	themoss@freeuk.com

SUTHERLAND

Caroline was up to her eyes in it the day we visited, but she still found time to rustle up venison sausages for lunch while keeping an eye on her new arrivals – six lambs that had been born that morning, one of which was asleep in front of the Aga. Outside, 21 hens and eight ducks roamed the garden, and you eat their eggs at breakfast, which is served either in the kitchen with Caroline, or in the dining room with the view. Bedrooms are snug: library steps for bedside tables, electric blankets, old *armoires*, tartan blankets. Rogart's hills await your feet. *2% credit card charge. Dogs by arrangement.*

rooms	2 doubles, both with private bath.
room price	£80. Singles £40.
meals	Dinner, 2-4 courses, £14-£25. B.Y.O.
closed	Occasionally.
directions	From Inverness, A9 north. Cross Dornoch bridge. 14 miles on, A839 to Lairg. Cross small bridge in Rogart & sharp right uphill, for St Callan's church. House 1.5 miles on, on right, next to church.

Robert & Caroline Mills
St Callan's Manse,
Rogart, Sutherland IV28 3XE

tel	01408 641363
fax	01408 641313
e-mail	saintcallan@aol.com
web	www.miltonbankcottages.co.uk

An early-1800s ivy-clad farmhouse, Chlenry stands in its own glen by the Southern Upland Way. Delightful flowers, fresh fruit, bathrobes and biscuits await in your bedroom – and you fall asleep to the country sounds of the tumbling burn, the hoot of the owl and the stir of retiring pheasants and sheep. Bathrooms are large with deep old-fashioned tubs and everything that you may have left behind. The dining room is painted a deep, warm red – it's flower-filled in summer, fire-lit in winter. Meals can be simple or elaborate, often with game or fresh salmon. There are some beautiful gardens to visit nearby.

A gorgeous home, run with great charm by Liz and Peter. Chief among its many architectural virtues is the garden room, spectacular with original windows, books, maps, rugs, wall hangings and local art – all the colours of the rainbow. In the dining room ancestors peer down from the walls; in the hall, the paintings are modern. Georgian windows give country views, there's an open fire in the drawing room, and the odd sloping floor. Bedrooms are just as good, very private (in a different wing). One is huge, with room for a sofa, and an armchair in the bathroom. People who come vow to return.

rooms	2: 1 twin, 1 double, 1 with private bath, 1 with shared.
room price	£60. Singles £35.
meals	Breakfast until 9.30am. Packed lunch £5. Supper, 2 courses, £12.50. Dinner, 4 courses, £26.
closed	Christmas & New Year.
directions	A75 for Stranraer. In Castle Kennedy, right opp. Esso station. Approx. 1.25 miles on, after right bend, right signed Chlenry. Down hill, farmhouse 300 yds on left.

rooms	2: 1 twin/double with bath/shower; 1 double with bath.
room price	£56. Singles £34.
meals	Breakfast 7.30-8.30am. Dinner, 3 courses, £20.
closed	Rarely.
directions	From Stranraer, A77 for Portpatrick for 1.5 miles. Straight on at A716 for Drummore. Drive on left after approx. 1 mile, at junction with B7077 signed Newton Stewart.

David & Ginny Wolseley Brinton
Chlenry Farmhouse,
Castle Kennedy, Stranraer,
Wigtownshire DG9 8SL
tel   01776 705316
fax   01776 889488
e-mail   wolseleybrinton@aol.com

Peter & Liz Whitworth
Kildrochet House,
By Stranraer,
Wigtownshire DG9 9BB
tel   01776 820216
fax   01776 820216
e-mail   kildrochet@compuserve.com
web   www.kildrochet.co.uk

map: 17 entry: 653

map: 17 entry: 654

www.thirdangle.com

WALES

ANGLESEY

Our inspector was blown away by it – "unbelievable!" An adventure from the moment you leave your car and are taken in the 4x4 vehicle along the cliffs to this isolated outpost on an RSPB Reserve. The old Fog House (a former signal station for Trinity House) is now converted into a bird-watching observatory. Philippa cares deeply about guests and is generous with everything, food included. The dining room and quiet sitting areas have panoramic views. The bedrooms, part of the former keeper's quarters, are simple and attractive. Don't forget waterproofs and binoculars. *Advance request for brochure and booking essential.*

rooms	2: 1 double next to private shower; 1 twin with shared/private bath.
room price	£60. Singles £32.
meals	Dinner, 3 courses with wine, from £20.
closed	November–March.
directions	On Holyhead seafront, take upper road on left. After 2 bridges, Warden's House at Breakwater Country Park on left. Phone to be collected. If coming by train or ferry, ring from station.

Philippa Jacobs
North Stack,
c/o 4 Lower Park Street, Holyhead,
Anglesey LL65 1DU
tel   01407 761252

map: 12 entry: 655

CARDIFF

Minutes from the beach, the limestone house with pretty terraced cottage garden and veranda has a thoroughly relaxing feel. On fine days, breakfast outside and watch the boats on the Bristol Channel as you tuck into Glamorgan sausages (leek and Caerphilly cheese) and home-grown tomatoes. Bedrooms are fresh and light with mahogany furniture, unusual paintings, comfy beds, goosedown duvets and lovely patterned and crocheted antique bedspreads. Jane and David are easy-going, generous hosts – there's even a small bottle of wine in your room. It's a short hop to Cardiff centre and airport.

rooms	3: 1 double with bath & shower; 2 doubles with shared bath (second let only to members of same party).
room price	£40-£60. Singles £35.
meals	Packed lunches £4. A short walk from excellent restaurants.
closed	Rarely.
directions	At r'bout with clock in Penarth centre, go straight on. Take 1st left (Church Rd), 1st right (Bradford Pl) & 1st right onto Beach Lane.

Jane & David Maw Cornish
Rock House,
9 Beach Road, Penarth,
Cardiff CF64 1JX
tel   02920 704314
fax   02920 704314
e-mail   rockhouse@eidosnet.co.uk
web   www.rockhouse-penarth.co.uk

map: 3 entry: 656

CARMARTHENSHIRE

CARMARTHENSHIRE

A white peacock greets you at this 1708 mansion in the foothills of the Black Mountains. Katy and Carole's work continues on the restoration of both house and beautiful garden with crumbling dovecote and 25-foot-deep icehouse — you'll forgive the odd unkempt thing. They produce their own honey, fruit and free-range eggs for breakfast and informal dinner. Big, simply furnished bedrooms have long views; the sitting room an open fire and baby grand. Farmyard doves coo and pot-bellied pigs waffle; wallow in the sights and sounds of a passing pastoral age. *Self-catering available. See back of book.*

For 300 years praise has been heaped upon this unique estate overlooking the Towy Valley; Mandinam means 'untouched holy place'. Daniella and Marcus, an artist, are its guardians today: you'll stay as friends, encouraged to enjoy both house and garden. Stay all day — Daniella treats you to delicious meals in the farmhouse kitchen. Here are log fires, shutters, rich rugs on wooden floors and, in the woods and fields, wildlife and wild flowers. The charming bedroom in the ancient Coach House has a private terrace and woodburner. As you watch the sun go down before dinner you'll agree this is a magical place.

rooms	3: 1 double with bath; 1 double, 1 twin/double, both with shower.
room price	From £46. Singles by arrangement.
meals	Breakfast 8-9.30am. Dinner, 3 courses, from £15.
closed	January-February.
directions	From M4 to Pont Abraham services, 2nd exit marked Ammanford. There, left at 2nd set of lights. After 2 miles, 2nd right after Llandybie sign; house 1 mile up on right.

rooms	3: 1 double with private bath, 1 single (only let to same party); 1 twin/double in Coach House with shower.
room price	£70. Single £35.
meals	Lunch or picnic from £7.50. Dinner with wine, £15-£25. Pub 2.5 miles.
closed	Christmas.
directions	Between Llandeilo & Llandovery on A40, exit for Llangadog. Left at Mace shop. 50 yds on, right for Myddfai. Past cemetery, 1st right for Llanddeusant. 1.5 miles on, track through woods on left. Signed.

Katy & Carole Jenkins
Glynhir Mansion,
Glynhir Road, Llandybie,
Ammanford,
Carmarthenshire SA18 2TD
tel 01269 850438
fax 01269 851275
e-mail enquiries@theglynhirestate.com
web www.theglynhirestate.com

Daniella & Marcus Lampard
Mandinam,
Llangadog,
Carmarthenshire SA19 9LA
tel 01550 777368
e-mail info@mandinam.co.uk
web www.mandinam.co.uk

The views to the Black Mountains are breathtaking: "This must be the best view from any bed in the UK," enthused one guest. Generous bedrooms have more than a touch of luxury with lovely large beds and embroidered sheets. Sue is an interior decorator and a brilliant cook – she uses local lamb, beef and organic veg, and her delicious vegetarian dishes are well worth making a note of. After dinner play a game of billiards or relax in front of a lovely log fire in the sitting room. Aberglasney and the National Botanic Gardens are both nearby.

From the highest point on the Dents' 270 acres you look down the valley to the rushing salmon river and the view takes in long lawns, woodland, bluebell woods, a Norman hill fort and the Towy Valley. The house is Georgian and the flagstones on the ground floor have been lifted to install underfloor heating – so cosy. The drawing room is grand and smart, the dining room has original panelling. Bedrooms are plainer but large, with long windows and lovely views. Big British breakfasts, vegetarian or continental options. *Children over 10 welcome.*

rooms	3: 1 twin/double with bath; 1 twin/double, 1 single, sharing bath (let only to members of same party).
room price	£56. Singles £30.
meals	Packed lunch £5. Dinner, 3 courses with wine, £15.
closed	Christmas.
directions	From Llandovery, A40 for Llandeilo. At Llanwrda, right for Lampeter (A482). Out of village, 1st right after mounted pillar box in lay-by on left. Over bridge & up hill; 1st left. House 1st on right.

rooms	2: 1 twin with shower; 1 twin with bath/shower.
room price	£50. Singles £30.
meals	Excellent pubs/restaurants within 2 miles.
closed	Rarely.
directions	From Carmarthen A40 east to Pont-ar-gothi. Left before bridge & follow small lane for approx. 2 miles keeping to right-hand hedge. House on right. Call for precise details.

Sue & Nick Thompson
Mount Pleasant Farm,
Llanwrda,
Carmarthenshire SA19 8AN
tel   01550 777537
fax   01550 777537
e-mail   rivarevivaluk@aol.com

Charlotte & Gerard Dent
Plas Alltyferin,
Pont-ar-gothi, Nantgaredig,
Carmarthenshire SA32 7PF
tel   01267 290662
fax   01267 290662
e-mail   dent@alltyferin.fsnet.co.uk
web   www.alltyferin.co.uk

Freddie holds up a standard for B&B – she is dedicated to the comfort of guests without being intrusive. Pilgrims used to stay in this 14th-century chapel high up the River Towy and you'll love the restorative peace. This is a designated SSSI and you can fish on the private stretch of water. Brass beds and beams, patchwork and chintz, ornaments aplenty and beautifully laid tables for dinner and breakfast. There's a new fairweather terrace for summer teas and there will be plants for sale. Her vegetable garden feeds her guests and nearby is the National Botanic Garden of Wales. *Stabling for horses. Self-catering available. See back of book.*

The setting is so deeply rural that this Grade II-listed Georgian mansion has its own water supply. You can stable your horse, play tennis and revel in 16 acres of beautiful grounds complete with pond and mature woodland; brilliant for bird-watching. Furnishing is traditional; rooms, including bathrooms, are big and light; the oak-floored sitting room has French windows onto the walled garden while the dining room is simpler with separate tables. A hum from the A40 if the wind's from that direction, but this is wonderful value, and 15 minutes from the National Botanic Garden of Wales.

rooms	3: 1 double with bath/shower; 1 double with shower; 1 twin with private bath.
room price	£60. Singles £40.
meals	Breakfast 8-9am. Dinner £25.
closed	Christmas.
directions	B4300 from Carmarthen to Capel Dewi. Leaving village follow sign on left & down drive off main road.

rooms	3: 2 doubles, 1 twin, all with bath/shower.
room price	£50-£55. Singles £30-£35.
meals	Dinner, 3 courses, approx. £18. B.Y.O.
closed	Rarely.
directions	From Carmarthen A40 west for 4 miles. Right for Bancyfelin. After 0.5 miles, right into drive on brow of hill.

Fredena Burns
Capel Dewi Uchaf Country House,
Capel Dewi Road, Capel Dewi,
Carmarthenshire SA32 8AY

tel	01267 290799
fax	01267 290003
e-mail	uchaffarm@aol.com
web	www.walescottageholidays.uk.com

Cynthia & David Fernihough
Sarnau Mansion,
Llysonnen Road, Bancyfelin,
Carmarthenshire SA33 5DZ

tel	01267 211404
fax	01267 211404
e-mail	fernihough@so1405.force9.co.uk

CEREDIGION

Carole and Allen, who are devoted to conservation, unfussily draw you into their home and serve Welsh cakes on your arrival. The organic farm is Soil Association-registered and they have their own small beef herd — you will eat well. Broniwan is a cosy house, with warm, natural colours from paintings and woollen tapestries. Plentiful birdlife in the wonderful garden adds an audible welcome: tree-creepers, wrens and redstarts nest in ivy-covered walls and mature beech trees. There are views to the Preseli Hills, and the National Botanic Garden of Wales and Aberglasney are nearby.

rooms	2: 1 double with shower; 1 double with private bath.
room price	£50-£54. Singles £26-£28.
meals	Breakfast 8-9.30am. Light supper £12. Dinner £18.50.
closed	Rarely.
directions	From Aberaeron A487 for 6 miles for Brynhoffnant. Left at B4334 to Rhydlewis; left at Post Office & shop, 1st lane on right, then 1st track on right.

Carole & Allen Jacobs
Broniwan,
Rhydlewis, Llandysul,
Ceredigion SA44 5PF
tel   01239 851261
fax   01239 851261
e-mail broniwan@compuserve.com

map: 7 entry: 663

CONWY

The solid Victorian exterior belies a surprising interior. Patricia, a former restorer, has brought together a fascinating collection of furniture, each piece with a history. Her careful paintwork and use of colour bring light and life to her seaside home. Above is the Little Orme with stunning views; below, across the main coast road, the sweep of Llandudno Bay. The Marina Room is fresh yellow with a turquoise ceiling and a painted Neptune on the cupboards; all the bedrooms, double-glazed with lovely views, feel special, and have crisp white linen, delicious fabrics and fresh flowers.

rooms	3: 2 doubles, 1 twin, all with bath/shower.
room price	£55-£60. Singles £35-£40.
meals	Breakfast 8.30-9am. Enjoyable walk to many restaurants.
closed	Mid-December-mid-January.
directions	B5115 Llandudno & Colwyn coast road (sea on left). Pass turn for Bryn Y Bia on right. House on right.

Patricia Richards
Lympley Lodge,
Craigside, Llandudno,
Conwy Ll30 3AL
tel   01492 549304
fax   0870 1383370
e-mail clive@lympleylodge.co.uk
web   www.lympleylodge.co.uk

map: 12 entry: 664

CONWY

A haven for musicians, walkers and those who love the simple life. Fresh air, birdsong, good conversation and hot scones for breakfast – could you want more? Alan is a pianist who might play after your (excellent) supper; Irish Ger plays the fiddle and the organ. The small bedrooms in this long, low, wonky-floored granite cottage are whitewashed and simple, personalised with cheerful rugs and friends' paintings. The bathroom is overlooked only by sheep – and there's a guests' sitting room with a woodburner. An atmospheric, riverside retreat. *Children over 10 welcome.*

rooms	3: 1 double with bath/shower; 1 twin with private shower. Single room also available.
room price	£45. Singles £22.50.
meals	Supper £7.50. Dinner £12.50-£15. B.Y.O.
closed	November-March.
directions	From A5, B4406 through Penmachno. Left at The Eagles pub. On for 2 miles until 'S' bend sign; cottage on left just before bridge.

Ger Tunstall
Rhyd-y-Grô,
Cwm Penmachno, Betws-y-Coed,
Conwy LL24 0RB
tel   01690 760144
fax   01690 760144
e-mail afonig@btinternet.com
web   www.afonig.com

map: 8 entry: 665

DENBIGHSHIRE

The 15th-century wattle-and-daub house and former cow byre sit in a glorious position. The honey-coloured barn has been sensitively converted for guests, keeping its low sloping ceilings, beams and small windows; you can still see the outlines of the original thick stone walls. Simple country feel with a sitting room that looks over the Vale of Clwyd and jolly hosts who will drop and collect you from Offa's Dyke walks. Irene runs craft courses, including textiles, creative canvas work and paper-making: ask for details. Good value. *Children over 10 welcome.*

rooms	2: 1 double, 1 triple, both with shower.
room price	£44. Singles £27.
meals	Packed lunch £3.50. Pub 0.75 miles.
closed	Rarely.
directions	A494 east from Ruthin. Left opp. Griffin Hotel onto B5429. After 0.5 miles, right to Llangynhafal. After 2 miles, Esgairlygain signed on right 100 yds past Plas Draw. House left of courtyard.

Irene Henderson
The Old Barn,
Esgairlygain, Llangynhafal, Ruthin,
Denbighshire LL15 1RT
tel   01824 704047
fax   01824 704047

map: 8 entry: 666

Walk down through bluebell woods and parkland to the river, with only pheasants and lambs for company. This is such a peaceful place, a large, stone-built Georgian house on the upper reaches of the river Dee. Wholly modernised inside, it dates in part from the 14th century and is one of the oldest sites on the river. Fresh, immaculate rooms include a deep red drawing room with French windows that open to the terrace, and floral bedrooms looking towards the river or the Berwyn hills. A sunny walled garden hides a tennis court — and you can swim in the indoor pool under the painted gaze of an Egyptian god.

Welcoming dogs and Welsh air will soothe the weary traveller; so, too, will the stunning mountain and river views — and the Harmans, who entertain guests without fuss. Rambling, 18th-century, slate-floored, the farm is in the most glorious setting with the River Dee rolling by at the bottom of the valley. Comfortable antique furniture, old beams and simple, good Aga-cooked food; most vegetables come from the well-tended garden. Guests have two sitting rooms, one upstairs, charming, with a lovely view. There is absolutely nothing here to ruffle you.

rooms	2: 1 twin, 1 double with extra single, both with bath.
room price	£80. Singles £50. Children's rates on request.
meals	Supper £12. Dinner, 3 courses, £22.
closed	Christmas & New Year
directions	From A5, turn right onto B5437. Over river, left; through Carrog village after 0.25 miles; keep left. House on right after 300 yds.

rooms	3: 1 twin with shower; 1 twin with private bath; 1 single for members of same party.
room price	£48-£52. Singles £24-£26.
meals	Breakfast until 9.30am. Packed lunch £4. Supper £12.50. B.Y.O. Pub 200 yds.
closed	November-February.
directions	Leave Llangollen on A542 signed Ruthin. After 1.5 miles left onto B5103 for Rhewl. After 2.5 miles, note red brick chapel on right. 400 yds further on, farm on left before Sun Inn.

Frances Bradshaw
Rhagatt Hall,
Carrog, Corwen,
Denbighshire LL21 9HY

tel   01490 412308
fax   01490 413388
e-mail   fjcb@btopenworld.com

Mary Harman
Dee Farm,
Rhewl, Llangollen,
Denbighshire LL20 7YT

tel   01978 861598
fax   01978 861598
e-mail   harman@deefarm.co.uk

Pure Elizabethan, magical and intriguing – Golden Grove was built by Sir Edward Morgan in 1580. The Queen Anne dog-leg staircase, oak panelling and furniture are set off beautifully by the rich jewel colour schemes (the breakfast room is red, the dining room a subtle aquamarine). The two Anns are wonderful hosts, serving breakfast from kitchens at each end of the morning room. The family foursome tend the formal garden, organic vegetable garden and nuttery and run a sheep farm as well as their relaxed B&B. Friendly and worth the trip.

A farmhouse with an Elizabethan panelled drawing room – it's been in the family for 500 years. A spring runs beneath the dining room and on a beam above the fireplace is carved *Aelwyd a gymhell* ("a welcoming hearth beckons"). It is a treat to come across a genuine Arts & Crafts interior: good, solid furniture, not a frill or a flounce in sight. Bedrooms have hill views to Offa's Dyke, beds are comfortable, towels the best. A copper beech rustles in the west wind, and you are six miles from St Asaph with the smallest medieval cathedral in the country.

rooms	3: 1 double with bath; 1 twin, 1 double, both with private bath & wc.
room price	£80. Singles £50.
meals	Breakfast 8-9.30am. Dinner £25.
closed	December-January.
directions	Turn off A55 onto A5151 for Prestatyn. At Spar shop before Trelawnyd, right. Branch left immed. over 1st x-roads & right at T-junc. Gates 170 yds on left.

rooms	2: 1 double, 1 twin, both with shower.
room price	£50-£54. Singles £25-£28.
meals	Packed lunch £3. Dinner £13.50.
closed	Rarely.
directions	From Chester, A55, B5122 left for Caerwys. There, 1st right into High St. Right at end, on for 0.75 miles to x-roads & left, past camp, straight for 1 mile. House on left, signed.

Ann & Mervyn, Ann & Nigel Steele-Mortimer
Golden Grove,
Llanasa, Nr. Holywell,
Flintshire CH8 9NA
tel   01745 854452
fax   01745 854547
e-mail   golden.grove@lineone.net

Mrs Nest Price
Plas Penucha,
Peny Cefn Road, Caerwys, Mold,
Flintshire CH7 5BH
tel   01352 720210
fax   01352 720881
e-mail   nest@plaspenucha.freeserve.co.uk
web   www.geocities.com/plaspenucha

map: 13 entry: 669

map: 13 entry: 670

Church records show that the house was built in Elizabethan times with some Victorian additions. It is beautiful, surrounded by bluebell woods, and a two-acre terraced garden adds to the magic. Beams everywhere, open fires and lovely views across the valley from every window. Cosy bedrooms are full of comfort: goosedown duvets, cushion-bedecked sofas, soft carpets, fluffy towels and bathtime goodies. Much of the food is organic and local and Charmian often adds a Mediterranean touch to her cooking, which is delicious; the wines are carefully chosen, too. *Children over eight welcome.*

Such a sense of adventure as you climb the steps to the tower bedrooms: the age and history of the place permeate your skin. Bedrooms have latticed mullioned windows, dark traditional furniture, pale walls, big beds. This is the only remaining fortified house on the border and it was built over 500 years ago by the family who occupy it now. The medieval dining hall in the tower displays the coat of arms and the family motto: "without God there is nothing". A full Welsh breakfast is served by delightful hosts at the library end of the huge drawing room. All this, and four acres of formal gardens in which to dream.

rooms	2: 1 twin/double, 1 double, both with bath/shower.
room price	£80. Singles £55.
meals	Breakfast 8-9.15am. Packed lunch £5. Dinner, 5 courses, £25.
closed	Rarely.
directions	From Mold A494 for Ruthin. Past Rainbow Inn & left for Maeshafn. In Maeshafn, past phone box, left fork (yellow sign) through woods; follow to end. House on right through gates & courtyard.

rooms	3: 1 double with bath; 1 double, 1 twin/double, both with private bath.
room price	£70–£80. Singles £50.
meals	Dinner available within 2 miles.
closed	22 December-3 January.
directions	To traffic lights in centre of Mold, onto Wrexham Street (B5444). After 0.7 miles, fork right to Nercwys. After 0.4 miles, entrance on right, through large black gates.

Charmian & Ted Spencer
Pentre Cerrig Mawr,
Maeshafn, Nr. Mold,
Flintshire CH7 5LU

tel	01352 810607
fax	01352 810607
e-mail	pentre.cerrig@virgin.net
web	www.pentrecerrigmawr.com

Charles & Mairi Wynne-Eyton
Tower,
Nercwys, Mold, Flintshire CH7 4EW

tel	01352 700220
fax	01352 700220
e-mail	bookings@towerwales.co.uk
web	www.towerwales.co.uk

A former rectory with breathtaking views of hills and the lake which lies shimmering below. Olwen loves poetry, people and gardening and has created the cosiest of country homes; waxed pine shutters protect you from the rigours of wind and rain, bedrooms are bright and modern. One palatial bathroom has pretty stained glass salvaged from a local chapel and there's a sampler detailing the house's owners – from 1318 to Olwen. She is the kindest of hosts and will happily drop walkers off at the right spot... or you can catch the steam railway on its way to Bala.

The sort of retreat that has city dwellers vowing to leave for the country. There are valleys, mountains and beaches and the pretty terraced garden tumbles down from the house and merges with the scenery. Light-filled bedrooms have long views, and there are fresh flowers in each one; bedspreads are fresh white and blue. There's a guests' sitting room, beamed and warmed by the fire in the inglenook, that opens into the dining room. Eat in and be spoiled: Jane is a professional Cordon Bleu chef and uses fresh local produce and home-grown vegetables whenever possible.

rooms	2: 1 double with bath; 1 twin with private bath.
room price	£48–£50. Singles £28.
meals	Good choice of pubs/restaurants within 3 miles.
closed	Rarely.
directions	On entering Bala on A494, left & drive across head of lake. Right on B4403 to Llangower & cross bridge. Large stone house straight ahead.

rooms	2: 1 double, 1 twin, both with bath.
room price	£48–£52. Singles by arrangement.
meals	Packed lunch from £5. Dinner, 1-3 courses, £12.95–£21.95. B.Y.O.
closed	Rarely.
directions	A487 from Machynlleth for Dolgellau. Left onto B4405, through Abergynolwyn. 2nd farmhouse on right after 1 mile.

Olwen Foreman
Plas Gower,
Llangower, Bala, Gwynedd LL23 7BY
tel   01678 520431
fax   01678 520431
e-mail   olwen@plasgower.com
web   www.plasgower.com

Mrs J Howkins
Tan-y-Coed Isaf,
Bryncrug, Tywyn,
Gwynedd LL36 9UP
tel   01654 782639
fax   01654 782639
e-mail   tanhow@supanet.com
web   www.tanycoedisaf.co.uk

Watch the waves roll in from the room with the vast four-poster: you feel a million miles from city hustle and bustle. Walkers love Llwyndû; it's warm and earthy, generously simple, with bold colours on ancient stone walls, spiral stone stairways, inglenook fireplaces, quirky touches. Comfy bedrooms are split between the old 16th-century house and the granary. Candlelight and old lamps create their magic in the evening when Peter, a historian turned cook, treats you to organic Welsh Back beef and other feasts at a big table. It's an easy walk down to the beach at Cardigan Bay.

Trudie's quest for the last word in style and comfort has ended here and bedrooms and bathrooms — with excellent lighting, jumbo towels and organic shampoos — are equally memorable. Edwardian Erw is a fine house that sits in an acre of grounds: gasp as you take in the sea and estuary views. Then take advantage of Trudie's deep knowledge of Snowdonia, enjoy the light, bright atmosphere and her sumptuous organic cookery, and admire the way this evolving home has been planned in meticulous detail by a hostess who is larger than life and full of fun. The beaches are glorious.

rooms	7: 2 doubles, 1 twin, 2 four-posters, 2 family, all with bath/shower.
room price	£64–£76. Singles £32–£41.
meals	Packed lunch £4–£5. Dinner, 3 courses, from £18.95.
closed	Christmas Day & Boxing Day.
directions	A496, 2 miles north of Barmouth when street lights stop. Llwyndû signed on right.

rooms	2: 1 twin/double with bath & shower; 1 double with shower.
room price	£90–£110. Singles £65–£80.
meals	Dinner £25.
closed	Rarely.
directions	On A496 in Llanfair; entrance directly opposite signposted Slate Caverns.

Peter & Paula Thompson
Llwyndû Farmhouse,
Llanaber, Barmouth,
Gwynedd LL42 1RR
tel   01341 280144
fax   01341 281236
e-mail   intouch@llwyndu-farmhouse.co.uk
web   www.llwyndu-farmhouse.co.uk

Trudie Hunt
Erw,
Llanfair, Harlech,
Gwynedd LL46 2SA
tel   01766 780780
fax   01766 781010
e-mail   erwharlech@waitrose.com
web   www.erwharlech.co.uk

map: 7 entry: 675

map: 7 entry: 676

An immaculate drive leads to the Georgian rectory in three acres of grounds; grand, but not intimidatingly so. The energetic Gabrielle wants guests to relax completely and come and go as they please; she gives you comfortable beds, good linen, luxurious towels and super food and wine. All is harmony and light: seagrass and Persian rugs, big mirrors and family antiques, log fires on chilly evenings, a smart drawing room with paddock views – Gabrielle rides and Roger sails. So many beaches and mountains to explore, without the traffic and crowds. Guests often book for one night and stay for more.

Under clear skies there can be few more beautiful views: the long lake and miles and miles of Snowdonia. Linger on the lawn, perhaps with a drink as the sun sets; the lawn ends with a rail, then fields plunge down to the water. Each bedroom – large, modest, traditionally furnished – has the same glorious view. Barbara is easy-going and relaxed, happy to give you a key so you can pop in and out... perhaps to roam – the walking is stupendous – or to the lake to sail, canoe or swim. Bryniau Golau means 'hill of lights', a reference to the time when lime kilns glowed on the hills.

rooms	4: 2 twins, both with bath; 1 double with bath; 1 double with shower.
room price	£80. Singles £40-£50.
meals	Breakfast 8-9.30am. Packed lunch £5. Light supper £17.50. Dinner, 3 courses, £22.50.
closed	Christmas.
directions	From Pwllheli, A499 to r'bout. Right onto A497 Nefyn & Boduan road for 3 miles. Left opp. church. House set back, on right.

rooms	3: 2 doubles with spa bath & shower; 1 double with bath/shower.
room price	£55-£80. Singles £35-£55.
meals	Several restaurants nearby.
closed	Rarely.
directions	From Bala B4391 (Ind. Estate). After 1 mile, right on B4403 to Llangower. Pass Bala Lake Hotel; look for sign showing left-hand turn; approx. 20 yds after tree sign on right; left up hill, over cattle grid. House 1st on right.

Gabrielle & Roger Pollard
The Old Rectory,
Boduan, Nr. Pwllheli,
Gwynedd LL53 6DT
tel	01758 721519
fax	01758 721519
e-mail	thepollards@theoldrectory.net
web	www.theoldrectory.net

Hugh & Barbara Emsley
Bryniau Golau,
Llangower, Bala, Gwynedd LL23 7BT
tel	01678 521782
fax	01678 521790
e-mail	emsley@bryniau-golau.fsnet.co.uk
web	www.bryniau-golau.fsnet.co.uk

MONMOUTHSHIRE

MONMOUTHSHIRE

Step inside the old farm cottage to an interior that makes the heart sing. The feel is fresh, with stripped beams, soothing colours, garden flowers and unusual pieces of art and pottery tucked into every corner. Nancy and Piers are lovely, too, and treat you to the finest local and organic breakfasts in front of the woodburning fire. Bedrooms are serene and cosy, dotted with delightful things: a burnished lamp, a feathered cushion, a gilt mirror, three African bowls. Beds are dressed in lambs wool blankets and crisp white linen, the garden has walkways, birds and fresh scents at every turn. A joyfully stylish place.

The approach is majestic and the house, deep in countryside between England and Wales, meets all expectations; the lines of the Welsh longhouse blend beautifully with the Georgian and the Victorian. Surrounded by 140 acres of farmland, with gardens sloping down to a small lake and a stream that meanders through the woodland, there's plenty to explore. Lovely wallpapers, curtains and good linen in the large bedrooms, and you breakfast in an upstairs gallery overlooking the garden. The peace and the seclusion are soothing, and there is a tennis court and a swimming pool, too.

rooms	3: 1 twin, 1 single with private/shared bath/shower; 1 double with shower.
room price	£70. Singles £35.
meals	Breakfast until 9.30am. Dinner occasionally available.
closed	Rarely.
directions	A466 to Chepstow racecourse; left at racecourse r'bout onto B4293 for 4 miles; left at T-junc. signed Kilgwrrwg, Newchurch, Gaerllywd; pink cottage 0.5 miles along, on x-roads.

rooms	3: 1 double, 1 twin, 1 family, all with private bath.
room price	£70. Singles £40.
meals	Dinner £17.50–£20.
closed	December.
directions	Please ask for directions when booking.

Nancy & Piers Propert
Corner Cottage,
Kilgwrrwg, Chepstow,
Monmouthshire NP16 6PL

tel	01291 650646
fax	01291 650794
e-mail	nancy_propert@btinternet.com

Mrs Susan Inkin
Court St Lawrence,
Llangovan, Monmouth,
Monmouthshire NP25 4BT

tel	01291 690279
fax	01291 690279

map: 8 entry: 679

map: 8 entry: 680

MONMOUTHSHIRE

A large Edwardian house in the lovely Usk valley. The Boyles have been here for 27 years and pour most of their energy into the garden: big and beautiful, with a summer house you may use. Catriona sells plants and runs a garden school. The house is pretty and rambling; breakfast round the mahogany table, relax in the comfortably old-fashioned sitting room. Bedrooms have lacy bedcovers and garden views; small bathrooms share a corridor. Fine walking all around in the nearby Brecon Beacons National Park, swimming in the summer pool. Good, solid B&B.

rooms	2 twins, both with private bath.
room price	£60-£70. Singles £40.
meals	Good pub within walking distance.
closed	Rarely.
directions	A40 to Abergavenny; at big r-bout on edge of town, B4598 to Usk for 2.5 miles. Left at King of Prussia pub, up small lane; house 200 yds on left.

Catriona Boyle
Penpergwm Lodge,
Abergavenny,
Monmouthshire NP7 9AS
tel   01873 840208
fax   01873 840208
e-mail   boyle@penpergwm.co.uk
web   www.penplants.com

map: 8 entry: 681

PEMBROKESHIRE

This was the Quay Master's house, with the best views of the Cleddau Estuary. The Wights have decorated boldly, but with respect for the Georgian interior; in one bathroom there's a ball-and-claw bath and gilt mirror, in others, Philip's fine handmade furniture. The food is memorable – organic and wholesome with a modern twist: their own wild smoked salmon, local fish and home-grown organic produce. Miles of river footpaths – spot kingfishers, herons and shell ducks – and a fine inn a minute away. It's fun, vibrant and relaxing and the Wights are brilliant hosts. *Self-catering available. See back of book.*

rooms	3: 1 double with shower; 1 four-poster with bath; 1 twin with private bath/shower.
room price	£50-£60. Singles £40.
meals	Packed lunch from £7.50. Dinner £25.
closed	Christmas.
directions	From A477, right onto A4075. Left at brown sign for Cresswell House. House on left after 1.4 miles, just before bridge.

Philip Wight
Cresswell House,
Cresswell Quay, Nr. Pembroke,
Pembrokeshire SA68 0TE
tel   01646 651435
e-mail   phil@cresswellhouse.co.uk
web   www.cresswellhouse.co.uk

map: 7 entry: 682

PEMBROKESHIRE

Left column

The Cleddau Estuary winds its way around the boundary of this 1,000-acre organic arable and dairy farm; the lush grass feeds the cows that produce milk for their organic 'Rachel's' yogurts. It's quite a collection of quirky farm buildings, best seen from the back lawns where you can picnic, barbecue and explore the woods. Ginny is a helpful and unobtrusive host and rustles up delicious organic dinners in the formal dining room rich with dark wood antiques. Bedrooms are simple yet comfortable; there are floral curtains and bedspreads, comfy beds and fresh woodland flowers.

rooms	3: 1 double with bath; 1 double with shower; 1 twin with private bath.
room price	£50–£55. Singles £25–£32.
meals	Packed lunch £6. Supper from £12. Organic dinner, 4 courses, £22.
closed	Rarely.
directions	A4075 to Cresselly. Turn right. Follow signs for Lawrenny to first x-roads. Straight over. Next x-roads right. 100 yds on left.

Ms Virginia Lort Phillips
Knowles Farm,
Lawrenny, Kilgetty,
Pembrokeshire SA68 0PX
tel   01834 891221
fax   01834 891344
e-mail ginilp@lawrenny.org.uk
web   www.lawrenny.org.uk

map: 7 entry: 683

Right column

PEMBROKESHIRE

An ancient bluebell wood pulsates with colour in the spring and wild flowers of all kinds bloom generously. If you're lucky, you might see a badger lumbering into the garden. This is a friendly, gracious house, filled with gorgeous Welsh antiques, candles and crystal. One of the bedrooms has a fine, restored half-tester bed and a giant private bathroom with Victorian washstand where fluffy bathrobes envelop you. In readiness for a day's walking, breakfast on local produce, home-made jams and marmalades, fresh fruit salad and yogurt… the Pembrokeshire coastal path runs through the farm.

rooms	3: 1 double, 1 twin, both with private bath; single available for members of same party.
room price	£50–£55. Singles £30.
meals	Breakfast 8-9.30am. Packed lunch £5. Pub/restaurant 0.5 miles.
closed	Mid-October-Easter.
directions	B4320 from Pembroke centre for Hundleton. After woods, house 1st on right. House is approx. 1 mile from Pembroke centre.

Ann Morris
Bowett Farm,
Hundleton, Pembroke,
Pembrokeshire SA71 5QS
tel   01646 683473
fax   01646 683473
e-mail bowett@pembrokeshire.com
web   www.bowettfarmhouse.co.uk

map: 7 entry: 684

A country seat in medieval times, this long, white country house has the sandy beaches and clifftop walks of the Pembrokeshire coast on its doorstep. It is secluded and surrounded by rolling farmland, with horses, peacocks and a croquet lawn. Inside is space without fuss, with antiques and a large orangery which opens onto the walled garden; it is a grand yet modest place. Ben's welcome is wonderfully warm and he can ferry you to or from walks. The air here is so fresh it is a different substance and the sunset views over St Bride's Bay defy all efforts to paint them. *Pets by arrangement.*

A wonderful spot for birdwatchers, fishermen or walkers – the Pembrokeshire Coastal Path runs past the house. Jane and Anthony will give you lifts back from walks, and the setting is breathtaking: you could take your breakfast coffee to the edge of the cliff and still drink it piping hot. Or simply admire the views from the sunny dining room. The 60s house is formal, traditional, colourful; there's *bara brith* and tea on arrival and lots of suggestions for things to do, and it's the perfect spot from which to explore the bird sanctuary islands of Skomer, Skokholm and Ramsey. *Children over eight welcome.*

rooms	3: 2 doubles, both with bath; 1 twin/double with private bath.
room price	£50-£60. Singles from £40.
meals	Packed lunch £4. Good pubs & restaurants 1.5-3 miles.
closed	Rarely.
directions	B4341 to Broad Haven through Portfield Gate. After 2 miles turn for Timber Hill Holiday Lodges & keep following lodge signs. On right about 0.5 miles before lodges.

rooms	5: 1 twin with conservatory & shower; 1 double, 1 single, both with bath; 1 double, 1 single, both with private bath.
room price	£24-£64.
meals	Breakfast 8.30-9.30am. Pubs/restaurants within 1 mile.
closed	November-February.
directions	From Haverfordwest, B4341 for Broad Haven. Right at sea front, then up hill signed Nolton. House 1st on left.

Ben & Judith Stewart-Thomas
Haroldston Hall,
Portfield Gate, Haverfordwest,
Pembrokeshire SA62 3LZ
tel	01437 781549
e-mail	benjamin@stewart-thomas.fsnet.co.uk
web	www.haroldstonhall.co.uk

Jane & Anthony Main
Lion Rock,
Broad Haven, Haverfordwest,
Pembrokeshire SA62 3JP
tel	01437 781645
fax	01437 781203
e-mail	lion.rock@btinternet.com
web	www.stayatlionrock.co.uk

A decanter of port in your room, mints on your pillow. Such atttention to detail: the Swedish-style décor echoes the serene west coast light – white floorboards, seagrass matting, pale antiques, original shutters. The Georgian house borders the National Park with its coastal path and all bedrooms have sea views. Hire bikes, play croquet, head off with a picnic (home-made, delicious) to unspoilt beaches. Caroline, a potter, offers tuition in her studio; art and craft courses are being planned, along with a special garden for guests in wheelchairs. *Self-catering available. See back of book.*

What an entrance: the hallway has deep raspberry and pistachio walls with Arts and Crafts lamps and medieval-style chandelier. Mary and Tony are easy-going and fun and have spent seven years restoring the house. Sir Evan Jones built Pentower to have the best views of the harbour, for which he was the civil engineer. Pretty bedrooms are modern, light and airy with sheer curtains and huge showers. Breakfast in the formal, quarry tiled dining room or on the terrace; curl up in the evening with a cat on rattan chairs by the French windows and watch the comings and goings in the harbour below.

rooms	5: 3 doubles, 2 twins, all with bath/shower.
room price	£60–£85. Singles £40–£60.
meals	Packed lunch from £4. Restaurants, pubs & cafe 1.5 miles.
closed	Rarely.
directions	From Fishguard A487. Right at Croesgoch x-roads, 6 miles from St David's. After 1 mile, left at Llanrhian x-roads. House on left, 0.5 miles on.

rooms	2: 1 twin, 1 double, both with shower.
room price	£60. Singles £40.
meals	Packed lunch £5. Pubs/restaurants 5-minute walk.
closed	Rarely.
directions	A40 to Fishguard town; at r'bout, 2nd exit onto Main Street. Before sharp left bend, right fork onto Tower Hill; 200 yds on, through house gates.

Caroline Flynn
Trevaccoon,
Llanrhian, St David's,
Haverfordwest,
Pembrokeshire SA62 6DP
tel   01348 831438
fax   01348 831438
e-mail   flynn@trevaccoon.co.uk
web   www.trevaccoon.co.uk

Tony Jacobs & Mary Geraldine Casey
Pentower,
Tower Hill, Fishguard,
Pembrokeshire SA65 9LA
tel   01348 874462
e-mail   pentowerpembs@aol.com

PEMBROKESHIRE

A cosy home overlooking pretty Fishguard harbour – you'll feel like part of the family. Fanny and Vivian are generous, great company and love having guests to stay; she was a professional chef and her meals are wonderful: fresh vegetables from the garden and local meat, served in the gorgeous mulberry dining room. Take a glass to the bottom of the sloping garden and watch the ferry and fishing boats set sail for Ireland. Wonderful antique finds are dotted around the house and everything feels just right. Bedrooms are fresh, very comfortable with spoiling smellies, and one has sea views.

rooms	2: 1 double with bath/shower; 1 double with shower.
room price	£70. Singles £50.
meals	Packed lunches £8. Dinner (min 4), 3 courses, £20. B.Y.O.
closed	Rarely.
directions	Cardigan exit off main r'bout in Fishguard; on for 600 yds, do not go left down hill but carry straight on; at Tower Hill, house 200 yds on left.

Fanny & Vivian Brogden
The Towers,
Tower Hill, Fishguard,
Pembrokeshire SA65 9LA
tel 01348 875489
e-mail fanny@frances14.freeserve.co.uk

PEMBROKESHIRE

The views to the Preseli hills are magical, and the oldest part of the farmhouse goes back 300 years. Bedrooms are light and airy, the dining room is elegant with mahogany table and glass chandelier, and the sitting room yours to share – lovely sash windows painted white, shelves dotted with family photos and books, fresh flowers in vases, log fires for chilly nights. Morris and Christine are excellent hosts; she concocts breakfasts from organic sausages and home-grown fruits, he bursts with enthusiasm for their new garden. *Min. stay two nights.*

rooms	2: 1 twin with bath/shower; 1 double with shower.
room price	£60. Singles £35.
meals	Pub/restaurant 1 mile.
closed	Rarely.
directions	From A487 to Nevern, past pub, over bridge; 1st left before church, up hill, bear right at fork; 100 yds on left after Trefach Farm, driveway marked.

Morris Hywel Evans
Glasdir Bach,
Nevern, Nr. Newport,
Pembrokeshire SA42 0NQ
tel 01239 820623
fax 01239 821257
e-mail glasdirbach@btopenworld.com

PEMBROKESHIRE

The guest book is full of praise for the food and the setting. David and Patricia go to great lengths to bring you the freshest, tastiest, most local organic produce, and there are good wines, too – even Welsh ones – and beer. Britain only has one Coastal National Park and the Old Vicarage is in it; the most challenging section of the path – a stunning bay and great cliffs – is only a mile away. Inland are woodland walks and the Preseli Hills. The Edwardian house, filled with books and family paintings, has an acre of lawned gardens and large bedrooms that drink in the coastal light.

rooms	3: 2 doubles, 1 twin, all with shower.
room price	£65. Singles £40.
meals	Breakfast 8.30-9am. Picnic lunches available. Dinner, 3 courses, £19.
closed	December-February.
directions	From Cardigan bypass for Cardigan at southern r'bout. Left by Eagle Inn to St Dogmaels. Sharp right at end of High Street to Moylegrove. There, 1st left to Glanrhyd, then up hill. House on right, past church.

Patricia & David Phillips
The Old Vicarage,
Moylegrove, Nr. Cardigan,
Pembrokeshire SA43 3BN
tel   01239 881231
fax   0870 1362382
e-mail   stay@old-vic.co.uk
web   www.old-vic.co.uk

POWYS

There are two donkeys (Coppelia and Ophelia) in the garden and a weeping ash that is over 140 years old. Pistyll Rhaeadr, Wales' highest waterfall, is up the lane. In this superbly preserved example of neo-Gothic architecture (1861), the hall is dominated by the oak staircase winding to the galleried landing full of pictures and the décor painstakingly restored. Beautiful shower rooms are totally up-to-date and from the bright sunny bedrooms (Sunflower, Orchid and Bluebell) you can see the bracken-gilt Berwyn Mountains. The work on the lovely garden continues.

rooms	3: 1 double, 1 twin, 1 family, all with shower.
room price	£50-£60. Singles £30-£35. Family room £75-£85.
meals	Breakfast from 8.30am. Packed lunch on request. Excellent restaurants nearby.
closed	Rarely.
directions	12 miles west of Oswestry on B4396. In village, right after HSBC bank into Waterfall St. 1st large house on right.

Karon & Ken Raines
Bron Heulog,
Waterfall Street,
Llanrhaeadr Y-M Mochnant,
Powys SY10 0JX
tel   01691 780521
e-mail   kraines@enta.net
web   www.kraines.enta.net

Wild Wales at its best; drive across the moor where the ponies run free, or arrive via the Route 25 cycle track. This was the first brick house built in the area in 1815 and it's now a working farm. There's a big organic vegetable plot (you should sample the results), a landscaped garden, and a large sheltered terrace with wooden loungers and long, lush views. Inside, your hosts have gone for a pleasingly simple style: bedrooms have plain wooden furniture and colourful throws and rugs. Curl up by the woodburner, or sit in the dining room with its flagstones, rugs, painted murals and oodles of books to blissfully unwind.

For lovers of Victoriana, the house, designed by Sir George Gilbert Scott, is sheer delight. Behind the French Gothic façade lies the evidence of a lifetime's collecting by Paul: splendid brass beds, cast-iron radiators, period light fittings, original porcelain loos. Sumptuous bedspreads and fabrics add to the exotic mood. Dine by gaslight (the food is superb), ring the servants' bell for early morning tea. You are on the English side of Offa's Dyke: look north to the heavenly Radnorshire hills, south to all of Herefordshire. Paul is cultured, charming and fun.

rooms	2: 1 double, 1 twin/double, both with bath/shower.
room price	£50. Singles £30.
meals	Dinner, 3 courses, £15. B.Y.O
closed	Rarely.
directions	From A483 to Llanboter on B4356. Follow for 2 miles past chapel on right; across common. Immed. sharp left to Llanbadarn Fynydd; follow hedge on right for 0.3 miles to gate.

rooms	3: 1 double with bath/shower; 1 double with bath; 1 twin with shower.
room price	£80. Singles £45.
meals	Dinner, 4 courses, £24.
closed	Rarely.
directions	B4355, between Presteigne & Knighton; in village of Norton, immed. north of church.

Mr John Rath & John Underwood
Cwmllechwedd Fawr,
Llanbister, Llandrindod Wells,
Powys LD1 6UH
tel   01597 840267
fax   01597 840267
e-mail postmaster@cwmllechwedd.u-net.com
web   www.cwmllechwedd.u-net.com

Paul Gerrard
The Old Vicarage,
Norton, Presteigne, Radnorshire,
Powys LD8 2EN
tel   01544 260038

POWYS

The food is plentiful and truly delicious and the dining room has been created amid a jumble of corn-milling machinery; B&B guests and campers can eat here together in the evening. The Grade II*-listed watermill has wood, flagstone, terracotta, woodburning stoves, comfortable chairs, simple pine bedrooms and a riverside garden. The bunkhouse and camping facilities in the old cider orchard give the mill a relaxed and informal air. A good base from which to explore on foot, horseback, bicycle or canoe — lovers of the outdoors looking for good value with a planet-friendly bias will be in heaven.

rooms	3: 1 twin, 1 double, both with continental bath/shower; 1 double with shower.
room price	£46–£52. Singles from £33.
meals	Simple supper £6. Dinner, 3 courses, £14.
closed	Rarely.
directions	12 miles north of Brecon on A470. Mill set slightly back from road, on left, between Llyswen & Erwood.

Alistair & Nicky Legge
Trericket Mill Vegetarian Guesthouse
Erwood, Builth Wells,
Powys LD2 3TQ
tel 01982 560312
e-mail mail@trericket.co.uk
web www.trericket.co.uk

POWYS

A fascinating medieval cruck-built hall house on a hillside overlooking the Wye valley. In the restoration Annie and John have imbued the former bishop's summer house with their own distinctive and delightful personalities: the eccentric mix of Venetian mirrors, Indian rugs, gorgeous fabrics and 1930s photos works well. Both double rooms have antique patchwork quilts; one has a dramatic half-tester. The ancient, Grade II*-listed house is reached by a bumpy, private track across farmland — and is wonderfully secluded. Just chickens, cats, goats, birds… a unique place.

rooms	3: 1 double, 1 family, both with bath; 1 twin with private shower.
room price	£43–£48. Family room £60. Singles from £35.
meals	Dinner, 2 courses, £12; 3 courses, £15. B.Y.O.
closed	Christmas.
directions	From Hay-on-Wye, A479 then A470 to B. Wells. Through Llyswen, past forest on left, down hill. Next left for Trericket Mill, then immed. right & up hill. Straight through gate across track to house.

Annie & John McKay
Hafod Y Garreg,
Erwood, Builth Wells,
Powys LD2 3TQ
tel 01982 560400

POWYS

Gleaming oak floors and staircases are a proud feature of this 17th-century, Grade II-listed cottage. Bedrooms are large and beds comfortably firm. The welcome from Linda is friendly but reserved, with guests free to come and go as they please; she and Ed tend to keep to their own part of the house. A postbox by the front door is all that remains of the cottage's past. Tired walkers can recover here after a stint in the Black Mountains; bookworms can seek out the second-hand bookshops of Hay-on-Wye. Whichever activity you choose, you'll be captivated by the beauty of the area. Superb vegetarian breakfasts are served.

rooms	3: 1 double/family, 1 twin/double, 1 double, all with shower.
room price	£56. Singles £28.
meals	Breakfast from 8.30am. Good pub 2 miles. Pubs/restaurants in Hay-on-Wye.
closed	Rarely.
directions	From Hay-on-Wye on Brecon road. After 0.5 miles, left, signed to Llanigon. On for 1 mile & left before school. White building on right opp. church.

Linda Webb & Ed Moore
The Old Post Office,
Llanigon, Hay-on-Wye,
Powys HR3 5QA
tel   01497 820008
web   www.oldpost-office.co.uk

POWYS

It's all there: croquet and boules, a piano upon which to tinkle, a jacuzzi for one of the bedrooms, log fires in the sitting rooms and acres of gardens to roam. The Brecon Beacons National Park is close by and there are two huge magnolias — among other ancient trees — to sit and dream under. Inside all is solid and traditional, rather than informal, and almost luxurious: fitted carpets, antiques and modern furniture, big pelmeted floral curtains and perfect comfort — everything reliable, nothing out of place. It is impressive, and terrific value.

rooms	5: 1 family, 1 twin, both with shower; 1 master suite, 1 West Wing double, both with bath/shower; 1 twin with jacuzzi.
room price	£55-£80. Singles £45-£70.
meals	Packed lunch £5. Good restaurants nearby.
closed	Rarely.
directions	From Abergavenny, A40 for Brecon & Crickhowell. Approx. 2 miles on, pass car sales garage on right & 200 yds on, a county sign. Next drive on right with lodge at gate.

Mrs Christina Jackson
Glangrwyney Court,
Crickhowell, Powys NP8 1ES
tel   01873 811288
fax   01873 810317
e-mail glangrwyne@aol.com
web   www.glancourt.com

WHAT'S IN THE BACK OF THE BOOK?

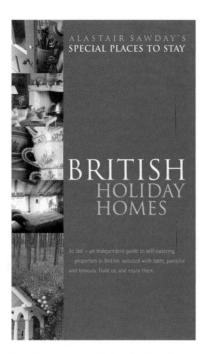

Below is a list of owners in this book who also appear in our *British Holiday Homes* (£9.99).

Cornwall • 40 • 81 • Cumbria • 89 • 92 • Derbyshire • 98 • 99 • 104 • Devon • 112 • 120 • 121 • 130 • Dorset • 161 • 179 • Gloucestershire • 194 • Herefordshire • 249 • Kent • 262 • Norfolk • 325 • Northumberland • 349 • Oxfordshire • 371 • 372 • Shropshire • 384 • 401 • 402 • Somerset • 420 • Staffordshire • 426 • Suffolk • 440 • Warwickshire • 489 • Wiltshire • 518

Isle of Skye • 623 • Perth & Kinross • 630 • 632 • 640 • Sutherland • 652

Carmarthenshire • 657 • 661 • Pembrokeshire • 682 • 687

BED & BREAKFAST FOR
GARDEN LOVERS

The B&Bs below also appear in our *Bed & Breakfast for Garden Lovers* (£14.99).

Bath & N.E. Somerset • 11 •12 • Cheshire • 28 • Cornwall • 34 • 49 • 51 • 64 • 66 • Derbyshire • 99 • Devon • 120 • 125 • 137 • 141 • Dorset • 183 • Essex • 193 • Gloucestershire • 195 • 201 • 206 • 216 • 217 • Hampshire • 224 • 231 • Herefordshire • 237 • 238 • 246 • 249 • Isle of Wight • 257 • Kent • 260 • 273 • 277 • London • 306 • Norfolk • 320 • 335 • 336 • Northamptonshire • 343 • Oxfordshire • 363 • 368 • Shropshire • 387 • 388 • Somerset • 401 • 402 • 403 • 420 • Suffolk • 430 • Sussex • 471 • 482 • 486 • Warwickshire • 487 • 489 • 491 • 497 • 499 • Wiltshire • 503 • 506 • 518 • Yorkshire • 528 • 534 • 537 • 540 • 541 • 560 • 561

Ayrshire • 578 • Renfrewshire • 641 • Wigtownshire • 654

Carmarthenshire • 661 • Ceredigion • 663 • Monmouthshire • 680

WHAT IS ALASTAIR SAWDAY PUBLISHING?

Twenty or so of us work in converted barns on a farm near Bristol, close enough to the city for a bicycle ride and far enough for a silence broken only by horses and the occasional passage of a tractor. Some editors work in the countries they write about, e.g. France; others work from the UK but are based outside the office. We enjoy each other's company, celebrate every event possible, and work in an easy-going but committed environment.

These books owe their style and mood to Alastair's miscellaneous career and his interest in the community and the environment. He has taught overseas, worked with refugees, run development projects abroad, founded a travel company and several environmental organisations. There has been a slightly unconventional streak throughout, not least in his driving of a waste-paper-collection lorry, the manning of stalls at jumble sales and the pursuit of causes long before they were considered sane.

These books owe their style and mood to Alastair's miscellaneous career and his interest in the community and the environment

Back to the travel company: trying to take his clients to eat and sleep in places that were not owned by corporations and assorted bandits he found dozens of very special places in France – farms, châteaux etc – a list that grew into the first book, *French Bed and Breakfast*. It was a celebration of 'real' places to stay and the remarkable people who run them.

The publishing company grew from that first and rather whimsical French book. It started as a mild crusade, and there it stays – full of 'attitude', and the more appealing for it. For we still celebrate the unusual, the beautiful, the individual. We are passionate about rejecting the banal, the ugly, the pompous and the indifferent and we are passionate, too, about 'real' food. Alastair is a trustee of the Soil Association and keen to promote organic growing and consuming by owners and visitors.

It is a source of deep pleasure to us to know that there are many thousands of people who share our views. We are by no means alone in trumpeting the virtues of resisting the destruction and uniformity of so much of our culture – and the cultures of other nations, too.

We run a company in which people and values matter. We love to hear of new friendships between those in the book and those using it, and to know that there are many people – among them farmers – who have been enabled to pursue their decent lives thanks to the extra income our books bring them.

FRAGILE EARTH SERIES

The Little Earth Book

Now in its third edition and as engrossing and provocative as ever, it continues to highlight the perilously fragile state of our planet.
£6.99

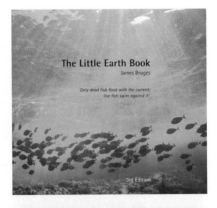

The Little Food Book

Makes for a wonderfully stimulating read — one that may change your attitude to the food choices you make daily.
£6.99

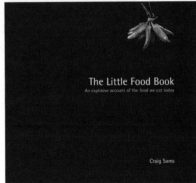

The Little Money Book

Could make you look at everything financial — from your bank statements to the coins in your pocket — in a whole new way.
Available November 2003
£6.99

This fascinating series has been praised by politicians, academics, environmentalists, civil servants — and 'general' readers. It has come as a blast of fresh air, blowing away confusion and incomprehension.

www.fragile-earth.com

SIX DAYS

Celebrating the triumph of creativity over adversity.

An inspiring and heart-rending story of the making of the
stained glass 'Creation' window at Chester Cathedral by a
woman battling with Parkinson's disease.

*"Within a few seconds, the tears were running down my cheeks. The
window was one of the most beautiful things I had ever seen. It is a
tour-de-force, playing with light like no other window ..."*

Anthropologist Hugh Brody

In 1983, Ros Grimshaw, a distinguished designer, artist and
creator of stained-glass windows, was diagnosed with Parkinson's
disease. Refusing to allow her illness to prevent her from
working, Ros became even more adept at her craft, and in
2000 won the commission to design and make the 'Creation'
Stained Glass Window for Chester Cathedral.

Six Days traces the evolution of the window from the first
sketches to its final, glorious completion as a rare and wonderful
tribute to Life itself: for each of the six 'days' of Creation
recounted in Genesis, there is a scene below that is relevant
to the world of today and tomorrow.

Extracts from Ros's diary capture the personal struggle involved.
Superb photography captures the luminescence of the stunning
stained glass, while the story weaves together essays, poems,
and moving contributions from Ros's partner Patrick Costeloe.

Available from Alastair Sawday Publishing £12.99

ORDER FORM UK

All these books, are available in major bookshops or you may order them direct. **Post and packaging are FREE within the UK.**

		Price	No. copies
French Bed & Breakfast	Edition 8	£15.99	
French Hotels, Châteaux & Inns (Nov. 03)	Edition 3	£13.99	
French Holiday Homes	Edition 1	£11.99	
Paris Hotels	Edition 4	£9.99	
British Bed & Breakfast	Edition 8	£14.99	
British Hotels, Inns & Other Places (Nov. 03)	Edition 5	£13.99	
Bed & Breakfast for Garden Lovers	Edition 2	£14.99	
British Holiday Homes	Edition 1	£9.99	
London	Edition 1	£9.99	
Ireland	Edition 4	£12.99	
Spain	Edition 5	£13.99	
Portugal	Edition 2	£9.99	
Italy (Oct. 03)	Edition 3	£12.99	
Europe with courses & activities	Edition 1	£12.99	
India (Oct. 03)	Edition 1	£10.99	
Morocco (Nov. 03)	Edition 1	£10.99	
The Little Earth Book	Edition 3	£6.99	
The Little Food Book	Edition 1	£6.99	
The Little Money Book (Oct. 03)	Edition 1	£6.99	
Six Days		£12.99	

Please make cheques payable to Alastair Sawday Publishing   **Total £** _____ _____

Please send cheques to: Alastair Sawday Publishing,
The Home Farm Stables, Barrow Gurney, Bristol BS48 3R N.
For credit card orders call 01275 464891 or order directly
from our web site **www.specialplacestostay.com**

Title   First name   Surname
Address

Postcode   Tel

If you do not wish to receive mail from other like-minded companies,
please tick here ☐

If you would prefer not to receive information about special offers on our books,
please tick here ☐

BBB8

ORDER FORM USA

All these books are available at your local bookstore, or you may order direct. Allow two to three weeks for delivery.

		Price	No. copies
Europe (Spring 04)	Edition 1	$19.99	
Morocco (Dec 03)	Edition 1	t.b.c	
Spain	Edition 5	$19.95	
Ireland	Edition 4	$17.95	
French Bed & Breakfast	Edition 8	$19.95	
Paris Hotels	Edition 4	$14.95	
British Holiday Homes	Edition 1	$14.95	
British Hotels, Inns and other places (Jan 04)	Edition 5	$17.95	
French Hotels, Châteaux and Inns (Jan 04)	Edition 3	$19.95	
Portugal	Edition 2	$14.95	
London	Edition 1	$12.95	
Italy	Edition 3	t.b.c	
French Holiday Homes (Mar 04)	Edition 2	$17.95	
	Total $		

Shipping in the continental USA: $3.95 for one book,
$4.95 for two books, $5.95 for three or more books.
Outside continental USA, call (800) 243-0495 for prices.
For delivery to AK, CA, CO, CT, FL, GA, IL, IN, KS, MI, MN, MO, NE,
NM, NC, OK, SC, TN, TX, VA, and WA, please add appropriate sales tax.

Please make checks payable to: **Total $**
The Globe Pequot Press

To order by phone with MasterCard or Visa: (800) 243-0495,
9am to 5pm EST; by fax: (800) 820-2329, 24 hours;
through our web site: **www.GlobePequot.com**; or by mail:
The Globe Pequot Press, P.O. Box 480, Guilford, CT 06437

Date

Name

Address

Town

State

Zip code

Tel

Fax

Britain

France

Ireland

Italy

Portugal

Spain

Morocco

India...

all in one place!

On the unfathomable and often unnavigable sea of online accommodation pages, those who have discovered **www.specialplacestostay.com** have found it to be an island of reliability. Not only will you find a database full of trustworthy, up-to-date information about all the Special Places to Stay across Europe, but also:

- Links to the web sites of all of the places in the series
- Colourful, clickable, interactive maps to help you find the right place
- The opportunity to make most bookings by e-mail – even if you don't have e-mail yourself
- Online purchasing of our books, securely and cheaply
- Regular, exclusive special offers on books
- The latest news about future editions and future titles

The site is constantly evolving and is frequently updated with news and special features that won't appear anywhere else but in our window on the worldwide web.

Russell Wilkinson, Web Producer
website@specialplacestostay.com

If you'd like to receive news and updates about our books by e-mail, send a message to newsletter@specialplacestostay.com

REPORT FORM

If you have any comments on entries in this guide, please let us have them. If you have a favourite house, hotel, inn or other new discovery, anywhere, please let us know about it.

Existing Entry:

Name of property: _____

New recommendation:

Name of property: _____

Address: _____

_____

_____

_____

Tel: _____

Comments: _____

_____

_____

_____

_____

_____

_____

_____

Your name: _____

Address: _____

_____

Tel & e-mail: _____

Please send the completed form to:

Alastair Sawday Publishing, The Home Farm Stables, Barrow Gurney, Bristol BS48 3RW
or go to www.specialplacestostay.com and click on 'contact'.

BBB8

Thank you.

QUICK REFERENCE INDICES

QUICK REFERENCE INDICES

Singles These houses either have a single room or charge no single supplement.

Bath & N.E. Somerset • 10 • 11 • Cornwall • 41 • 48 • 65 • 68 • 70 • Devon • 120 • 122 • 125 • 129 • 141 • 142 • 143 • 144 • Dorset • 175 • 176 • Durham • 189 • 190 • Essex • 192 • Herefordshire • 244 • 248 • Kent • 262 • 266 • Leicestershire • 283 • Lincolnshire • 286 • Norfolk • 336 • Nottinghamshire • 361 • Oxfordshire • 374 • Somerset • 406 • Suffolk • 436 • 440 • Surrey • 459 • Sussex • 475 • Wiltshire • 510 • 523 • Yorkshire • 529 • 544 • 558

Argyll & Bute • 572 • Dumfries & Galloway • 586 • 590 • Edinburgh & the Lothians • 610 • Inverness-shire • 620 • 621 • Perth & Kinross • 627

No Car? These owners have told us that they are happy to collect you from their nearest public transport drop-off point.

Bath & N.E. Somerset • 2 • 11 • Berkshire • 17 • Cambridgeshire • 24 • Cheshire • 28 • Cornwall • 38 • 40 • 41 • 42 • 44 • 46 • 48 • 56 • 58 • 59 • 62 • 73 • Cumbria • 83 • 86 • 94 • 96 • Derbyshire • 98 • Devon • 114 • 118 • 120 • 123 • 125 • 135 • 143 • 146 • 147 • 148 • Dorset • 158 • 159 • 163 • 166 • 180 • 181 • Durham • 189 • Essex • 192 • Gloucestershire • 197 • 199 • 208 • Hampshire • 226 • Herefordshire • 232 • 239 • 251 • Kent • 274 • 276 • Leicestershire • 282 • Lincolnshire • 284 • 286 • London • 295 • 307 • 309 • Norfolk • 331 • 336 • Northumberland • 345 • 346 • 349 • 356 • Nottinghamshire • 360 • Oxfordshire • 365 • 378 • Shropshire • 382 • 394 • Somerset • 396 • 403 • 410 • 411 • 415 • 421 • Staffordshire • 425 • Suffolk • 433 • 434 • 437 • 442 • 446 • 456 • Surrey • 459 • 461 • Sussex • 469 • 473 • 484 • Wiltshire • 507 • 513 • 520 • Yorkshire • 529 • 530 • 531 • 532 • 533 • 552 • 554

Angus • 570 • Dumfries & Galloway • 589 • 590 • East Lothian • 607 • West Lothian • 610 • Inverness-shire • 621 • Perth & Kinross • 627 • 635

Anglesey • 655 • Cardiff • 656 • Carmarthenshire • 658 • 661 • 664 • Gwynedd • 674 • Monmouthshire • 679 • Pembrokeshire • 683 • 684 • 688 • 689 • Powys • 694

QUICK REFERENCE INDICES

Horse B&B   Want to travel with your trusty steed? Stabling available here.

Bath & N.E. Somerset •2 • Cambridgeshire • 24 • Cornwall • 38 • 63 • 67 • Cumbria • 93 • Devon • 122 • 124 • 125 • 129 • 133 • 144 • 146 • Gloucestershire • 197 • 213 • Herefordshire • 232 • 234 • 243 • 247 • 251 • Leicestershire • 282 • 283 • Lincolnshire • 284 • Norfolk • 315 • 330 • 331 • Northamptonshire • 339 • Northumberland • 357 • Shropshire • 382 • 394 • Somerset • 415 • 422 • Staffordshire • 425 • Suffolk • 429 • 434 • Surrey • 462 • Sussex • 468 • Warwickshire • 489 • 493 • Wiltshire • 514 • 524 • Yorkshire • 530 • 532 • 542 • 549 • 551 • 552 • 558

Dumfries & Galloway • 590 • Peeblesshire • 626 • Perth & Kinross • 629 • 635 • 638

Carmarthenshire • 658 • 660 • 661 • 662 • Denbighshire • 667 • Gwynedd • 674

Tennis   There's a tennis court in the grounds of these houses which owners are happy for you to use, by arrangement.

Bath & N.E. Somerset • 2 • Cambridgeshire • 24 • Cheshire • 28 • Cornwall • 39 • 52 • 67 • 76 • Cumbria • 95 • Devon • 127 • 135 • 148 • Dorset • 158 • 169 • Durham • 190 • Essex • 192 • Gloucestershire • 194 • 195 • 196 • 204 • 205 • 213 • Herefordshire • 232 • 242 • 247 • Kent • 260 • 271 • Leicestershire • 283 • Lincolnshire • 290 • Norfolk • 328 • 329 • 331 • Northumberland • 353 • 355 • Oxfordshire • 365 • 374 • 376 • Shropshire • 387 • 390 • Somerset • 399 • 403 • 415 • Staffordshire • 424 • Suffolk • 434 • 436 • 447 • 453 • 454 • 456 • Surrey • 462 • 469 • Sussex • 478 • Warwickshire • 492 • 497 • Wiltshire • 502 • 506 • 508 • 522 • Worcestershire • 525 • Yorkshire • 528 • 540 • 550 • 557 • 562

East Lothian • 609 • Perth & Kinross • 629 • 640 • Scottish Borders • 647 •

Carmarthenshire • 662 • Denbighshire • 667 • Monmouthshire • 680 • Pembrokeshire • 690

QUICK REFERENCE INDICES

Pool   These are houses with a swimming pool in the grounds which owners are happy for you to use, by arrangement.

Bath & N.E. Somerset • 2 • Berkshire •18 • Cornwall • 34 • 39 • 48 • 69 • Devon • 126 • 132 • 142 • Durham • 190 • Gloucestershire • 194 • 195 • 196 • 202 • 204 • 205 • 214 • Hampshire • 229 • Herefordshire •232 • 239 • 242 • Kent • 278 • Leicestershire • 283 • Norfolk • 316 • 320 • 330 • 333 • Nottinghamshire • 359 • Oxfordshire • 367 • 374 • Shropshire • 387 • 390 • 401 • 403 • 405 • 406 • 410 • Suffolk • 454 • 465 •470 • 472 • 477 • 478 • Wiltshire • 516 • 522

Perth & Kinross • 629 • Roxburghshire • 646

Denbighshire • 667 • Monmouthshire • 680 • 681

Limited mobility   Need a ground-floor bedroom and bathroom? Try these.

Bath & N.E. Somerset • 7 • Buckinghamshire • 22 • Cambridgeshire • 23 • 26 • Cornwall • 33 • 36 • 37 • 42 • 60 • 64 • 75 • Cumbria • 88 • 91 • Devon • 111 • 113 • 121 • 138 • 144 • 145 • Dorset • 159 • 162 • 172 • 174 • 178 • 182 • Gloucestershire • 194 • 203 • 206 • Hampshire • 224 • Herefordshire • 241 • Hertfordshire • 254 • Kent • 261 • 264 • 265 • 268 • 270 • 275 • Leicestershire • 282 • 283 • Lincolnshire • 285 • 286 • London • 299 • 311 • Norfolk • 325 • 327 • 332 • 338 • Northamptonshire • 339 • Northumberland • 347 • 354 • 359 • Oxfordshire • 365 • 370 • 373 • 375 • Shropshire • 386 • 389 • Somerset • 410 • Staffordshire • 425 • Suffolk • 432 • 437 • 443 • 450 • Surrey • 457 • 463 • Sussex • 464 • 467 • 469 • 479 • 485 • Warwickshire • 489 • 493 • 495 • Wiltshire • 505 • 507 • 523 • Yorkshire • 532 • 539 • 554

Argyll & Bute • 572 • 574 • 576 • 577 • Ayrshire • 579 • Banffshire • 581 • Dunbartonshire • 591 • 592 • Edinburgh & the Lothians • 597 • 601 • 607 • Fife • 613 • Highlands • 615 • 616 • Inverness-shire • 618 • Perth & Kinross • 628 • 629 • 638 • Ross-shire • 642 • Scottish Borders • 647 • Selkirkshire • 650

Anglesey • 655 • Gwynedd • 675 • Pembrokeshire • 686 • Powys • 696

INDEX BY SURNAME

INDEX BY SURNAME

INDEX BY SURNAME

INDEX BY SURNAME

INDEX BY SURNAME

INDEX BY SURNAME

INDEX BY SURNAME

INDEX BY TOWN NAME

HOW TO USE THIS BOOK

sample entry

CONWY

A haven for musicians, walkers and those who love the simple life. Fresh air, birdsong, good conversation and hot scones for breakfast – could you want more? Alan is a pianist who might play after your (excellent) supper; Irish Ger plays the fiddle and the organ. The small bedrooms in this long, low, wonky-floored granite cottage are whitewashed and simple, personalised with cheerful rugs and friends' paintings. The bathroom is overlooked only by sheep – and there's a guests' sitting room with a woodburner. An atmospheric, riverside retreat. *Children over 10 welcome.*

	rooms	3: 1 double with bath/shower; 1 twin with private shower. Single room also available.
❶	room price	£45. Singles £22.50.
❷	meals	Dinner £12.50–£15. Supper £7.50. B.Y.O.
❸	closed	November–March.
❹	directions	From A5, B4406 through Penmachno. Left at The Eagles pub. On for 2 miles until 'S' bend sign; cottage on left just before bridge.

	Ger Tunstall
	Rhyd-y-Grô,
	Cwm Penmachno, Betws-y-Coed,
	Conwy LL24 0RB
tel	01690 760144
fax	01690 760144
e-mail	afonig@btinternet.com
web	www.afonig.com

❻ 🚴 🖊 🚲

❼ map: 8 entry: 665

explanations

❶ rooms
We do not use the words 'en suite'.
WITH bath or **WITH shower** = **en suite**

If a room is not 'en suite' we say with private bathroom or with shared bathroom: the former you will have to yourself, the latter may be shared with other guests or family members; both will have a wc, basin and either a bath or a shower.

❷ room price
The price shown is for B&B for two people sharing a room. A price range incorporates room/seasonal differences. We also give single occupancy rates – the amount payable by one person staying in a room for two.

❸ meals
Prices are per person. All meals must be booked in advance. Ask the owner if you may bring your own wine. Some entries say B.Y.O.

❹ closed
When given in months, this means for the whole of the named months and the time in between.

❺ directions
Use as a guide; the owner can give more details.

❻ symbols
see the last page of the book for fuller explanation:

🐑 working farm
🧸 all children welcome
🐾 pets can sleep in your bedroom
🖊 vegetarians catered for with advance warning
🚶 step-free access to bathroom/bedroom
♿ wheelchair facilities for one bedroom/bathroom
🚭 no smoking anywhere
🏠 this house has pets
💳 credit cards accepted
🍷 licensed premises
🚬 smoking permitted in certain rooms only
🚲 borrow or hire bikes here
🥾 good hiking from house or village

❼ Map & entry numbers
Map number; entry number.

INDEX BY TOWN NAME

INDEX BY TOWN NAME

INDEX BY TOWN NAME